THE

HOME

ENVIRONMENTAL

SOURCEBOOK

THE
HOME
ENVIRONMENTAL
SOURCEBOOK

◆ 50 ◆

Environmental Hazards
to Avoid When Buying, Selling,
or Maintaining a Home

ANDREW N. DAVIS, PH.D., ESQ.

AND

PAUL E. SCHAFFMAN, P.E.

An Owl Book

HENRY HOLT AND COMPANY · NEW YORK

Henry Holt and Company, Inc. / *Publishers since 1866*
115 West 18th Street / New York, New York 10011

Henry Holt® is a registered trademark
of Henry Holt and Company, Inc.

Published in Canada by Fitzhenry & Whiteside Ltd.,
195 Allstate Parkway, Markham, Ontario L3R 4T8.

Library of Congress Cataloging-in-Publication Data
Davis, Andrew N.
The home environmental sourcebook: 50 environmental
hazards to avoid when buying, selling, or maintaining a home /
Andrew N. Davis & Paul E. Schaffman. — 1st ed.
p.   cm.
"An Owl book."
Includes bibliographical references and index.
1. House buying—Handbooks, manuals, etc.   2. Dwellings—
Inspection—Handbooks, manuals, etc.   3. Environmental health.
I. Schaffman, Paul E.   II. Title.
TH4817.5.D37   1996
643'.12—dc20   96-17749
                                                            CIP

ISBN 0-8050-4177-X

Henry Holt books are available for special promotions
and premiums. For details contact: Director, Special Markets.

First Edition—1996

*** LEGAL NOTE ***
The information contained in this book is believed to be
up-to-date and accurate, but is in no way guaranteed.
This book is intended as a reference and is offered for sale to
the general public with the understanding that neither the
authors nor the publisher are engaged in rendering legal,
technical, financial, or medical services. If you encounter a
situation where expert assistance is required, seek the services
of a competent professional of your choice. The views
presented in this book reflect the authors' personal beliefs
about environmental issues and do not in any way reflect the
views of their employers or clients.

Printed in the United States of America
All first editions are printed on acid-free paper. ∞

2   4   6   8   10   9   7   5   3   1

For our families—
past, present, and future

CONTENTS

Part III: Off-Site Environmental Hazards

ACKNOWLEDGMENTS

Numerous friends and colleagues generously shared their time, knowledge, and support during all stages of the development of this book. We are grateful to the following, who, based on their expertise in a variety of environmental disciplines, provided invaluable critiques of various portions of the book: Skip Averill, Joyce Bennett-Church, Tim Briggs, Steve Connelly, Maria Dittmar, Joe Gall, Evan Glass, David Greene, Peter Hapke, Lee Hoffman, Bob Jontos, Ed Kaplan, Micah Kaplan, Brian Klingler, Joel Levin, Mark Lichtenstein, Santo Longo, Arnold Reitze, Donna Schwartz, Jim Sima, Jim Thompson, Bill Williams, Jim Yates, and Paul Zimmerman. We are indebted to all of them in helping make this book a reality and success; any errors and omissions, however, remain ours alone.

Special thanks go to Cindy Wilson and Sarah Butler of Connecticut College for their diligent research assistance. We are grateful to Sean White and Paul DePaolo for fruitful discussions early on in helping shape the format of this book. Thanks also to Dennis Flemming and Dolores Pellegrini for patiently typing various versions of the manuscript (and translating our chicken-scratch edits).

We appreciate the efforts of our agent Kathi Paton, who exhibited great patience in working with first-time book authors and provided needed guidance on the ins and outs of publishing. We thank our editor David Sobel, his assistant Jonathan Landreth, our production editor Alessandra Bocco, and designer Victoria Hartman at Henry Holt and Company, Inc./Owl Books for their professional assistance.

Finally, we are most grateful to our families—Suzanne, David, and Hannah, and Varda, Alana, and Scott—for their encouragement and patience, and for having to do without us on too many occasions during the long process of researching and writing this book.

PART I

Introduction

Why We Wrote This Book

For years we have dealt with environmental hazards associated with commercial real estate in our day-to-day professional lives. Frequently, colleagues, friends, and family ask us questions about environmental problems associated with their homes, such as lead-based paint, asbestos, underground storage tanks, well water, or nearby toxic dumps. In many instances we've been able to provide answers by drawing on our work experiences. However, there were (and are) many times when we needed to research an issue in order to provide some advice—and, when looking for answers, we could not find any comprehensive book on how to identify and manage environmental hazards associated with homes.

Typical buyers do not focus on possible environmental issues when they are in the midst of deciding on the purchase of a home. The primary reason is that they are dealing with other important questions, like: Can we afford this home? How many bathrooms do we need? Are the local schools any good? . . . and so on—not to mention sometimes also trying to sell their own home at the same time. As a result, problems that can affect health and safety, cost a lot to fix, and devalue a home often are ignored until it's too late.

We have all heard of home owners who have incurred significant costs or suffered serious health problems as a result of environmental hazards. Many people mistakenly link environmental problems only to industrial properties. However, there are many sources of environmental hazards in and around homes, and unsuspecting home buyers often have to bear the costs to rectify problems caused by previous owners or nearby residential, commercial, and industrial activities. These costs can, and do, run into thousands of dollars.

Unlike residential purchases, the commercial transactions we work on routinely use what is known as an "environmental site assessment." Such an assessment is a significant undertaking, typically costing thousands of dollars, whereby an environmental consultant identifies the environmental issues, estimates the associated financial risks, and provides necessary information that helps buyers and sellers decide how best to address any problems and manage the risks. While a number of environmental consultants will perform residential environmental site assessments for less than $1,000, this is a lot of money for home buyers. The cost of the average home cannot justify the expense of a full-blown site assessment, especially since the buyer might not go through with the deal if a significant environmental problem is uncovered. In terms of relative risk, however, that faced by a home owner is just as significant, if not greater, than that faced by a business executive evaluating a commercial deal.

Most buyers just don't think about, or can't afford, a costly site assessment before purchasing a home. With all the other financial pressures associated with closing, many buyers resist such costs. Instead they rely on inspectors, appraisers, and real estate agents to identify problems that can affect the value or safety of their investment. Unfortunately, for most environmental hazards, such reliance simply doesn't work. Home inspectors usually do *not* include an assessment of the full range of environmental hazards, whether on the property or nearby. Sure, a prospective buyer can get an inspector to test for radon, lead paint, or water. But the basic home inspection rarely goes beyond looking at a home's structural integrity and an evaluation of its mechanical and electrical systems. The same goes for appraisers; environmental issues are usually not factored into the calculation of a home's worth. If you read the fine print on a typical appraisal report, you'll see an "environmental disclaimer" that reads something like:

> The value estimated is based on the assumption that the property
> is not negatively affected by the existence of hazardous substances
> or detrimental environmental conditions. The appraiser is not an
> expert in the identification of hazardous substances or detrimental
> environmental conditions.

What this boils down to is that most appraisers will not do your environmental homework for you. Unless a problem is obvious, no buyer (or lender) should believe that a property's appraised value includes any environmental concerns.

When trying to understand environmental hazards, real estate agents are generally not much help either. Boilerplate real estate contracts generally avoid all but the most common environmental problems. In addition, agents have a duty to their clients, the sellers—although increasingly, agents are required by law to ensure that environmental problems are disclosed. And don't expect your lawyer to save you. Real estate lawyers are generally not trained to spot environmental hazards; rather, they focus on traditional concerns, such as documenting the deal and conducting the title search.

This book provides up-to-date information on the major environmental hazards that can arise in the normal residential real estate setting— whether in an old house, a new house, or undeveloped land. We raise the critical environmental questions that must be asked and answered about buying and selling residential property, whatever your role is in the residential real estate market.

Who Should Read This Book—and Why

When we began to write this book, we felt it would be used primarily by buyers and sellers. However, the more we wrote, the more we recognized that the book would also be useful for others working in residential real estate who face real financial risks and must satisfy professional standards and legal responsibilities associated with environmental hazards. Therefore, we have addressed the concerns of both the residential consumer and the various real estate professionals who must understand the environmental landscape and their associated obligations.

Both *buyers* and *tenants* must identify any environmental hazards associated with a home, evaluate the financial and health risks, and then factor them into the decision-making process. The bottom line for the buyer is simple: you don't get the price you deserve, you get the price you negotiate. When you buy a home, its environmental problems become yours. And, of course, most buyers will someday become sellers and must recognize that potential buyers may shy away from the home when it is put back on the market (what we call the shrinking pool of potential buyers). A home owner also may be forced to address an environmental problem if the laws change and so require it.

Sellers, landlords, and *property managers* need to identify possible environmental hazards up front so they can address them according to their own time frame, at their expense, and in the manner they choose. This will reduce or eliminate any leverage a prospective buyer or tenant may have during negotiations and minimize potential future liability. A seller who addresses environmental problems before putting a home on the market can turn a traditional adversary (the home inspector) into an ally and minimize the likelihood of losing a sale due to a prospective buyer's discovery of a problem.

Home owners, even if not currently buying or selling, must be aware of the environmental risks, whether health-related or financial, that are posed just by living (and, sometimes, working) in a home. And if any construction or renovation work is planned, a home owner must anticipate potential environmental hazards that may be encountered.

Real estate agents and *brokers* must understand environmental hazards to properly represent their clients and minimize their potential liability. Understanding and satisfying disclosure obligations, especially as they apply to environmental hazards, is and will continue to be an important issue for agents (see pages 13–19). Buyer's brokers must also be aware of environmental hazards to properly serve *their* clients.

Builders and *developers* face many of the same issues as sellers and agents concerning disclosure of environmental hazards. And because builders and developers continually buy land for new development, they must understand environmental issues and liabilities and factor them into any business decision.

Home inspectors and *environmental consultants* need to keep abreast of developments in the environmental field, as many buyers now want their home inspection to include an evaluation of potential on-site and off-site environmental hazards.

Banks, mortgage companies, and other *lenders* generally have not applied the stringent environmental policies and procedures used for commercial loans to residential loans. This practice poses significant financial risks to the lender. Today lenders need to identify environmental hazards associated with residential properties (whether owned, foreclosed, or held in trust or as collateral) to meet changing government standards and reduce potential environmental liabilities. The same goes for *trustees* involved with residential property.

Appraisers are increasingly being asked to incorporate pertinent environmental information into the residential property valuation process, whether for a new loan, for a property tax assessment, or for expert witness testimony in lawsuits involving property devaluation claims. Organizations like the Federal National Mortgage Association (Fannie Mae) and the Federal Home Loan Mortgage Corporation (Freddie Mac), which buy up large numbers of home loans on the secondary market, have stringent appraisal standards that often require an appraiser to comment on and evaluate on-site *and* off-site environmental hazards. Thus, appraisers must understand the environmental hazards associated with homes.

Real estate attorneys too must understand potential environmental hazards to effectively represent their clients, who rely on them to protect their investments and minimize the potential for financial and health risks or liability to others.

Home owner's insurance companies regularly face claims for environmental damage or liability coverage, and need to evaluate environmental hazards when underwriting residential insurance policies and when making decisions about whether a property will require a professional environmental site assessment prior to providing a home owner's policy.

State and local government officials, such as those involved with building, planning, zoning, or wetlands, are often asked about possible environmental hazards associated with a home, property, or locality by owners and prospective buyers.

Our Environmental Philosophy

Recognizing the variety of reader perspectives concerning environmental hazards affecting residential property, we wish to stress a few points about our philosophy and approach to environmental issues. For simplicity, we chose the word *hazard* to describe the fifty environmental issues that may be of concern in the residential setting. However, just because something is listed in the book as a "hazard" does *not* mean that it is necessarily "hazardous" or "unsafe" in a particular situation. Rather, it becomes a problem only when it presents health or financial risks. Further, don't be overwhelmed by the fifty hazards. If every hazard were an issue in every transaction, no one would ever buy a home— including us. But that's not the case. Remember, a home may have only one or a few hazards; many will have none. Although environmental hazards should be taken seriously, most are manageable and need not kill a real estate deal. While occasionally a deal may fall apart due to an environmental problem, in most situations environmental issues need not be "deal stoppers."

Virtually every choice in life presents risks and options. But the key is being able to distinguish minor risks from major risks. This book should help you identify the significant risks, from both a health perspective and a financial perspective, and assist you in making educated decisions about how to respond to them. All players in the residential real estate market need a way to evaluate the issues and make their own assessment about these risks. If an environmental hazard is identified, you have several options. Buyers, for example, can: walk away from a deal if the health risks are too great or the problem might cost too much to fix; require the seller to fix the problem as a condition of closing; or figure the repair costs into the price offered for the home. You can also choose to ignore the risks you decide are minimal or manageable—but you should do it with full knowledge of the potential problems. Whatever your role in the home-buying process, you must face environmental issues with your eyes wide open. This book will help you identify potential environmental problems *before* they turn into nightmares.

Another tenet of our philosophy is to educate the consumer and protect all parties—whether buyer, seller, or agent—by facilitating the *disclosure* of environmental hazards. In many situations, disclosure is the "grease" needed to allow a deal to proceed to closing; it should assist parties to reach a fair price and to minimize the number of lawsuits filed against sellers and agents.

This book is a "living" document and will be updated as new environmental hazards are identified* and as available information and requirements change. Peculiar hazards associated with a particular home, geographic area, or climate are inevitable. We'd be pleased to learn about your own experiences with the environmental hazards discussed in this book or any that may have escaped our attention. Send your suggestions to us in care of Henry Holt and Company, Inc., 115 West 18th Street, New York, NY 10011.

This book must be a mere starting point in identifying the environmental hazards, if any, in your particular situation. Be prepared to contact an environmental professional or attorney, or to call the appropriate environmental or health agency, for specific advice.

From the above was borne the idea for this book. For six years we researched and gathered the information with the goal to develop a comprehensive guide to environmental hazards that arise in the residential setting. We organized it into what we believe is a usable format, and this book is the result. We trust that it will serve the purposes we intended.

Your Home: The Biggest Investment You'll Ever Make . . . and How to Protect It (and Your Health)

Every year more than four million homes change hands in the United States, and more than another million or so new houses are built. In addition, millions of people lease apartments, condominiums, and houses every year. For many people, the purchase of a home is the biggest investment they will ever make. The average house in the United

---

* For example, some health and safety experts are currently questioning whether fiberglass insulation will become the asbestos of the twenty-first century.

States sells for about $115,000, a large chunk of money for just about anyone. People do not change homes often, and when buying, they usually allow their emotions to drive the deal. Buyers tend to concentrate only on the observable qualities of a home—location, aesthetics, square footage, construction features, and the like.

Financial and Health Risks

No one should buy or live in a home today without considering the environmental hazards. The potential for harm to health, as well as financial well-being, is significant. After spending your life savings on a new home, the last thing you need is to spend thousands of dollars more to deal with an environmental surprise—or worse, to be unable to resell your home in the future. Especially if it's something you should have or could have known about beforehand. Most buyers, however, just don't give environmental hazards the attention they deserve.

Consider the following examples of on-site financial impacts:

- $6,000 to clean up a leaking underground oil tank
- $500 or more per room to abate lead-based paint finishes
- $10,000 to replace a faulty septic system
- $2,000 to install a radon ventilation system in your basement
- $5,000 to drill a new drinking water well

In addition, potential environmental hazards can be located near your property, such as:

- contamination from leaking underground tanks at a nearby gas station
- noise from an airport
- electromagnetic fields from nearby power lines
- pollution from a nearby toxic waste dump and
- odors from a sewage treatment plant

In addition to the direct costs to address an environmental hazard or to clean up contamination, home owners face other financial risks. *Financial risk* means different things in different situations. We use the term to include all potential costs that could arise from an environmental hazard, such as expenses to install treatment equipment or repair damage to a home or personal property; lost income; costs to investigate and clean up a problem (and dispose of any associated wastes); costs to comply with environmental or land use laws (including possible fines);

costs to comply with disclosure requirements (including loss of a sale); liability to others for property damage or personal injury; limitations on the use of, ability to build or expand, or ability to sell a property; increased financing costs (or an inability to refinance); insurance expenses; legal and expert fees; short- or long-term medical treatment and monitoring costs; inconvenience and relocation costs due to forced evacuation following an accident; and loss of value due to stigma (see pages 10–13).

Financial risks can pale in comparison to the health risks to home owners and their families, such as retarded learning and development in a young child caused by eating lead paint chips or lung cancer brought on by years of exposure to asbestos or radon gas. The health risks from exposure to environmental hazards generally range from minor problems, such as headaches, interruption of sleep, or the inability to fully use and enjoy a property, to long-term, more serious problems, such as cancers, birth defects, and nerve, kidney, or liver damage. People may be exposed to those hazards by eating, drinking, or breathing contaminated food, water, dirt, or air. These environmental hazards and their associated health risks are particularly troublesome for children, for whom the risks tend to be magnified.

Remember, the goal of our book is not to scare you or impede real estate deals but to assist you in identifying the environmental conditions, whether in your home, on your property, or nearby, that can have health or financial ramifications. Once identified, an environmental hazard can then be evaluated to determine if it presents any unacceptable threat or risk. This process is called a "risk assessment." Informally, we all do this, whether we're aware of it or not, every time we decide to drive a car or fly in an airplane, drink a diet soda or a glass of wine or beer, or choose to live near a highway.

Defining Risk and Stigma for Yourself

Being aware of risks is important to all involved with residential real estate deals. The fact that a hazard is discussed in this book does *not* mean we consider it to be a problem in *all* circumstances. There is risk, and then there is risk that matters. Risk matters when the potential impacts are unacceptable to you. In many cases, the environmental hazard will not pose any real health or financial risks, or if it does, the risks may be effectively managed (depending on your tolerance level). As with any aspect of a home sale, the risks associated with an environmental hazard should be fully identified and understood, and the costs associated with the correction or cure should be quantified. You must make a risk assessment based on the specific facts about the property—how it will be used, who will live there, its location, and other criteria.

Take an on-site hazard, such as lead-based paint, as an example. For a couple with young children, lead-based paint should be a significant concern. However, for an older couple whose children are grown, potential health risks from lead-based paint may not matter. However, they will need to take precautions when their grandkids visit, and should recognize that when it comes time for them to sell the home, the pool of potential purchasers willing to buy a home with lead-based paint may be small. Also, new laws may require them to de-lead the house at some point. While either couple may choose to go ahead with the purchase, they should do so understanding the specific risks and factor them into their valuation of the home. Thus, when presented with the same set of facts about a home with an environmental problem, each potential buyer will assess the problem and the risks it presents differently depending on their particular circumstances and level of risk tolerance.

Likewise, off-site environmental hazards, such as gas stations and landfills, may not be a problem, but each should be identified and considered, because in the event that they are, health and financial impacts can be major. For example, *if* an underground gas storage tank were to leak, there *could* be groundwater pollution. If there is, and your home has a well and it is located in the path of the migrating pollution, then there may be a health concern that must be addressed. Whether or not there is an actual problem, the mere presence of an off-site hazard tends to affect property values negatively (what we call stigma, as discussed below). Unfortunately, spurred by media hype, environmental issues tend to become oversimplified, generalized, and exaggerated, often creating problems that aren't grounded in reality.

With many environmental hazards, homes may become guilty by association—that is, they become "stigmatized." Stigma means that there is a decrease in property value due to a perception that the property poses health or financial risks. Stigma can arise where there actually is an environmental problem, where there is the potential for a problem, or where there is the fear of a problem. Increasingly home owners are bringing stigma lawsuits against sellers, agents, industry, and others for diminished market value of their homes allegedly caused by environmental hazards.

Power lines and their associated electromagnetic fields (EMFs) are a good example. The scientific data that demonstrate EMFs from power lines cause health problems is inconclusive and controversial, and even the studies suggesting a problem say that any actual health risk appears to be low. To some extent, we all fear what we cannot comprehend or explain; because of this, homes close to power lines can be devalued. The scientific uncertainty associated with power lines (or any other environmental hazard) only adds to the problem. Many home buyers wonder: If the scientists aren't certain, why should I take a chance? And "what ifs" abound: What if horror stories about power lines are in the newspaper the month I go to put my house on the market? What if, ten years from now, EMFs from power lines are a proven cause of health problems?

Stigma is especially common for homes near an industrial site. Because of past environmental problems at some facilities, many people fear *all* industries, regardless of actual threat. This is the root of the NIMBY ("not-in-my-backyard") phenomenon (also called NOPE, "not on planet Earth," and BANANA, "build absolutely nothing anywhere near anything") that has thwarted the siting and start-up of countless industrial operations, such as trash-to-energy facilities and manufacturing complexes. We all know how important a home's location is in determining its desirability and value. While local zoning requirements often separate residential areas from industrial zones, home buyers *must* recognize that in many locations commercial and industrial zones overlap or abut residential zones. Generally, zoning has not provided any transition or buffer area from industrial to residential, an underlying source of many conflicts and stigma lawsuits. These problems have been compounded with the expansion of suburbs, as more and more residential developments have sprung up near agricultural, commercial, and industrial operations.

There is no simple bottom line regarding environmental risk in residential real estate—in this context, risk is very personal. The question is not whether some hypothetical one person in ten thousand is at risk, it's whether *you* are at risk. If there is an environmental hazard, you need to make an informed decision based on the specific facts of the situation. Ask yourself (and answer them honestly) important questions like: How much is known about the hazard? Is the possible impact catastrophic or merely a nuisance that I can live with? Can problems, if they occur, be fixed, and at what cost? Are other options available? And, most important, what are my own attitudes about risk? One thing is certain: risks that are understood and undertaken voluntarily are more easy to accept than those imposed on you. That is why people choose to smoke, scuba dive, ride motorcycles, hang glide, undergo cosmetic surgery, or live near the San Andreas Fault in southern California. With an awareness and understanding of environmental hazards, we can all make better informed choices about risks in the context of buying and selling homes. We ask that you understand these risks and keep them in perspective.

In the final analysis, when all environmental hazards are understood, the purchase price of the home should fairly reflect them. This process puts all players in the residential real estate market on a level playing field where the rights and responsibilities of buyers, sellers, and all the other participants are understood and properly integrated into the home-buying process. If not, the buyer might not buy, the seller might not sell, the lender might not lend . . . or there may be lawsuits down the road.

Disclosure Obligations

Today, disclosure of a property's existing conditions by the seller is fundamental to ensuring that transactions proceed to closing. More and more buyers want to (and should) know everything about a property before making a decision to purchase. And, as a result of legislation and court decisions across the country, sellers, agents, and others face an expanding range of disclosure obligations for environmental hazards associated with homes. These new laws and cases are dissolving the old doctrine of "let the buyer beware" (caveat emptor); sellers and agents have a growing legal responsibility to inform buyers about any major issues affecting a home's value, including any on-site and off-site environmental hazards. Penalties for a false disclosure, or nondisclosure, can be significant—in many instances home sales have been canceled.

Because of the importance of disclosure, the following section discusses the obligations that apply to sellers, real estate agents and brokers, builders, developers, landlords, and property managers. Disclosure obligations vary from state to state; many of the issues discussed may not necessarily apply in your state. Talk to a real estate lawyer or call your state's consumer protection office to find out what disclosure requirements apply in your situation.

Obligations of Sellers and Real Estate Agents

Up until the last few decades, buyers had little or no recourse against sellers or agents for defects discovered after the purchase; it was "tough luck" for the buyer of a house with a major problem that the seller knew about but didn't reveal. Today this is no longer true—many states now have mandatory disclosure laws or court rulings that require thorough disclosure.

What types of problems must be disclosed? Generally those considered "material defects," a broadly interpreted legal concept meaning problems that could adversely affect the value of a property and the buyer's decision to purchase it. Examples of material defects include leaky roofs; insect infestation; faulty heating and septic systems; defective or polluted drinking water wells; presence of formaldehyde insulation, lead-based paint, or asbestos; building code violations; flood damage; and presence of an underground storage tank (leaking or not). It used to be that only problems on the property were subject to disclosure, but recent court cases in some states have also required disclosure of off-site conditions, such as nearby toxic waste dumps or power lines, that can affect property values.

In many states the liability of a real estate agent equals that of a seller. Be aware that the agent works for the seller and must disclose this fact to the buyer. The agent is not an uninterested party and stands to make a profit *only* if the deal goes through.* In the past, real estate agents were required only to *not* make false representations or actively conceal material defects. However, the halcyon days of "hear no evil, see no evil, speak no evil" are gone; some courts have ruled that an agent's mere silence about a known defect was the same as a false representation and that when a seller informed an agent about the problem, the agent was required to inform the buyer. In other instances, sellers have been found liable for an agent's failure to disclose defects the seller told the agent about. As a result, more and more agents have been named as defendants in lawsuits between buyers and sellers.

In some ways, real estate agents should be even more concerned than sellers about disclosure obligations and potential liability. First, real estate agents are experienced, licensed professionals—they are in the business of selling homes and dealing with the types of issues, environmental and otherwise, that commonly arise. Because of this, when disclosure issues arise, judges and juries look closely at the real estate agent's role in the transaction. Second, real estate agencies are generally perceived to have deeper pockets than a seller and are thus able to sustain greater penalties. And in some states, a real estate agent's license can be revoked for violation of disclosure requirements.

The National Association of Realtors (NAR) supports the concept of seller disclosure. Its code of ethics and standards of practice (which are *not* law) require members to discover and disclose adverse conditions that a reasonably competent and diligent inspection by someone with their expertise would turn up, and to avoid exaggeration, misrepresentation, or concealment of material facts.

---

* To protect themselves, some buyers utilize "buyer brokers," who are legally obligated to disclose defects to the buyer.

Court Cases on Disclosure

Before states enacted disclosure laws, "common law"—legal doc-trines that have evolved from years of court decisions—was used to place liability for nondisclosure of a property's known conditions on sellers and real estate agents. Buyers can still use common law principles to establish liability for sellers and agents, whether or not there is an appli-cable state disclosure law. Court cases abound where sellers and agents have been held liable for violation of contract provisions (like an ex-press warranty of habitability) or under various other theories (such as breach of an implied warranty of habitability, negligent or intentional misrepresentation, and fraudulent concealment). Though the details of these legal theories are beyond the scope of this book, as a general statement of common law, sellers and their agents have a duty to: relay accurate information; not make false representations or conceal defects; and disclose facts about which they have knowledge that would affect the value, desirability, or condition of the property.

In addition to an affirmative duty to disclose known defects, common law generally does not allow sellers and agents to remain silent, espe-cially (but not only) if asked. Nondisclosure can be as much a problem as a false disclosure. Courts in several states have also imposed liability for "innocent" misrepresentations where the buyer relied on a state-ment such as, "You'll have no problem getting a permit for the septic system." And in a few states, courts have gone so far as to require dis-closure of not only known defects, but those that are "reasonably discov-erable." Under these rulings, agents *may* have an obligation to inspect the property before it's sold.

Buyers in many states have also relied on consumer protection, unfair trade practice, and fraud laws to impose liability on sellers and agents who have failed to meet disclosure obligations. These laws list prohib-ited acts and allow for specified damages that may be recovered by a buyer, including rescission (where a contract is voided and the seller must return the buyer's money and take back the house). For example, a Connecticut court required a seller to take back a property because the seller had not informed the buyer that a permit for a septic system had been denied, and a Louisiana court awarded a buyer damages and legal fees for the seller's concealment of a flooding problem. In many states, sellers have been found liable under fraud statutes for failing to disclose such things as defective water, heating, and sewer systems. Con-sumer protection laws in some states may apply only to business transac-tions, such as where a home is purchased from a real estate agent, builder, or developer. Typically the sale of a new home by a builder or developer carries with it an implied warranty of habitability or fitness.

Damages awarded by courts in disclosure lawsuits vary from state to state and case to case. They range from cost recovery by the buyer (that is, reimbursement for out-of-pocket costs to fix the problem, including legal fees and costs), to cost recovery with damages (sometimes even double or triple damages), to rescission. Many courts have awarded damages for impacts to property value (including stigma damages), personal injury, mental anguish, and inconvenience. In one tragic case, a Vermont seller who failed to disclose that a driveway heating system was faulty was convicted of manslaughter when a couple and their child died from carbon monoxide poisoning.

Disclosure of Off-Site Environmental Hazards

There have been a number of recent state court decisions (in California, Connecticut, New Jersey, New York, Oregon, and Pennsylvania) where sellers have been found liable for not disclosing the presence of known off-site environmental conditions that could affect the value of a property, such as landfills, toxic waste sites, power lines, oil spills, planned new highways, street conditions, or noisy businesses.

In a significant disclosure case, the New Jersey Supreme Court ruled in 1994 that residential builders, developers, and their agents had a duty to inform buyers that a new home development was near a toxic waste dump. This case sent shock waves through the real estate community across the country because it expanded disclosure obligations to nearby or off-site conditions. The case involved a class action against a builder and developer and its brokers by more than one hundred home owners. The properties had been advertised as being in a rural area where residents could enjoy a pristine environment. The builder did not tell prospective buyers that a toxic waste dump was less than one mile from the homes. The court ruled that the builder and its brokers had had a duty to inform buyers about conditions off-site that could affect the enjoyment and value of their properties, especially when the off-site environment was an inducement that was advertised as a benefit of the development. The court also found that the developer had falsely represented the development by failing to inform buyers that the dump could leach toxic substances and affect the properties being sold.

We caution that the result in this case is limited to its specific facts and applies only in New Jersey. While no such duty may exist in other states, similar situations will undoubtedly arise as residential property developments are built near contaminated sites. Eventually courts in other states may follow New Jersey and expand disclosure obligations to include off-site hazards; therefore, all sellers, real estate agents, and builders and developers would be wise to understand the implications of this case.

State Disclosure Laws

Along with the expansion of buyers' rights through the courts, many states have passed laws requiring sellers and/or their agents to disclose problems with residential property. In general, these laws benefit all parties by defining the rights and responsibilities (and any limitations) of buyers, sellers, and agents. Today more than half of the states have some type of *mandatory* "property condition disclosure law," also known as seller disclosure laws: Alaska, California, Connecticut, Delaware, Hawaii, Idaho, Illinois, Indiana, Iowa, Kentucky, Maine, Maryland, Michigan, Mississippi, Nebraska, Nevada, New Hampshire, North Carolina, Ohio, Oklahoma, Oregon, Rhode Island, South Dakota, Tennessee, Texas, Virginia, Washington, and Wisconsin.

Most other states have *voluntary* property disclosure programs, typically run by the state real estate association, including: Arizona, Arkansas, Colorado, District of Columbia, Georgia, Kansas, Louisiana, Massachusetts, Minnesota, Missouri, Montana, New York, North Dakota, Pennsylvania, South Carolina, Utah, Vermont, West Virginia, and Wyoming. Many of these states are considering mandatory disclosure legislation.

Some states have separate and specific environmentally related disclosure laws. For example, a Massachusetts law requires sellers and landlords to determine if formaldehyde insulation (known as UFFI) is present and to disclose levels of formaldehyde gas in the indoor air.

Because new laws get enacted and existing laws change frequently, always check with your real estate agent, lawyer, or state real estate association as to the requirements in your state. Also remember that in addition to the remedies provided by state disclosure laws, buyers normally retain all existing common law remedies. Further, in states without mandatory disclosure programs, buyers can use common law remedies as well as consumer protection or fraud statutes if they have been harmed by a seller's misrepresentation or failure to disclose.

The details and scope of disclosure requirements vary considerably from state to state; they typically require sellers to provide buyers with some type of completed form or report describing the condition of the property *before* any binder, contract, or purchase and sale agreement is signed (or within some specified time after execution, along with an examination and rescission period). In some states, owners who sell their own homes need not provide a disclosure form. In many states, the text of the disclosure form is mandated by statute and developed by the state consumer protection office or real estate association. The disclosure form must usually be attached to the contract and signed by both the buyer and the seller (and the agent). The real estate agent may be required to inform the prospective purchaser if a seller refuses to complete or sign a disclosure form.

Contact your real estate agent or state consumer protection office to get a copy of your state's law and the disclosure form, and for additional guidance. Review the law and the form to see what information must be disclosed. The form may cover structural, zoning, or building code issues, and environmental conditions, such as drinking water wells, septic systems, termites, insulation, radon, and asbestos. Disclosure of lead-based paint is now mandatory in all states under federal law (see Hazard 13, Lead-Based Paint).

State disclosure requirements usually apply to single-family properties as well as some multifamily properties (usually fewer than four units), but many do not apply to sales of new or never-occupied homes. In some instances, these laws also cover leases, lease-options, or exchanges. There are also certain exemptions from disclosure in particular state laws.

Damages that may be recovered by a buyer under state disclosure laws vary considerably. Some states do not allow for rescission, while others do. Other damages include civil penalties and recovery of actual damages (including legal costs) as well as other specified damages.

Summary

Despite the risk of losing some deals, full disclosure of environmental hazards (both on-site and off-site) by sellers and agents is by far the best policy. In states where disclosure forms are mandated, sellers and agents who properly utilize them will be best protected. Even where disclosure is not mandatory, the prudent seller and agent should opt for full disclosure, because this will avoid deals being killed at the last minute and the last thing a seller needs is a lawsuit after selling a home. And for developers and agents with reputations to protect and other deals in the works, in the long run, full disclosure is clearly in their best interest. With this in mind, we offer the following tips for sellers and agents:

- investigate and disclose to prospective buyers all information that can affect the value and use of the property;
- do *not* minimize potential problems or exaggerate about the property (don't make statements like, "These soil conditions will have

no problem supporting a septic system," or "Don't worry about the nearby landfill"); and

- document your disclosures (to the buyer and to the agent) early on and continuously.

Finally, buyers must remember that a disclosure form is *not* a warranty or a substitute for an inspection. Just because a seller provides a completed disclosure form does not mean it is accurate or complete. A buyer should always proceed with an independent inspection of a home, property, and its surroundings and examine all information that could affect its value. Buyers should hire and use experts as needed, based on the age, condition, and other variables about the property. Also, all disclosures made by the seller or agent should be documented, and accurate records should be kept of how questions about the property are answered.

Buyers will not always succeed in claims against sellers and agents. Because of this, a buyer's diligence in the form of a home inspection up front is doubly valuable. First, it may allow the buyer to avoid a nondisclosure problem altogether; an informed buyer can better establish a fair price for a home that includes costs for issues that might not have been disclosed. Second, an up-front inspection provides a baseline of information in the event that the buyer does encounter a problem and is forced to take action against the seller or agent for damages. A buyer who can establish that a thorough investigation conducted before the purchase did not reveal a problem the seller knew about will be in a better position in the event of a lawsuit than one who cannot.

The Home Inspection

A purchase of a home or an undeveloped parcel of land is a significant investment, and an inspection—although not foolproof—is a good way to reduce or eliminate exposure to unexpected environmental hazards and the financial costs to address them. While the decision to perform a home inspection is usually the buyer's, some lenders require limited inspections for things like termites, well water quality, or lead-based paint before approving a mortgage. Sellers also can have inspections done before putting their home up for sale to identify problems that might arise with a buyer. Economic issues aside, whether buying or maintaining a home, you owe it to yourself and your family to be aware of any health risks that might be associated with an environmental problem. Despite their importance, home inspections are conducted on fewer than half the homes sold every year in the United States.

Scope of an Inspection

A typical home inspection entails an evaluation of the property and the structural, electrical, and mechanical aspects of a house, which few people have the expertise to do themselves. The inspector usually looks at exterior features such as the foundation, roof, siding, gutters, decks, windows, and trim; the plumbing, heating and cooling, and electrical systems; the attic and basement or crawl spaces; and the condition of the interior rooms. Many of the environmental hazards discussed in this book are generally *not* addressed by a home inspection. Although some inspectors may look at some on-site environmental conditions as an option (and at an additional cost), few are trained to properly identify most environmental hazards. In many instances, special certifications or licenses are needed to inspect, remove, and dispose of certain hazards, such as lead-based paint and asbestos. And as for off-site environmental hazards, most inspectors never look for them.

We recommend that a home inspection include an assessment of all potential environmental hazards in the home and on adjacent and nearby properties that could adversely impact health or finances. The specific issues that should be addressed will be dictated, in part, by the home's age, location, and proximity to potential pollution sources. The environmental part of the inspection can be conducted by a home inspector, if qualified, or by an environmental consultant with specific expertise. Recognize that you may not need to hire someone at all to do the environmental research—at a minimum you can do some of the work yourself (see the Self-Help section on pages 22–25).

Contract Negotiation Tips for an Inspection

The purchase and sale contract for a house should allow the buyer sufficient time to conduct an inspection and to be able to walk away from the deal if the inspection results are not satisfactory. That is, the purchase should be contingent upon a "satisfactory inspection"—and it should be clear that it must be to the *buyer's* satisfaction. The contract should specify what inspections will be performed (well water, radon, septic, and lead-based paint, for example), their purpose, and who will conduct and pay for them. If the seller agrees to do repairs as a result of an inspection, the contract should be revised to reflect this. The contract should also require the seller to supply proof that repairs were completed (in the form of paid receipts) at or before closing. For example, if the property has a septic system, the buyer should require the seller to have it checked for proper operation and pumped out, and to provide a paid receipt for this work at closing. For the protection of all involved, any agreements and contingencies should be in writing.

Sellers should put wording in the contract that requires a buyer to provide them a copy of the inspection report, especially where a buyer can walk away or renegotiate the price based on the report. Buyers can request that a seller share the cost of the inspection in exchange for a complete copy of the report, regardless of its findings. For sellers, paying for part of a report may not be bad if a problem is identified and—worst case—the buyer backs away from the deal; the seller will at least be aware of what needs fixing without having to pay the full cost of an inspection.

To avoid unanticipated problems, buyers should not accept a contract that specifies a particular date when the inspection results are to be completed and beyond which they cannot walk away from the deal. For example, suppose a well water sample is taken for testing but the lab misplaces it and can't get the results to the buyer before the date specified in the contract. In such a case, the buyer could be stuck. The best option for buyers is for the contract to specify that the inspection will be conducted within so many days of both parties signing the contract (remember to allow a week or two to line up an inspector) and that the buyer has X number of days *after receipt of the final report and all results* to inform the seller as to whether the deal will go forward.

Choosing a Home Inspector

Choosing a home inspector can be tricky, especially when looking for one qualified to evaluate environmental hazards. Ask your real estate agent or attorney for referrals. You will find a range of qualifications, as there is no national governmental licensing or certification board for home inspectors; only a handful of states require any inspector registration. One organization, the American Society of Home Inspectors (ASHI), is a private, national, nonprofit professional organization with stringent requirements for home inspectors. There are also many state associations of home inspectors.

The home inspector you choose should be knowledgeable about all areas of concern and should have access to and be fully trained in the use of any required equipment. To determine exactly what will be covered in an inspection, read the materials provided by the inspector. Better yet, ask for a sample contract and review the scope of services and other contract language carefully. This will help you understand what you will—and won't—be getting. To maintain their independence, home inspectors *generally* should only *inspect* homes—however, if they are also in business to repair homes or sell equipment as a follow-up to their inspections, get a second estimate.

The inspector you hire should be bonded and insured. Inspectors should have both "errors and omissions" insurance, which covers the inspector's negligence, and liability insurance, to protect the prospective buyer in case the inspector damages the home during the inspection.

A ballpark cost for a standard home inspection is $300 to $500. This doesn't include an evaluation of all the environmental hazards discussed in this book, or any associated lab analyses. Often an inspector will look at some environmental issues, like lead-based paint or radon, for an extra charge. Costs for environmental tests can range from $25 for a simple radon test to $250 for a pesticide scan of drinking water. If you can't find an inspector to look at the environmental issues you are concerned about, you can hire an environmental consultant with special expertise to do this work. Not counting laboratory fees, the cost for such an undertaking will range from $500 to $1,000.

The Report

A home inspection report should summarize all features inspected, note any problems, and provide some guidance as to the overall soundness of the home. Some inspectors may provide rough estimates of how much it should cost to replace or repair any defect. The report should identify what may be expected from the buyer in terms of maintenance and remediation costs after the sale. Just because an inspection identifies some problems does not mean you shouldn't buy the property. Rather, you'll want to know if the problems can (or should) be fixed, and if so, at what cost. By being fully apprised of conditions up front, a buyer can choose not to buy the house, renegotiate the contract price to reflect costs to address any problems (including any permanent devaluation), or require the seller to address the issue(s) before closing.

Self-Help

If you have the time and are so inclined, you can do some of the information gathering and even conduct some limited tests as part of an environmental home inspection. By doing so, you will not only save money, you will find out more about your future home and neighborhood. Helpful background information is readily available—you just need to know the right questions to ask and where to find the answers. Keep in mind that much of an actual environmental inspection is best left to an expert—testing pipe insulation for asbestos, inspecting a septic system or underground storage tank, and evaluating water test results are a few examples. However, the money you save by doing the initial legwork can be used to hire an expert to address those environmental issues that require special qualifications. Even if you don't choose to do any of your own research, this section will be useful in helping you understand what the inspector did to evaluate your property and in reviewing the inspector's report.

The following are a few useful tools to obtain environmental information about a home and its surroundings:

Visual Inspection—The Self-Help Checklist

The simplest way to get a feel for a home and its surroundings is to visually check it out yourself. But just taking a walk around isn't enough—you need to be aware of the warning signs that indicate potential problems (what are referred to as "red flags" in the real estate industry). To assist you in your visual inspection, we've prepared a self-help checklist of the red flags to look for in a home, outside a home, and in a neighborhood. This checklist, which is provided in Appendix 5, contains the aspects and areas in and around a home that you can preliminarily inspect. Photocopy this checklist and take it with you as you walk around. In addition, each of the fifty hazards presented in this book contains a section called "What to Look For," where we've identified conditions that should raise red flags for you as you inspect a home. The point of the visual inspection is not to make definitive conclusions about possible hazards but to identify the red flags and raise questions that should be answered to your satisfaction before you proceed with a deal.

Do your site walk *before* hiring an inspector. You may have questions that are easily answered to your satisfaction by the seller or agent (for example, that the truck traffic is from a road project that will end in a week, or that the sellers use bottled water only because they like the way it tastes). Or during your inspection of a property and surrounding area, you might identify an issue for your inspector to address (do those old shingles contain asbestos?). Finally, you might uncover something that will just not be acceptable to you, no matter what the price of the home (for example, you may refuse to live near a landfill). If so, you can walk away and will have saved yourself the time and expense of negotiating a contract and hiring an inspector.

Environmental Tests You Can Do

Most environmental laboratories will work for individual home owners or buyers, providing sample containers and instructions and analyzing the samples. Some labs may even help you select the tests you need and assist in interpreting the results—you may need to search for a lab with qualified chemists who are willing to work with a home owner. You can collect the drinking water sample for the lab to analyze, test for radon, as well as conduct limited tests for the presence of lead-based paint—most types of lead tests, as well as sampling, testing, and removal of asbestos, must be done by certified experts. Also the inspection of heating and cooling systems, septic systems, and underground storage tanks is best left to experts. Check the phone book under "water testing" or "laboratories—testing," or any other specific category (such as "radon testing") to find an appropriate laboratory. You can also call your state or local environmental or health agency to find qualified consultants and labs.

Always follow laboratory instructions exactly—sampling technique is crucial to be able to properly interpret and trust the results. Poor sampling procedures can lead to false positive results (that is, the test results indicate a problem that really doesn't exist) or, worse, false negative results, which could lead you to ignore a situation that may present a health hazard. When a high reading occurs, retest to confirm results. Ask the lab to help you understand results and discuss the situation with your state or local health or environmental agency. Always review results with an expert before hiring a contractor, undertaking costly repairs, or buying an expensive treatment system.

Municipal or Town Records

A property's ownership history can be reviewed through an informal title search at the town hall. You may find that a property was once used for agricultural, industrial, or commercial purposes, or that a prior owner had a home business, such as photography or furniture stripping, that would raise questions about the condition of the soil and groundwater. In addition, information about the property and past uses may be gleaned from old building, sewer, and underground storage tank permits. Talk to the local officials and review their files—look at the zoning maps and ask about the zoning classification or if there are any industrial or commercial activities targeted for nearby properties. Find out about zoning, wetlands, forestry, or conservation restrictions. The town sanitarian or engineer should be able to answer questions about sewers, septic systems, municipal water supplies, well water, and where the local landfill or dump is, or was, located. The fire marshal should have records on residential underground oil storage tanks and past spills on or near a property.

Environmental Databases, Maps, and Photos

The Environmental Protection Agency (EPA) and state environmental agencies maintain records and computer databases with useful information about the environmental practices of industries and the environmental conditions of various properties. In order to access the information, you may need to visit your EPA regional office or the appropriate state environmental or health agency. See Appendix 4 for a list of these agencies. Call first to find out how to access the agency's files and databases.*

Some companies collect publicly available environmental information from federal, state, and local sources and compile it into their own databases. For a fee, they will then provide a report about a specific property (costs for these services can run $200 to $300 or more). Be cautious in using these services; the information is only as accurate as the person loading it into the system and may not be up-to-date. The Internet also offers access to information useful in evaluating environmental hazards.

There are also a number of publicly available maps and photos that can be used to find out about historical uses of a property or about a nearby industry.

Some examples of the most useful publicly available environmental databases, maps, and photos are summarized in Appendix 3.

Home Owner's Insurance and Environmental Hazards

Most home owner's (or renter's) insurance policies do *not* cover property damage or liability resulting from environmental hazards. However, coverage for damage from some environmental hazards is available—you may already have coverage for a specific problem, like flooding, and have limited coverage for other damages, or specific coverage may be available at additional cost. Read your policy or talk to your insurance agent to learn the scope of your policy and its exclusions. Because you cannot count on insurance coverage to protect you from most environmental hazards, it is critical that you understand the specific environmental hazards and their associated health and financial risks *before* you purchase a property.

Despite the importance of home owner's insurance, most people give

---

* To find information about some industries, you may be required to submit a written Freedom of Information Act (FOIA) request. Under federal and state FOIA laws, government agencies must make available documents requested by the public about a particular property or facility. Start your research early, as this can be a time-consuming process; don't count on getting back all necessary information within the time frame necessary for real estate buyers to evaluate a home and make a decision on whether to go forward with the purchase. Call the EPA or your state environmental agency for assistance in developing a written FOIA request.

little thought to choosing their policy and generally consider it a hassle. With the stress of closing on a home and all of the other details that need attention, selecting an insurance policy is often a last-minute decision. While almost all home owners have some coverage (as do many renters—about 50 percent), few ever take the time to read or understand their policy.

Every home owner should have a policy. In most instances, you'll have no choice. If you have a loan from a bank or other lender, you will be required to maintain a policy (naming the lender as a beneficiary) as part of your mortgage obligations. The lender's rationale is simple: since your home serves as collateral for the loan, it wants to ensure its investment is protected in case of damage. Sellers who finance a sale privately should also require the buyer to maintain appropriate insurance. Even if you don't have a mortgage, insurance coverage is important, as you cannot control everything that may happen to your property, especially from off-site sources.

A quick primer about the basics of home owner's insurance is warranted. A policy is simply a contract between you and your insurance company—you pay the premium; in exchange, the company assumes certain risks. Two types of coverage are typically provided: (1) property coverage—compensation for damage to your home, other structures, and your personal property (your earthly possessions, *not* your land, which is "real property"); and (2) liability coverage—financial protection for when you are responsible for another person's property damage or physical injuries. Liability coverage usually encompasses related legal costs.

Not all home owner's policies are created equal. The scope of coverage and exclusions vary greatly from one policy to another. Your policy is probably derived from a standard industry form that provides coverage only for damage resulting from specific named causes (or perils), such as fire, lightning, hail, explosion, smoke, and many others; environmental hazards are rarely, if ever, named. The wording of every policy differs, so these are just a few examples of named causes. Other insurance policies provide coverage for all damage except those specifically *excluded*. All policies have exclusions, such as for losses caused directly or indirectly by floods, earthquakes, or acts of war. (Flood insurance is available only through the federally subsidized National Flood Insurance Program, while earthquake coverage can be obtained from private insurers—see Hazard 7, Floods and Other Natural Disasters, page 82.)

Almost all home owner's insurance policies have a "pollution exclusion" provision that excludes coverage for damage to property relating

to, for example, "the discharge, seepage, release or escape of pollutants." The term *pollutant* typically includes just about every possible
contaminant or chemical under the sun. In addition, pollution exclusions usually don't cover costs for environmental testing or to remove or
clean up contaminated soil or debris. These exclusions usually apply
regardless of the cause of the problem.

Insurance companies may also deny coverage for pollution on other
grounds—for example, coverage for cleanup of contaminated well water
may be denied because "water" is not considered "covered property"
under a policy. Or the cleanup of contaminated soil might not be covered because "land" (literally) is usually not considered "covered property." Insurance policies often won't cover costs to remove lead-based
paint because lead is considered a "pollutant." Because of this, an insurance company would argue that any health problems arising from
lead-based paint are not covered (say, if a neighbor's child got lead
poisoning in your home).

Most policies also do not cover costs associated with, or loss caused
by, construction, demolition, remodeling, or renovation, including the
removal and disposal of any associated debris. Thus, under a debris
exclusion, costs to dispose of asbestos-containing materials or lead-
contaminated debris, for example, generally will not be covered. Even if
you have a policy that provides debris-removal coverage, *contaminated*
debris may not be within the policy's definition of covered property.

There are several approaches to *try* to recover on a loss due to an
environmental hazard. First, the environmental hazard itself may be
considered a "covered peril." Second, the cost of cleaning up and disposing of any associated contamination may be covered in a "debris-
removal" provision. Third, some policies cover environmental hazards
arising *as a result of* a covered peril. For example, even if your policy
specifically excludes leaks from underground heating oil storage tanks,
if such a leak is caused by a covered peril, such as lightning or a fire,
then damage to your (or a neighbor's) property may be covered.
Fourth, costs associated with the removal and disposal of lead- or
asbestos-contaminated building debris may be covered if a covered peril
was the primary cause of the damage.

Despite what we've said above, the question of coverage for environmental claims under home owner's policies is not well settled by the
courts. There are many cases where courts have interpreted policies
broadly in favor of the home owner. We expect the claims by home
owners in this area to grow in the coming years as governmental agencies increase the pressure on property owners to correct environmental
hazards, and as public awareness of the financial and health risks associ-

ated with environmental hazards increases. This will undoubtedly lead to more lawsuits as home owners mount challenges to denials of coverage by insurance companies. The wording of the policy and the facts in any given situation will determine the result.

The lesson for the home owner or tenant is straightforward: a standard home owner's insurance policy is generally not going to ease your financial burden in the event of an environmental hazard or problem. However, yours may provide some degree of coverage for certain environmental hazards. The best way to avoid costly surprises is to understand what type of coverage you are buying and the limitations and exclusions of your policy. Choose a policy that's best for you, your location, and your budget. If you encounter an environmental problem, review your policy—and you may be surprised, it might be covered. The Insurance Information Institute provides a hotline (800/942-4242) to answer consumer questions about insurance coverage issues.

Environmental Hazards and Taxes

The unlucky home owner who discovers an environmental problem should first act to minimize financial and health risks. Thereafter, other issues can be considered, such as whether costs to remedy the environmental hazard can be used to offset income tax liability, or the effect that an environmental issue has on property taxes.

Income Taxes

Under current Internal Revenue Service (IRS) policy, a home owner cannot deduct the cost of a "capital improvement" or a "repair," even when the cost is incurred in response to some environmental problem. However, if the remedy of an environmental hazard can be considered an "improvement," while still not deductible, the cost can be added to the home's basis and used to decrease the capital gains tax when you sell. Work that doesn't qualify as an improvement is a repair, with no tax benefits; repairs are simply part of being a home owner. The trick is to distinguish an improvement from a repair. The test is that an improvement must prolong the life of the property *and* increase its value. While the second part of the test may be easily met, it is difficult to satisfy the first part—to demonstrate that an environmental "fix" (venting radon or treating water, for example) prolongs the life of the property. There are no clear lines on how the IRS will rule in any situation. You bear the burden of supporting your claim.

The cost to remedy an environmental hazard *may* be a deductible medical expense. To be deductible as a medical expense, the purpose of the expense must be to "alleviate or prevent" medical illness. For example, the removal of lead-based paint is allowed as a medical expense deduction in certain circumstances, such as where a child has, or has had, lead poisoning (IRS Rev. Ruling 79-66). While limited only to lead-based paint, the rationale behind this ruling *may* support a claim that costs to remove and prevent exposure to other environmental health hazards, such as asbestos and radon, are no different and so should also be deductible medical expenses.*

If you own rental property (including multifamily property), the tax rules are different. Landlords can deduct costs to make repairs and can depreciate capital improvements per standard IRS rules. As discussed above, distinguishing repairs from improvements isn't easy and the IRS has no bright line test for determining where the cost to remedy an environmental hazard falls.

There are no hard and fast rules as to how the IRS will view a deduction taken for costs to fix or respond to an environmental hazard. The IRS makes decisions on a case-by-case basis. Seek the advice of an accountant or call the IRS (800/829-1040) for assistance. (Be careful—the IRS does *not* guarantee the verbal representations of its employees.)

Real Estate Tax Issues

If an environmental hazard lowers your home's market value, you may be able to obtain relief through a lower tax assessment. The reduction in property taxes may offset, at least in part, out-of-pocket expenses to address the environmental hazard or any loss suffered when a devalued home is sold.

In almost all states, property owners pay real estate taxes. The formula for calculating property taxes varies from state to state, but real estate taxes are typically 1 percent to 4 percent of the property's fair market value (FMV). To determine the tax assessment, the assessed value of the property is measured as a percentage of its FMV, the price a willing buyer would pay to a willing seller under normal circumstances. FMV is based on the property's highest and best use.

Environmental hazards will devalue a property. For example, on-site hazards such as high radon levels can substantially lower property values. And proximity to off-site hazards such as toxic waste dumps can stigmatize neighborhoods and devalue individual properties. The extent of devaluation depends largely on the hazard and the site-specific circumstances.

---

* Medical expenses are not straight deductions—unreimbursed medical expenses must come to more than 7.5 percent of your adjusted gross income in order to be deductible. However, costs to fix environmental hazards can add up quickly.

Encountering an environmental problem is not good news, but there can be some financial offset. If you can demonstrate to the local government tax assessor that the environmental hazard devalued your property, you may be able to lower your tax assessment. For example, several Michigan home owners successfully demonstrated property devaluation from contamination migrating from a nearby landfill; the assessed value of their homes was reduced to $100 each. Similarly, in a New York residential development impacted by contaminated groundwater from a nearby petroleum storage terminal, assessed values on two hundred homes were reduced, on average, by more than 30 percent.

To appeal a property assessment, *you* bear the burden of showing that it is incorrect. You'll need adequate data, such as a recent appraisal, to support such a position. It is difficult to document the impact on property value of an environmental hazard, and for an assessor to determine the extent to which the environmental hazard or contamination affects property values. The best evidence might be recent sales of comparable homes subject to the same or a similar environmental hazard where an owner had to sell below the appraised value.

How to Use Parts II and III of This Book:
On-Site and Off-Site Environmental Hazards

The next sections of this book contain our priority list of fifty environmental hazards that can impact health, finances, and the ability to sell, refinance, or lease a property—whatever your role in a real estate transaction. Although you must be aware of all environmental hazards before you can rule any of them out, unless you are unlucky, few (if any) will turn out to be significant problems. The environmental hazards are not listed in order of importance; rather, they're listed alphabetically within two groups: on-site environmental hazards (Hazards 1–23) and off-site environmental hazards (Hazards 24–50).

On-site environmental hazards are those that can be found *in* a home or *on* the property. Figure 1 (see page 39) shows a cutaway view of a hypothetical home which, for informational purposes, depicts most of the on-site environmental hazards discussed in Part II. For example, in older homes, asbestos, lead-based paint, and formaldehyde insulation may be present. Old and new homes alike may contain unhealthy or even toxic levels of radon, carbon monoxide, or other indoor air pollutants. Or there may be residual contamination in the well water or soil from past industrial or agricultural activities on what is now residential property.

Off-site environmental hazards are nearby sources of environmental contamination that can migrate to, and affect, residential property. The single most critical pathway for off-site pollution is groundwater, especially where private wells are used as the source of drinking water. Groundwater contamination occurs when toxic chemicals, such as pesticides, gasoline, hazardous wastes, or dry-cleaning solvents, seep down through the soil into underground water supplies (known as aquifers) that are the source of water for both private wells and public supply wells. Groundwater contamination does not recognize property boundaries, and where there is a problem, numerous properties may be affected. Even if a home does not rely on groundwater as its source of drinking water, properties with contaminated groundwater can still be devalued and pose health and financial risks. For example, one possible threat to people living in homes situated above contaminated groundwater is that certain organic chemicals can volatilize and enter indoor air through the home's foundation.

Residential properties can also be impacted by surface water runoff, air pollution, odors, and noise, as well as the threat of any of these impacts from off-site hazards. Off-site hazards include toxic waste dumps, farms, dry cleaners, gas stations, mines, industries, and many others. Figure 2 (see pages 186–87) depicts the variety of off-site environmental hazards which could be located near, or impact, a home, as discussed in Part III. Distance and direction between the off-site hazard and the home is a key factor in determining whether or not there has been or will be an actual impact. Generally, those environmental hazards within seeing or hearing distance of a home require the most attention and scrutiny. However, homes thousands of feet away from a pollution source may be affected due to groundwater movement, stream flow, air pollution, or catastrophic accident.

In the Environmental Hazard Matrix on pages 32–33, the fifty on- and off-site environmental hazards discussed in this book are cross-referenced against four generic categories of property: (1) older, pre-1980 homes; (2) post-1980 homes; (3) undeveloped land; and (4) new construction, to help you focus on those potential hazards you should review for your particular home and eliminate those that are not applicable to your situation. More likely than not, the hazards you will need to read about and look for will depend on the type of property in question. If, for example, you are considering an older home, look especially at those hazards checked in that column; however, any hazard that is *not* checked may be of concern in certain limited circumstances for a particular property, no matter what category it is in. Note also that while

ENVIRONMENTAL HAZARD MATRIX

	Type of Property			
	Existing Homes		Undeveloped Land	New Construction
Hazard	Older (Pre-1980)	Newer (Post-1980)		
1. Asbestos[1]	X			X
2. Biological contaminants[1]	X	X		X
3. Combustion sources and carbon monoxide[1]	X	X		X
4. Drinking water: private wells	X	X	X	X
5. Drinking water: public water supplies	X	X		X
6. Erosion and sedimentation[2]	X	X	X	X
7. Floods and other natural disasters[2]	X	X	X	X
8. Formaldehyde insulation[1]	X			
9. Heating oil storage tanks	X	X	X	X
10. Historic disposal activities	X	X	X	X
11. Household chemicals and hazardous waste	X	X		
12. Indoor air pollution sources: carpets and building materials[1]		X		X
13. Lead-based paint[1]	X			
14. Lead in water	X	X		X
15. Miscellaneous on-site hazards	X	X	X	X
16. PCBs	X			X
17. Pressure-treated wood	X	X		X
18. Radon in air[1]	X	X	X	X
19. Radon in water	X	X	X	X
20. Septic systems	X	X	X	X
21. Termites and other wood-destroying pests	X	X		X
22. Wetlands[2]	X	X	X	X
23. Zoning and other land use restrictions[2]	X	X	X	X

ON-SITE

OFF-SITE

24.	Airports
25.	Autobody shops
26.	Dry cleaners
27.	Electric power plants
28.	Electromagnetic fields[3]
29.	Farms and agricultural properties[3]
30.	Gas stations
31.	Golf courses
32.	Hazardous waste facilities
33.	Highways and roads
34.	Incinerators
35.	Industrial manufacturing plants
36.	Landfills
37.	Military bases
38.	Mines and quarries
39.	Miscellaneous off-site hazards
40.	Municipal garages
41.	Nuclear power plants
42.	Pesticides[1,3]
43.	Petroleum storage terminals
44.	Print shops
45.	Radio and communication towers
46.	Railroad yards and tracks
47.	Salt storage areas
48.	Sewage treatment plants
49.	Superfund sites
50.	Zoning

All off-site hazards can apply to any type of property, depending on the location.

NOTES:
1. An indoor air pollution concern.
2. A particular concern for waterfront properties.
3. Also an on-site concern.

many on-site environmental hazards are limited to certain categories of property, virtually *any* off-site environmental hazard can be an issue for any type of property.

A few words about the format of Parts II and III. First, acronyms and abbreviations are common in the environmental field—Appendix 1 contains a complete list of those we use. Second, the information is presented in the same manner for each of the fifty environmental hazards discussed in this book. The summary box at the beginning of each hazard identifies: (1) the environmental hazard; (2) *where applicable for on-site hazards only,* where the hazard is found (including relevant dates and locations); and (3) what the *potential* risks are if the hazard is present (the symbols indicate health risks, ⊕ [low] to ⊕⊕⊕ [high]; and financial risks, $ [low] to $$$ [high]).

Note that, particularly for the off-site hazards, these rankings are our estimates of the seriousness of the risks from the subject hazard relative to other hazards. Therefore, even where we have given a hazard a low ranking, if there is a problem, the *actual* risks can be high.

Following the hazard summary box, eight informational sections are presented for each hazard, as described below.

Background This section describes what the environmental hazard is and where it may arise, contains a brief historical perspective, and provides other relevant information.

Health Risks This section describes health risks and typical exposure scenarios associated with the hazard. Potential impacts to health can be short term (acute) or long term (chronic). The actual health impacts from environmental hazards are determined by the type of contaminant, the level and duration of exposure, and the age and health of the exposed individual. The health risks discussed vary with the hazard and range from minor problems such as headaches, interruption of sleep or the use and enjoyment of a property, to such long-term, more serious problems as cancers, birth defects, and nerve, kidney, or liver damage. Exposure pathways include eating, drinking, or breathing contaminated food, water, dirt, or air. Except for some common hazards like lead-based paint and radon, an in-depth discussion of the health risks associated with specific chemicals is beyond the scope of this book. (Consult with a medical professional as necessary.)

Financial Risks This section identifies the range of *estimated* financial impacts from the environmental hazard (as well as the risk to any pending sale or lease), including: costs to install equipment and fix damage to a home or personal property; costs to investigate, clean up, and dispose of a hazard; costs to comply with applicable environmental or land use laws; costs to comply with disclosure requirements; liability to others for property damage or personal injury; limitations on the ability to use, build, expand, and transfer a property; increased financing (or an inability to refinance) or insurance expenses; legal and expert fees; medical costs; inconvenience and relocation costs due to forced evacuation following an accident; and loss of value due to stigma.

Managing the Risks This section offers tips on managing the health and financial risks associated with the hazard, including information about available treatment options, other practical ways to reduce or eliminate problems, and how to plan for resale.

Regulatory Outlook This section provides a *general* discussion of relevant federal, state, and local requirements associated with the environmental hazard, and offers projections on where regulations might be headed.

What to Look For This section outlines ways to spot the red flags associated with the environmental hazard and determine whether it might be a problem *before* you sign a contract or incur the expense of getting professional advice.

Where to Find Help and Further Information This section identifies tests that can be performed (and their associated costs), and where to go for further assistance and information, other suggested readings, and relevant hotlines. (Federal and state environmental and health agency phone numbers and addresses are listed in Appendix 4.)

The Bottom Line This section briefly summarizes the key facts about the environmental hazard, including the associated health and financial risks.

One final point: We do not expect this book to be read from cover to cover—utilize it as a reference guide and skip around and read about those hazards relating to your particular situation. Recognizing this, we have attempted to make the information contained in each of the fifty hazards as complete as possible. In doing so, this has created some unavoidable but necessary redundancy.

PART II

On-Site Environmental Hazards

ON-SITE ENVIRONMENTAL HAZARDS

1. Asbestos
2. Biological contaminants
3. Combustion sources and carbon monoxide
4. Drinking water: private wells
5. Drinking water: public water supplies (not shown)
6. Erosion and sedimentation
7. Floods and other natural disasters (not shown)
8. Formaldehyde insulation (UFFI)
9. Heating oil storage tanks
10. Historic disposal activities (not shown)
11. Household chemicals and hazardous waste
12. Indoor air pollution sources: carpeting and building materials
13. Lead-based paint
14. Lead in water
15. Miscellaneous on-site hazards
16. Polychlorinated biphenyls (PCBs)
17. Pressure-treated wood
18. Radon in air
19. Radon in drinking water
20. Septic systems
21. Termites and other pests
22. Wetlands
23. Zoning and other land use restrictions (not shown)

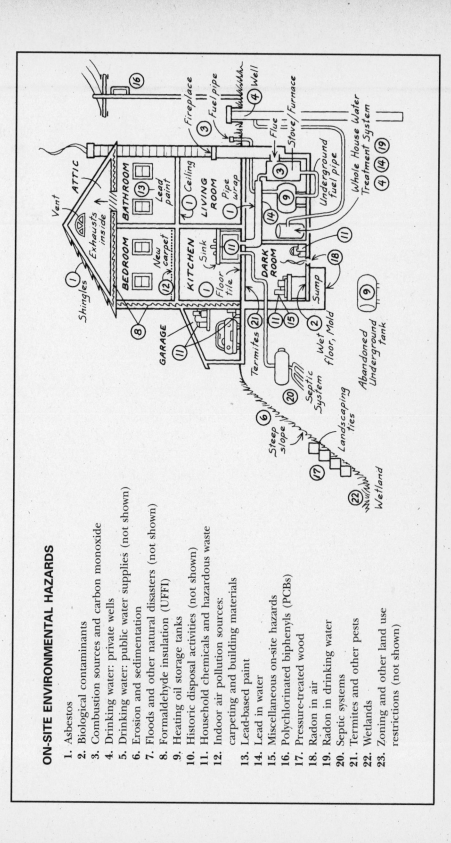

1. ASBESTOS

Homes built before around 1980; found in interior and exterior
building and insulation materials

Risks: HEALTH ⊕⊕   FINANCIAL $ $

Background

, Asbestos is a naturally occurring fibrous mineral found in rocks and
soils throughout the world. From the turn of the century until the late
1970s, asbestos was widely used in all sorts of construction materials
because it is strong, durable, fire retardant, and a good insulator. It can
be found in flooring, walls, ceiling tiles, exterior shingles, insulation for
electrical and heating systems, and other materials.

Asbestos and asbestos-containing materials (ACMs) pose health risks
when they are friable (easily crumbled) and a disturbance releases asbestos fibers into the air. Because of their small size and shape, once
released, asbestos fibers can remain airborne for several days and can be
inhaled. The health hazards from asbestos exposure are well documented and include cancers and other diseases.

Friable ACMs have the greatest potential to be dangerous. Nonfriable
ACMs (such as floor tiles) will not, under normal use, release fibers and
are thus considered less hazardous. However, nonfriable ACMs can release asbestos fibers under certain conditions, such as if floor tiles containing asbestos are sanded or drilled. Since the late 1970s, the use of
asbestos in building materials has been restricted and is gradually being
phased out.

Health Risks

Inhalation or ingestion of a significant amount of asbestos fibers over time is dangerous. These microscopic fibers (they are less than one micron in width—there are twenty-five thousand microns per inch—and more than a thousand times finer than a human hair) are hazardous because, once inhaled, they lodge deep in the lungs. Asbestos is very persistent—once in the lungs, it is not readily expelled or destroyed by the body's natural defense mechanisms; it will persist virtually forever and concentrate in tissues if repeated exposure occurs.

Asbestos is a "group A" human carcinogen; it is known to cause lung cancer (including mesothelioma—cancer of the lining of the lungs) and degenerative lung disease (asbestosis) following prolonged, repeated exposure. Asbestos fibers that are ingested can also cause stomach or gastrointestinal cancer. The symptoms of these diseases may not appear for twenty or more years. The health effects to people from exposures to low levels of asbestos in the home are less certain, but there is no known level of exposure to asbestos fibers that is completely safe. Although some scientists speculate that exposure to a single fiber is enough to cause cancer, the risks increase with duration and amount of exposure.

Financial Risks

Due to safety concerns and regulatory requirements, costs to test, monitor, and comply with laws (where applicable) to remove and dispose of ACMs in a home can run into several thousands of dollars, depending on the type, amount, and location of ACM. Asbestos-abatement contractors typically charge $4 per square foot to remove vinyl flooring (tiles and linoleum), $4 to $5 per square foot to remove ceiling tiles, $10 to $15 per square foot to remove textured ceiling paint or plaster, up to $20 per linear foot to remove asbestos pipe insulation, and $30 per square foot to remove furnace insulation. For example, the cost to hire a licensed contractor to remove and dispose of ACM around a furnace could be $1,000 to $2,000.

A home with ACMs may be devalued merely because of the presence of asbestos, even if it is not friable. Some buyers will walk away from a home with asbestos, while others may utilize its presence as a negotiating point, require it to be removed prior to closing, or ask for a credit at closing. Even if you have only nonfriable ACMs in your home, always consider the possibility that you might have to deal with the issue when you sell the home. For example, to avoid losing a sale, a friend had to recently spend $5,000 to remove undamaged ceiling tiles containing asbestos from his basement.

Here's two worst-case examples of the financial risks associated with asbestos. In 1988, a Florida family had to abandon its home following renovation work that scattered asbestos everywhere. They couldn't afford to clean the house up, no one would buy it, and they could not find a contractor willing to demolish it. Further, their insurance company would not cover their losses.

In 1989, a plumbing contractor contaminated an entire house in Massachusetts while removing asbestos-containing furnace and duct insulation. Testing showed contamination in *every* room and inside the ducts. Evidently the asbestos was spread through the hot air heating system. The family was forced to evacuate the home; clothing, carpeting, furniture, and some appliances had to be discarded as contaminated. They were able to return to the house only after repeated decontamination procedures and reoccupancy testing that took more than four months.

Other financial risks:

▸ Liability for nondisclosure; see Disclosure Obligations, pages 13–19.

▸ Costs for short- or long-term medical treatment and monitoring; legal and expert fees; and inconvenience and relocation costs due to forced evacuation following an asbestos release.

Managing the Risks

First, find out if any asbestos is present. Friable ACMs should immediately be repaired (encapsulated or enclosed) or removed to prevent a release. *If the ACM is in good condition and located in an area where it is not likely to be disturbed, leave it alone.* Known or suspected ACMs should be checked regularly for damage. Extreme care must be taken when working around suspected ACM to prevent damaging or disturbing it; remember, asbestos fibers are easily released. For example, routine cleaning operations such as dusting, brushing, vacuuming, and scrubbing can release asbestos fibers. If an ACM becomes damaged, it should be repaired or removed by a qualified asbestos contractor.

Construction and renovation activities ranging from drilling, sawing, and sanding to demolishing a wall will release asbestos fibers if ACMs are present. If there is a release, *do not* vacuum or sweep up the asbestos, which will further disperse the asbestos fibers—call a qualified expert. Nonfriable ACMs do *not* normally present health risks. For example, vinyl flooring containing asbestos can be cleaned in the usual manner; however, fibers can be released if the flooring is sanded, drilled, filed, or scraped. Before renovating a home built before around 1980, test any materials suspected of containing asbestos (particularly ceilings, walls, and vinyl flooring). If ACMs are present and likely to be disturbed by any construction activities, hire an experienced, licensed contractor for guidance.

Removal of ACMs from a home can be a complicated task, depending on the amount, type, and location of the ACMs. Check with your state environmental or health agency to find out if home owners are allowed to remove asbestos or if you must hire certified or licensed professionals to do so. Even if home owners are allowed to remove asbestos, we maintain that, because of the risks, *asbestos removal is not a do-it-yourself project.* Its repair or removal should be performed only by properly trained and qualified contractors; be careful who you hire because many home repair contractors don't have the equipment, training, or experience to work with asbestos or remove it from a home safely. Total removal of an ACM is typically the last, and most expensive, alternative. Exterior ACMs usually do not pose health risks. However, if asbestos-containing roof or siding shingles are worn or damaged, they may need to be sealed or removed. Recently a Nevada apartment building owner was *criminally* convicted for illegally removing asbestos from his buildings and violating federal asbestos laws. Contact your state environmental or health agency *before* deciding on a course of action and trying to identify a qualified contractor (see Appendix 4).

Regulatory Outlook

Under federal law, any material containing more than 1 percent asbestos is considered to be a regulated "asbestos-containing material," or ACM. Federal and state asbestos rules generally do not force individual home owners to remove asbestos, even if it is friable or damaged. However, we strongly recommend that any damaged or friable ACM be properly repaired or removed. Licensed contractors must follow applicable state worker protection and abatement requirements. Multifamily homes are covered by more rigid state and federal rules—landlords and building managers generally must survey for and repair or remove friable ACMs that could lead to exposure scenarios.

The EPA and state environmental or health agencies may regulate asbestos-abatement activities in homes. Asbestos removal from a home, such as that which must occur during remodeling, that involves a certain number of square feet of ceiling or floor tile or a certain number of linear feet of asbestos pipe insulation, may need to be done by licensed professionals and require compliance with notification, removal, packaging, or storage regulations. Your town or state may also have special disposal requirements for asbestos.

The EPA and the Occupational Safety and Health Administration (OSHA) have taken steps to reduce exposures to asbestos by setting permissible exposure levels in public buildings (such as schools) and for workers, and by requiring labeling of products containing asbestos. Because of the health risks, asbestos use is being phased out. Since 1980, asbestos has not been allowed in common household materials like insulation or ceiling tiles; by the end of 1996, asbestos will be virtually banned from all consumer goods in the United States.

What to Look For

In new homes or those built since 1980 or so, asbestos should not be a problem. In older homes, asbestos may be found in many types of applications, including, but not limited to:

- vinyl wallpaper
- vinyl floor tiles,* linoleum, and flooring adhesives (''mastic'')
- wall and attic insulation
- acoustical ceiling tiles
- decorative ''popcorn''-textured or ''cottage-cheese'' ceilings
- exterior siding
- roof tar, felt, and shingles
- coated plaster
- wallboard
- textiles (fire blankets, theater curtains, and cordage)
- insulation around pipes, furnaces and breeching, and hot air ducts (interior and exterior)
- door gaskets on wood and coal stoves, furnaces, and ovens
- fuse boxes
- light fixture insulation
- materials troweled or sprayed around pipes, ducts, and beams
- patching or joint compounds, such as putty, caulking, and spackling (including chimney patch)
- textured paints

---

* 9″ × 9″ vinyl tiles in pre-1980 homes usually (about 90 percent of the time) contain asbestos; 12″ × 12″ vinyl tiles about 50 percent of the time.

- paper products, such as corrugated paper, cardboard, and mill-board
- pegboards typically used in workshops
- gypsum-based Sheetrock
- greenhouse plant boxes and outdoor tree planters

When doing a self-inspection of an older home, look for any of the materials listed above. Asbestos may appear as fluffy-looking plasterlike material in ceilings and walls, or white or grayish cloth or feltlike, fibrous insulation wrapped around pipes or furnaces. Assume that vinyl floor coverings contain asbestos. If in doubt, treat the material as if it is an ACM until you can have it tested. *The only way to know for certain if a material contains asbestos is to have it analyzed.*

Where to Find Help and Further Information

To evaluate and test for asbestos, hire a home inspector or consultant trained and experienced with asbestos—a professional should know where to look, how to take samples properly, and how to interpret results. An asbestos inspection of a home, including sampling, may cost $300 to $500 as a stand-alone project, or an extra $100 to $300 if added onto a full-blown home inspection. Lab analyses for asbestos cost between $20 and $35 per sample. Inspectors should be able to help you decide what remedial actions, if any, are needed, and should recommend reputable asbestos contractors if repair or removal is needed. The only way to verify if there has been a release of asbestos is to take air samples or dust wipes and have them analyzed by a lab—talk to an asbestos consultant about this type of testing.

Most states require contractors to be licensed to remove asbestos. Information about qualified asbestos consultants, contractors, and laboratories may be obtained from the EPA or your state environmental or health agency (see Appendix 4). The manufacturer of a suspected ACM may be able to tell you, based on the model number and age, whether it contains asbestos.

For more information about asbestos, contact the Consumer Product Safety Commission (CPSC) (800/638-CPSC) or the EPA's Asbestos Hotline (202/554-1404). For further information, see American Lung Association, U.S. Consumer Product Safety Commission, and U.S. Environmental Protection Agency, *Asbestos in Your Home,* n.d.; U.S. Consumer Product Safety Commission and U.S. Environmental Protection Agency, *Asbestos in the Home,* n.d.; U.S. Environmental Protection

Agency, *Managing Asbestos in Place: A Building Owner's Guide to Operations and Maintenance Programs for Asbestos-Containing Materials*, 2OT-2003, 1990.

The Bottom Line

You do not want to breathe asbestos fibers. Homes built before 1980 or so should be inspected for asbestos. The mere presence of asbestos is not necessarily a health risk or financial problem—if the ACM is not friable and in good condition and not in a place where it is likely to be disturbed and release asbestos fibers, it can be left alone indefinitely. However, known or suspected ACMs should be periodically checked for damage. Because loose or damaged friable ACMs can present significant health risks that may not show up for years, they should be repaired or removed—often an expensive undertaking. Always hire experienced, licensed professionals for asbestos testing, repair, or removal. Asbestos is generally not a concern for newer homes.

2. BIOLOGICAL CONTAMINANTS

Homes with damp basements, forced-air heating and cooling systems, or poor ventilation

Risks: HEALTH ⊕ ⊕ FINANCIAL $ $

Background

We each spend about 90 percent of our lives indoors, and about 65 percent of that time is in our homes. The indoor air we breathe often carries diverse pollutants that can impair human health and pose financial risks to home owners and their families. One major category of pollutants is biological airborne contaminants—"biocontaminants" for short—which include a wide range of microscopic "beasts" such as: bacteria; mold; mildew, fungi; viruses; pollen; insects; dander and saliva from cats, dogs, and birds; and dust mite and cockroach feces. Some experts estimate that biocontaminants, which can trigger allergies, transmit diseases, and cause a wide range of other health problems, are the largest source of indoor air pollution and may affect tens of millions of people in the United States. Exposure to biocontaminants is compounded in energy-efficient homes constructed since the 1970s—airtight homes with little air exchange increase the likelihood of an indoor air problem.

Some biocontaminants are a direct result of the lifestyle of those living in a house, while others are related to the construction features and location of the house itself. Biocontaminants can be carried by humans, pets, and rodents, and thrive in homes with poor ventilation, excessive humidity or moisture, and where cleanliness is not a priority. Musty furniture and carpets, wet basements and walls, poorly maintained heating, ventilation, and air-conditioning (HVAC) systems, window air conditioners, humidifiers and dehumidifiers, and refrigerator drip pans can be a breeding ground and distribution center for biocontaminants.

Health Risks

Biocontaminants can trigger respiratory allergic reactions, including various forms of asthma, and transmit infectious diseases such as influenza, measles, and chicken pox. Certain types of molds and mildews can release toxins associated with diseases, such as Legionnaires' disease, which affect the lungs, intestines, kidneys, and central nervous system, and can even cause death. For example, in 1976, more than thirty American Legion members died following the spread of a deadly virus through the HVAC system of a Philadelphia hotel. And an outbreak of a pulmonary virus, carried by deer mice into homes, killed more than fifty people in the Southwest in 1993–94. Children, the elderly, and those with breathing problems, allergies, and lung diseases are particularly susceptible to biocontaminant-induced ailments.

Exposure to biocontaminants can occur through inhalation, ingestion, or skin absorption. Symptoms can include chills, headaches, muscle aches, sneezing, watery eyes, shortness of breath, nausea, diarrhea, coughing and sore throat, lethargy, fever, and digestive problems. Allergic reactions caused by biocontaminants may occur immediately or can be the result of previous exposures that a person may not be aware of.

Financial Risks

Alternatives and costs to remedy or minimize a biocontaminant problem depend on its source and location. For example, the costs to moistureproof a basement might be minimal if all that is needed is to divert roof drains away from a foundation or seal minor seeps; or moderate to purchase and use a dehumidifier ($200 to $500); or high to hire a contractor to waterproof a basement or install a foundation drain

($1,000 to $10,000). For biocontaminants in musty carpets, furniture, and draperies, a several-hundred-dollar vacuum cleaner with a special filter, known as a high-efficiency particulate air (HEPA) filter, may be necessary. Forced-air HVAC systems can be professionally cleaned (from $300 to over $1,000) to remove many biocontaminants. Costs to install new fan exhausts or energy-efficient ventilation systems may range from less than $20 (for a do-it-yourself dryer exhaust) to thousands of dollars (if significant home renovations are necessary).

A damp or wet basement will deter some would-be buyers. People sensitive to (or aware of) problems from biocontaminants may not be interested in a home with a damp basement or poor ventilation or may use the repair cost as a bargaining chip during negotiations. Potential buyers may view a biocontaminant problem in a home as a stigma; the financial impact of this is real but difficult to quantify.

Other financial risks:

▶ Liability for nondisclosure; see Disclosure Obligations, pages 13–19.

▶ Costs for short- or long-term medical treatment and monitoring; legal and expert fees; and inconvenience and relocation costs due to forced evacuation following discovery of a biocontaminant problem.

Managing the Risks

Installing adequate ventilation throughout a house and reducing or eliminating moisture in the basement will lower the potential for bio-contaminant problems. Sealing cracks in the foundation and providing proper ventilation reduces indoor humidity levels and acts as a barrier to disease-carrying organisms. For most homes, relative humidity levels should be maintained between 30 and 50 percent. Exhaust fans should be vented to the *outdoors* for kitchens, bathrooms, and the clothes dryer, and attics and crawl spaces should be properly ventilated. Room or whole-house air-cleaning units can be purchased and installed, although their effectiveness in eliminating many biocontaminants is questionable. Air exchangers provide a source of clean outside air and are particularly useful in energy-efficient, "airtight" homes. In some states, they are required for new home construction.

Routine housekeeping chores can reduce the risks of biocontaminants: keep the house clean to minimize dust (use a vacuum cleaner with a HEPA filter if there is a problem), replace filters on the HVAC system, change the water in a humidifier regularly, and don't let water produced by a dehumidifier or air conditioner stand for more than two days. Consider having a HVAC system professionally cleaned every three to five years. Damp carpets and other home furnishings should be steam cleaned and dried thoroughly, and if the problem persists, they should be replaced.

Regulatory Outlook

Currently there is no federal program applicable to residential indoor air quality generally, or biocontaminants specifically. OSHA, the EPA, and many state environmental and health agencies regulate indoor air under various programs—for such contaminants as asbestos and tobacco smoke—but only in public buildings (such as schools) and commercial buildings for the protection of workers. However, Congress has indicated that reducing indoor air pollution is a priority and someday may pass laws concerning indoor air, including standards for biocontaminants. Your state environmental or health agency can provide further details on the outlook for, or status of, regulation of indoor air pollution in your state. However, because OSHA and the EPA (and parallel state agencies) focus on commercial buildings and the protection of workers, if and when we see indoor air quality standards, we expect that initially they will apply only to offices, stores, and the like, and then later they may apply to residential properties. With increased public awareness of indoor air problems, there may come an increase in toxic tort and disclosure lawsuits against landlords, property owners and managers, and sellers and their agents, as well as against manufacturers, designers, and installers of HVAC systems and other building materials.

What to Look For

Wet or damp basements, and attics or crawl spaces with mold or mildew growing on walls and other surfaces (especially wood joists, rafters, and the backs of walls or stairways), are indications of conditions where biocontaminants thrive. Mold and mildew can appear as any color stain on wood, concrete, or wall surfaces. Also check for signs of mold and mildew or accumulated dust in the forced-air HVAC system or ducts. Check to see whether kitchen and bathroom fans and clothes dryer exhausts vent indoors or outside; examine bathtubs, refrigerator drip pans, dehumidifiers, and humidifiers for signs of mold.

Where to Find Help and Further Information

Home inspectors look at many problems associated with biocontaminants, but they may not be aware of health concerns. Indoor air can be tested to determine levels of biocontaminants; this work should be done by a qualified indoor air specialist or industrial hygienist. OSHA workplace standards for some biocontaminants can be used as a guide in the home. Check with your state environmental or health agency for laboratories certified to sample for indoor air pollutants (see Appendix 4). Testing costs range from $100 to $500. Because conditions in a home vary, samples may need to be collected more than once to adequately characterize levels of biocontaminants.

The EPA as well as many state environmental and health agencies have designated contacts who can provide information on indoor air issues (see Appendix 4). If you suspect you have a biocontaminant-related health problem, discuss your concerns with a doctor. Before undertaking a significant effort to address an indoor air issue, talk to an expert and consult with the appropriate environmental or health agency.

The Bottom Line

Biocontaminants, which thrive in wet and humid places in houses, can pose significant health risks. There are many possible sources of biocontaminants in a home and many ways to reduce them—the costs can become significant. By eliminating or minimizing a wet or moldy basement, a seller will decrease potential biocontaminant problems and improve the appeal of the home to prospective buyers. Homes with a biocontaminant problem may be devalued. All buyers, and especially those susceptible to biocontaminant-related health problems, should identify biocontaminant sources and remediation costs when considering the price they are willing to pay for a home.

3. COMBUSTION SOURCES AND CARBON MONOXIDE

Furnaces, fireplaces, stoves, and heaters

Risks: HEALTH   FINANCIAL $

Background

Combustion sources include furnaces, fireplaces, stoves, and space heaters that burn gas, oil, kerosene, wood, or other fuel. With the exception of all-electric houses, most homes have at least one combustion source. Although these sources are generally safe, under improper conditions. they pose health and financial risks through the emission of the byproducts of combustion—toxic gases and particulates. (The risks of fire and explosion hazards and the dangers of gas leaks from combustion sources should also be considered.) The major toxic byproducts of combustion are *carbon monoxide* (CO) and *nitrogen dioxide* (NO_2), which are commonly produced whenever fuel is burned. High emissions can result from incomplete burning of gas or oil from an improperly operating furnace. Woodstoves, fireplaces, and kerosene space heaters can also release small particles and combustion dust—known as *particulates*—into the indoor air if they are not properly installed or used.

Combustion of fuels produces a variety of potentially harmful byproducts—that is why furnaces and other fuel-burning appliances are almost always vented to the outside. If combustion sources are not properly installed, operated, or maintained, they can result in fires or cause a variety of health problems, ranging from minor throat irritation to death. Incidents of CO poisoning have received extensive press coverage in recent years; tennis star Vitas Gerulaitis, who died in 1994 from breathing CO fumes from a faulty propane heater, is a well-known example. Common venting problems include blocked, leaking, or damaged furnaces, flues, and chimneys, and cracked furnace heat exchangers. Animals, such as birds and squirrels, often build nests in chimneys, and that can cause problems. Woodstoves that are not sized correctly or those without tight-fitting doors can also be a problem. Some combustion sources are not usually vented, including space heaters (kerosene or gas) and gas stoves. To avoid the release of toxic gases into the home, these appliances must be maintained and used in strict conformance with manufacturer's directions. Car exhaust fumes that enter the home from an attached garage are another common source of CO buildup in homes and townhouses where the garage is situated underneath or alongside the living space.

Health Risks

Carbon monoxide is a colorless and odorless gas that interferes with the delivery of oxygen throughout the body. At low levels CO causes fatigue in otherwise healthy people; at higher concentrations it can cause headaches, weakness, dizziness, or confusion. Thousands of people each year are affected by CO; many confuse the symptoms with those of the flu or food poisoning. At high levels CO causes unconsciousness, brain damage, and death. According to the CPSC, CO is responsible for more than two hundred deaths each year in the United States (although the Centers for Disease Control put the figure at about six hundred deaths per year and other estimates are as high as fifteen hundred). Death from CO poisoning can take anywhere from several minutes to an hour, depending on the concentration of CO in the air. In November 1993, three sleeping Connecticut teens died from CO fumes emanating from an improperly ventilated first-floor gas-fired furnace. Pregnant women, infants, the elderly, and people with anemia or respiratory or heart problems are especially sensitive to CO exposure, even at low levels. Pets are also susceptible to CO poisoning.

Exposure to *nitrogen dioxide* can irritate mucous membranes in the eyes, nose, and throat and cause shortness of breath. Children and those with asthma or other respiratory diseases are particularly sensitive to NO_2. There is some evidence that exposures to low levels of NO_2 for long periods of time can increase the chance of respiratory infections or contribute to more serious lung diseases.

Particulates can cause eye, nose, and throat irritation, respiratory infections, and bronchitis. They can also act as a carrier for much more dangerous pollutants, such as radon.

People who are concerned that they may have health problems related to exposure to CO, NO_2, or particulates should talk to their doctor.

Financial Risks

Costs to remedy problems associated with combustion sources may range from almost nothing (to make minor adjustments to a furnace), to several hundred dollars (to professionally clean a chimney), to thousands of dollars (if a new furnace or chimney is required). Replacing an unsafe woodstove can cost from $500 to over $2,000. Unvented space heaters can be replaced with ones that are vented; costs will range from $250 to over $1,000, depending on the size of the unit and how much renovation is required to install a vent. The cost to install an outdoor vent for any unvented gas-fired appliance will be site specific and range from less than $100 for a simple do-it-yourself project to over $1,000 if a contractor is hired to do significant renovations.

The cost to fix problems or replace a combustion source can become a factor during negotiations when a house is sold. Prior to listing their homes, sellers should repair major problems, such as a broken flue or chimney, first because they are unsafe, and second because these problems may be considered a major negative to would-be buyers. If building code violations exist, they can delay a closing, especially for new homes, where inspections are usually required prior to issuance of a certificate of occupancy.

In the course of a transaction, financial risks can also arise in the context of disclosure obligations (see Disclosure Obligations, pages 13–19). Most state disclosure laws do not specifically identify CO as a disclosure item; however, failure to disclose such a problem to a potential buyer could present serious legal ramifications for the seller (or landlord) and his or her real estate agent—such as liability for injuries to buyers (or tenants). In an extreme case, a Vermont home owner who failed to disclose that the furnace used to run a driveway heating system was faulty when he sold the house was convicted of manslaughter when a couple and their child died from CO poisoning.

Home owners who have a CO problem may also incur costs for short- or long-term medical monitoring and treatment; legal and expert fees; and inconvenience and relocation costs due to forced evacuation following a CO accident. For example, in a recent Maryland case, several tenants sued the landlord and his insurance company when debris from an old chimney liner fell into the base of the chimney, blocked the exhaust from the building's boiler, and caused CO to spread throughout the multifamily building.

Managing the Risks

Don't ignore problems with combustion sources—they can be deadly. Check for problems often and have a professional inspect for leaks, and clean and tune up your chimney, furnace, and other appliances frequently (typical recommended frequencies are annually for oil-fired appliances and every three years for gas-fired appliances). Repair any problems immediately and take any necessary additional steps. If nests in a chimney are a problem, have a professional install a screen or grating (it must be properly sized so as not to restrict air flow).

Minimize risks by installing and using all combustion sources—especially space heaters—strictly as directed by the manufacturer. Routine maintenance (like keeping gas appliances properly adjusted and replacing furnace filters) and common sense (using the proper fuel, opening flues, and making sure exhaust fans work) will also minimize risks. Enclosures that restrict air movement should never be built around a furnace—when the air supply to a furnace is reduced, combustion is affected, increasing the production of CO. Make sure the door on a woodstove fits tightly. Do not leave cars running inside an attached garage for any length of time. Never barbecue indoors or in an enclosed space.

While maintenance of combustion sources is the best way to minimize the risk of CO buildup, the use of a CO detector—used in only about 5 percent of the homes in the United States today—is a critical supplement. If you have a combustion source in your home, use a CO detector. There are many on the market for residential use, and they come in all types, sizes, and with various features (see the July 1995 issue of *Consumer Reports,* which reviews several brands and models). CO detectors are similar to smoke detectors, are typically installed in hallways or bedrooms (but for early warning can be installed in the basement or wherever else a combustion source is located), and range from $40 to $100 or more. Not all detectors are the same—some are hypersensitive and have been criticized for frightening consumers and burdening fire safety officials with false alarms. CPSC officials suggest that home owners use CO detectors that have been tested and certified to meet the voluntary industry UL standard established by Underwriters Laboratories Inc.

Regulatory Outlook

In most areas of the United States, local building codes regulate the installation and use of furnaces, woodstoves, and fireplaces, and some form of permit or approval is often required. Some cities, like Chicago, require the use of CO detectors in all new single-family homes and in existing homes with oil or gas furnaces (failure to comply can result in significant fines). Although workplace standards for CO, NO_2, and particulates have been published by the EPA and OSHA, we are not aware of any indoor air standards applicable to residential properties. In recent years, the EPA has focused attention on indoor air pollution problems in general. We expect to see more research in this area in the future, and perhaps some specific guidance or regulation for CO and other toxic gases in indoor air.

What to Look For

Look for gas or wood-burning fireplaces, portable gas space heaters, gas clothes dryers or refrigerators, and fuel-burning furnaces, ranges, water heaters, and woodstoves. Telltale signs of possible problems include black soot or smoke stains around the furnace, vent pipe, flue, or the connection point to the chimney, black stains above a fireplace or space heater, and a clogged chimney or blocked chimney opening (from bird and squirrel nests, fallen bricks, or accumulated soot). All ventilation pipes and flues should be securely attached to each other and to the flue. Check for corroded piping, loose-fitting equipment, or cracks in the flue or chimney, inside and out.

Exhausts are normally found adjacent to or above other appliances, such as stoves and space heaters. If vents exit inside the house, they should be inspected to ensure they are not blocked or clogged. Homes with forced-air systems may be particularly susceptible to problems because ducts can spread the toxic gases around the home.

Check the flame on any gas appliance. If it's yellow tipped—and not blue—excess CO is being released and the burner should be adjusted. Remember, CO is colorless and odorless, and the only way to know if there's a problem is to test.

Where to Find Help and Further Information

Home inspectors normally evaluate combustion sources during a home inspection. Make sure they look at all sources (not just the furnace), check for the problems mentioned above, and verify that they are installed to meet the building code. *A qualified professional should inspect all combustion sources regularly.*

The local building department may have records and approvals for furnaces, fireplaces, and woodstoves. A fire department official may conduct a free safety inspection. Other sources for inspections are the gas or fuel company and heating equipment or chimney-cleaning contractors. The cost to inspect and service most heating systems should be under $100.

Samples of the indoor air can be tested to determine levels of CO or particulates and compared to guidelines set by the EPA or OSHA for commercial settings. The EPA's guideline for CO in ambient air is 9 parts per million (ppm) for an eight-hour day; OSHA's standard is 35 ppm. Because of the cost, testing is not normally done unless a health problem is suspected. If this type of sampling and evaluation is desired, it should be done by a home inspector or an industrial hygienist. Some gas companies and heating contractors can also perform these tests, which run between $50 and $200. Because conditions in a home vary, samples may need to be collected more than once to adequately characterize levels.

Information about CO detectors can be obtained from the CPSC (800/638-2772; see Appendix 4).

The Bottom Line

Improperly functioning combustion sources that emit toxic gases, such as carbon monoxide, present health and financial risks to home owners. To ensure their safety, all home owners, as well as potential buyers, should take precautions to ensure that furnaces, woodstoves, portable heaters and stoves, as well as chimneys and flues, are properly installed, inspected, and maintained. All buyers should factor in the cost to fix problem combustion sources when considering a purchase. Carbon monoxide poisoning is serious but can be prevented easily and relatively cheaply—all homes with gas or oil-fired appliances should have CO detectors.

4. DRINKING WATER: PRIVATE WELLS

Homes in rural and semirural areas that are not served by public drinking water supplies

Risks: HEALTH ⊕⊕⊕ FINANCIAL $ $

Background

According to the EPA, about 15 percent of the U.S. population (forty million people) rely on private wells for drinking water and about 50 percent rely on groundwater, including public supply wells, for drinking water. Homes in rural, semirural, and lightly developed suburbs often have wells. Homes in developed neighborhoods may also use wells, even where public water supplies are available. Many well owners believe they have better water than those relying on a public water supply because they own the well and their water is not chemically treated or piped from an off-site source. However, the quality of well water can be problematic, due to naturally occurring compounds or human pollutants— and the problems range from minor nuisances to significant health and financial risks.

Wells are categorized by their depth and how they are constructed. Local soil conditions, the presence of bedrock, and groundwater depth govern what type of well can be built and used. "Shallow wells" include those that are "dug," "driven," or "bored" and are typically less than 100 feet deep. "Deep wells" are almost always drilled and may be 100 to 1,000 or more feet deep.

- Dug wells are just what their name implies: a hand- or machine-dug hole in the earth below the seasonal groundwater table, lined with brick, stone, or other material. They are usually 50 feet or less deep and 3 to 10 feet wide.
- Driven wells are the cheapest and easiest wells to build. A driven well consists of a small diameter metal pipe (3 inches or less), with a point and slotted screens on one end, that is driven by hand or by power tools to a depth of up to 50 feet.
- Bored wells are constructed using a rotating auger bit in soils without large rocks. Bored wells are usually 4 to 6 inches in diameter and may be 20 feet deep, if made by hand, or 100 or more feet deep if a machine auger is used.
- Drilled wells are normally constructed using a large truck-mounted "drill rig" machine. For private homes, they are usually 4 to 6 inches in diameter. There are many different types of drilled wells—one common construction method is to use a pneumatic hammer under high pressure, drilling down to the desired depth.

After the well hole, the most important components of a well include: the "casing" (the pipe that runs from the ground to the aquifer or bedrock); the "screen" (in nonbedrock wells, the slotted portion of the casing where water enters the well); the "packing" (the fill material outside the casing that keeps the screen from getting clogged); the "grouting" (an impermeable material used to seal and protect the well water from contaminants); and the cover at the top of the well (this should always be tightly sealed). When a new well is built or an existing well is opened for maintenance, it should be disinfected with bleach.

The well pump is also an important part of a home's water supply system. Depending on the well type, depth, and area, a variety of well pumps are available. Some pumps are located at the bottom of the well (called "submersible pumps"); others are located at the surface of the well or in a basement.

Storage capacity is an important consideration in any water system. Pressure tanks, which are located in the basement, provide some storage, but have limited capacity. Sometimes an additional storage tank or cistern may be used; often the well itself can serve as a reservoir for water (a 6-inch well with a 200-foot water column contains almost 300 gallons of water).

The *quantity* of water that a well will produce (its yield) is an important factor in determining whether or not a well can provide reliable service. A typical home of four people uses around two hundred gallons of water a day, not counting activities like watering the lawn or washing cars. More important than daily requirements are the peak water demands—when someone is taking a shower at the same time the washing machine or dishwasher is running, there may be a need for ten gallons of water per minute or more. The ability of a well to meet these requirements is very important; living in a home with a poor water supply can be a major nuisance.

How much water a well will yield is influenced by a number of factors: its construction and depth, the type of pump, and, most important, shallow and deep groundwater conditions. Some groundwater aquifers just don't have much water. And overuse or drought can result in temporary shortages or long-term problems. Shallow wells are most susceptible to short-term drought conditions as well as to contamination from nearby sources. In addition, nearby construction or blasting activities can reduce the yield of a well.

The range of possible problems in water *quality* and their consequences is broad. Some naturally occurring elements, like iron, may be a nuisance and an aesthetic problem (such as making your water look rusty) but do not represent any health concern, while others, like radon, can cause serious health problems. Private wells can be contaminated as a result of such on- and off-site hazards as septic systems (by nitrates and bacteria), salt storage piles (sodium), leaking underground tanks (gasoline or oil), industries (toxic waste or solvents), agricultural activities (pesticides), or landfills (organic compounds or metals). Since groundwater is not static, the water in a well can be impacted by activities thousands of feet, or even several miles, away. (Off-site hazards that can impact wells are discussed in Part III.)

Groundwater usually moves in a downhill direction. Soil conditions and geology greatly influence the natural quality and quantity of groundwater supplies. Groundwater entering deeper, drilled wells is more likely to have originated far away. Remember that groundwater supplies are a renewable but complicated, dynamic, and fragile resource. Wells that currently provide excellent quality and quantity of water can be impacted through new real estate development or contamination from historic or new nearby sources of pollution.

Below are short summaries of the major well water contaminants that may be encountered, their sources, associated health risks, and typical treatment options. The EPA has established drinking water standards for over one hundred chemical substances. Because of their importance, we have reproduced the EPA's list of drinking water standards in Appendix 2. Although the EPA's standards do not apply to private drinking water wells, home owners who rely on a private well can use them as guidance. Remember that health risks depend on the compound, the amount, and the duration of exposure—just because a certain compound is present in a water supply doesn't necessarily mean that it is unsafe to drink. Also remember that these problems aren't unique to well water—public water systems may be plagued by the same problems.

Compounds Associated with Aesthetic Problems

Iron and Manganese The naturally occurring metals iron and manganese can make water taste bad and discolor plumbing fixtures and clothes with reddish to black stains. Reddish, slimy bacteria also thrive in water with high iron levels. Treatment options include water softeners, specially designed iron filters, and chlorination where iron bacteria are a problem.

Hard Water Caused by calcium and magnesium, two naturally occurring minerals, hard water can present problems with laundry and other washing activities because it prevents soap from lathering properly. It also causes white scales to form on appliances and fixtures. Water softeners (see page 65), which are typically used to treat hard water, put small amounts of sodium into the water, which can be a health problem for some. Potassium can be used instead of sodium in these situations.

Sodium, Chloride, and Dissolved Solids Sodium, chloride, and dissolved solids occur naturally in water but are often the result of contamination from improper salt storage, landfills, and industrial activities. Use of a water softener can also increase the sodium level in water. These compounds can impart a bad taste to water. A high level of dissolved solids can result from intrusion of brackish water into a well from natural or man-made sources. Elevated sodium levels may pose a problem for people with high blood pressure. Treatment options include distillation and reverse osmosis systems (see page 66).

Acidic or Corrosive Water Acidic or corrosive water is a result of natural conditions and can cause blue-green staining of plumbing fixtures and corrosion that can ruin pipes and appliances such as water heaters. Acidic water can increase the leaching of lead and therefore may pose a health risk if the water pump has parts containing lead, or if lead piping, soldering, or fixtures are in the house. Water neutralizers (see page

65) are normally used for treatment of acidic water but may raise hardness levels.

Compounds Associated with Health Problems

Nitrate Nitrate contamination can come from natural soil conditions or from agricultural activities (application of chemical fertilizers and manure), failing or improperly sited septic systems, or improper disposal of sewage sludge. The major health concern from drinking nitrate-rich water or baby formula mixed with such water is methemoglobinemia ("blue baby disease"), which impairs the ability of infants to exchange oxygen and can be fatal. Some adults, especially pregnant women, are also susceptible to developing methemoglobinemia. Nitrate treatment options include reverse osmosis, distillation, or anion exchange systems (see page 66).

Bacteria and Viruses Bacteria and viruses can get into well water if the well is too close to a septic system, or if it is poorly built, shoddily maintained, damaged, or contaminated as a result of flooding, from nearby agricultural activities, from landfill leachate, or from improper sewage sludge disposal. Poorly maintained deep wells (with cracked collars or open tops) and shallow "dug" wells can allow bacteria-contaminated surface water to get into the groundwater. Bacteria and viruses cause gastrointestinal or more serious health problems. Treatment may require disinfection of the water (usually with bleach), boiling of the water, or the use of specialized filters. If there is a recurring bacteria problem, identify and address the cause.

Radon The naturally occurring radioactive gas radon can cause lung cancer. Treatment options include carbon filters and air strippers (see pages 65–66 and Hazard 19, Radon in Water).

Lead Lead can get into well water from off-site sources but is more likely to occur as a result of a home's plumbing or fixtures being corroded by acidic water. Well pumps may contain brass parts that can leach lead when they come into contact with acidic water. Ingestion of lead can cause brain, nervous system, or kidney damage. Children and pregnant women are at greatest risk. Treatment options for lead include reverse osmosis, distillation, and some carbon filters. In some cases, a water neutralizer can prevent lead from leaching out of plumbing (see page 65 and Hazard 14, Lead in Water).

Other Metals The EPA has published drinking water standards for other metals, including arsenic, barium, cadmium, chromium, mercury, selenium, and silver. While sometimes of natural origin, these toxic metals can stem from industrial, municipal, or hazardous waste sites, or from pesticides, and can easily contaminate groundwater. Treatment for metals can be difficult; one option is to use a water softener or anion exchange system (see pages 65–66).

Pesticides Pesticides include a number of chemicals used for agricultural, commercial, and residential purposes that are linked with a variety of health problems. Carbon filters are the most common treatment option for organic pesticides (see pages 65–66 and Hazard 42, Pesticides).

Organic Chemicals Organic chemicals associated with industrial and commercial activities, waste disposal sites, or underground tanks include fuel components (benzene or toluene) and industrial or dry-cleaning solvents (xylene or trichloroethylene). Carbon filters and air strippers are the most common treatment option for organic chemicals (see pages 65–66).

Oil Oil contamination can result from spills, leaking storage tanks, or past disposal activities. Oils used in well pumps have been known to leak and pollute a well. Pump motors installed before 1979 may contain polychlorinated biphenyls (PCBs), which have also contaminated wells as a result of leaks. Dealing with oil contamination is difficult—carbon filters may be a treatment option (see pages 65–66).

Health Risks

The health risks from drinking contaminated well water depend on the compound, its concentration, and the period of exposure. In addition, certain organic compounds, if present in drinking water, can volatilize and be released into the indoor air when showering and pose a variety of health risks. A discussion of the health risks from every potential groundwater contaminant is beyond the scope of this book. A brief summary of the health concerns of a few of the most common well water contaminants is provided above, in Background. See Appendix 2 for the list of the EPA's drinking water standards, which include descriptions of potential health effects.

Financial Risks

The cost to install a well varies greatly, depending on the area of the country and type of well required. Costs may be less than $1,000 for a shallow well, can range from $1,500 to $5,000 for a "normal" deep well, and can reach $10,000 or even more for a very deep well (well drillers often charge by the foot). Sometimes the yield of an existing well can be improved by physical methods (one method is called "hydrofracturing"); costs for such a program can be $1,000 to $5,000. Often a new well must be drilled with the hope that it will have a better yield, or a holding tank must be used to provide buffer water storage capacity.

Potential buyers will ask about well water quality and quantity, and costs to deal with problems should be factored into any offer. Some buyers may be put off if a water treatment system is in use, even if it is for a conventional problem like hardness.

Aesthetic problems, like those caused by hardness and iron, can usually be solved with commonly available and inexpensive treatment systems. Such problems are not uncommon, and except for the cost of installing and operating a system, they should not impact property values significantly. Other, primarily aesthetic problems, like excess salinity from dissolved salts and chloride, may be difficult to treat and may require use of bottled water or an alternate drinking water supply.

Properties with contaminated wells will be significantly devalued (at best) and difficult to sell (at worst). Even if a problem is corrected (by installing a treatment system), a property may be devalued due to stigma. Often bottled water may be the only short-term option, and possibly the only affordable (although inconvenient) long-term solution. The cost to treat or otherwise correct a problem can be:

- relatively low, if a small, under-the-sink treatment system is all that is needed (such systems cost between $50 and $500), or if a one-time treatment is required (disinfection with bleach to treat a bacteria problem);
- moderate, for a simple water treatment system (a basic water-softening system should cost between $800 and $1,500), or if a well must be repaired ($300 to $1,000);
- relatively high, if a new well or sophisticated treatment system ($1,000 to $10,000) is required; or
- exorbitant, if a home owner is assessed for connection to a distant public water supply.

It costs money to operate a well—while electricity usage is usually low, periodic maintenance and replacement of the well pump (which may last five to twenty years, depending on the quality of the water and how the pump is installed and used) will be required at a cost of around $500 to $1,000. Water treatment systems will also have operating and replacement costs. For example, water softeners must have salt added to them fairly often (this may cost between $5 and $20 a month) and can require new treatment media after five to ten years ($100 to $300).

Other financial risks:

► Liability for nondisclosure; see Disclosure Obligations, pages 13–19.

► Costs for short- or long-term medical treatment and monitoring; legal and expert fees; and inconvenience and relocation costs due to forced evacuation if a well becomes contaminated.

Managing the Risks

Routine preventative maintenance of a well and any water treatment device can reduce health and financial risks. First, make sure the well has a good cover and is sealed to prevent contamination by surface water (plywood sheets or an upside-down bucket are *not* appropriate covers). For dug wells, make sure the top of the cover is above grade and the area is landscaped or graded so that any surface water flows away from the well. For wells contaminated with bacteria, it may be possible to disinfect the well water using bleach for up to twenty-four hours (call your local health department for instructions). However, if surface water runoff carrying bacteria is a recurring problem, it may be necessary to recase the well or extend the casing above the ground surface.

The pump and pressure tank controls should be checked regularly to make sure the pressure is correct, the pump is running smoothly, and there is no corrosion or leakage. Water treatment systems should be maintained according to the manufacturer's instructions—to avoid headaches and emergency service calls, make sure filters are replaced, chemicals are added, and the system components are all working properly. Some water treatment companies will provide these services under a separate service contract.

Houses should not be electrically grounded to copper pipes in the basement—this can increase corrosion of metals, like copper or lead from solder, into the water. Instead they should be "earth grounded."

Treatment systems for more conventional problems, like hardness or iron, as well as systems that can treat other contaminants, are readily available from plumbers or local companies specializing in water treatment. Two nationally recognized trade groups—the Water Quality Association (708/505-0160) and the National Sanitation Foundation International (800/673-6275)—offer product testing and certifications for water treatment devices and provide information to consumers. A detailed description of water treatment systems is beyond the scope of this book. Nevertheless, because of the importance of this topic, some of the more common types of treatment systems available are discussed below.

Two general categories of water treatment devices are available:

whole-house systems, where a relatively large system is installed to treat the water as it enters the house; and "point-of-use" systems, which are smaller and are installed to treat water at a faucet or under a sink. Always discuss your specific situation with an expert before buying a system. Be sure to consider the volume of water you need to treat, the capacity of your well, its operating costs (electricity and replacement chemicals), and the maintenance and routine attention it will require. Some may come with alarms; some may have options for varying degrees of automation. Make sure the installer is qualified and have the water tested before and after the system is installed to make sure it is working properly.

Solids Filters Solids filters remove fine particles, sand, grit, and solids from the water. Because many compounds which cause health problems are either dissolved or too small to be removed by a filter, sand filters alone cannot usually eliminate problems. However, when suspended particles are the only problem, a filter should work fine; they are also used in front of other treatment systems. Filters range from disposable paper or plastic cartridges that are dropped into a plastic housing, to automatic backwashing sand filters that require installation by a plumber.

Water Softeners Also known as cation exchange systems, water softeners replace calcium and magnesium salts associated with hard water with less harmful sodium or potassium salts. The "good" salts must be periodically added to the system to keep it working. Under certain conditions, softeners can also remove low levels of iron or other metals from the water. Most water softeners require the installation of two small tanks and have an automatic backwashing system that produces a waste brine solution that may be regulated by state or local health codes.

Iron Removal Systems Iron removal systems precipitate iron dissolved in the water into a solid (using air, bleach, ozone, or other chemicals) that is then captured by a filter. As with water softeners, these types of systems must be backwashed periodically.

Water Neutralizers Water neutralizers "sweeten" acidic water by passing it over a bed of marble chips or limestone or by injecting a neutralizing solution (like soda ash or sodium hydroxide) directly into the water. These systems require periodic replacement of the treatment chemical and maintenance of the chemical feed pumps.

Activated Carbon Filters A variety of compounds can be removed by activated carbon filters, including radon, chlorine, and some other pollutants (lead, certain pesticides, or compounds like benzene, or solvents—check with an expert to make sure activated carbon works on the specific compound you are concerned about). Use of a carbon filter can also be a very effective way to improve water's taste and odor and to remove color. These filters are often used in conjunction with a solids filter. Carbon systems cannot be reactivated at home and must be routinely discarded or replaced to ensure proper functioning and to prevent bacterial buildup. The filters range in size from small point-of-use systems connected to a tap or under the sink to large whole-house systems.

Air Strippers Air strippers purge radon and some volatile organic pollutants (like solvents or gasoline) out of the water and allow them to be vented outside the house. They are typically large whole-house systems.

Reverse Osmosis "RO" systems remove metals, salts (including sodium), bacteria, fluoride, and nitrates from water supplies. These systems consist of ultrafine membranes that separate many contaminants from water under pressure. They can be expensive and are usually installed as point-of-use systems. These systems produce a waste brine solution.

Distillation Units Distillation units can remove bacteria, metals (like lead), and dissolved solids from a water supply by boiling the water and then condensing the steam that forms as water. These units can be expensive to operate and usually have a small capacity.

Anion Exchange Systems Anion exchange systems are usually used for the treatment of nitrates but are also effective at removing sulfates and certain toxic metals (such as arsenate). They are normally large whole-house systems that look and function like a water softener.

Chlorination and Ultraviolet Light Systems Chlorine and strong ultraviolet (UV) light are used to disinfect water and to kill bacteria and other potentially harmful microorganisms. The chlorination systems are older, tried and true, but may impart a chlorine taste and odor to the water (carbon filters can be used to remove the chlorine taste). Chlorination can result in the production of low levels of trihalomethanes, which are suspected of causing health problems (see Appendix 2). The UV light systems are newer, generally effective, but expensive.

In addition to on-site treatment, there are many other options for responding to a well water problem. In some cases, installing a new well may be the best option (if allowed); however, no new well can be guaranteed to yield water. A new well may often have the same problem as the original if, as is usually the case, it is located nearby. The use of bottled water for drinking and cooking may be an interim solution, although inconvenient, in some cases. Connection to a nearby public supply, if available, may be the only solution in some instances.

In situations where pollution has impacted private drinking water wells, state or local authorities should be involved and can sometimes help locate the responsible parties and force them to clean up the problem and provide bottled water or install treatment systems at impacted properties, or connect a home to a public water supply. However, this is often a time-consuming and frustrating process. Another option open to home owners is to sue the responsible party. This too will be a time-consuming and potentially costly undertaking.

Regulatory Outlook

In general, federal and state drinking water laws and regulations *do not* apply to private drinking water wells. The EPA, under the federal Safe Drinking Water Act of 1974 (and its 1986 amendments), has adopted standards that set maximum contaminant levels (MCLs) and MCL goals for over one hundred compounds that can be found in drinking water. The standards typically apply only to public and private water supply systems serving more than twenty-five people (see Hazard 5, Drinking Water: Public Water Supplies). The EPA has also developed unenforceable standards relating to taste, color, odor, and other aspects that do *not* present a health risk. Tables containing the primary and secondary standards are included in Appendix 2. Many state and local environmental and health departments have adopted these standards. While these standards usually do not apply to private wells, state and local agencies will use them as guidelines for determining whether or not well water is safe to drink.

Where groundwater contamination by others is suspected, local or state environmental agencies may undertake investigations and cleanup actions. All state environmental and health agencies have the ability to issue orders and penalize those suspected of causing contamination problems.

In many areas, there are local health requirements that must be met when installing a new well, such as a minimum distance from a septic system; permits may be required before drilling and documents about the new well may need to be filed with local or state agencies. In certain areas of the country where groundwater supplies are scarce, you may *not* automatically be entitled to use the groundwater under your property. In addition some state and local governments (such as the state of Washington) have restricted the installation of new wells to protect water resources used for fish and wildlife. For new homes, health departments usually require a water test prior to issuance of a certificate of occupancy. In some areas, wells must also have some minimum yield (often between five and fifteen gallons per minute) before a certificate of occupancy will be issued.

What to Look For

The seller or agent will know whether or not a property is served by a well and if it has a water treatment system. This information is often included in the real estate listing information. Newer wells can be hundreds of feet deep—the top parts of deep wells are often located above ground (they may be four- to six-inch-diameter pipes). Tops of shallow wells are often covered with a concrete or metal plate. Check to see that the well cover is tightly sealed; if there is a concrete collar, it should be free of cracks. Make sure the well is not located near the septic system.

Well pumps can be submerged at the base of a well or located at the surface (in a basement or a well house), where they effectively pull the water out of the ground. A pressure tank is often located in the basement to maintain water pressure in the home. To get a feel for the supply volume and pressure, don't simply flush the toilets a couple of times—run the bathwater and dishwasher at the same time for a while. Ask about the water supply volume.

Buyers should look for a water treatment system under the sink or in the basement. Whole-house water treatment systems usually have one or more tanks (six to eighteen inches in diameter, two to four feet high) or cartridges next to the water pressurization tank in the basement. Smaller systems may also be placed under a kitchen sink or on the tap. If a water treatment system or bottled water is used, find out why.

Look at, smell, and taste the water—problems may be apparent. For example, water containing large amounts of iron will taste metallic and may be tinged brown, and water contaminated by oil or gasoline may smell bad. Examine sinks, tubs, showers, and appliances (toilet bowl tanks, washing machines, dishwashers) for stains; blue stains may be due to acidic water corroding copper water pipes, black stains may indicate a high manganese content, and red-brown stains may indicate high iron levels in the water. A rotten egg odor may indicate a sulfur or sulfate problem. *However, in most cases, pollutants can be detected only by laboratory tests.*

Look for activities near the house that might cause a groundwater problem: gas stations, farms, landfills, industrial parks, and any of the others discussed in Part III. Knowledge of potential pollution sources can help you determine which (if any) specific laboratory tests are needed.

Where to Find Help and Further Information

Local health agencies may have records or reports containing information on a well's construction, initial yield, potability test records, and lab data filed by the contractors who installed the well. All home owners with wells should test the water for bacteria and other compounds every few years to ensure good water quality. Sellers should consider water tests to troubleshoot possible questions asked by buyers, as well as to allow time to fix a problem that could later kill a deal if it is discovered by a prospective buyer. Buyers of new homes where the well has not yet been drilled or the water tested should consider including a clause in the purchase agreement specifying what acceptable well yield and water quality will be, when a treatment system will be installed, and who will pay for it.

Buyers should have the water tested during a home inspection. Samples of water should be drawn as close to the well as possible (usually from a tap next to the water pressure tank) after letting the water run for several minutes. Other samples should be taken after any treatment equipment is installed (to see how it works) or, directly from a tap, first thing in the morning (to see if any metals are leaching from the home's plumbing system). Tests normally include common drinking water constituents, as recommended by a testing lab or health agency. A test of ten to fifteen basic parameters (not including organics, pesticides, or other site-specific possible contaminants) should cost between $75 and $150. Basic parameters to test for include:

- corrosiveness—pH and alkalinity
- bacteria
- hardness
- ammonia and nitrates
- color
- iron and manganese
- lead
- turbidity
- dissolved solids
- sodium and chloride

You may also want to test for some of the following compounds, depending on your particular location:

- copper and lead (if the water is corrosive)
- radon (if indoor air tests indicate high levels)

- fluoride (particularly if you are giving fluoride supplements to your children)
- metals like arsenic or chromium, or radioactivity (if natural or off-site sources are a concern)
- pesticides (for agricultural activities)
- hydrocarbons (if leaking underground tanks are a concern)
- volatile organic compounds (VOCs) (if contamination from solvents or other off-site sources is possible)

Since it may be impossible to determine which chemicals to test for, a more expensive, generic test for several groups of common pollutants (such as metals, petroleum products, or pesticides) may be necessary if a problem is suspected. Home inspectors and local laboratories offer testing services and can provide advice about specific situations.

Get sampling instructions and help from private laboratories if you do the sampling yourself, or let your inspector do the tests. Some labs (see your phone book under "water" or "water testing") will mail out bottles and instructions—you take the sample and ship it to the lab. Where and how you sample the water is important to ensure that results are representative. If a sample shows high levels of some contaminant, retest the water to verify initial results before purchasing a treatment system or taking other actions—laboratory error is always a possibility, especially when some compounds are being measured at levels of parts per billion.

The EPA and state and local environmental or health agencies or agricultural extension offices may be able to provide information about a specific existing well or whether there are any known groundwater problems in an area (see Appendix 4). Neighbors are another good source of information about well water problems in an area.

Private water treatment companies often have experts available to discuss contamination problems and will provide cost estimates for treatment systems. Keep in mind, however, that these people make their living selling treatment systems; beware of buying a system you don't need or one that may be ineffective in your situation. All water tests should be done by an independent laboratory, not by the seller of the treatment system. For more information, see U.S. Environmental Protection Agency, *Is Your Drinking Water Safe?*, EPA 810-F-94-002, 1994; U.S. Environmental Protection Agency, *Home Water Treatment Units—Filtering Fact from Fiction*, EPA 570/-90-HHH, 1990.

The Bottom Line

Safe drinking water is such a basic and essential part of good health that it is imperative that you be comfortable with your home's supply. Some knowledge about the water quality, through testing, may be required for this comfort. Living with an inadequate or tainted water supply will be, at best, an inconvenience and, at worst, a health threat and a source of worry. Common well water problems can usually be remedied by treatment. Costs should be factored into the price offered for a home. In areas where more serious groundwater contamination problems exist, homes may be significantly devalued—in these cases, buyers and sellers must understand the risks and have a plan to cope with them before a home is bought or sold.

5. DRINKING WATER: PUBLIC WATER SUPPLIES

Most city, urban, and suburban areas

Risks: HEALTH ⊕ ⊕ ⊕   FINANCIAL $ $

Background

Over 85 percent of the U.S. population relies on public water supplies for their drinking water needs. Drinking water in urban, suburban, and many rural communities is supplied by the almost 200,000 public water suppliers (i.e., local governmental agencies or private or quasi-public utility companies). The source of water varies depending on the area of the country: greater than 90 percent comes from surface water supplies, like lakes, reservoirs, and rivers; less than 10 percent of publicly supplied water comes from wells. As with other natural resources, the quality of water supplies can be impacted by natural or man-made pollution, drought, or overuse. The U.S. Centers for Disease Control reports that an average of only seventy-four hundred cases of disease caused by contaminated public drinking water supplies are reported each year. This number is low, as many cases don't get reported.

Problems that may be encountered with public water supplies range from objectionable odors or taste, to the staining of plumbing fixtures and high hardness (which causes problems because soap won't dissolve), to contamination with bacteria or man-made toxic compounds. The possible contaminants that can impact publicly supplied water are generally the same as those for well water (see Hazard 4, Drinking Water: Private Wells, pages 60–62). The EPA has established drinking water standards for over one hundred chemical substances (see Appendix 2). However, while drinking water quality may meet the EPA standards when it leaves the water treatment plant, it can deteriorate by the time it reaches your tap, as compounds like lead can leach out of pipes (see Hazard 14, Lead in Water).

Most of the large water suppliers (and many small ones) treat the water before it is delivered to customers to soften it, remove turbidity or other contaminants (such as iron and manganese), and to kill pathogens (bacteria and viruses). Treatment may include some combination of chemical addition, aeration, settling, filtration, carbon adsorption, and disinfection (typically by adding chlorine). Some communities run desalinization plants because their groundwater supplies have become brackish due to saltwater intrusion or overuse. Fluoride is added to many public water supplies to help prevent dental problems.

Health Risks

The health risks associated with contaminated public drinking water supplies depend on the specific pollutant, its concentration, and the period of exposure. A discussion of the health risks from every potential contaminant is beyond the scope of this book. In Hazard 4, Drinking Water: Private Wells, we provide a brief summary of health concerns of a few of the most common water contaminants (also see Appendix 2 for the EPA's drinking water standards, which include a description of potential health effects).

A common complaint about publicly supplied water is that it smells and tastes "funny." This is usually due to chlorine, which is added to kill microorganisms. Chlorine is not suspected of causing health problems at the low levels used in drinking water (except to goldfish). A by-product of chlorination is the formation of small amounts of chlorinated organic compounds (known as trihalomethanes) such as chloroform, some of which are toxic and are suspected of causing cancer and birth defects at high levels. Levels of these compounds should be monitored by the supplier and should be below the EPA threshold of 100 ppb (see Appendix 2).

Recently, bacterial contamination in public water supplies has been identified as a major problem that causes gastrointestinal illness. Symptoms of illnesses caused by bacteria include nausea, vomiting, and diarrhea. An outbreak in Milwaukee in 1993 reportedly caused hundreds of thousands of people to become sick from exposure to a drinking water–borne microbe known as "cryptosporidium." Many people are believed to have died as a result of complications induced by the illness. These organisms managed to pass through water that had been filtered and chlorinated.

Many other cities, large and small, have had similar public outbreaks of health problems (though not as large or as well covered by the national media as the one in Milwaukee). Other common bacteria include coliform, which come from contamination by human and animal waste and can cause gastrointestinal problems such as dysentery, and *Giardia,* a parasite that causes diarrhea. Some scientists believe that the problem of gastrointestinal diseases caused by public water supplies is greatly underestimated, since the overwhelming majority of people don't get sick enough to see a doctor or go to the hospital, and even when they do, unless there is some obvious outbreak, most doctors will treat the patient without identifying the water as the problem.

Fluoride is added to many public water supplies because, at low levels (about 1 ppm), it helps prevent tooth decay. However, fluoride levels in water can be naturally high and cause discoloration of teeth, especially in children.

Other possible health risks associated with public drinking water depend on the particular contaminant (see pages 60–62). In some areas of the country, low levels of radon or toxic metals may be in the water or there may be high levels of solids that make the water taste bad. Some public water supply wells have problems with organic pollutants, such as cleaning solvents or gasoline. For example, a dozen companies in an industrial park in Burlington, Massachusetts (where one of the authors grew up), were forced to spend millions to clean up groundwater contaminated by VOCs which shut down nine public supply wells that served more than 80 percent of the town's residents with drinking water.

The water supplier should be made aware of any problems and is required to take corrective measures.

Financial Risks

Homes with water supplies that are known to cause or are suspected of causing health problems may be devalued. Aesthetic problems (such as odor or high hardness) are not uncommon and generally won't reduce property values. In many of these situations, the home owner could purchase bottled water or, if feasible, use a treatment system. Efforts should always be made to have the costs of any treatment borne by the water supplier. Costs vary substantially—simple filters for the faucet can be installed by a do-it-yourselfer for under $100; a more complicated system might involve an under-the-sink distillation system that could cost up to $500; whole-house water treatment systems can cost $1,000 to $10,000. Bottled water costs depend on the location and the amount needed and can range from $5 to $50 a month. See Hazard 4, Drinking Water: Private Wells, page 63, for more details concerning costs associated with water treatment systems.

Home owners often have to pay large assessments (which can run into thousands of dollars) for connection to a public water supply system—these assessments are often paid over several years. Problems may arise at closing if assessments have not been fully paid or if the buyer isn't aware of them. As a result of mandates included in the federal drinking water law, many suppliers will be upgrading their treatment plants over the next few years at substantial costs—costs that likely will be passed along to consumers in the form of new capital assessments or increased user charges.

Potential buyers should ask about water quality; costs to deal with a problem should be factored into the offer. Some buyers may be concerned if a water treatment system is in use, even if it is for a common problem like hardness, and may use a water problem as a bargaining chip during negotiations.

Other financial risks:

▶ Liability for nondisclosure; see Disclosure Obligations, pages 13–19.
▶ Costs for short- or long-term medical treatment and monitoring; legal and expert fees; and inconvenience and relocation costs due to forced evacuation if the public water supply becomes contaminated.

Managing the Risks

Your water supplier should be aware of specific problems with its water and be able to suggest needed home treatment systems. Contact the water supplier to find out if there is a plan to fix the problem, and if so, when it will be implemented. Water suppliers are regulated by the EPA and/or state environmental or health agencies—if the supplier cannot answer your questions, you may need to contact one of these agencies (see Appendix 4).

Options for the home owner range from use of bottled water to installing a treatment system (see pages 64–66). For some contaminants, simply running the tap for several minutes before drinking or cooking with the water can lower risks considerably. Carbon filters can be used to reduce chlorine taste and odor, and also remove trihalomethanes. For bacterial problems, treatment options include boiling the water; on-site disinfection using chlorine, ozone, or ultraviolet light systems; or use of a specialized filter.

Regulatory Outlook

In 1974, Congress enacted the Safe Drinking Water Act (SDWA), which directs the EPA to establish minimum national drinking water standards. These standards set limits on the amounts of various substances found in drinking water. Owners of public water supplies that serve more than twenty-five people (or fifteen homes) are regulated under the SDWA. In 1986, Congress amended this law to accelerate the EPA's regulation of drinking water contaminants, ban future use of lead pipes and lead solder, mandate better protection of groundwater sources of public drinking water, and streamline enforcement to ensure that water suppliers comply. Under the SDWA, there are two types of drinking water standards. The National Primary Drinking Water Standards, which are designed to protect public health and are enforceable, set maximum contaminant levels for dozens of compounds (see Appendix 2). These standards reflect the levels the EPA believes we can safely consume in our water. In addition to the primary standards, the EPA has also issued Secondary Drinking Water Standards for fifteen compounds, which are *unenforceable guidelines* recommended to states as goals concerning taste, odor, color, and other aspects of drinking water (see Appendix 2). States may adopt their own enforceable regulations concerning these secondary standards.

Many states run the SDWA program or at least share the responsibility with the EPA. State drinking water laws must be at least as stringent as the SDWA. Many county or local governments also have agencies that control public water supplies. Under the SDWA, water suppliers must regularly test their water to verify that it meets the primary standards. If tests fail, they must notify their customers (by newspaper, radio or TV, or letter, depending on the circumstances); for certain contaminants that exceed acute standards, notification must be given within seventy-two hours. Whenever lab reports are requested by a customer, the supplier must provide them. In cases where the water is substandard, suppliers are supposed to install treatment systems to correct the specific problem—in any case, many have had to install basic treatment systems (filters and chlorination) under this law. The SDWA has provisions for significant penalties for suppliers who fail to meet its requirements and deadlines.

Building new water treatment plants, or upgrading existing ones, are often major public works projects that can cost millions of dollars—even when a supplier has identified and committed to fixing a water quality problem, it will probably take years before home owners see results. Remember also that while the SDWA covers systems that serve up to 80 percent of the U.S. population, small systems (those serving fewer than twenty-five people) are exempted from much of this program—these companies may be subject only to state and local requirements.

What to Look For

The presence of a water treatment system, whether a whole-house system located in the basement or an under-the-sink unit, or use of bottled water, may be an indication of some problem with the public water supply. If a water treatment system or bottled water is used, find out why. The seller or real estate agent should be able to tell you if a home uses a water treatment system.

Look at, smell, and taste the water—in some cases, problems will be apparent. For example, water containing large amounts of iron will taste metallic and may be tinged brown, or water contaminated by gasoline may smell bad. Likewise, examine sinks, tubs, showers, and appliances (toilet bowl tanks, washing machine, and dishwasher) for stains—blue stains may be due to acidic water corroding copper pipes, black stains may indicate high manganese, and red-brown stains may indicate high iron levels in the water. *However, in most cases, pollutants can be detected only by laboratory tests.*

Where to Find Help and Further Information

Ask the seller and neighbors about any problems. The water supplier must provide information about the water and how it is treated. Request copies of recent water-testing reports and ask if there have been any complaints or problems and how they have been handled. The water supplier may be willing to do water tests for you at no cost. To find the name and number of the water supply company, look at a water bill or call your local health department. Information on drinking water quality and treatment is available from the EPA as well as your state environmental or health agency (see Appendix 4). The EPA also maintains a toll-free Safe Drinking Water Hotline (800/426-4791).

Depending on the area, all home owners (and especially buyers) should test the water for at least the basic parameters: pH and alkalinity (to see if the water is corrosive), hardness, bacteria, and lead are a few basic tests that can be run for under $75. More expansive testing may be warranted in some cases, depending on the water supply—talk with the water supplier, your home inspector, or an environmental expert (see Hazard 4, Drinking Water: Private Wells, page 69, for more on possible test parameters). Private laboratories provide water-testing services—check the phone book or call your state or local environmental or health agency to find out what labs are approved in your area (see Appendix 4). Home inspectors may provide water testing as part of their services. Make sure that water samples are collected *before* the water has passed through any existing treatment system, and, depending what you're testing for, at the tap, too (see page 69). Commercial water treatment companies often employ experts in treatment problems and will provide cost estimates for treatment systems. Keep in mind, however, that these people make their living selling treatment systems—beware of buying a system you don't need or one that won't work for your problem, and never buy one without first testing the water. All water tests should be done by an independent laboratory, not a seller of treatment systems.

For more information, see U.S. Environmental Protection Agency, *Is Your Drinking Water Safe?*, EPA 810-F-94-002, 1994; U.S. Environmental Protection Agency, *Home Water Treatment Units—Filtering Fact from Fiction*, EPA 570/-90-HHH, 1990.

The Bottom Line

Public water suppliers must meet their responsibility to provide safe water to their customers. Under the SDWA, you have a right to expect that your water meets minimum standards and to be told if it doesn't.* Most water supplies *are* safe; however, some do not consistently meet health standards due to overdevelopment, lack of funding, poor operation, or natural or man-made events. Since drinking water is such a basic and essential part of life, it is important that your water supply is safe. Good information about the water can provide this comfort. Living with tainted water can be an inconvenience or, at worst, a health risk and a source of worry. Home owners with a bad water supply will have financial problems and health risks to deal with, and homes with contaminated water will be devalued. Buyers should factor the cost to remedy a water problem into the valuation of a home.

---

* In August 1996, Congress amended the SDWA to require public water suppliers to mail customers annual "Consumer Confidence Reports" identifying the levels of contaminants found in the water and the associated health risks.

6. EROSION AND SEDIMENTATION

Waterfront properties, newly constructed homes, or those on steep slopes

Risks: HEALTH None   FINANCIAL $ $

Background

Soil erosion is caused when wind, water, or ice strips topsoil away from the land, leaving bare ground that can form gullies and other depressions that, if not repaired, get progressively worse with time. While natural erosion usually occurs slowly, on properties abutting bodies of water, shoreline erosion can be rapid, particularly during the winter season, spring runoff, and stormy weather. Natural erosion can also be accelerated when the land is disturbed and vegetation is removed—either by fire, for example, or through human action, such as construction, the clearing of rights-of-way by utilities and railroads, timber harvesting, stream channeling, filling of wetlands, and farming. Exposed soil is then susceptible to increased erosion by wind and water action. Erosion leads to sedimentation—the movement and deposition of soil particles carried by storm water onto nearby properties and into lakes, rivers, streams, and oceans.

Properties most susceptible to erosion and sedimentation include new construction sites, those in or downhill from hilly areas, homes with steep slopes, and those that border bodies of water. In addition, homes near or below residential or commercial construction sites may have erosion and sedimentation problems if surface water runoff from the construction site is not managed properly. Erosion can expose and weaken a home's foundation and other structural features, including walls and driveways, and affect the ability of a property to support landscaping, gardens, or a septic system. In extreme cases, erosion can lead to a landslide that could completely destroy a home on a steep slope. Severely eroded properties, beside being an eyesore, can require costly repairs and can damage neighboring properties by channeling water onto them.

Health Risks

Health risks are not directly caused by erosion. However, erosion can damage a property, the weakened structures of which could cause bodily harm. In addition, erosion can destroy a septic system's leaching field and cause bacterial contamination of drinking water, thereby posing certain health risks (see Hazard 20, Septic Systems).

Financial Risks

Erosion problems can present significant financial risks to home owners. For example, in 1994, homes near a creek outside St. Louis experienced several erosion-related problems: cracked foundations, collapsed decks, eroded backyards—some homes were even condemned. Dredging activities in the San Jacinto River in Texas have caused significant erosion problems for riverfront property owners. In 1993, many multi-million-dollar homes in Laguna Beach, California, were severely damaged—many even slid down hills—from erosion caused by heavy rains in areas that had been denuded of vegetation by wildfires. A Toronto family whose home sits on a cliff saw more than twelve feet of their property drop into the river, and were looking at more than $300,000 to permanently fix the problem. Generally, home owner's insurance will not cover erosion problems, although some policies and flood insurance may. Controlling erosion requires a combination of landscaping and structural controls. Costs are minimal for simple problems but, when major controls such as building barriers or dikes are required, can increase to thousands or even tens of thousands of dollars.

Local building or soil conservation officials may require property owners to fix serious erosion problems. During new construction, they sometimes require bonds or other financial assurance that work will be completed properly. Local building authorities can also withhold issuance of a certificate of occupancy until erosion problems are solved.

Properties with erosion problems can be devalued. Potential buyers may ask about erosion from nearby construction or from natural occurrences, especially for waterfront properties. For example, home owners in a Hollywood, Florida, neighborhood have seen property values decline as a result of erosion caused by runoff from a nearby highway drainage ditch. For one family, a cracked foundation and water seepage cost an estimated $30,000 to repair. Buyers may demand that erosion problems be repaired or use the cost of fixing them as a negotiating point. In a California case, buyers bought a home on a one-acre parcel that suffered massive erosion just after the sale. Due to improperly engineered and compacted soil, a portion of the property slid away, damaging the driveway and cracking doors and walls. Costs to repair the damage were approximately $40,000. The real estate agents had observed indications of a potential problem, but had not warned the buyer.

Homes near construction projects or farms that create erosion problems may be affected by storm water runoff containing sediments or redirected flows that can cause on-site erosion or property damage. Home owners who have been impacted by erosion and sedimentation in some way may also incur costs to fix damage to a home's lawn and gardens, wetlands, ponds or lakes, or well water.

Expensive and time-consuming lawsuits can also result if neighbors sue when their properties are impacted by erosion caused by problems on your property.

Other financial risks:
- ▶ Liability for nondisclosure; see Disclosure Obligations, pages 13– 19. Some state and local laws specifically require sellers to disclose to prospective buyers that a property is in a designated erosion zone.
- ▶ Legal and expert fees.

Managing the Risks

Erosion problems can be prevented by minimizing disturbances to natural vegetation and grading a property to reduce slopes and prevent uncontrolled channeling of storm water. Physical structures like berms, retaining walls, rock cover, and surface drains are sometimes required. Carefully planned landscaping—using "vegetative buffers" comprised of the right combination of grasses, trees, and shrubs—can help to prevent erosion problems. Using porous substances such as flagstone, gravel, or crushed stone in lieu of asphalt or concrete can also reduce soil erosion around a home.

If the cause of erosion is an off-site activity or a builder's or developer's error, contact the responsible party for financial or technical help in correcting the problem, and for help managing the associated risks.

Regulatory Outlook

The EPA and many state and local environmental and land-use agencies require certain large construction and development projects to control erosion and sedimentation, as well as storm water runoff generally. Many states set sedimentation limits, but the enforcement of these limits is variable. For new home construction, erosion prevention and control is regulated by local building or conservation departments which approve plans that must address erosion and may require problems to be fixed before allowing occupancy. Some cities and towns restrict building on steep slopes and may require a soil analysis and structural engineering report before approving construction. Many towns and counties require developers to post bonds to secure the installation of erosion and sedimentation controls, such as hay bales, silt fences, soil-retaining sod, retaining walls, and special vegetation to minimize erosion and storm water runoff. For existing homes, unless a problem is severe or neighbors complain, there is usually no regulation of erosion. Many states and towns have shoreline protection rules that regulate the use of coastal properties and what types, if any, of erosion controls may be used.

What to Look For

Impacts of erosion are seen as gullies, exposed rock or sand, or areas with little vegetation. Areas around foundations and walls and other structures should be examined for signs of erosion damage. Look for unusual topography, such as steep slopes or plateaus, that may indicate large amounts of filling during a property's development; natural drainage patterns (swales, gullies, and flattened vegetation); and other signs of soil disturbance.

For waterfront properties, look for evidence of shore erosion, which can be caused by waves, high stream flows, steep slopes, large storms, human and vehicle traffic, ice damage, and tidal fluctuations. In some cases, you may need to go out on a boat to get a good look.

Where to Find Help and Further Information

A home inspector or professional engineer can evaluate structures damaged by erosion and help solve any problems. Experts can test soil conditions for the ability to provide a good foundation for a home. Landscaping contractors can help solve erosion problems. Local land use or building officials can provide information on known erosion problems and any erosion/sedimentation requirements for home construction, as well as copies of plans showing filling needed during property development and erosion and floodplain maps. Check aerial photographs that go back in time, if available, to see the history of site erosion (see Appendix 3).

If you are buying a waterfront property, find out about soil conditions, the slope of the property, and the history of erosion or flooding. Ask about any shoreline protection laws that you may have to deal with.

State and county agricultural offices, as well as the U.S. Department of Agriculture's Soil Conservation Service, recently renamed the Natural Resources Conservation Service (14th and Independence Street, SW, Washington, D.C. 20250, 202/720-4525), provide free literature on how to prevent and control soil erosion. The United States Geological Survey (USGS) may be able to provide additional information about a property's soil conditions and erosion history (see Appendix 3).

The Bottom Line

Erosion can be a problem for homes everywhere, and especially for those in new developments, near construction areas, and on waterfronts. Problems may be most severe during and immediately after new construction. Costs to prevent and control erosion can be minimal or significant depending on the situation—in all cases they should be factored into a property's value.

7. FLOODS AND OTHER NATURAL DISASTERS

Risks: HEALTH ⊕ ⊕ ⊕   FINANCIAL $ $ $

Background

Floods and other natural disasters, such as earthquakes, sinkholes, wildfires, and landslides, pose significant financial and health risks to home owners. Flooding is the most costly natural phenomenon in the United States. About 7 percent of the land area in the United States (containing more than eight million properties) is considered floodplain. Every year, floods cause millions of dollars' worth of property damage to thousands of homes and the loss of hundreds of lives. For example, the great flood of 1993 in the Midwest caused thirty-eight deaths, extensive damage to more than 100,000 homes, required the evacuation of tens of thousands of people, and created large-scale disruptions in transportation, business, and water and sewer services. More than five hundred counties were declared federal disaster areas and damage estimates were in the $16 billion range.

Although flooding is typically associated with coastal or lowland areas, floods can, and do, occur in many other areas. As new residential communities are built, large areas of land are paved over with impervious concrete and asphalt. The rainwater, which would naturally soak into the ground, must run off somewhere, and finds its way to rivers, lakes, and streams, creating flood problems for home owners.

Earthquakes, though not as common as floods, threaten large areas of the United States, especially California and Alaska, and cause extensive and costly damage. Damage to walls and foundations of homes, as well as their contents, can be caused by an earthquake's shock waves and the resulting shifting ground. The threat of an earthquake is not limited to the San Andreas Fault area of California—the most significant earthquakes to hit the United States occurred in Missouri in 1811, South Carolina in 1886, and Alaska in 1964. There are major fault lines in many areas, and the possibility of earthquakes threatens more than two-thirds of the United States.

Sinkholes are common in many areas (estimated at about 20 percent of the United States) where limestone deposits or other rocks susceptible to dissolution are prevalent below the surface of the earth. Large holes or depressions in the ground can form when limestone dissolves from natural causes or from various land use activities. Sinkholes can severely damage homes and impact the ability to develop land—experts calculate that hundreds of millions of dollars in damage has occurred in the last twenty years from more than six thousand sinkholes in the eastern United States. Sinkholes contribute to flooding, building and property damage or collapse, and groundwater contamination.

Other natural disasters, like wildfires, landslides, mudslides, and tornadoes, also cause a lot of property devastation and some deaths. In the arid western portion of the United States, for example, home owners brace themselves each summer for their annual encounter with wildfires. In 1994, wildfires claimed thirty-four lives, required the expenditure of more than $1 billion to fight them, and caused untold millions in property damage. Like wildfires, many natural disasters are limited to certain parts of the country. The catastrophic impacts of natural disasters cannot be controlled.

Many communities have stringent construction standards for homes in areas subject to flooding, earthquakes, sinkholes, or other natural disasters. These standards incorporate design features to minimize property damage. Local zoning may limit building in dangerous areas.

Health Risks

Health risks, while statistically small, are not insignificant. Hundreds of people die each year in the United States from floods, earthquakes, tornadoes, landslides, and wildfires, and many more are injured.

Financial Risks

Floods and other natural disasters present significant financial risks by causing damage to land, houses, and personal property. Home owner's insurance does not cover floods or other natural disasters unless coverage is specifically provided; without coverage, out-of-pocket costs can be enormous and financially debilitating. Costs can be as minimal as replacing a wall damaged by a minor flood to as high as the value of the entire property. Properties that experience floods or other natural disasters (or those with certain restrictions imposed on them) can be devalued. Potential buyers may ask about these problems, especially for waterfront properties. Buyers may demand that any problem be repaired, or use the cost to fix it as a negotiating point. In some areas, the mere possibility of a natural disaster may devalue a home.

Home owners who have been impacted by a natural disaster may incur other costs to fix damage to lawn and gardens, wetlands, private ponds or lakes, or well water. Temporary inconvenience and relocation costs are another very real possibility. Floods, for example, have contaminated homes with PCBs, and sinkholes have channeled surface-water runoff contaminated with pesticides, metals, and petroleum residues into private drinking water wells.

Banks and other mortgage lenders may require flood insurance as a condition for a loan for a home in a flood- or mudslide-prone zone. The average yearly premium under the National Flood Insurance Program (NFIP) (discussed below) is about $300. Premiums vary with the length of the policy, the deductible, the age of the house, the amount of building and contents coverage, and the hazard ranking of the area.

Earthquake insurance has not typically been required by banks, but this is changing; many home owners and their mortgage holders are simply unprotected. Annual costs for basic earthquake coverage starts at about $300, where it is available (the issue of cost and availability is a major problem in California).

Safety features can be built into new homes, but these can be costly. Local building ordinances require certain measures, such as mandatory flood walls, restrictions on the placement of doors and windows in floodplains, and additional structural protection in earthquake zones. Additional safety features can also be installed, depending on the buyer's finances and level of concern. Local zoning laws may severely curtail your ability to build on or develop in certain areas subject to natural disasters.

Although it's hard to imagine a buyer of a home in Los Angeles, or on a barrier island in South Carolina, or in the Oklahoma Panhandle, not being aware of the possibility of earthquakes, floods, or tornadoes, it doesn't mean that a seller is relieved of disclosure obligations. In addition, there are many areas where less threatening floods routinely occur, and buyers may not be aware of risks or requirements. In the context of a deal, if there is a known problem or a restriction on the property and it isn't disclosed, sellers and agents may face significant liability for failure to disclose the problem (see Disclosure Obligations, pages 13–19). Federal law, and some state and local laws, require sellers to disclose to prospective buyers that a property is in a designated flood (or other natural disaster) zone. Some state laws (such as in California) require that buyers be told if a home is on or near an earthquake fault.

Managing the Risks

If you live in an area subject to flooding, earthquakes, or other natural disasters, consider purchasing insurance to minimize your risks. No matter where you live, you may need special hazard insurance. Standard home owner's policies do not provide coverage for most natural disasters. Review your policy to see what is, and what is not, covered. For floods, property owners in eligible areas can obtain coverage through the NFIP—about 3.5 million policies are in effect nationwide. Coverage is provided only up to $250,000 for the home, and up to $100,000 for personal contents. A few insurers offer coverage beyond NFIP limits. Most people do not have insurance for earthquakes, but coverage is available from some companies as an endorsement to a standard policy and for an additional premium (special deductible provisions typically apply). Some natural hazards, such as fires, lightning, windstorms, hail, and tornadoes, are often covered by standard home owner's policies.

Become familiar with safety measures to take in the event of a disaster as well as precautionary measures to take to minimize risks to your health and property. Many local and state disaster-planning agencies can provide useful information. For new homes, consider incorporating safety features into the construction to address natural disasters that fit your budget and general attitude about risk. If your property is identified as being in a floodplain, and you believe this is incorrect, consult with your attorney about options to challenge the determination.

Regulatory Outlook

The primary federal agency involved in flood control is the U.S. Army Corps of Engineers. After a series of disastrous floods in the early 1900s, Congress enacted the Flood Control Act of 1936 (which has been amended over the years), establishing a national policy for flood control and a cooperative program with the state and local governments to carry out flood control activities. Overall the Corps' flood control programs are aimed at reducing the potential for property damage and human losses. The Corps performs emergency activities, such as fighting floods, repairing and restoring flood control works, and supplying emergency clean water to communities. The U.S. Department of Agriculture is also involved in flood control in agricultural watersheds.

Many states have specific programs for dealing with floods and other natural disasters. Most states are responsible for the overall coordination of floodplain management activities and regulation of local land use when towns and counties are unable or unwilling to take the actions needed to reduce the risk of flooding. Every state has given its local governments the authority to meet the regulatory requirements of the flood insurance program of the Federal Emergency Management Agency (FEMA), the National Flood Insurance Program (NFIP). Established in 1968, the NFIP identifies flood-prone areas, makes subsidized flood insurance available to home owners and businesses located on coastal areas and in floodplains *in communities that join the program,* and encourages floodplain management efforts. Under the flood program, FEMA prepares maps designating the one-hundred-year floodplain in communities (areas where the annual probability of a flood is 1 percent). In exchange for providing insurance, FEMA requires that the community adopt floodplain regulations, and that all buildings be protected to the base flood elevation (the height that a one-hundred-year flood would reach). This is usually accomplished by building structures above the base flood elevation or by floodproofing buildings. To satisfy FEMA's requirements, local governments develop laws that: (1) impose certain building codes for floodplain development; (2) limit the types of land use allowed in the floodplain; and (3) require that all development incorporate strategies and structures to minimize potential flood problems. With the passage of the federal National Flood Insurance Reform Act of 1994, major changes will take place with the NFIP, which governs the types of coverage available and how local insurers administer the program.

For other natural disasters, state and local land use laws and building codes must be consulted with respect to allowable locations and construction requirements for residential development.

We continue to make strides in flood and other natural disaster control projects. While new technology and early warning systems help prepare us for, and to some extent control, the damage, natural disasters will continue to occur and wreak unpredictable havoc.

What to Look For

Look around the property and the neighborhood for signs of property, tree, or house damage from natural disasters. For example, impacts from past floods are seen as gullies, exposed rock or sand, or areas with little vegetation. Areas around foundations and walls and other structures should be examined for signs of erosion damage. Look for natural drainage patterns and signs of soil or vegetation disturbance. Of course, the absence of these signs does not guarantee that floods or other natural disasters will not occur.

For waterfront properties, look for evidence of landscape erosion and damage to the house itself. Many low-lying areas can be subject to major or minor flooding problems. Even small creeks can vastly increase in size during floods. Sinkholes, common in areas of the southeast United States, can often be seen as large depressions on a property.

Where to Find Help and Further Information

A qualified home inspector or professional engineer can evaluate structures damaged by floods or other natural disasters and help solve any problems. Local land use or building officials can provide information on natural disasters in the area (such as sinkholes) and should have maps designating areas that have been subject to flooding or mudslides. The best bet for flood risk is to check local flood insurance maps (see Appendix 3). Areas referred to as "flood zones" or "floodplains" are mapped by the frequency of flooding—a one-hundred-year flood is more severe but occurs less frequently than a twenty-year flood. Check aerial photographs that go back in time, if available, to see the history of site erosion, sinkhole formation, or flooding (see Appendix 3). If you are buying a waterfront property, check into the history of flooding. Local officials can also provide information about specific rules for locating and building in these areas. Emergency organizations, like FEMA (800/462-9029), can supply information on planning for and coping with natural disasters. These agencies may be good sources of information on areas most at risk and techniques for minimizing your risk. Local fire departments often have general information on area fire risks. The National Weather Service (301/413-0900) can provide information on various natural disasters. For more information on flood insurance, call the NFIP (800/638-6620), or contact your local insurance agent for questions about coverage for natural disasters generally.

The Bottom Line

Floods and other natural disasters strike many homes throughout the United States, especially those in certain geographic areas or located near rivers, lakes, oceans, and other bodies of water. Homes in areas prone to natural disasters can be devalued because of associated health and financial risks. Property insurance requirements and options for homes in areas subjected to floods and other natural disasters should be evaluated and selected based on your budget and attitudes about risk. While you may or may not live by choice in an area prone to earthquakes, floods, tornadoes, or mudslides, the prudent course is to take steps to minimize financial risks to your property and add safety features to your home to protect you and your family.

8. FORMALDEHYDE INSULATION

Homes built (or where insulation was added to existing homes) during the 1970s and early 1980s, particularly in the Northeast

Risks: HEALTH ⊕   FINANCIAL $ $

Background

During the 1970s and early 1980s, formaldehyde insulation—also known as urea formaldehyde foam insulation (UFFI)—was installed as an energy-saving measure in about half a million homes in the United States (especially throughout the Northeast) and almost 100,000 homes in Canada. UFFI, a wet foam material, was pumped under pressure into walls through small holes, where it hardened to form a layer of effective and relatively inexpensive thermal insulation. Immediately after installation and as it hardened, UFFI released significant amounts of formaldehyde gas into the indoor air. A colorless gas with a pungent odor, formaldehyde can cause a number of health problems.

UFFI isn't the only possible source of formaldehyde gas in homes. Other sources include such construction materials as particleboard, plywood, and paneling; heating systems; tobacco smoke; automobile exhaust; and household items such as carpets, drapes, furniture, upholstery, and paper products. See Hazard 12, Indoor Air Pollution Sources: Carpets and Building Materials, for a discussion of formaldehyde and other indoor air problems and their sources.

Health Risks

Formaldehyde gas causes a range of adverse health effects in humans, including irritation to the eyes, nose, and throat, respiratory illnesses, skin irritations, dizziness, headaches, and nausea. Formaldehyde has been shown to cause cancer in animals, and the EPA has classified it as a probable carcinogen for humans.

While there is no indoor air standard for formaldehyde in homes, the gas can be smelled down to levels of about 0.1 ppm, the level commonly used as a guideline in homes. (However, formaldehyde is a "sensitizer," i.e., a chemical that, after periods of exposure, requires higher and higher levels to be detected at all.) This is also the level above which health impacts may arise. The American Society of Heating, Refrigerating, and Air-Conditioning Engineers (ASHRAE) recommends that indoor formaldehyde concentrations in the home not exceed 0.1 ppm. OSHA allows 0.75 ppm exposure for an eight-hour average, and 2 ppm as a 15-minute short-term exposure limit, for employees in the workplace. OSHA typically receives complaints when the concentration is between 0.45 and 0.60 ppm or more in commercial buildings. Some people (as much as 20 percent of the population, according to some sources) are highly sensitive to formaldehyde, even at very low levels.

Studies have shown a strong correlation between the age of UFFI and levels of formaldehyde in air. Formaldehyde levels in UFFI houses across the country dropped significantly since the insulation was installed during the 1970s and 1980s, and health complaints have sharply diminished since then. Today formaldehyde exposure from UFFI is not the public health threat it once was. For the vast majority of homes containing UFFI, formaldehyde levels are below the level at which concern would be warranted. However, formaldehyde can be released from UFFI if it is allowed to get wet or damp, or if it is exposed to excessive heat.

Financial Risks

Since most homes containing UFFI no longer have levels of formaldehyde in the air that pose any risk, you probably do not need to spend any money to remove the material or otherwise address the UFFI issue. UFFI removal is extremely invasive and disruptive to a home, not to mention costly (as high as $20,000 or more for a single-family home).

However, due to stigma alone, the mere presence of UFFI can devalue a home. The financial impact of this is real but difficult to quantify. For example, immediately after the Canadian government banned

UFFI in 1980, owners of homes with UFFI saw the value of their properties plunge up to 35 percent, and reports indicate that some U.S. homes were devalued by more than $25,000. If you are the seller, your pool of potential buyers, especially those with children, may shrink. Recognize also that if you buy a home with UFFI, you may have some difficulty reselling it in the future. Many buyers still demand information about the presence of UFFI as part of the purchase and sale agreement; some will undoubtedly use the UFFI issue as a bargaining chip during negotiations.

Other financial risks:
▸ Liability for nondisclosure; see Disclosure Obligations, pages 13–19. Most state disclosure laws generally encompass UFFI, and some states specifically require disclosure of the presence of UFFI.
▸ Costs for short- or long-term medical treatment and monitoring; and legal and expert fees.

Managing the Risks

Increased technology and the development of energy-efficient, airtight building materials have increased the occurrence of indoor air quality issues, including formaldehyde gas. For peace of mind, it is a good idea to conduct at least one air test to measure formaldehyde levels in homes insulated with UFFI. As with many other environmental issues, testing for UFFI should be part of an addendum to your real estate contract. Your state environmental or health agency may even conduct the test for free. Although generally not a health concern, there are houses where UFFI was improperly installed as insulation in attics and ceilings. There are various solutions to best manage the risks if testing indicates elevated formaldehyde levels.

In most instances, removal of UFFI is not recommended because there is usually no longer any significant health risk, removal costs are extremely high, and the benefits of the removal procedure are uncertain. Because UFFI hardened in place after it was installed, removal is a costly and difficult endeavor that can require tearing down walls; it is typically employed only as a last resort. If removal of UFFI is necessary, check with your state environmental or health agency to see if it has funds available for removing the material. Other, less costly treatment options exist where there is a known problem. Formaldehyde vapors can be significantly reduced or eliminated by covering walls with vapor-barrier paint, vinyl wallpaper, or other special coatings, such as polyurethane; sealing cracks in walls; and installing gaskets in electrical outlets. Carbon-based air filtration systems can also be used, but these are costly and require constant monitoring. To prevent problems, keep UFFI from getting damp or wet.

Formaldehyde levels tend to be highest during the summer months (due to high temperatures and humidity). Increasing air exchange or ventilation in a home is a simple way to reduce indoor formaldehyde levels, but may result in significantly increased heating and cooling costs. Forced air systems (air/heat exchange ventilation systems) draw in fresh air while retaining heat. Their efficiency in reducing formaldehyde levels is not certain, but the frequent air exchange should help.

Regulatory Outlook

During the late 1970s, home owners who experienced health problems from exposure to formaldehyde gas from UFFI began to express concern over the use of UFFI. Some states banned its use in the late 1970s, and in February 1982, after receiving thousands of complaints, the Consumer Product Safety Commission (CPSC) determined that UFFI presented an unreasonable health hazard and banned its future sale and installation as a home insulation. Canada had already banned it in 1980. The CPSC did not set a level of acceptable exposure for formaldehyde. Although the ban was subsequently reversed in April 1983 by a federal court because the CPSC could not provide evidence that formaldehyde was harmful to human health, the year-long ban and associated bad publicity effectively wiped out what had been a multibillion-dollar UFFI market and put its manufacturers and installers out of business.

There are currently no federal or state requirements for formaldehyde levels in the indoor air of homes. In the future, we may see federal and state laws governing indoor air contaminants, including formaldehyde. Your state environmental or health agency can provide further details on the regulation of UFFI where you live. Some states, such as Massachusetts, specifically require sellers and landlords to determine whether a home contains UFFI, and if so, to disclose this fact (and the levels of formaldehyde in the home) to potential buyers or tenants. Massachusetts also has a public fund (created by taxes on the companies that manufactured and installed UFFI) that home owners may tap for financial assistance with air testing and removal of UFFI.

What to Look For

During the 1970s and early 1980s, UFFI was used primarily in insulating older, existing homes, but was also used in then-new construction because it could be pumped into hard-to-reach places. Houses built or renovated during that time may have UFFI, while those built before 1970 that did not have insulation added probably do not contain UFFI. (UFFI also was used extensively in mobile homes built in the 1970s and early 1980s.) Ask the owners if UFFI was installed or used in construction.

If present, UFFI can be seen as an irregular-shaped, hardened, shaving-cream-like foam inside the walls. Remove electrical outlet covers and light switch plates and check behind them in the walls for a crumbly, styrofoamlike mass. You may also be able to see UFFI in areas where there are unfinished walls, such as the wall separating a home from an attached garage or in an unfinished basement. Where UFFI was added, the foam was often inserted through small holes uniformly spaced in the exterior wall cavity. In some instances, the holes patched up after installation can be seen—carefully inspect the outer walls (however, just because there are some patched holes on the walls does *not* mean that UFFI is present).

Where to Find Help and Further Information

Although a UFFI inspection is not part of a routine home inspection, a qualified inspector can determine the presence and estimated age of UFFI. Air testing is the only way to determine if formaldehyde levels in a home with UFFI are a problem. Relatively inexpensive, do-it-yourself formaldehyde home test kits are available, typically for less than $40. The reliability of these kits varies. To ensure that the sampling period is representative, be sure the monitoring takes place for a minimum of twenty-four hours. If the test comes out high, repeat it. Remember that even if elevated formaldehyde levels are found in a house, the source may not be UFFI. Although they are more expensive ($200 to $500), laboratory analyses of air samples are always the best option. Check with the EPA or your state environmental or health agency for qualified laboratories that can sample for indoor air pollutants, including formaldehyde. Before removing UFFI, discuss your options with a qualified expert and consult with the EPA or your state environmental or health agency (see Appendix 4).

The Bottom Line

The vast majority of homes containing UFFI do not now present any increased health risks. Because UFFI is no longer installed, and most has sufficiently aged and "off-gassed" formaldehyde, homes with UFFI today generally have low formaldehyde levels. However, it is prudent to look for UFFI in older homes, and where present, to consider having the indoor air analyzed for formaldehyde. Although in most cases there will be no health risks, financial risks associated with UFFI should be considered. The stigma of UFFI may devalue a home and reduce the number of potential buyers, although most people will buy a home with UFFI if formaldehyde levels are acceptable. Finally, if you experience any health problems, consult with your doctor and consider testing your air for formaldehyde as well as other contaminants.

9. HEATING OIL STORAGE TANKS

Homes with (or those that previously had) oil furnaces
Risks: HEALTH ⊕ ⊕   FINANCIAL $ $

Background

Tanks used to store heating oil may be located inside (usually in the basement) or outside a home, and may be either aboveground or underground. Although underground storage tanks (USTs) are the riskiest of the various tank types and, therefore, the main focus of this section, aboveground tanks can present similar problems.* Until the late 1970s, many homes with oil-fired furnaces had USTs installed for storing heating oil. During the Arab oil embargo in the 1970s and other periods of oil shortage, many more USTs (often one-thousand-gallon tanks, to store enough oil for a winter) were installed for backup storage and as a hedge against rising oil prices. For economic reasons, many homes subsequently converted from oil heat to natural gas or electric, often leaving the UST buried in the ground. While USTs are not often installed at homes today, many remain in use—though most are nearing or past the end of their useful life and need to be removed or properly abandoned in place (where allowed).

Most USTs are built of steel, which can corrode over time, resulting in leaks that contaminate soil, groundwater, and lakes and streams. UST leaks are usually not noticeable because they develop slowly and the rate at which oil is released is low. The effective life of a steel UST is fifteen years and older tanks are likely to leak. The biggest threat posed by a

_____
* Therefore, in many places where we refer to a UST, the same issues may apply to aboveground tanks.

leaking UST is its impact on on-site or nearby drinking water wells. Oil can also migrate into basements of nearby homes. Also, spills during tank filling can cause significant problems if not cleaned up immediately.

Health Risks

Heating oil and other petroleum products can render a water supply unfit for drinking because of health and aesthetic considerations; prolonged skin contact with oil can be problematic; and fumes can cause persistent headaches and nausea. Heating oil also contains toxic organic compounds, such as benzene, a known human carcinogen. Fumes from leaking tanks can migrate into nearby homes and present health risks if inhaled. In addition, these fumes can also present a potentially explosive situation and could ignite from an electrical spark or pilot lights on appliances in the basement.

Financial Risks

The costs to test a tank's structural integrity range from $250 to $1,000. Costs to remove or abandon (if allowed by law) a UST range from $1,500 to $5,000 or more if the tank is beneath a paved driveway or the house or garage. Higher costs may be incurred as a result of oil leaks or spills from underground or aboveground tanks. Where the amount of soil contamination is small, cleanup costs can be less than $5,000; where there is a significant impact to soil or groundwater, costs can skyrocket to tens or even hundreds of thousands of dollars. For example, in 1991, a Massachusetts man used up his retirement nest egg of more than $50,000 cleaning up soil contaminated from a leak in his home's UST. In some instances, cleanup costs can even exceed a property's value. If a leaking UST is found, or if there's a spill, state or local officials may be called in; emergency response costs can add thousands of dollars to a cleanup bill. Installation of a new tank generally costs less than $1,000, depending on its size. Additional costs may be incurred if public water supplies or off-site private wells are contaminated.

A home with a leaking UST will be devalued and may be difficult to sell. Buyers may ask for information about a UST and any possible contamination. A home with a UST (even if it isn't leaking) is likely to be devalued due to stigma and its mere presence will undoubtedly affect a buyer's decision and the offer. Lenders may also be concerned about the presence of a UST on a property and may require testing or removal before making a loan.

Other financial risks:
- ► Liability for nondisclosure; see Disclosure Obligations, pages 13–19.
- ► Costs associated with contaminated drinking water; see Hazard 4, Drinking Water: Private Wells.
- ► Costs for short- or long-term medical treatment and monitoring; property damage (such as harm to livestock, crops, or landscaping); legal and expert fees; and inconvenience and relocation costs due to forced evacuation following a spill.

Managing the Risks

Sellers should know if a UST is present, when it was installed, what it contained, or, if it was removed, when, how, and by whom. Home owners who have a UST removed should keep records and get a certificate detailing the removal for a future buyer or lender. Sometimes a home owner may not know the location or even be aware of the existence of a UST installed by a prior owner. If there are no wells on or near a property, the presence of a UST may be acceptable to a buyer. USTs can be tested for leaks, but results are not always definitive.

If there is a UST, consider having it removed and replaced with an aboveground tank. This is *not* a do-it-yourself job—use a qualified contractor. A tank removal follows a general procedure: the tank is accessed and any leftover oil and sludge is pumped out and sent for recycling or disposal (in some areas, charities collect leftover oil and give it to lower-income families, and a tax deduction is available); the tank is pulled out of the ground; underlying soil is checked for contamination (this is often required by a fire marshal or other authority to document that no contamination was left behind); any contaminated soil is removed; the tank "grave" is backfilled with sand and gravel, topsoil is replaced, and the area is reseeded. The tank may be disposed of or cut up and sold as scrap, as allowed. In many cases, the removal process will go smoothly; however, where there has been a spill or leak, the task becomes complicated and expensive.

We recommend removing a UST before putting a home on the market, as a property with a UST will be difficult to sell, especially where a private drinking water well is used. Some buyers will put the burden of taking the UST out of service on the seller (and ask for a comprehensive and expensive removal) or use the UST as a negotiating tool. However, when a UST is removed, there is a chance that a major problem will be found, leaving the owner responsible for huge cleanup bills. An alternative approach (if allowed by local law) is to have the tank emptied, cleaned, and abandoned in place (usually a tank is filled with inert solid material, such as sand or cement), but this option can be almost as expensive as pulling the tank itself. Keep all records of the removal or abandonment, and if a local official inspects the project, ask for a letter or report approving the process.

Check aboveground tanks and fuel lines to make sure they are in good condition, supported securely, and not corroded or leaking. Consider installing a catch pan under the tank to contain any oil leaks or spillage.

Check the vent pipe for all tanks—it must not be clogged or restricted because of ice, snow, or animal or insect nests. If it is clogged, the tank could become overpressurized when filled and leak or burst. Installing a screen over a vent can prevent these problems. Never leave an old abandoned fill pipe in place—oil companies have been known to pump oil into these pipes by mistake and put hundreds of gallons of oil directly into a basement! For example, an Indiana home was filled with six hundred gallons of heating oil when it was mistaken for another house two streets away. The home's furnace had been converted to gas heat years earlier but the fill pipe was left in place, so the oil was pumped directly into the basement. Also, make sure your oil company knows the location of the fill pipe so oil isn't accidently pumped into your well, as recently happened to a Massachusetts home owner. Consider labeling both your well and your fill pipe.

Leaking USTs, particularly in older homes, are common. If a leaking tank contaminates groundwater, treatment of your well's drinking water is possible. As discussed in Hazard 4, Drinking Water: Private Wells, bottled water or connection to a public water supply, if available, may be the best, and most cost effective, option in the long run.

It's not always possible to put a tank in a cellar or garage, and some apartment or condominium buildings may need a UST. If you must install a new UST, buy the best state-of-the-art system available incorporating fiberglass tank materials, corrosion protection, double-walled construction and piping, and leak-detection devices.

Some home owner's insurance policies cover costs associated with leaking USTs, others do not—check your policy. Some states have special insurance programs for heating oil tanks that cover personal injury, property damage, and cleanup costs for accidental spills. You can sue neighbors if their leaking UST damages your property (or vice versa), but lawsuits are costly and often take years to resolve.

Regulatory Outlook

There are millions of USTs used for heating homes around the country and many others are inactive and abandoned. While the EPA and many state environmental agencies regulate USTs at commercial and industrial sites, these rules typically do not apply to USTs of the size commonly used in most single-family homes, but may apply to larger USTs in multifamily apartment buildings and condominiums. In the absence of federal or state regulations pertaining to residential USTs, many towns and counties have enacted laws, often enforced by the fire marshal, that regulate USTs and may require permits for their installation, use, and removal, as well as spill reporting and cleanups. The range of requirements varies tremendously and may include: prohibitions on the installation of USTs in new building lots· (but existing tanks may be allowed to remain in use); registration of all USTs; regular testing of USTs fifteen or more years old for leaks; removal or, where allowed, proper abandonment in place of inactive USTs; and the use of overfill protections, double-walled construction, monitoring devices, cathodic protection for steel tanks, impervious liners, or secondary containment structures. Some states and towns also require USTs to have fill pipes and covers painted a bright color for identification. In environmentally sensitive areas, such as public water supply watersheds, installation of USTs may be prohibited. "Groundwater protection zoning" is a new concept tightly controlling or prohibiting environmentally risky activities in areas where groundwater is used for drinking supplies. These rules can require testing, and sometimes removal, of existing USTs.

The average lifespan of an unprotected steel tank is only fifteen years, and it is estimated that more than half of the USTs in the country are leaking. In most towns, any leak or spill from a UST is an illegal and regulated discharge—home owners can be required to undertake large-scale cleanups, particularly if public or private water supplies are threatened. Some states have special funds to help home owners pay for cleanups. Problems from USTs will diminish as older tanks are removed from service and replaced with aboveground tanks (which are lower risk and can be visually inspected for leaks) or more environmentally sound USTs.

What to Look For

Home heating oil is typically stored in tanks of 275 gallons or larger that, if not located in the basement, are outside, either aboveground or underground. If you *suspect* that a UST is buried on a property, inspect the basement and yard for telltale signs. USTs are often found in homes without a basement (built on slabs), in remote areas where access for oil delivery was difficult, and in apartment buildings and condominiums. You can find a UST by locating its fill pipe (with a cover) or vent pipe (without a cover), which may be sticking out of the lawn or side of the house. Even if the home is now heated by natural gas, there may be an abandoned UST somewhere. Check an older, gas-fired boiler or furnace for a manufacturer's label that reads "oil-fired"; the furnace may have been converted some time ago. Look for oil stains near the furnace and sniff around for heating oil odors.

Ask the seller and agent if any USTs are or were previously on the property. Remember, even if there is a tank in the basement, there still may be a UST somewhere on the property, especially if the home was built before 1980. Abandoned USTs may be difficult to locate, especially if the fill and vent pipes have been removed. Cracks or patches in a basement wall, unusual settlement, cut or patch marks on pavement, or places where grass won't grow may indicate the presence of a UST (or where one was), as can fill pipes that are not connected to anything.

A warning sign that a UST is leaking is a sudden increase in the amount of oil used (check the oil usage records). Look for signs of spills around the fill and vent pipes. Make sure the tank vent is not clogged or restricted. Check the overspill protector (and ensure that the overfill whistle and electronic overfill device, if there is one, work). Outside, check for petroleum odors and look for oil sheens in nearby streams, wetlands, or drainage ditches. Look for signs of distressed vegetation over, or downhill from, the UST.

Where there is an aboveground tank, look for evidence of spills, such as oil stains on the floor, soil, or grass under or next to the tank or around the fill pipe. Find the fill pipe and vent location; the vent should be clear and the fill pipe connected. There should not be any loose fittings on an aboveground tank. Also, check to make sure that the tank is in good condition, is properly supported, and is not in danger of falling or being knocked over. Check if the fuel line between the tank and furnace (usually a small copper tube) runs underground. If this pipe leaks, it can cause the same problems as a UST.

If a well is in use, taste and smell the water; minute quantities of oil will produce odors. However, laboratory tests are usually needed to detect contamination (see Hazard 4, Drinking Water: Private Wells). If a water treatment system or bottled water is used, find out why.

Where to Find Help and Further Information

Check with the town's land use or building officials or the fire marshal to find out if there are records of a UST ever being installed or removed (ask about nearby properties too). State and local environmental agencies often maintain records of USTs for apartment complexes and commercial or industrial properties, but they rarely do so for residential properties. These agencies can help you understand the requirements for the installation, use, maintenance, and removal of USTs; identify qualified consultants who can evaluate the structural integrity of a tank or clean up a spill; and develop a strategy to handle a problem. Your fuel oil supplier can also provide a list of qualified contractors. Check publicly available Sanborn Fire Insurance Maps, which may show the location of aboveground or underground storage tanks (see Appendix 3).

If a drinking water well may be affected by a leaking UST, the water should be tested for petroleum hydrocarbons. The cost to add this test to other well water analyses is about $25 to $50. If a UST is suspected but cannot be found, a survey using a metal detector or other methods can be performed by a qualified consultant (costing between $200 and $500). Many private contractors will also pressure test a UST at a cost of $500 to $1,000. However, due to variations in tank construction and size, these tests may not be reliable. An alternative test, known as a "soil vapor survey," checks the soils around a UST for vapors that would indicate a leak (costs are $500 to $1,000).

Contact the EPA or your state environmental or health agency for additional information or assistance (see Appendix 4).

The Bottom Line

USTs should be considered environmental time bombs. Home buyers are becoming increasingly wary of homes with USTs, even if there's been no problem. The mere presence of a UST can devalue a home and impact property transactions—a home owner's best option is to remove a UST and switch to an aboveground tank before entering into a real estate deal. USTs don't present a health risk unless there's been a leak or spill, but because they have the potential to leak, they are a financial risk. Costs to address contaminated groundwater are high, and the value of a property with a groundwater problem will be significantly reduced. Health risks are greatest in areas where well water is contaminated as a result of a leaking UST located on your property or on a neighbor's property. Aboveground tanks can also pose serious health and financial risks—the most common problems are spills when the tank is filled. While catastrophes are rare, leaking USTs are common; buyers of homes with USTs and wells should test the water to eliminate concerns about health issues. Buyers of older homes should check to ensure that a property does not have an abandoned tank still buried in the yard.

10. HISTORIC DISPOSAL ACTIVITIES

Risks: HEALTH   ✚✚   FINANCIAL $ $

Background

Information about how a piece of land was used in the past is crucial to ascertain and evaluate possible environmental contamination. This is true for all properties, whether a small lot in an old subdivision or a huge parcel of undeveloped land—severe financial and health risks can be encountered where past disposal of wastes has occurred or where contaminated soils were used as fill.

A worst case and perhaps the most notorious example is Love Canal, a section of a small town near Niagara Falls, New York, where toxic wastes were disposed of for many years by filling in an old canal. After the canal was filled, the property was deeded over to the town, which allowed a residential neighborhood, including schools and playgrounds, to be built on top of what we would now call a hazardous waste dump. By the mid-1960s, residents were complaining of major health problems; by the end of the 1970s, the EPA and state and local environmental agencies began tests and cleanup work, and the area soon became one of the first "Superfund" sites (those sites considered most toxic to human health and the environment and targeted by the EPA for cleanup; see Hazard 49, Superfund Sites). Many homes were vacated; some residents were forced to leave by order of health authorities; still other homes were purchased and financial restitution was made to home owners.

Are there more undiscovered Love Canals out there? Undoubtedly yes, but because of increased public awareness, government regulation, and changed industry disposal practices, probably not many of that magnitude. However, problems continue to surface. For residential property, it is important for a potential buyer to rule out the possibility, no matter how remote, that the property was ever used for waste disposal—by a former landowner who used the "back forty" for a junk-yard, by the developer who dumped leftover hazardous construction debris, or by unknown "midnight dumpers" of hazardous waste. Many undeveloped, unsecured tracts of land historically have been used for dumping chemicals, lead- or asbestos-contaminated construction debris, or contaminated fill, or have become unofficial local dumps for appliances, water heaters, old cars, and rubbish.

For example, in 1994, while investigating a nearby property, the EPA stumbled upon a thirty-acre wooded site in Ohio with a large pit containing hundreds of drums full of PCBs, pesticides, and other hazardous waste. In another situation more than one hundred residential properties in an upstate New York community were contaminated with PCBs from fill used to landscape the properties. And a California family discovered more than five thousand pounds of radioactive materials in their backyard when they dug a barbecue pit. In the past, dumping was sometimes the result of ignorance—we know of an old summer camp where, in the 1950s, partially full drums of industrial solvents were emptied right on the property, rinsed, and then used as floats for rafts placed in the lake!

In a bizarre situation, in the 1930s a University of Pennsylvania professor conducted radioactive experiments in his basement and secretly buried contaminated waste on his and his neighbors' property. In the 1980s, the EPA placed the property on the Superfund National Priorities List (see Appendix 3 and Hazard 49, Superfund Sites) and spent almost $12 million razing the house and several neighboring garages and cleaning up more than 4,000 tons of contaminated soil.

Some contaminated residential properties are also the result of prior industrial use of the site—including many of the commercial and industrial activities discussed in Part III. For example, in the early 1980s, unsuspecting home owners who bought new homes in a Texas subdivision later found out that the site, formerly operated as a creosote wood-treatment plant for more than twenty-five years, was the target of an EPA investigation; cleanup is expected to cost millions of dollars and require the demolition of many homes.

Health Risks

Health risks depend on the kind and amount of toxic material present the duration and route of exposure (via air, contaminated soil, groundwater, or surface water). Hazardous contaminants in soil present a health risk through inhalation, ingestion, or direct skin contact, or through leaching into groundwater that can affect drinking water wells. Impacted drinking water wells are a common route of exposure, as is contamination of soil from historic dumping, especially for children (see Hazard 4, Drinking Water: Private Wells, for more details on health risks from contaminated well water). Some hazardous chemicals have been linked to elevated risks of cancer, damage to internal organs, respiratory problems, skin rashes, and reproductive and nervous system problems.

Financial Risks

Where there is minor soil contamination, cleanup costs can be several thousands of dollars; where lots of soil and groundwater are impacted, costs can skyrocket to hundreds of thousands of dollars. Other costs may be incurred for off-site cleanups if public water supplies or private wells are at risk; in instances where contaminated groundwater from your property impacts a neighbor's well, you could be responsible for damages even if you didn't cause the problem.

A home with contaminated soil or groundwater will be devalued and difficult to sell. Buyers may ask a seller for information about historical activities that took place on-site, where the fill used for landscaping the site came from, and possible contamination. Homes with contaminated soil or groundwater are also likely to be devalued due to stigma, even if the property has been cleaned up. The presence of such contamination will undoubtedly affect a buyer's decision and the amount of the offer.

Contaminated soil or groundwater on your property can affect your ability to use or develop the property as desired—you may need to obtain regulatory approvals and resolve any cleanup issues before being able to develop the property, and this can be expensive. In some cases, if the property is contaminated, you may not be able to initiate construction because doing so might exacerbate the hazardous conditions.

Other financial risks:
- Liability for nondisclosure; see Disclosure Obligations, pages 13–19.
- Costs associated with contaminated drinking water; see Hazard 4, Drinking Water: Private Wells.
- Costs for short- or long-term medical treatment and monitoring; property damage (such as harm to livestock, crops, or landscaping); and legal and expert fees.

Managing the Risks

A thorough inspection of the property and review of historical activities at the site is a critical step to avoid buying a contaminated parcel. If there is a potential problem, a professional environmental consultant should be contacted to evaluate suspected past on-site disposal activities—the evaluation and removal of toxic wastes from a property is *not* a do-it-yourself job for the home owner.

See Hazard 4, Drinking Water: Private Wells, for a discussion of how to manage risks if a drinking water well is contaminated.

Where appropriate, look to the source of the pollution (such as a prior owner or whoever contaminated the property) for financial or technical help in correcting any problem and in managing the associated risks.

Regulatory Outlook

The EPA and state environmental agencies have legal authority to require the cleanup of contaminated property, including residential property contaminated from past disposal activities. These authorities have broad power, particularly if there is potential for impact to public health or drinking water supplies. Unfortunately, many times the actual polluter doesn't get stuck with the cleanup bill; rather it's often the current owner who does, even if he or she did not cause the problem.

Recently a legal theory known as the "innocent landowner" doctrine has evolved in some states, either through laws or by court decisions. This doctrine protects the person who gets stuck with a contaminated property through no fault of his or her own from being forced to clean it up. Specific requirements to qualify as an innocent landowner vary from state to state—a significant one in many states is that the owner completed a thorough inspection or assessment of the property before the purchase and still did not discover the problem. The person who can truly succeed in claiming innocent landowner status is rare, and the legal costs to do so can be enormous. Finally, although an owner may not be *forced* to clean up a property, he or she will probably have to pay for a costly and time-consuming cleanup anyway to be able to develop or sell the property.

What to Look For

Things that should raise a red flag warning of possible problems include: piles of fill material of unknown origin; discarded garbage, building materials, drums, and paint cans; or, in the case of larger tracts of undeveloped land, areas where significant filling has taken place. Look for variations in terrain that might indicate previous construction or a possible dump site. If a well is in use, taste and smell the water; however, laboratory tests are usually needed to detect contamination (see Hazard 4, Drinking Water: Private Wells). If a water treatment system or bottled water is used, find out why.

Look around the property for physical evidence of contamination. Dark-stained areas of soil may be a hint of a past petroleum or solvent spill, and unnatural (blue-green or yellow-orange) colors may indicate a past spill of heavy metals. Areas where vegetation won't grow or where it appears stressed or dead are a good indication of potential contamination. Unusual odors or seepage is another clue to a possible problem.

Where to Find Help and Further Information

If past dumping is suspected, home owners and potential buyers of homes with wells should have the water tested (see Hazard 4, Drinking Water: Private Wells). Coordinate tests with a qualified laboratory, consultant, or inspector. Contact the EPA or your state environmental or health agency for additional information or assistance (see Appendix 4).

You can find out who the past owners were and what the land was used for by doing a quick and informal title search at your local land records office; or ask your home inspector to check this out. Your attorney can also identify past land use when doing a formal title review—however, at that stage of the game, you are probably near closing and may be penalized if you back out of the deal (unless you have the right contingencies built into your purchase and sale contract). Some state and local environmental and natural resource agencies have aerial photographic surveys of many areas taken at five- or ten-year intervals. These can indicate historic activities, like filling, that could require additional investigation (see Appendix 3).

You can also inspect files at your state or local environmental agency that may indicate any spills, disposal, or cleanup that occurred at a property.

The Bottom Line

Historic disposal activities on a property can affect the value of a home. While significant contamination is rare, soil or groundwater contaminated with toxic chemicals or waste can pose health risks and associated financial risks. Buyers of nearby homes with private wells should have the water tested to see if there is any reason for concern. The costs to address contaminated water are high and the value of a property with a water problem will be significantly reduced. Although the chance that a property was used for waste disposal is small, it is important to rule out the possibility altogether with some up-front sleuthing by you or your home inspector or environmental consultant. In particular, anyone who owns or is buying large tracts of undeveloped land should verify that there are no surprises associated with past disposal on some part of the property.

11. HOUSEHOLD CHEMICALS AND HAZARDOUS WASTE

Risks: HEALTH FINANCIAL $

Background

Household chemicals—while an innocuous-sounding term—can cause environmental and health problems if not used, stored, and disposed of properly. Most significantly, children are at risk of being poisoned. In addition improper disposal leading to contaminated drinking water supplies is a serious problem. The average household has more than ten gallons of hazardous chemicals that can jeopardize your family's health if improperly used, spilled, or ingested. The list of hazardous products used in homes is extensive: paints and paint thinners, ammonia, floor-care products, drain cleaners, air fresheners, oven cleaners, disinfectants, swimming pool chemicals, waxes and polishes, household and car batteries, furniture and paint strippers, pesticides and fertilizers, antifreeze, brake and transmission fluids, glues, epoxies, mothballs, cleaning solvents, used oil, and kerosene. Home hobbies or occupations, such as painting, auto repair, furniture restoring, and photography, to name a few, entail the use of all sorts of chemicals. Many of these same chemicals, when disposed of by industry, are regulated as hazardous waste!

Health Risks

Material is hazardous if it's toxic (causes injury or death if swallowed, inhaled, or absorbed through skin), corrosive (very acidic or basic materials that corrode tissue), reactive (explosive), or ignitable (flammable at low temperatures). Some materials are hazardous whether or not they meet these criteria. Repeated or excessive exposure to household chemicals or hazardous waste may lead to skin problems, headaches, lung problems like chronic asthma, brain and nerve damage, depression, cancer, and even death. Children and pregnant women are particularly at risk. Health risks are specific to the chemical compound and the type of exposure (inhalation, ingestion, skin contact). An excellent summary of the range of health risks posed by household chemicals may be found in Ruth Winter's *A Consumer's Dictionary of Household, Yard and Office Chemicals* (Crown Publishers, 1992).

Financial Risks

There are major financial risks associated with the improper use or disposal of household chemicals. Costs to clean up contaminated soil (outside or in a home's basement) and groundwater can run into the thousands or even tens of thousands of dollars. Pouring toxic chemicals down a sink or toilet can affect the operation of a septic system and lead to costly repairs (see Hazard 20, Septic Systems). The costs to dispose of unused household chemicals can be significant, although they have been reduced in recent years, as many towns now provide various inexpensive disposal options.

Buyers may be wary of properties where chemicals are improperly stored and may ask about past disposal activities. Where there is known soil contamination or if a well is impacted, a home will be devalued and difficult to sell; even if a problem is fixed, a property may be devalued because of stigma.

Other financial risks:
- ▶ Liability for nondisclosure; see Disclosure Obligations, pages 13–19.
- ▶ Costs associated with contaminated drinking water; see Hazard 4, Drinking Water: Private Wells.
- ▶ Costs for short- or long-term medical treatment and monitoring.

Managing the Risks

Hazardous chemicals and materials in the home are accidents waiting to happen—they should always be stored out of the reach of children, in tightly closed containers so they won't evaporate and pollute the indoor air, and kept labeled in their original containers. The best way to minimize exposures to toxic household chemicals and prevent health problems is to use safe, nontoxic alternatives whenever possible. When using toxic products, make sure there is sufficient ventilation. Try not to buy more chemicals than needed for a given job.

Hazardous chemicals that can't be used up or that have exceeded their useful shelf life should be disposed of properly. Home owners should regularly remove and dispose of unneeded household chemicals, and certainly should do so prior to showing their home. Buyers should put a clause in the contract that requires the seller to remove all household chemicals and clean up and dispose of any junk before closing, or else proceeds will be withheld at closing for removal and disposal costs. Remember: buyers should inspect the home again just prior to closing; if the stuff's still there, you will then be able to have your lawyer withhold the money needed to cover any costs you may incur in disposing of it.

Methods for collecting household chemicals which are hazardous waste from homes vary widely around the country. There may be drop-off facilities in your area that accept household hazardous waste directly from home owners. The town landfill or transfer station may serve as a collection point for some wastes, such as used oil, antifreeze, and latex paint, on a regular basis. In addition, household hazardous waste collection days are becoming a popular service offered by cities or towns at little or no cost. Towns (or several towns) will contract with licensed professional haulers, who staff the collection center and take the household hazardous wastes to their facilities for proper handling and disposal.

Home owners should take advantage of these opportunities, as access to a drop-off site may be unavailable and the cost savings can be great. Certain guidelines usually apply: proof of residency is often required, materials may need to be packed and sealed in their original containers, and there may be maximum limits (in gallons or pounds) per home. There are also items that may *not* be accepted. Examples include: explosives, fireworks, ammunition, gas cylinders, radioactive materials (in smoke detectors), PCBs, wood preservatives containing pentachlorophenol (commonly used for sealing outdoor decks and for which there is no known safe method of disposal). Call your town's land use or building officials to find out when the next household hazardous waste collection day is scheduled.

See Hazard 4, Drinking Water: Private Wells, for a discussion of how to manage risks if a drinking water well is contaminated.

Regulatory Outlook

Because of the small amount of waste generated by each home and the difficulty in enforcing compliance, the use and storage of hazardous chemicals at residential properties are not covered by the EPA or state hazardous waste programs. Some towns have hazardous materials storage laws that apply broadly or may be limited to water supply watersheds or other environmentally sensitive areas, but generally do not apply to homes. However, the illegal dumping of toxic chemicals can—and will—get you into trouble, perhaps criminally. Even today, toxic chemicals are poured down sinks and toilets, dumped "out back," spilled into storm drains, and put out with the weekly trash—eventually making their way into water supplies or solid waste landfills not designed to handle toxic chemicals. Nationwide, the EPA estimates that more than 250,000 gallons of used oil are dumped into storm drains or directly into the environment each year.

Your state and its environmental agency may have laws and regulations that apply to your household hazardous waste situation.

What to Look For

Look in the kitchen, bathroom, basement, garage, workshop, attic, and outbuildings (shops or barns where home hobbies take place) for stockpiles of household chemicals, including paints, cleaners, and pesticides. Keep an eye out for utility sinks, floor drains, or sumps in these areas— they may have been used for disposal and, if connected to a septic system or dry well, indicate a potential soil or groundwater contamination problem. Look outside for piles of debris, old paint cans or drums, and stained soil or areas of dead vegetation.

If a well is in use, taste and smell the water: however, laboratory tests are usually needed to detect contamination (see Hazard 4, Drinking Water: Private Wells). If a water treatment system or bottled water is used, find out why.

Where to Find Help and Further Information

Check with your town's public works or building officials to find out about household hazardous waste requirements. If there's a possibility that well water is impacted by improper chemical disposal, home owners and potential buyers should have the water tested (see Hazard 4, Drinking Water: Private Wells). Coordinate tests with a qualified laboratory, consultant, or inspector.

Contact the EPA or your state environmental or health agency for additional information (such as a list of qualified labs) or assistance (see Appendix 4).

The Bottom Line

Most households use many toxic chemicals. If improperly stored or disposed of, they can pose real health and financial risks. Good housekeeping practices are an important safety precaution for all home owners and a positive selling point. Get rid of old hazardous chemicals that are just sitting around. Do *not* throw them out with the trash, pour them down the sink or floor drain, or flush them down the toilet—it's illegal. Dispose of household hazardous wastes only in accordance with acceptable practices and the law. Buyers should require sellers to remove all unneeded chemicals prior to closing, and where a home has a private well or a septic system, consider testing to eliminate concerns about potential health problems from possible improper disposal practices in the past. Costs to deal with contaminated well water or fix a septic system are high, and the value of a property with a problem will be significantly reduced.

12. INDOOR AIR POLLUTION SOURCES: CARPETS AND BUILDING MATERIALS

Risks: HEALTH FINANCIAL $ $

Background

We each spend about 90 percent of our lives indoors, and about 65 percent* of that in our homes. The EPA estimates that indoor air pollution levels are two to five times higher than those found outside. The demand for energy-efficient, airtight homes has increased indoor air quality problems—as air loss or exchange from a home decreases, airborne chemicals can build up to high levels.

Among the possible indoor air pollutants of concern are a variety of toxic volatile organic compounds (VOCs) that are released into the home from glues, resins, and preservatives used to manufacture synthetic flooring (like linoleum), carpets, drapes, furniture, and uphol-

---

* And this number is rising as more and more people work at home.

stery, or are present in paneling, particleboard, and plywood used for building materials. The release of chemical fumes from products into the air is called "off-gassing." Off-gassing peaks right after a carpet, building material, or piece of furniture is brought into the home and then (usually) rapidly decreases with time. In addition, indoor air problems are common in new or remodeled homes. Indoor air problems peak in the winter, when homes are tightly sealed, and in the summer, when higher temperatures tend to maximize VOC off-gassing.

Formaldehyde, a colorless gas with a pungent odor, is a VOC commonly associated with indoor air problems (formaldehyde is also the chemical associated with UFFI—see Hazard 8, Formaldehyde Insulation). It is a component of adhesives used in particleboard (subfloors, cabinets, and shelving), plywood panels, and medium-density fiberboard (drawer fronts and cabinet doors). It is also a major component of pressed wood products used for exterior construction. Occupants of mobile homes (an estimated ten million people in the United States) and prefabricated homes, which contain a large amount of pressed-wood products, may be exposed to higher levels of VOCs than the rest of the public.

There are hundreds of different VOCs that can be released from carpeting, including benzene, xylene, ethylbenzene, and 4-PC, a chemical used for stain resistance and in latex backings. There is mixed information about carpeting as a source of formaldehyde—according to the Carpet and Rug Institute, formaldehyde use in carpets has been greatly reduced in the past ten years. In addition to releasing VOCs, carpeting, if not kept meticulously clean, can be a "sink" for dust mites and other biological contaminants that can create indoor air problems (see Hazard 2, Biological Contaminants). Many household or commercial carpet cleaners contain VOCs that can be emitted during and after cleaning applications.

Other specific indoor air contaminants are discussed elsewhere in this book: see Hazard 1, Asbestos; Hazard 2, Biological Contaminants; Hazard 3, Combustion Sources and Carbon Monoxide; Hazard 13, Lead-Based Paint; Hazard 18, Radon in Air; and Hazard 42, Pesticides.

Health Risks

Literally hundreds of possible VOCs can be emitted from carpets and other building materials—without testing, it is impossible to pinpoint the specific chemicals. As is the case with any chemical, health risks depend on the compound(s) as well as the level and duration of exposure. VOCs in indoor air may cause a range of adverse health effects in humans, including irritation to the eyes, nose, and throat, respiratory illnesses, skin irritations, and dizziness, headaches, and nausea. Asthma attacks, memory loss, and depression have also been reported. Of the huge number of indoor air pollutants, formaldehyde is among the most studied. Formaldehyde causes cancer in laboratory animals. According to the National Institutes of Health, a large percentage of the population (over 15 percent) may be allergic to formaldehyde and sensitive to other household chemicals. (For more information on formaldehyde, see Hazard 8, Formaldehyde Insulation.)

Except for the initial few days, the concentration of chemicals emitted by carpets and other building materials into the air is usually very low and may be of concern only to allergy-prone or hypersensitive individuals. One of the best-publicized health incidents associated with indoor air problems from carpets occurred at the EPA's Washington, D.C., headquarters in 1987, when hundreds of employees became sick after new carpeting was installed. The chemical 4-PC was suspected to be the cause of the problem.

Financial Risks

The cost to retrofit a house with an air exchanger and ventilation system can be $5,000 to $10,000 or more. For new construction, the costs to install such a system will be significantly less—it does represent an *added* cost, certainly, but far less than a future retrofit. Air filtration systems can cost anywhere from $100 to $200 for a single-room unit to $1,000 to $5,000 or more for a whole-house system.

The base price of an energy-efficient house built using nonemitting materials (such as tile and wood flooring instead of carpets and solid wood instead of pressed-wood products) and special ventilation equipment will be significantly more (around 15 percent) than a comparable conventional house. As indoor air problems from new carpets and building materials are often only of short duration, less costly options for air treatment may be effective unless you are hypersensitive to the chemicals.

Building owners, landlords, and property managers need to be responsive to indoor air quality complaints and may be liable for damages from indoor air problems alleged by tenants.

Other financial risks:

▶ Liability for nondisclosure; see Disclosure Obligations, pages 13–19.

▶ Costs for short- or long-term medical treatment and monitoring;

legal and expert fees; and inconvenience and relocation costs due to forced evacuation following an indoor air problem.

Managing the Risks

There are three basic strategies for reducing exposure to any indoor air contaminant: source control (taking steps to eliminate or minimize contaminant sources), increased ventilation, and air cleaning (where filters are used to physically remove pollutants from the air).

Ventilation is the term used to describe the introduction of fresh, outdoor air into a home. A home's "air exchange rate" is the rate at which outdoor air replaces indoor air. There are three general categories of ventilation: "infiltration" where air flows through the building joints, closed windows, or the foundation; "natural ventilation" through open windows and doors; and "mechanical ventilation" where fans, blowers, or other mechanical means are used to increase the air exchange rate.

Some low-cost ways to minimize indoor air pollution from carpets and other indoor air pollution sources include the following:

1. Avoid purchasing products containing significant amounts of toxic compounds in the first place (you can read labels and product literature, but this may be easier said than done). You can, for example, buy solid wood cabinets instead of ones made with particleboard, or use tile flooring instead of carpets. If building a new home, you can use exterior-grade plywood and particleboard indoors, as it contains less formaldehyde than the interior grades.
2. Look for and purchase carpets and underpadding tested and rated by the carpet industry to be low VOC emitters. If possible, avoid using carpet adhesives, as they usually emit significant amounts of organic compounds.
3. Remove new synthetic materials (e.g., carpets, cabinets, or flooring) from their packages and let them sit in a garage or other well-ventilated place for a few days before bringing them inside (ask your carpet supplier to unroll carpets for twenty-four hours prior to delivering them to your home). This will reduce the amount of organic compounds released inside your home.
4. After new carpets are installed, open the windows to increase ventilation, and minimize occupancy of the rooms for at least seventy-two hours. If possible, vacate the house and turn the heat up during this period to increase off-gassing rates (do *not* do this if anyone—or any pets—will be in the house).

5. After the initial installation period, off-gassing can be reduced by lowering the thermostat and running a dehumidifier.

Emissions from particleboard flooring and cabinets can be reduced by sealing them with special paints. Installing equipment like fans or ventilators to increase air exchange and ventilation in a home is a relatively easy way to reduce indoor pollutant levels, but may result in increased energy costs. You can install forced ventilation systems that draw in fresh air while retaining heat. Whole house or individual room air filtration systems using carbon filters can also be used.

Landlords and building owners should pay close attention to ventilation systems to minimize indoor air problems. They should be inspected and tested regularly. When installing carpets, landlords should take proper precautions to inform and protect tenants.

Regulatory Outlook

Currently there is no federal program applicable to indoor air quality in private homes. OSHA, the EPA, and many state environmental and health agencies regulate indoor air under various programs—for such things as asbestos and tobacco smoke—but only in the context of public buildings (such as schools) and commercial buildings for the protection of workers. There are a smattering of indoor air regulations; for example, the Department of Housing and Urban Development (HUD) set regulations in 1985 requiring mobile home manufacturers to comply with certain standards on indoor air pollutant levels.

Looking forward, Congress has indicated that indoor air pollution is a priority and may provide future laws. Your state environmental or health agency can provide further details on the outlook for, or status of, the regulation of indoor air pollution in your state. We expect that any future OSHA or EPA indoor air study will initially apply to offices, stores, and other commercial buildings—only later will they apply to residential properties. And with the increased public knowledge of indoor air pollution generally, there may be an increase in toxic tort and disclosure lawsuits against landlords, property owners and managers, sellers, and agents, as well as against manufacturers, designers, and installers of HVAC systems and various building materials.

What to Look For

You can't see indoor air pollutants—but you may be able to see their potential sources. Look for new carpets, paneling, and cabinets in new construction or where a home has been recently renovated. If possible, see if subfloors and walls are made from pressed-wood products like particleboard or plywood (for new construction, this should be easy). Your home inspector should be able to identify and assess the adequacy of the ventilation system.

Where to Find Help and Further Information

Where an indoor air problem is suspected, we suggest hiring an indoor air quality consultant to inspect the home. Air testing is the only way to determine if organic vapor levels in a home are elevated. Such an inspection with appropriate tests can cost $500 to $1,000. Relatively inexpensive do-it-yourself home test kits are typically available for less than $40. However, the reliability of these kits varies. Be sure the monitoring takes place for a minimum of twenty-four hours to ensure that the sampling period is representative. If the test comes out high, repeat it. Laboratory analysis of air samples is always the best option, although it can be expensive (from $200 to $500 generally).

The carpet industry is very aware of indoor air pollution—reportedly they have reduced the use of formaldehyde because of public concern. The Carpet and Rug Institute (800/882-8846) has developed an Indoor Air Quality Testing Program and can answer questions and provide additional information.

Ask your home inspector or an environmental consultant for recommendations about an indoor air specialist or testing laboratories. Contact the EPA or your state environmental or health agency for additional information or assistance (see Appendix 4).

For more information, see U.S. Environmental Protection Agency and U.S. Consumer Product Safety Commission, *The Inside Story—A Guide to Indoor Air Quality,* EPA/400/1-88/004, 1988.

The Bottom Line

Indoor air quality can be a significant issue for home owners, and one that goes largely unnoticed and unregulated. Formaldehyde-containing wood products and synthetic carpeting have been in wide use for over thirty years. Apparently, some individuals are especially sensitive to formaldehyde and chemical fumes from carpets and other building materials, whereas most are not. However, some brands of carpets, and even certain batches within a manufacturing run, may be higher VOC emitters than others. If you are sensitive to indoor air pollutants, consider alternatives to pressed-wood products and carpeting. Use solid wood products and carpets that are low-emitting. The easiest way to reduce any risk is to ventilate your home and avoid spending extended periods of time in rooms during the time in which carpeting or pressed-wood products are installed and for a few days after. Finally, if you experience health problems associated with air problems, see your doctor and consider testing the air for suspected contaminants, especially if symptoms appear after new carpets or other building materials are installed or you have just moved into a new home or renovated an older one. A home with an indoor air problem can pose serious health and financial risks, and suffer reduced property value.

13. LEAD-BASED PAINT

Interior and exterior of homes built before 1978

Risks: HEALTH ⊕ ⊕ ⊕ FINANCIAL $ $ $

Background

From the turn of the century through the 1940s, lead was used as a primary ingredient in many interior and exterior oil-based paints because of its adherence qualities, brightness, and durability. From that time and through the 1960s, the use of latex paints, which are generally lead-free, became widespread, and the use of lead-based paint (we refer to it as LBP for the rest of this section) gradually decreased. In 1978, the Consumer Product Safety Commission (CPSC) banned lead in house paint; many cities had stopped its use years earlier. However, as there was no recall of existing paint, cans of LBP were probably available for sale for some time after 1978.

LBP is found in homes and apartments in cities and suburbs, in both private and public housing. The EPA and HUD believe that fifty-seven million U.S. homes (three out of every four built before 1978) contain LBP. Reportedly, LBP is in almost all homes built before 1940, half of the homes built between 1940 and 1960, and almost half of all homes built between 1960 and 1978. LBP was used indoors on floors, walls, ceilings, woodwork, and windows, especially in bathrooms and kitchens. It was also used extensively on exterior surfaces, including doors, windows, siding, and trim. Lead can also enter a home from other outdoor sources, such as dust from lead-contaminated soil near busy roads and improperly contained bridge renovation activities.

Health Risks

For centuries, exposure to lead has been known to cause serious health problems. Recent research indicates that LBP represents a more significant health hazard than previously thought—and at lower levels than expected. The risk of lead poisoning from LBP depends on the age of the affected person, the amount ingested or inhaled, and the route of exposure. Lead is especially toxic because it accumulates in the blood, bones, and soft tissues of the body.

Airborne lead enters the body when lead dust is inhaled or swallowed. Lead dust* comes from the normal deterioration of LBP, from friction caused when opening and closing windows, or if LBP-covered surfaces are scraped, sanded, or heated in various paint-stripping procedures. Lead particles in dust settle onto carpets and fabric and are recirculated in the air by sweeping and dusting. Fine lead particles will pass through the filter systems of household vacuum cleaners and then be sent back into the air, where they can then be inhaled or ingested. Lead from exterior house paint can flake off or leach into the soil around the outside of the home, contaminating children's playing areas, and can be tracked into the home.

Much of the concern about LBP centers on its effects on small children; it is considered the number-one environmental health threat to children in the United States. Children frequently come into contact with lead dust, paint chips, leaded soil, and surfaces painted with LBP. Young children and infants are more vulnerable to lead than others because (1) they mouth protruding surfaces (such as windowsills) and put objects contaminated with lead in their mouths (lead has a sweet taste that children like); (2) lead is easily absorbed into growing bodies; and (3) their brains and nervous systems are extremely sensitive to the damaging effects of lead. Because of a child's lower body weight, exposure to a small amount of lead is more damaging to a child than to an adult. Overall, an estimated three to four million children in the United States have blood lead levels high enough to pose health problems. The Centers for Disease Control (CDC) estimate that more than 10 percent of all preschoolers may have elevated blood lead levels.

Lead causes a variety of health effects at all levels; it is called the "silent disease" because its effects occur gradually and imperceptibly. Children exposed to low levels of lead, if it is not detected early, can suffer damage to the brain and nervous system, kidneys, and blood

---

* Recently, the CPSC issued a warning concerning lead dust hazards from deteriorating cheap vinyl miniblinds.

formation system. Childhood lead poisoning can lead to behavior and learning problems (hyperactivity and lower IQ levels), slowed growth, hearing or coordination problems, and headaches. The Centers for Disease Control defines a blood lead level of concern as ten micrograms of lead per deciliter (ug/dl) of blood.

Exposure to high levels of lead can cause blindness, brain damage, convulsions, and even death. There are hundreds of tragic examples where children have suffered permanent blindness and retardation or died from lead poisoning following lead-abatement activities or from eating LBP chips. Recent studies have linked high lead levels to aggressive, antisocial behavior in children.

Lead is also poisonous to adults; low exposure to lead can cause high blood pressure, reproductive problems, digestive problems, nerve disorders, memory and concentration problems, and muscle and joint pain. Higher levels can cause brain damage or death. Women of childbearing age are at risk because lead poisoning can cause difficulties during pregnancy, including miscarriages and premature births, and can ultimately lead to problems with the baby's development. Lead can also poison your pets.

Financial Risks

The cost to abate—encapsulate (cover over) or remove and replace—LBP can be high, depending on where it is found and the abatement method used. Costs to remove LBP completely can be as much as $15,000 to $20,000 or more for a single-family home or $10,000 per unit in multifamily housing—these costs can even exceed the value of a home! Removal and replacement of window frames and doors coated with LBP may be $200 to $300 each. Where LBP can be left in place and encapsulated with approved materials, costs for a single-family home can be $500 to $1,000 per room. These estimates do not include costs for temporary housing during the de-leading process or testing and disposal costs.

Many buyers and tenants, especially those with or contemplating having children, are wary of homes with LBP. Some buyers may make an offer far below the asking price, make the offer contingent on the seller removing all LBP, or just walk away. In all cases, costs to abate LBP should be factored into the negotiations over price. Even if the LBP is not flaking or chipping, its mere presence can be a stigma for buyers—as a result, the pool of potential buyers may be smaller. If you buy a home with LBP, recognize that removal may be required if the LBP laws change in the future.

LBP may be an issue for insuring and financing a home. Most insurance policies today contain specific lead exclusions; even where there is no such exclusion, lead may be excluded through a broad pollution exclusion clause. And, many banks and mortgage companies require lead tests *before* they will provide financing. If you plan to rent out your home or apartment and it has LBP, be careful: liability can be high if a tenant's child ingests lead. In some states, landlords must relocate tenants at their own cost during abatement, and some have had to abandon marginally profitable apartment buildings after receiving orders to remove LBP. And, generally, landlords can't legally minimize their liability or escape compliance obligations by evicting, or refusing to rent to, families with children—it's discrimination.

Liability for LBP is significant for all players in the real estate market—sellers, agents, landlords, lenders, inspectors, property managers, and others increasingly have been targets of lawsuits stemming from lead-poisoning incidents around the country.

Other financial risks:
- ▸ Liability for nondisclosure; see Disclosure Obligations, pages 13–19. While several states (California, Connecticut, Delaware, Illinois, Indiana, Iowa, Maine, Maryland, Massachusetts, Michigan, Mississippi, New Hampshire, Ohio, Oregon, Rhode Island, South Dakota, Tennessee, Texas, Virginia, Washington, and Wisconsin) require LBP disclosure either under a property condition disclosure law or other state law, a recent federal law, known as Title X, and its implementing regulations will mandate LBP disclosure in all states by the end of 1996 (see Regulatory Outlook, below).
- ▸ Costs for short- or long-term medical treatment and monitoring; legal and expert fees; and inconvenience and relocation costs due to forced evacuation following a lead contamination problem.

Managing the Risks

LBP is an immediate hazard if it is chipped, cracked, peeling, or loosened in any way. Except where a state requires that LBP be removed from certain surfaces if children under a specific age (usually six) reside in the home, or where a child is found to have lead poisoning, addressing LBP is generally at the discretion of the home owner. Before starting any lead-abatement work, review applicable regulations, lender requirements (such as those of HUD or a private bank), availability of public grants, no- or low-interest loans, or other forms of financial assistance (e.g., a $1,500-per-unit tax credit is available in Massachusetts), and insurance policies (to see if coverage is provided for lead abatement or liability claims for a lead poisoning incident). Also, call your state or local environmental or health agency with jurisdiction over LBP for information on lead inspection services and testing laboratories in your area. Consider getting a qualified consultant's opinion before doing anything (they may not charge for an initial consultation). Those renting older homes or apartments should notify the landlord immediately of any chipping or peeling paint.

There are *interim* steps that will reduce some risks if your house has LBP until a permanent solution is implemented. Periodically inspect painted surfaces for damage. If you have young children, survey their play areas and keep them from chewing on exposed painted surfaces and away from paint chips and dust. Teach them to wash their hands frequently—and always before eating. Wash toys and pacifiers frequently. Wet-mop floors and wipe down surfaces often, especially where the walls and floors meet and where the window sash rests on the sill. A solution of trisodium phosphate (TSP) or powdered high-phosphate dishwasher detergent picks up lead dust better than ordinary cleaners. Do *not* sweep. Do *not* vacuum paint chips or dust with a typical household vacuum cleaner (if there is lead in the dust, it is so fine that it will pass through the bag and spread into the air). If exterior LBP has accumulated in surrounding soil, keep the yard well vegetated to minimize the chance of children being exposed to lead-contaminated dust.

Parents living in homes with known or suspected LBP should be aware of the symptoms of lead exposure in children: are they abnormally cranky? complaining of stomachaches and headaches? unable to concentrate? hyperactive? vomiting? frequently tired? unwilling to eat or play? Even if children don't exhibit these symptoms, they still may have been exposed to harmful levels of lead.

Most state health agencies recommend lead testing for all children under the age of six (beginning when the child is six months to one year old), regardless of whether there are any symptoms. Consult with your doctor about the need for testing; a simple blood test, done during a regular checkup, will indicate if your child has an elevated blood lead level (tests are inexpensive and sometimes free). Treatment for severe lead poisoning (known as chelation therapy) is expensive, painful, and can take days or even weeks (in many instances, the effects of lead poisoning are irreversible). The Centers for Disease Control uses a multilevel intervention strategy to deal with elevated blood lead levels. If any elevated blood lead levels are found, test your home for LBP.

Defective (chalking, flaking, chipping, or peeling) paint in an old house should be considered problematic until tested. If the home has

LBP that is chipping or flaking, or if a child in the home has an elevated blood lead level, you should address the problem (some states require it). Abatement methods range from removing LBP, to sealing or enclosing it with special materials, placing Sheetrock or plywood over existing LBP walls, or putting aluminum or vinyl siding over exterior painted wood, to removing and replacing the LBP-coated building materials (in some cases, it may be cheaper to just replace entire LBP-coated doors and windows). Special paints are needed to properly seal LBP; painting over LBP with *regular* paint will not eliminate the problem and is not considered an acceptable abatement method. What *is* allowable as proper abatement varies from state to state.

Check with your state environmental or health agency to find out if home owners are allowed to abate lead or if you must hire certified or licensed professionals to do so. Even if home owners are allowed to abate lead, we maintain that, because of the risks, *lead abatement is not a do-it-yourself project.* If you try to de-lead your home yourself, you could make things worse. While requirements mandating the removal of LBP or the use of certified lead-abatement contractors do *not* exist in many states, we recommend that in all situations you hire an experienced contractor with proper qualifications, training, and equipment to correct an LBP problem. We emphasize: removing lead improperly can increase the hazard by spreading lead dust around the home. Certified lead-abatement contractors should use trained workers and follow strict safety rules. Call your state or local environmental or health agency for assistance in locating a qualified contractor and to find out if financial assistance is available.

If you are remodeling or renovating an older home or one known to have LBP, to prevent a release of lead into the air, there are a number of precautions you should take *before* you begin any activities where painted surfaces will be disturbed. First, have the area tested for LBP. If LBP is found, have the repair or renovation done by a trained lead-abatement contractor. A dry scraper, belt sander, propane torch, or heat gun should never be used to remove LBP. Consider moving out (take your pets too) until the abatement work is completed. If you can't relocate your family, make certain the work area is completely sealed off so that there is no air exchange with the rest of the home. Ensure that proper safety measures are followed during the work and in cleaning up. Finally, if you've already completed renovations that may have released LBP or dust, have any young children tested and consider having a consultant do some follow-up testing (air sampling or dust wipes) to ensure that the home is safe.

Regulatory Outlook

In the 1950s and 1960s, many cities began to regulate the use of LBP, and several, such as Chicago, Cincinnati, New Haven, New York, Philadelphia, St. Louis, and Washington, D.C., banned it. On the federal level, the Lead-Based Paint Poisoning Prevention Act of 1971 prohibited the use of LBP in federally financed housing or construction; HUD passed regulations banning the use of LBP in HUD-associated housing the following year. The CPSC banned the use of paints with more than 0.06 percent lead by weight after 1978. This ban remains in effect today. Removal of LBP already in homes was not and is not required by these laws.

In a significant recent development, Congress passed the Residential Lead-Based Paint Hazard Reduction Act of 1992 (also called Title X). This law affects millions of sellers and landlords by mandating disclosure of LBP before the sale or lease of pre-1978 housing nationwide. The EPA and HUD issued their long-awaited rules on March 6, 1996,* which require sellers and landlords of pre-1978 housing to:

- disclose the presence of known LBP or LBP hazards in housing and provide the buyer/tenant any available information (including all records, reports, and test data);
- provide disclosure and acknowledgment language containing a "Lead Warning Statement" to the buyer or tenant in, or attached to, the purchase and sale contract or lease (Note: the Lead Warning Statement must be worded precisely as set forth in the regulations; the text differs for sales and leases) (see Appendix 6);
- provide the buyer or tenant with an EPA/HUD-approved lead hazard information pamphlet; and
- [for *sellers* only] allow the buyer ten days to conduct an LBP inspection or risk assessment before becoming obligated to purchase the house.

By signing the disclosure form, the buyer or tenant acknowledges that the seller or landlord has satisfied the disclosure requirements. Real estate agents must also sign the LBP disclosure form and must ensure that sellers and landlords fully comply with the requirements.

---

* EPA and HUD have provided for a phase-in of the effective dates of the regulations. Sellers and landlords who own *more than four* residential dwellings were subject to the regulations as of September 6, 1996, while those who own *one to four* residential dwellings were subject to the regulations as of December 6, 1996.

There are a number of exemptions from the disclosure requirements, including:

- foreclosures (however, subsequent sales of housing acquired through foreclosures are covered);
- the purchase, sale, and servicing of mortgages;
- sale or lease of "0-bedroom" dwellings where the living area is not separated from the sleeping area (e.g., efficiencies and studio apartments);
- rental housing that is free of LBP as determined by a state-certified lead inspector; and
- repeated disclosures are not required when renewing an existing lease, provided the landlord has previously disclosed all information and no new information exists.

These new requirements have significant implications for sellers and landlords of single-family homes, property owners and managers of multifamily buildings, real estate agents and brokers, and lenders. To comply with the regulations, sellers, landlords, and their agents should review and revise their standard purchase and sale contracts and leases to ensure compliance with the regulations. Lenders should review and revise loan documents for transactions involving pre-1978 residential housing to ensure that future borrowers will comply with the LBP disclosure requirements when they resell or lease their home.

Sellers and landlords, and their real estate agents, can be liable for triple damages, legal and expert fees, and court costs, not to mention possible fines and even imprisonment, for nondisclosure under the new law. Sellers and landlords must keep the required records and disclosure and acknowledgment contract for three years. Be aware that sellers and landlords of housing built *after* 1978 still may have LBP disclosure obligations if they have knowledge of the presence of LBP.

Under the new law, LBP is defined as paint containing 0.5 percent lead by weight or a "dry film area" concentration greater than or equal to 1.0 mg/cm^2. The law does not force sellers to inspect or test a home for lead before a sale or to fix a lead hazard, if discovered. The purchaser is responsible for financing any inspection or risk assessment. Remodeling or renovating contractors are required to give home owners and tenants a copy of the lead pamphlet before starting work.

Many state and local laws are similar to or even more stringent than Title X. Some trigger abatement of LBP surfaces that are defective or directly accessible to children (particularly those under age six), or where there is a lead-poisoning incident. Actual standards vary significantly from state to state, and many states have none. Contact your state or local health agency for appropriate standards and/or triggers for LBP abatement (see Appendix 4). Some states also have LBP regulations governing property condition disclosures; home inspections and testing; lead-poisoning prevention, screening/testing, control, and follow-up in poisoning incidents; training, licensing, and certification of inspectors and contractors; and abatement options. In such states, the federal requirements complement the state requirements but do not limit a state's authority to impose additional, more stringent requirements.

Some state laws require the abatement of chipping or flaking LBP only if children under six are present, and may require more stringent de-leading (such as on friction surfaces, surfaces less than five feet from the floor, and mouthable surfaces that protrude more than one-half inch, whether or not the LBP is defective) if there is a child with an elevated blood lead level. Other states are more stringent and may require abatement of LBP on surfaces under five feet or on mouthable surfaces where children under six reside, *regardless of its condition* or the fact that no child has an elevated blood lead level. Which abatement methods are allowed, and who may undertake them, depend on the particular state law and the facts of each situation. Some states maintain a list of approved procedures and products for encapsulation or enclosure. Other requirements may include reporting of a child's elevated blood lead level, notification of de-leading activities, or special requirements for disposal of lead-contaminated debris.

What to Look For

Unless fully renovated, expect a pre-1960 home to contain significant amounts of LBP. Likewise, there is a good chance that a home built before 1978 will contain LBP unless it has been renovated. Before 1978, lead was used in both interior and exterior paint (about 50 percent of the estimated fifty-seven million homes with LBP have it inside and out; 30 percent have it on the exterior only; the remaining 20 percent have interior LBP only).

While a general home inspection will not always include a lead inspection, it may identify whether there is chipping, flaking, or peeling paint that may contain lead. Ask the owner or seller if he or she knows if LBP was used on the property. Look in the garage or basement to see if any old cans of paint are still around. All areas inside a home may contain LBP, including: windows (including casings, sashes, sills, and aprons); doors (including doorjambs, casings, and headers); ceilings;

floors; stairways (including risers, treads, railings, baseboards, and banisters); walls (including chair rails and baseboards); and cabinets and furniture.

On the exterior, areas that may contain LBP include: doors; windows and associated parts; trim and cornerboards; porches (including the floor, railings, support columns, and ceilings); and fences. In many areas, the lead content in soil around a house, where LBP has flaked off, can be high.

Just knowing that a home has LBP will not tell you if there is a hazard. A qualified inspector can identify potential sources of lead exposure and the actions to take to address them.

Where to Find Help and Further Information

To properly analyze a home, each painted surface (inside and outside) should be tested. If you suspect LBP is present or you wish to have paint tested, call your state or local environmental or health agency for guidance and for help in choosing a qualified contractor and lab. Remember that different paints may have been used on walls, floors, doors, and so on. Paints may also differ from room to room and may have been applied at different times.

Do-it-yourself lead test kits are widely available, easy to use, and inexpensive, costing from $5 to $75. These kits contain chemicals that change color in the presence of lead. However, these are "qualitative" tests—they tell you only whether there is lead, not how much or at what levels. Not all home test kits are reliable; you should not depend on these tests to assess safety, as you may get false positive results or, worse, false negative results that will lull you into a false sense of security.

The only accurate way to know for sure if there is LBP is to hire a professional testing company. Laboratory tests of paint require the removal of small samples of paint from several rooms and areas of a home and analysis by a qualified laboratory. Lab costs generally run from $30 to $50 per sample—with numerous samples needed to properly test a home, costs can quickly reach several thousands of dollars. An alternative is to have a consultant trained in using a portable "X-ray fluorescence" (XRF) analyzer to test for lead throughout a home. These XRF detectors can measure the amount of lead in all layers of paint. An XRF survey for a typical one-family home can cost anywhere from $400 to $1,000 or more, and $200 or more per unit in a multifamily building.

The EPA has a toll-free hotline that provides lead information (800/LEAD-FYI); the National Lead Information Clearinghouse (800/424-LEAD) provides information on lead abatement, risk assessment, and inspection standards; and other federal and state environmental and health agencies and organizations offer LBP information and guidance (see Appendix 4).

For more information, see National Lead Information Center, *Lead: Some Questions and Answers,* 1993; U.S. Environmental Protection Agency, *Reducing Lead Hazards When Remodeling Your Home,* EPA 747-R-94-002, 1994; U.S. Environmental Protection Agency, *Lead Poisoning and Your Children,* 800-B-92-0002, 1992; U.S. Environmental Protection Agency and U.S. Consumer Product Safety Commission, *Protect Your Family from Lead in Your Home,* EPA 747-K-94-001, 1995 (this is the EPA/HUD-approved pamphlet to be provided buyers/tenants of pre-1978 housing).

The Bottom Line

About three out of every four homes built before 1978 contain some LBP. Have your home tested for LBP if it was built before 1978, especially if paint is chipping or if you are planning renovations. If there is LBP, but it's in good condition and there is no chance that it will affect children, keep an eye on it but, unless your state laws require otherwise, leave it alone—in most cases, it will not be a health hazard. However, recognize that the presence of LBP, no matter what the condition, poses a *potential* threat that at some point may need to be abated. If the LBP is being released into the environment or accessible to young children, or if you have a lead-poisoning incident, you will need to address the problem and should have children in the home tested for lead levels in their blood. Health risks from LBP can be significant. Do not try to de-lead a home yourself, as you could make things worse—use a certified or licensed lead consultant and contractor for testing and LBP abatement. New federal disclosure requirements that will be in effect in late 1996 will greatly impact sellers, landlords, and real estate agents—the residential real estate market will now be forced to account for LBP hazards in determining sale or rental price. Costs to address LBP should always be factored into negotiations over the price of a home.

14. LEAD IN WATER

Pre-1988 homes with lead pipes or lead-based solder in plumbing; homes connected to public water supplies by lead pipes; homes with brass well pumps or faucets

Risks: HEALTH ⊕⊕ FINANCIAL $$

Background

It is estimated that more than 10 percent of the U.S. population (around thirty million people)—particularly residents of large cities with lots of old houses and public works systems with lead pipes—consume drinking water containing lead levels above the EPA's safe drinking water standard. In most instances where lead in water is a problem, it comes from pipes connecting a home's plumbing system to a public water main or from a home's own plumbing fixtures. Lead can be a problem for homes using private wells and those served by public water supplies. Many older homes, especially those built before 1930, have lead pipes. And until less than a decade ago, lead solder was commonly used to join copper water pipes. Also, some well pumps and plumbing fixtures and faucets used today are made of brass and bronze and will leach lead under certain conditions.*

When corrosive water passes through lead-containing pipes, plumbing fixtures, or solder, lead can be dissolved in the water, a process known as leaching. Corrosive water is usually acidic and has a low pH. Softened water can also be corrosive. The concentration of lead may be highest when water has been stagnant for a period of time. Studies have shown that solder with lead will leach after five years and brass alloy faucet fixtures continue to leach lead even after ten years. While private well water and public water supplies do not naturally contain lead, they can become contaminated with lead from a variety of industries, landfills, and other pollution sources.

Health Risks

The EPA's current health-based standard for lead in drinking water is 0.015 milligrams per liter (mg/L) (which is equivalent to 15 parts per billion [ppb]) (see Appendix 2). Note that this standard applies only to

---

* In 1995, several major faucet manufacturers agreed to eliminate lead from their products by the year 2000.

public water systems serving more than twenty-five people (see Hazard 5, Drinking Water: Public Water Supplies). As discussed in Hazard 13, Lead-Based Paint, exposure to lead causes a variety of health effects. The EPA estimates that lead in drinking water affects more than four million children a year.

Financial Risks

Homes with significant lead-in-water problems will see a reduction in potential sales (particularly to buyers with children) and decreased market value due to treatment costs and stigma. If you are selling a home that has lead solder in the plumbing, test the water before putting the house on the market. If a home has a water treatment system, be ready to answer questions from potential buyers about lead levels and the system's operation and maintenance. If you are buying a home, ask the seller for any water test results. Costs to reduce lead levels in water (including replacing plumbing, if warranted) should be factored into the negotiations over the sales price. Only in extreme situations, it may be necessary to have the lead pipes replaced. Costs to do this will vary with the size of the home and the amount of plumbing; in most cases, this can be an expensive proposition.

Other financial risks:
- Liability for nondisclosure; see Disclosure Obligations, pages 13–19.
- Costs associated with contaminated drinking water; see Hazard 4, Drinking Water: Private Wells.
- Costs for short- or long-term medical treatment and monitoring; and legal and expert fees.

Managing the Risks

About 20 percent of all public water systems have some lead pipes. If you are connected to a system that has lead pipes, if your home has lead interior pipes or copper pipes with lead solder, or if you suspect your water has lead in it, there are some short-term precautions that you can take until the water is tested and a lead problem is either ruled out or corrected. Use only cold water for drinking and cooking, and always run the water for thirty seconds or so before drinking it, particularly if you haven't used the water for some time. One trick is to fill bottles with cold water after washing the dishes and store them in the refrigerator for drinking. You can also purchase bottled water for drinking and cooking needs. However, this can be expensive and a nuisance. Boiling water will *not* reduce the amount of lead.

Ways to remove lead from water include reverse osmosis, distillation, and some carbon filtration systems (see Hazard 4, Drinking Water; Private Wells, Managing the Risks, pages 64–67, for water treatment options). A treatment option for lead released from outdoor pipes is to neutralize the water as it enters the home so it will be less likely to corrode pipes and leach lead. Replacing lead pipes or solder is an option, although potentially expensive.

Regulatory Outlook

In 1986, Congress revised the Safe Drinking Water Act (SDWA) to include a total ban on materials containing lead, including pipe solder and flux, from use in public water supplies and in homes connected to public water supplies. (Plumbing materials are considered lead-free if solders and flux contain not more than 0.2 percent lead, and pipes and pipe fittings contain not more than 8.0 percent lead.) In 1988, the use of lead-based solder in plumbing applications within homes and buildings was banned. These bans, however, do not require the removal of existing plumbing containing lead.

Under the SDWA, public water suppliers serving more than twenty-five people must sample water from a representative portion of homes that are likely to have lead problems. Where lead levels in water exceed the EPA action level of 15 ppb, the suppliers must reduce the corrosiveness of the water and alert the public about the dangers of lead and how to reduce exposure. If lead problems persist, suppliers must provide additional treatment or remove lead pipes. Many states run the SDWA program for the EPA and have either adopted the EPA's standard or set a more stringent standard. States have their own monitoring requirements for the oversight of new hookups to public water systems.

Private drinking water wells are not governed by federal drinking water standards. However, state and local environmental and health agencies regulate the drilling and use of new wells and often set safe levels for contaminants such as lead.

What to Look For

For a home built before 1930, check to see if the water pipes are made of lead. Lead pipes are a dull gray metal color, are "soft" and will scratch easily with a key, and give a hollow, dull sound when hit with a metal object. Copper pipes are easy to distinguish by color and the ringing sound they make when struck. However, merely inspecting and whacking the pipes and plumbing fixtures is not enough to determine whether water in a home contains unsafe lead levels. If a home is hooked up to a public water supply, the network of pipes from the water source to the home may contain lead. In addition, many homes were built with copper pipes connected with lead solder, and even some brass faucets and plumbing fixtures in homes of any age can leach lead if the water is corrosive.

Lead in water is generally not a problem for homes built during the last decade so long as the pipes linking the home to a public water supply do not contain lead and the interior pipes do not have lead solder. Similarly, newly renovated older homes may not have a lead-in-water problem if lead pipes were replaced and lead-free solder was used in the new pipe joints. Check with the renovating contractor if possible.

Where to Find Help and Further Information

Since a visual inspection of a home's pipes is not an accurate means of determining whether there is lead in the water supply, some type of testing is needed. Your best bet is to have the water analyzed by a certified laboratory. In some instances, the public water supplier may do the test for you. If not, you or your home inspector can draw the water sample and take it to a lab for analysis. The sample should be drawn as a first flush after the water has remained in the pipes for at least six hours. If you take the sample yourself, follow the laboratory instructions carefully. If the lead level exceeds 15 ppb, or the relevant standard in your state, contact the appropriate agency or water supplier. While there are several do-it-yourself kits out there for testing lead in water, their reliability varies and it makes sense to have the test done right. The cost for a lab to analyze a water sample for lead is around $25 to $50; the lead test can be part of an overall water quality test.

In 1994, the EPA issued a lead-in-water warning that some well pumps that contain brass and bronze parts may leach lead into the water. It recommended that all users of wells test for lead.

If you suspect that your child has lead poisoning, have a blood test done. Testing is not expensive (between $10 and $75), and may be free in certain instances. Medical insurance may also cover the cost of testing blood lead levels.

Under the SDWA, all public water suppliers test their water for lead. Contact your supplier to find out test results for your area. If there is a problem, find out what they are doing about it. Contact the EPA or your state environmental or health agency for the applicable lead-in-water standard in your state, information about state-certified testing laboratories, or for further assistance (see Appendix 4). The EPA has a toll-free Safe Drinking Water Hotline (800/426-4791); several other lead hotlines are also available (see Appendix 4). See also U.S. Environmental Protection Agency, *Lead in Your Drinking Water,* EPA/810-F-93-001, 1993.

The Bottom Line

Lead in water can be a problem in old and new homes whether the home is connected to a public water supply or uses a private well for drinking water. As with lead paint, health effects from lead in water can be significant, especially for children. In the context of a transaction or if you suspect a problem, have the water tested for lead. Installation of water treatment systems or removal of problem pipes can be expensive remedies.

15. MISCELLANEOUS ON-SITE HAZARDS

Risks: HEALTH   ⊕   FINANCIAL $

Background

In this section, we highlight some other possible on-site hazards that are not specifically covered in Part II of the book; there may be others, depending on your situation and location.

Property History Land where agricultural, commercial, or industrial activities have occurred is sometimes converted to residential use, and these activities may have caused site contamination problems that may be of concern if a private drinking water well is used or if contaminated soil remains on the site. Old manufacturing buildings or mills are sometimes converted into apartments or condominiums and properties once used as gas stations, mines, or landfills may have been developed for residential use. For example, an old textile mill in New Jersey that was converted into a residential complex was recently evacuated due to contaminated indoor air. If a property had a prior agricultural, commercial, or industrial use, review the appropriate information as presented in Part III.

Hobbies Many popular home hobbies—photography, painting, pottery, flytying, bullet making, furniture stripping, and car repair and restoration, to name a few—involve chemicals that, if not stored, used, and disposed of properly, can cause environmental problems inside a home and outdoors. For example, on-site disposal of chemicals to a septic system (see Hazard 10, Historic Disposal Activities) can damage it, and also impact groundwater; careless storage of chemicals can put children at risk of poisoning (see Hazard 11, Household Chemicals and Hazardous Waste).

Local Creatures While almost everywhere there are local animals and insects that can be annoying pests, in some areas certain critters are more than nuisances—they can be dangerous. Poisonous snakes, spiders, scorpions, tarantulas, alligators, and coyotes can be a problem in certain areas. Deer ticks, which transmit Lyme disease, are one example of a real problem in many areas. It's best to find out about such problems ahead of time instead of being surprised later, especially if you're new to an area.

Others On-site issues—in the home or on the property—that may be of concern include:

- swimming pools (use, storage, and disposal of pool chemicals);
- gas or oil transmission pipelines under the property (leaks, explosions);
- junkyards for old cars and other machinery (solvents, gasoline and oil spills, and miscellaneous dumping);
- dental, medical, or veterinary offices (formaldehyde, medical waste, metals, pesticides);
- animal feeding and handling (manure);
- gardens, orchards, or nurseries (fertilizers and pesticides);
- barber and beauty shops (water usage, soaps, detergents); and
- funeral homes (formaldehyde, metals, incinerators).

Health Risks

See Hazard 4, Drinking Water: Private Wells, for a discussion of health risks if a drinking water well is contaminated by any of the above activities.

Risks to your health posed by local creatures, while rare, can be significant—some can kill you. Risks are greater in certain areas and even in specific neighborhoods in those areas. Children are often most likely to be hurt as they spend more time outside and may not know enough to avoid dangerous situations.

Financial Risks

Homes with contaminated wells will be devalued and difficult to sell. Some homes can be stigmatized and subject to devaluation if the pool of potential buyers, and thus the demand, shrinks due to a serious problem, such as with the water or some local pest. For example, where we live, there is a residential development in an area known to also be inhabited by thousands of rattlesnakes, and we know that some people won't even look at a home there.

Other financial risks:
- Liability for nondisclosure; see Disclosure Obligations, pages 13–19.
- Costs associated with contaminated drinking water; see Hazard 4, Drinking Water: Private Wells.
- Costs for short- or long-term medical treatment and monitoring; and legal and expert fees.

Managing the Risks

See Hazard 4, Drinking Water: Private Wells, for a discussion of how to manage risks if a drinking water well is contaminated.

In areas where some local pests may be dangerous, awareness and education are the first steps to minimizing your chances of having problems. If pesticides are used because of insects, make sure that they are used properly and that children are protected from poisoning.

Regulatory Outlook

Home hobbies and other on-site activities may be regulated by local land use agencies (see Hazard 23, Zoning and Other Land Use Restrictions). Chemicals in the home are discussed in Hazard 11, Household Chemicals and Hazardous Waste.

What to Look For

If a well is in use, taste and smell the water; however, laboratory tests are usually needed to detect contamination. If a water treatment system or bottled water is used, find out why (see Hazard 4, Drinking Water: Private Wells).

Look in the house, basement, garage, and outbuildings for workshops or other home hobby areas where chemicals may have been used. Check for floor drains or sinks connected to septic systems or dry wells for evidence that chemicals have been disposed of on-site.

Where to Find Help and Further Information

Check with the neighbors and the town land use or building officials to find out about historic uses of a property and ask about known groundwater or pest problems in an area. Find out if any of the off-site hazards covered in Part III have occurred on the property.

Home owners and potential buyers of homes with wells should consider testing the water (see Hazard 4, Drinking Water: Private Wells). Coordinate tests with a qualified laboratory, consultant, or inspector. Contact the EPA or your state environmental or health agency for additional information or assistance (see Appendix 4).

The Bottom Line

Miscellaneous activities vary with the nature of the property, historic uses, and local conditions. While they should rarely be a major problem, if present, they can pose health and financial risks. Try to find out if any activity that could have resulted in soil or groundwater pollution has occurred on a property, particularly if a well is used for drinking water. If local insects or other pests are a problem in your area, learn about them and take measures to protect yourself and your children.

16. PCBs

Some pre-1979 electric transformers on utility poles and capacitors in old well pumps, appliances, and fluorescent light ballasts

Risks: HEALTH ⊕⊕ FINANCIAL $

Background

Polychlorinated biphenyls (PCBs), a family of organic chemical compounds, were considered "wonder chemicals" and used extensively in electrical equipment, such as transformers, capacitors, circuit breakers, and switches, from the late 1920s to the mid-1970s. During this time, an estimated 1.4 billion pounds of PCBs were produced in the United

States. In the late 1970s, as the health hazards of PCBs became known, the EPA banned their manufacture, but they were not banned from use. Therefore, many transformers still contain PCBs; utilities can use these PCB-containing transformers until the end of their useful lives if they don't leak, or until they are taken out of service.

In residential areas, transformers, which reduce the higher voltages from electrical distribution lines to a lower voltage suitable for home use, are usually attached to telephone poles or located in aboveground or underground vaults. Apartment buildings and condominium complexes often use large PCB-containing transformers. Only pre-1979 transformers that contain PCBs are a potential problem. Transformers can leak oil, even during normal operation. If the oil contains PCBs, it can contaminate soil and groundwater and result in a possible health threat. Not all transformers pose a risk; if they are intact and do not leak, there is no direct threat. However, even nonleaking PCB-containing transformers are a *potential* threat, because hundreds of utility transformers around the United States rupture every year in storms and car accidents, showering residential properties with PCB-contaminated oil. For example, laboratory analyses of residential soil following several recent rupture incidents in Illinois showed significant levels of PCB contamination.

PCBs may also be found in a variety of other electrical equipment, posing similar risks. Many pre-1979 household items, such as air conditioners, dehumidifiers, refrigerators, microwave ovens, dishwashers, fluorescent light fixtures, and mercury vapor lamps, may also contain PCBs. Prior to 1979, PCB-containing capacitors even were components of some submersible pumps in drinking water wells; these capacitors have been known to fail and contaminate well water. In addition, until the early 1980s, PCB-laden oil often was sold as home heating fuel and used as a dust suppressant on dirt roads.

Homes can also be impacted by off-site PCB sources through air pollution, storm water runoff, and groundwater. Examples include:

- a landfill in upstate New York containing hundreds of tons of old PCB-containing capacitors contaminated groundwater near a residential development;
- more than three thousand residents had to leave their homes for three weeks following a 1988 fire at a Canadian warehouse where PCB-containing transformers were stored;
- in 1990, homes in Indiana were contaminated by PCBs following a flood;

- PCBs were discovered in natural gas lines leading to more than twenty-five homes in Indiana in 1990;
- in 1995, an Alabama PCB manufacturer was ordered to clean up soil tainted with PCBs at neighboring residences; and
- home owners near a Paoli, Pennsylvania, railroad yard have been embroiled in a dispute since 1986 over PCB contamination of their properties from railroad transformers.

Health Risks

Exposure to PCBs can occur by inhalation of fumes (from transformer fires), by skin contact with PCB-containing fluid or contaminated soil, and by consuming tainted food or water. PCBs are most harmful if ingested—the EPA drinking water standard for PCBs is extremely low (0.5 ppb). Chronic exposure to PCBs causes a range of health problems, from skin problems (known as chloracne) and eye irritation to liver damage and impairment of the nervous system. PCBs also have been linked to reproductive problems, such as low birth weight, and have been listed by the EPA as a probable human carcinogen because they cause cancer in laboratory animals. PCBs accumulate and persist in food chains and do not degrade easily in the environment.

Financial Risks

If PCB-containing items rupture or leak, soil and groundwater contamination can pose significant financial risks. Cleanup and disposal of contaminated soil can run into the thousands or even tens of thousands of dollars. In most cases, the owner of the electrical equipment—often the local utility (although many are privately owned, such as in multifamily properties)—will foot the bill for a cleanup. For example, in the mid-1980s, the EPA forced a utility to clean up hundreds of homes in northern Illinois where PCB-containing capacitors and transformers mounted on telephone poles had ruptured.

Because of potential cleanup costs, as well as health risks, a property with PCB-containing equipment or any known PCB contamination can be devalued. In 1987, a California jury awarded $25,000 to a family as compensation for devaluation of their home as a result of an explosion of a utility-owned PCB-containing transformer, which contaminated their property. Even if a PCB-containing transformer has never leaked, its mere presence can lower a property's value due to stigma.

The cost to dispose of and replace a PCB-containing transformer can be thousands of dollars, depending on its size and location. A home owner is rarely responsible for costs to replace a transformer—this is normally the local utility's domain.

Sellers of a property with items that contain PCBs should be prepared for questions from prospective buyers. Buyers may require items to be replaced or may factor in the cost of replacement when negotiating the price.

The cost to replace a well pump installed before 1979 containing PCBs should run between $500 and $1,000. However, most pumps of that vintage have already been, or are probably ready to be, replaced.

Other financial risks:

- ▶ Liability for nondisclosure; see Disclosure Obligations, pages 13–19.
- ▶ Costs associated with contaminated drinking water; see Hazard 4, Drinking Water: Private Wells.
- ▶ Costs for short- or long-term medical treatment and monitoring; property damage (such as harm to livestock, crops, or landscaping); and legal and expert fees.

Managing the Risks

If a transformer is owned by a public utility, that company will be able to tell you if it contains PCBs. If it does, ask the utility to replace it. Where there is evidence that a PCB transformer has leaked, the utility should be required to clean up any contamination immediately. For example, in 1987, a gas company was forced to supply bottled water to more than twenty-two hundred residents of a New Jersey town after PCB contamination from its pipeline was discovered in private drinking water wells. And in 1982, a California utility had to cut down trees, remove topsoil from lawns, and steam clean houses when a transformer exploded during a storm and contaminated several homes with PCBs. Do *not* try to clean up a PCB spill yourself, and avoid all skin contact with PCBs. Call the EPA or your state environmental or health agency for further assistance in dealing with contamination problems from transformers or other PCB-containing equipment (see Appendix 4).

Older well pumps with PCBs can be replaced. Other PCB-containing equipment on the property—such as fluorescent light fixtures and old appliances—should be inspected, and if damaged in any way, removed from the home or properly disposed of. Buyers should have the seller get rid of any such equipment *before* closing the deal.

See Hazard 4, Drinking Water: Private Wells, for a discussion of how to manage risks if a drinking water well is contaminated.

Contact the owner of the PCB equipment for financial or technical help in correcting a problem and in managing the associated risks.

Regulatory Outlook

The federal Toxic Substances Control Act (TSCA) of 1976 prohibited the manufacture or use of PCBs after 1979 but allowed their continued use under certain conditions. The EPA essentially banned all PCB production and use after July 1, 1979, however, *existing* PCB equipment could continue to be used "in a totally enclosed manner"—in essence, as long as the equipment didn't leak. Today the EPA and some state environmental agencies regulate the use, marking, storage, disposal, and cleanup of PCBs and PCB-containing equipment and set acceptable PCB levels for soil and water. Among the requirements is one under which utilities must identify and label PCB-containing equipment and then inspect all such equipment regularly for leaks. Residential property owners normally are not required to clean up PCB contamination. Since the ban, utilities have been gradually replacing equipment containing PCBs as they reach the end of their useful lives. Thus, over time, as more and more PCB-containing items are taken out of service and disposed of, PCBs will diminish as a potential hazard for home owners.

What to Look For

Electrical items and appliances manufactured after 1979 should not contain PCBs. An inspection of the property will allow you to locate utility poles and any transformers that may be present. Pole-mounted transformers are usually barrel-shaped metal containers, about two feet in diameter and two to three feet tall, although they can also be square or rectangular boxes. Transformers are often located on telephone poles but are also placed on the ground (they should be within a fence or inside a box) or in an underground vault. Utilities usually place square yellow labels with black lettering on PCB-containing transformers. However, some PCB-containing transformers may not be labeled. Most telephone poles and electrical equipment are identified by a code number that can be used as a reference when calling the local utility. Transformers in buildings or vaults are more likely to be the ones containing PCBs.

Look for oily streaks on the outside of the transformer or on the telephone pole. PCBs are dark or amber-colored oily liquids that have a faint odor some liken to mothballs. Oil-stained soil or pavement or stressed vegetation beneath or adjacent to a transformer may be a sign that it has leaked.

If the home has a well, you'll want to find out the age of the well pump (see below).

Although rare, look around the house for old appliances and fluorescent light fixtures—they may contain PCBs. During normal operation of a fluorescent light, the PCBs are entirely enclosed. However, when the capacitor wears out, it may burn or break and leak PCBs. New ballasts for fluorescent lights that do not contain PCBs should be labeled ''No PCBs.'' Check any equipment suspected of containing PCBs for a label that gives the date of manufacture and the trade name of the fluid— then call the EPA or your state environmental or health agency to find out whether the fluid contains PCBs (see Appendix 4).

If a water treatment system or bottled water is used, find out why. Laboratory tests are needed to detect PCB contamination (see Hazard 4, Drinking Water: Private Wells).

Where to Find Help and Further Information

If there is a transformer on the property, ask the seller if it contains PCBs. If the seller doesn't know, ask the local utility company, using the number on the pole as a reference guide. If the utility doesn't know if it contains PCBs, request that someone be sent out to inspect it (and to test it, if necessary). Check with your town's land use or building officials or the local fire marshal to find out about historic problems from PCB-containing transformers.

If you have an older well, find out when the pump was last replaced— if before 1979, see if any records about the pump were maintained. If so, try to contact the manufacturer. If there are no records, contact a plumber or a well installer to check whether the pump contains PCBs.

If there's a possibility that soil or well water is contaminated by PCBs, have laboratory tests conducted. Samples of contaminated soil should *never* be taken without first discussing the situation with an environmental consultant or home inspector. The cost for testing water for PCBs is $50 to $100. Contact the EPA or your state environmental or health agency for additional information (such as a list of qualified labs) or assistance (see Appendix 4).

The Bottom Line

PCBs are generally not a problem for home owners. If there is a transformer on a property, find out from its owner—usually the local utility—if it contains PCBs. Old appliances, fluorescent light fixtures, and well pumps may also contain PCBs. While there is no immediate threat to human health or the environment unless PCBs have been released, there are possible future liabilities. PCB-contaminated properties present major health and financial risks and warrant significant concern. Costs to deal with contaminated well water are high and the value of a property with a PCB problem will be significantly reduced.

17. PRESSURE-TREATED WOOD

Wood decks, playground equipment, landscaping materials, and other outdoor construction

Risks: HEALTH   ⊕   FINANCIAL $

Background

Pressure-treated wood (PTW) is popular for outdoor use because it resists rot and attack by bacteria, mold, fungi, and insects so well that it lasts more than ten times longer than untreated wood. Many manufacturers offer lifetime guarantees for PTW. Commercial products such as railroad ties, telephone poles, ranch fences, docks, and piers are made from PTW. It is also used around homes for decks, porches, fences, gazebos, picnic tables, sandboxes, play gyms, and docks, and for gardens and other landscaping projects.

PTW, which has been manufactured since the early 1900s, is made just as its name implies—wood is placed in a pressure chamber and liquid preservatives (various pesticides) are forced into the pores of the wood, forming a chemical barrier against wood-destroying pests and microorganisms. Three different wood preservatives are commonly used: creosote, pentachlorophenol ("penta" for short), and chromated copper arsenate (CCA). Generally, creosote and penta are used to preserve wood for commercial use, while CCA and other water-borne preservatives are used for residential application. We say "generally" because many of the PTW products produced for residential use are derived from recycled telephone poles and railroad ties preserved with creosote or penta.

With the benefits of PTW come a few potential problems. Wood preservatives are toxic and can be harmful to humans unless certain precautions are followed. Exposure can occur when working with PTW and inhaling PTW sawdust, or if a young child or pet chews or eats it. Because arsenic and other toxics can leach out of PTW, questions have been raised about its use near drinking water sources and vegetable gardens and around sandboxes and other play areas. PTW may also pose a threat to aquatic organisms, birds, and other wildlife. In addition, when PTW reaches the end of its useful life and begins to decompose, additional leaching of its toxic preservatives may occur.

Leaching rates of wood preservatives from PTW products made from telephone poles or railway ties may be significantly higher than from CCA-preserved products; the amount of wood preservative contained in commercial PTW tends to be higher because the wood was not originally intended for residential application. Therefore, potential health problems may be more significant from PTW that was originally manufactured for nonresidential use.

Health Risks

Wood preservatives that are toxic enough to kill insects and microbes may also have harmful effects on humans. *Normal,* restricted use of PTW products outdoors in a residential setting is not believed to cause health risks; indoor use may pose more of a risk—a woman in Massachusetts developed a severe skin rash from a log home in which the logs had been treated with penta. However, health problems can arise if anyone ingests PTW or breathes PTW dust. For example, it is dangerous to have skin contact with, breathe, or ingest arsenic, a strong poison, which is a component of CCA. Short-term effects from exposure to arsenic include headaches, dizziness, muscle spasms, delirium, and convulsions. Long-term ingestion or inhalation of even low levels of arsenic compounds can cause a variety of health problems including stomach irritation; liver, kidney, nervous system, or blood damage; and cancer of the lungs and skin. Wood preservatives, such as penta, are suspected of causing birth defects in the developing fetus. Long-term exposure to creosote is linked to dermatitis and skin cancer.

Wood preservatives can also be harmful or fatal to pets, wildlife, and aquatic organisms.

Financial Risks

In most cases, financial risks associated with PTW are not significant. Although not usually necessary for prevention of health risks, some people *may* want to have creosote- or penta-containing PTW replaced with other products in some situations (such as in a vegetable garden, where it comes into contact with drinking water, or in children's play areas).

PTW will need to be removed and disposed of when it reaches the end of its useful life. The costs of replacement, removal, and disposal vary with the amount and type of PTW and local disposal options. During a construction or renovation project involving PTW, there may be some PTW debris that will require proper disposal, but costs should be minimal. If PTW were to leach toxic chemicals that impact soil or groundwater, addressing the contamination could be costly.

Sellers of a property may be asked questions by prospective buyers about where PTW structures are located.

Other financial risks:
- Liability for nondisclosure; see Disclosure Obligations, pages 13–19.
- Costs associated with contaminated drinking water; see Hazard 4, Drinking Water: Private Wells.

Managing the Risks

If there is PTW on the property, check its location and age. PTW should not be used in kitchens for cutting boards or countertops—there really is no need for it indoors. Outdoors, PTW should not be used near drinking water supplies, as compost or animal bedding, or as posts or perches for bird feeders. Most experts, including the American Wood Preservers Institute, recommend that creosote- and penta-containing PTW *not* be used in playground equipment (e.g., swing sets and sandboxes); some also caution against the use of such PTW around vegetable gardens. If PTW is found in any of these locations, remove and replace it with something that does not have the *potential* to leach harmful chemicals. Concerns about potential impacts from other outdoor uses of PTW, such as for picnic tables, or around vegetable gardens, well heads and ponds, have also been raised by various organizations. Although some children's playground equipment made from PTW is finished with a sealant to minimize leaching of the pesticides, children and pets should be kept from chewing or mouthing PTW.

If there is unused PTW lying about, and you don't anticipate using it, require the seller to get rid of it *before* closing the deal.

When sawing or drilling PTW, wear a dust mask and take precautions to avoid breathing the dust, and wash your hands thoroughly afterward. Debris and dust should be removed and properly disposed of. PTW should never be left lying around where it could be ingested or contaminate a drinking water well. Never burn PTW scraps outdoors or indoors in woodstoves or fireplaces. In one case, high levels of copper, chromium, and arsenic found in dust and dirt in a home were linked to burning CCA-treated wood in a wood stove. A variety of health problems were identified in family members, including severe skin and respiratory problems in the youngest children, who played on the floor.

If you don't want to use PTW, naturally resistant woods, like cedar and redwood, are an alternative.

Regulatory Outlook

While we are not aware of any federal laws mandating how or where private home owners can use PTW products, the EPA has issued a warning that PTW should *not* be used near drinking water supplies or where it can come into contact with food or animal feed. The chemicals used in PTW are toxic, "restricted-use" pesticides that are not available to the general public. The EPA requires those working in the PTW industry to be certified to handle the pesticides and requires sellers of PTW products to provide information sheets to consumers detailing handling and use procedures and informing them of the chemical hazards and any associated health risks.

Some state and local laws restrict PTW use in certain circumstances, such as wetlands or bodies of water, or in public areas. For example, in California, the use of state funds to purchase playground or recreational equipment made from PTW is prohibited.

Waste materials containing arsenic or other wood preservatives generated by industry are considered hazardous and subject to strict control under EPA and state laws. These laws do not apply to private home owners, but some state and local agencies may have special rules for disposing of PTW, which may be considered household hazardous waste in your area (see Hazard 11, Household Chemicals and Hazardous Waste).

Local building codes may require the use of PTW or naturally resistant woods in construction where the wood will be in contact with exposed soil, concrete, or masonry to prevent rotting and damage from insects.

What to Look For

A visual inspection of the property should allow you to locate any PTW—look around the yard for landscaping timbers around shrubs and bushes, vegetable gardens, and sandboxes. Decks, backyard play gyms, fences, and other outdoor structures may also be made from PTW. When it is new, CCA-treated PTW has a green tint that gradually fades upon exposure to light; even old PTW may still be green on the underside. CCA-treated PTW is typically marked with words like "20 year." Also look for piles of PTW dust outside, such as near a deck, or indoors in a basement or wood shop.

Where to Find Help and Further Information

If PTW is used in any of the areas of concern listed above, ask the seller how old it is and if there have been any problems. If contamination is suspected, test the soil and water. Laboratory tests of well water for arsenic, copper, and chromium can be performed for around $50; tests for other wood preservative chemicals can be more expensive. Coordinate tests with a qualified lab or consultant. Lumber supply yards and contractors, the American Wood Preservers' Institute, 1945 Old Gallows Road, Suite 150, Vienna, VA 22182 (800/356-2974), and the National Coalition Against the Misuse of Pesticides, 1701 E Street, SE, Suite 200, Washington, D.C. 20003 (202/543-5450), can also provide information about PTW products. Contact the EPA or your state environmental or health agency for additional information or assistance (see Appendix 4).

The Bottom Line

Pressure-treated wood is favored by home owners because it is cheaper in the long run and requires less maintenance than conventional wood products. If PTW is used and handled properly, health and financial risks are minimal. Because some types of PTW, especially those products not originally intended for residential application, can contain toxic levels of wood preservatives, do not burn PTW, use it indoors, or place it near drinking water supplies, where leaching of toxic chemicals could contaminate drinking water, and harm wildlife. Creosote- and penta-containing PTW should also not be used in playground equipment and around vegetable gardens.

18. RADON IN AIR

Everywhere, particularly in the Northeast

Risks: HEALTH ⊕ ⊕ ⊕   FINANCIAL $ $

Background

Radon is a colorless, odorless, tasteless gas produced by the natural breakdown or "radioactive decay" of uranium naturally found in soil, rock, and water. Radon is recognized as a significant indoor air health threat—if inhaled for significant periods, radon can increase the risk of lung cancer. The EPA has indicated that radon is the second leading cause of lung cancer in the United States, estimated to cause as many as twenty thousand deaths per year.

Radon has been found in homes throughout the United States (especially the Northeast), whether new or old, well insulated or drafty, with or without basements. The EPA estimates that more than eight million homes in the United States have radon levels above what it considers safe. Radon enters a home from underlying soil, typically through openings in the foundation, such as cracks in a basement floor, drains, sump pump openings, wall or floor joints, and the pores in hollow block walls. Radon gas collects in the areas of a home closest to the ground and levels generally decrease as you move higher up in a house. Radon can also enter a home via its water supply, whether from a private drinking water well or public water source (see Hazard 19, Radon in Water).

Health Risks

Radon gas breaks down into radioactive particles, called decay products, that remain in the air. As you breathe these particles, they become trapped in your lungs and continue to break down and release radiation—these bursts of energy are known as "radon daughters"—and can damage lung tissue. Prolonged inhalation of radon gas has been shown to significantly increase the risk of lung cancer. The risk increases as the level of radon and duration of exposure increase. Smokers who live in homes with elevated radon levels are at even greater risk.

The concentration of radon in the air is measured in units known as picocuries per liter (pCi/L). Most homes have radon levels between 1 and 2 pCi/L, which is below the EPA's recommended maximum of 4 pCi/L. Congress has stated that a long-term goal for indoor radon levels should be no more than outdoor levels (about 0.4 pCi/L).

Homes built on granitic rock ledge containing radium are more likely to test higher. For example, in Connecticut (a state with a lot of granitic ledge), many homes have tested at 20 pCi/L or even higher. At that level, the EPA calculates the risk of contracting lung cancer to be about fifteen times the risk of a normal population (at 2 pCi/L).

The EPA's risk assessments are *conservative;* they assume that a person will be exposed to a given concentration of radon over a lifetime of roughly seventy years and spends 75 percent of his or her time in the home. The EPA believes that short-term exposure to high levels of radon is not as serious as long-term exposure to lower levels. However, the EPA believes that no level of radon exposure is known to be safe, as there may be risks associated with even very low levels. It estimates that the risk of dying from lung cancer as the result of lifetime exposure to an annual radon level of 4 pCi/L is the same as the risk of dying from lung cancer from smoking ten cigarettes a day or having two hundred chest X rays a year. A radon level of 40 pCi/L equates to smoking two packs of cigarettes a day, while a level of 100 pCi/L equates to two thousand chest X rays a year. The highest levels we've heard about occurred in 1984, when a nuclear power plant engineer in Pennsylvania set off the radiation detection device at work because his home had a radon level of 2,700 pCi/L (equivalent to smoking about two hundred packs of cigarettes a day).

The tables following illustrate radon risks for smokers and non-smokers (based on the assumption that a person spends 18 hours each day exposed to the same radon level for 74 years).

Financial Risks

Homes with elevated radon levels can be devalued due to health concerns and costs relating to radon reduction. Buyers and tenants, especially those with or contemplating children, may be wary of homes with radon problems. Some buyers may make an offer far below the asking price, make a sale contingent on the seller reducing the radon level, or simply walk away from the deal. Elevated radon levels can be a stigma for future buyers, so the pool of potential buyers may become smaller. If you buy a home with a radon problem, recognize that you may be required to address the problem if, in the future, a law requiring such action is enacted.

Costs for radon tests generally range from $25 to $200, depending on the size of the home, the number of samples collected, and whether a do-it-yourself kit is used or an outside company is hired to do more expansive tests. The cost to reduce radon or install radon-reduction

RADON RISK IF YOU SMOKE

Radon Level	If 1,000 people who smoked were exposed to this level over a lifetime . . .	The risk of cancer from radon exposure compares to . . .	What to Do: Stop Smoking and . . .
20 pCi/L	about 135 people could get lung cancer	←100 times the risk of drowning	Fix your home
10 pCi/L	about 71 people could get lung cancer	←100 times the risk of dying in a home fire	Fix your home
8 pCi/L	about 57 people could get lung cancer		Fix your home
4 pCi/L	about 29 people could get lung cancer	←100 times the risk of dying in an airplane crash	Fix your home
2 pCi/L	about 15 people could get lung cancer	←2 times the risk of dying in a car crash	Consider fixing between 2 and 4 pCi/L
1.3 pCi/L	about 9 people could get lung cancer	(Average indoor radon level)	(Reducing radon levels below 2 pCi/L is difficult)
0.4 pCi/L	about 3 people could get lung cancer	(Average outdoor radon level)	

NOTE: If you are a former smoker, your risk may be lower.

RADON RISK IF YOU HAVE NEVER SMOKED

Radon Level	If 1,000 people who never smoked were exposed to this level over a lifetime . . .	The risk of cancer from radon exposure compares to . . .	What to Do:
20 pCi/L	about 8 people could get lung cancer	←The risk of being killed in a violent crime	Fix your home
10 pCi/L	about 4 people could get lung cancer		Fix your home
8 pCi/L	about 3 people could get lung cancer	←10 times the risk of dying in an airplane crash	Fix your home
4 pCi/L	about 2 people could get lung cancer	←The risk of drowning	Fix your home
2 pCi/L	about 1 person could get lung cancer	←The risk of dying in a home fire	Consider fixing between 2 and 4 pCi/L
1.3 pCi/L	less than 1 person could get lung cancer	(Average indoor radon level)	(Reducing radon levels below 2 pCi/L is difficult)
0.4 pCi/L	less than 1 person could get lung cancer	(Average outdoor radon level)	

NOTE: If you are a former smoker, your risk may be higher.

From U.S. EPA, *Home Buyer's and Seller's Guide to Radon*, March 1993, 402-R-93-003.

equipment ranges from several hundred to several thousands of dollars, but most typically runs between $500 and $2,500, depending on several factors, such as the number of radon sources, the radon levels in the underlying soil or water supply, and the type of construction used in the home. If a radon-reduction system uses fans or pumps, operating these devices may significantly increase utility bills.

Many buyers will require information about the presence of radon as part of the purchase and sale agreement. Incidents of tampering with radon testing have been frequently reported; both sellers and agents may be liable for improper interference with a radon test that could lead to false results. Contractors, real estate agents, landlords, and others may also face potential liability for injuries to buyers or tenants from exposure to radon. Some lenders require radon testing *before* providing financing.

Other financial risks:
▶ Liability for nondisclosure; see Disclosure Obligations, pages 13–19. Almost half of the states specifically require radon data disclosure.
▶ Costs for short- or long-term medical treatment and monitoring; and legal and expert fees.

Managing the Risks

In general, an elevated radon level will be a significant issue in homes that use the basement for living or recreational space, or in split-level homes without a basement. Radon is not usually a problem for people living above the first floor in apartment or condominium buildings.

While there are no laws that require that radon levels in a home be reduced, we recommend confronting the issue of radon head-on. The first step is to test for radon. All buyers should do so, making sure their contract spells out entitlement to conduct a test, when and how it will be done, and how the cost of the test and its results will be shared. If you are selling a home, consider testing for radon before putting the home on the market to save time and preserve potential buyers during the transaction. Save test results, all information and documentation concerning the test(s), and steps taken to fix any problem discovered. What might otherwise be a problem can be turned into a positive selling point. Buyers will be likely to test anyway and can be expected to use any necessary remediation costs as a negotiating point. Even if you're not selling your home, testing for radon is a good idea because of the potential health risks.

In some cases where there is an elevated radon level, home owners will be able to perform the repairs needed to reduce radon levels. However, often it will be necessary to hire an expert to identify the radon sources and to design and install an effective radon-reduction system. Consult with your state environmental or health agency for assistance in choosing a qualified radon-reduction contractor (see Appendix 4). Always retest after completing any radon abatement work.

There are many effective and relatively inexpensive ways to reduce radon levels in a home. Some systems can reduce radon levels by up to 99 percent. The methods used vary depending on the location, the source of the radon, the ways in which it enters the home, and the type of construction used. Sealing holes and cracks in the foundation and basement walls can be an effective way to prevent radon from entering the home. A major factor influencing radon levels is ventilation. Opening windows or installing systems to increase ventilation, usually starting in the basement, is a common way to reduce radon; as a rule of thumb, doubling the ventilation rate can reduce radon levels by 50 percent.

In many cases, a method known as "sub-slab depressurization" is often recommended and proves effective in radon reduction by preventing the gas from entering the home through the foundation. Pipes are installed through the basement floor and radon-laden air is pulled up through the pipes by an exhaust fan that vents the air to the outside. These systems may cost $1,500 or more. Many other radon-reduction systems are available, depending on the design of your home and other factors.

If you are buying a newly constructed home or are building a home, especially in an area known to have radon problems, consider using radon-resistant construction techniques and features (a requirement of some state and local building codes).

Regulatory Outlook

In 1985, the EPA announced a voluntary "action guideline" of 4 pCi/L, above which radon-reduction measures should be implemented. The EPA also oversees two voluntary proficiency programs: (1) the Radon Measurement Proficiency (RMP) program and (2) the Radon Contractor Proficiency (RCP) program. The RMP program determines the accuracy of radon detectors and the RCP program evaluates the proficiency of radon mitigation companies. These programs are often run at the state level.

In 1986, Congress enacted the Radon Gas and Indoor Air Quality Research Act. While this law provides a vehicle for information gathering, research, and other aspects of the radon issue, it did not set action levels or mandate requirements for dealing with radon. For several years, Congress has been debating a law that would require disclosures about radon in every sale or lease of residential real estate. While we have no such law, many state disclosure and consumer protection laws do specifically require the disclosure of radon problems to buyers. To date, federal and state environmental and health agencies have funded research in the area of radon risk and abatement, developed recommended safe levels, and provided information to the public. While there are numerous state laws governing certification and licensing of radon mitigation companies and contractors, disclosure, and radon in public buildings, we are not aware of any laws currently in place requiring home owners to test for radon or to reduce levels below some threshold for private homes or for leased residences.

In recent years, the EPA has focused a lot of attention on indoor air pollution problems in general and radon risks in particular. At some point, Congress may require radon tests and disclosures in residential real estate purchases, much like the Title X program for lead-based paint. Also, many states regulate various aspects of radon, including: disclosure, consumer protection/unfair trade, radon mitigation and testing companies, the licensing and registration of contractors, building codes for radon-resistant buildings, and the indoor air quality in public buildings such as schools. Overall, we expect to see more research and guidance in this area in the future, and may see more certification requirements and controls over radon professionals.

What to Look For

Since you cannot smell or see radon, testing is the only way to know if a home has a problem. While local or neighborhood radon levels may suggest a trend, you cannot rely on radon tests taken in nearby homes to estimate the level in your home—houses that are next to each other can have very different radon levels. Buyers should ask the seller for any radon test results, and if the home has a radon-reduction system, request information and any documents about the system.

Where to Find Help and Further Information

You can test your own home or hire an EPA-listed or state-certified radon tester. Call the EPA's RCP program (202/233-9370) or your state environmental or health agency (see Appendix 4). Also ask for information concerning the types of radon-testing devices or kits available and for general recommendations about the appropriate device for your needs and expected testing conditions. Make sure the radon device is listed by the EPA's testing program or is state certified.

There are several ways to test for radon. Preliminary-screening test kits can be bought over-the-counter in many hardware, grocery, and convenience stores. Or you can send away for radon-testing devices from laboratories that offer mail-order services. Most initial radon tests are short-term, ranging from two to five days (in no case should a test be fewer than forty-eight hours), and involve opening small test canisters and placing them in the desired rooms—usually the basement or the lowest level suitable for occupancy. Instructions with the kit should be followed carefully to ensure that proper measurements are obtained. Environmental consultants and many home inspectors now do radon tests. Be sure that the person you hire has expertise regarding the tests and knows which device is appropriate for your situation. Buyers should discuss ways to prevent or detect interference with the radon test with an inspector or a radon expert.

If preliminary tests indicate radon levels greater than 4 pCi/L in living areas of the home, the EPA recommends that a follow-up test be conducted. For home owners, long-term testing, lasting up to one year, is a more accurate way to determine radon levels and exposure. Both short- and long-term testing devices are relatively easy to use and inexpensive. Recognize that radon levels will be higher in the winter, when there is less ventilation.

For further information, you can call the Radon Hotline (800/SOS-RADON). Also see U.S. Environmental Protection Agency, *Home Buyer's and Seller's Guide to Radon*, 402-R-93-003, 1993; U.S. Environmental Protection Agency, *Consumer's Guide to Radon Reduction*, 402-K92-003, 1992; U.S. Environmental Protection Agency, *Reducing Radon Risks*, 520/1-89-027, 1992; U.S. Environmental Protection Agency, U.S. Department of Health and Human Services, and Centers for Disease Control, *A Citizen's Guide to Radon*, 2d ed., 402-K92-001, 1992.

The Bottom Line

About one out of every fifteen homes in the United States has elevated radon levels, representing significant health and associated financial risks. The EPA is currently working closely with state and local governments and the private sector to identify cost-effective methods for reducing radon levels. Radon is considered the second leading cause of lung cancer; while some argue that the dangers have been blown out of proportion, testing is the only way to ensure that a home does not have high radon levels. Whether buying, selling, or just living in a home, have it tested for radon. If the radon level is 4 pCi/L or higher, fix the problem. If building a home, talk to your builder about radon-reducing construction techniques to head off any problems down the road.

19. RADON IN WATER

Homes with wells and airborne radon problems

Risks: HEALTH ⊕   FINANCIAL $ $

Background

As discussed in Hazard 18, Radon in Air, radon, a radioactive gas that comes from the breakdown of naturally occurring uranium in soil and rock, has been found in homes throughout the United States. Groundwater that flows through uranium-bearing rocks and soils will also contain radon. Thus, in addition to radon moving from the ground into the indoor air of a home, it can also enter through water drawn from a drinking water well. If water contains high radon levels, exposure can occur directly, through drinking, as well as from the release of radon into the air by showering, doing the laundry, boiling water, or running the dishwasher.

Radon in water contributes to overall indoor radon levels—estimates suggest that the level of contribution is between 1 and 5 percent. The EPA estimates that indoor air levels increase by about one picocurie per liter (pCi/L) of air for every 10,000 pCi/L of radon in water. While the average level of radon in groundwater in the United States is less than 1,000 pCi/L, tests have indicated levels above 1,000,000 pCi/L in some areas, such as northern New England. While radon in water can be a problem in any area of the United States (in one study, more than 17 percent of all homes in Georgia exceeded the EPA proposed standard of 300 pCi/L), radon in water appears to be more problematic in three areas of the country: New England, the western mountain states, and the New Jersey–New York–Pennsylvania area (a 1992 study found radon in water levels exceeding the EPA's proposed action level in fifty-seven out of fifty-eight private wells in one Pennsylvania county).

Radon in water is generally not a problem in homes served by public water supplies, such as reservoirs, which typically use some type of water treatment that aerates the water and releases radon. Homes served by community or municipal supply wells can, however, be impacted by radon in water.

Health Risks

Radon in water can increase levels of radon in indoor air and, as discussed in Hazard 18, Radon in Air, breathing air containing radon increases the risk of getting lung cancer. Preliminary studies by the EPA suggest that drinking radon-laden water can lead to stomach or intestinal cancer and possibly leukemia. Nationwide, radon in water is estimated to cause between one hundred and eighteen hundred deaths per year—more than any other water contaminant. However, the risks from radon in water are considered to be much lower than those from breathing air containing radon.

Financial Risks

Homes with a radon problem may be devalued and difficult to sell, particularly to buyers with children. Even if the problem is addressed, the property may be devalued because of stigma.

Costs of water treatment systems for radon range from $1,000 to $5,000, depending on the type (see Hazard 4, Drinking Water: Private Wells). Aeration systems can cost between $3,000 and $4,500 and will need an annual cleaning to work effectively and prevent contamination (parts and labor can run more than $250 per year). These systems also use fans, which add $50 to $100 a year to electric bills and can cause a loss of heated or air-conditioned air. Granular activated carbon (GAC) treatment systems cost about $1,000 to $2,000; the long-term operating costs for GAC systems should be lower than those for aeration systems.

Potential buyers may ask about a radon-in-water problem. Costs to reduce radon in water, if warranted, should be factored into the negotiations over the sales price.

Other financial risks:

▶ Liability for nondisclosure; see Disclosure Obligations, pages 13–19.

▶ Costs for short- or long-term medical treatment and monitoring.

Managing the Risks

If drinking water is contaminated by radon, treatment is possible. If a large contribution of the radon in a home is from the water, reducing it in the water can help reduce the overall indoor air radon level. Given today's technology, overall radon levels in most homes can be reduced to 2 pCi/L or less. The most effective treatment for reducing radon in water is to remove it *before* it enters the home—"point-of-entry" treatment. Treatment at a specific tap or under a sink, known as "point-of-use" treatment, is not as effective in reducing indoor air radon levels as it treats only a small amount of water. However, point-of-use treatment can be an effective way to reduce radon levels in water which is to be used directly for drinking.

Radon can be removed from water by one of two treatment methods: aeration or carbon filtration through GAC. Aeration systems, which force the radon gas from the water by spraying or using air bubbles to vent it outside the home, can achieve 95 to 99 percent radon reduction. The other option, GAC treatment, filters radon-bearing water through a specialized charcoal filter; although GAC treatment is a little less efficient than aeration (85 to 99 percent), its up-front and long-term operating costs are much lower. There is no added electricity requirement that can increase energy bills, but there are other operating costs for maintaining a GAC system, including replacement and disposal of the charcoal filters, which may need special handling for disposal (radon by-products can build up on the carbon if the filter has been used for high radon levels or for a long time). The water should be tested for radon every couple of years to ensure that the system is operating properly, which also adds to the cost.

If you are selling a home that has a well and you have a radon problem, test the water before putting it on the market and, if necessary, lower the radon level. Save the test results and all information that you have about steps that were taken to fix the problem—it could be a positive selling point. Sellers of homes with radon in water treatment systems should be prepared to answer questions from potential buyers about the radon levels and the system's operation and maintenance.

Regulatory Outlook

Congress, in its 1988 amendments to the Toxic Substances Control Act (TSCA), stated as a long-term goal that indoor radon levels should be no more than outdoor levels (about 0.4 pCi/L). To the extent that radon in water contributes to the overall indoor air levels, accompanying reductions in radon-in-water levels will be necessary to reach this goal.

Although never officially adopted, in 1991 under the Safe Drinking Water Act (SDWA), the EPA proposed a maximum contaminant level (MCL) of 300 pCi/L for radon in water. This number is controversial, and some health officials have suggested the level is too low—a final standard has not been set.*

What to Look For

You cannot smell, see, or taste radon in water. Testing is the only way to know for certain whether there is a problem. Buyers should look for water treatment systems under the sink or in the basement. If they're present, or if bottled water is used, find out why.

Where to Find Help and Further Information

If a home has a high indoor air level of radon, the water should be tested—whether from a well or a public supply. In addition, home owners who rely on private drinking water wells should consider testing for radon in water because of the independent health risks posed from ingesting radon-laden water. However, remember that the EPA radon-in-water standard is only proposed, and remains controversial.

Contact a lab certified to measure radon or a home inspector to have the water tested. While mail-order kits for testing radon in water are available for around $50, they are generally unreliable. The cost for a professional radon-in-water test ranges from $30 to $100, depending on the home owner's role in taking the sample and dropping it off at the lab. Water-testing devices and procedures are different from those used to test indoor air radon levels. You cannot rely on a neighbor's results, as radon levels vary from house to house.

Based on the results of a radon water test, you can estimate how much the radon in the water is contributing to the indoor air radon level according to the following procedure: subtract 1 pCi/L from the indoor air radon level for every 10,000 pCi/L of radon in the water (for example, if there are 40,000 pCi/L of radon in the water, then 4 pCi/L of the indoor air radon level may come from radon in water). If the

---

* In August 1996, Congress amended the SDWA to preempt EPA adoption of the proposed standard and authorized the National Academy of Sciences to prepare a risk assessment for radon in drinking water. Thereafter, the EPA must set a national primary drinking water standard for radon.

radon-in-water level is relatively low (below 1,000 pCi/L), then treating the water will not appreciably reduce radon levels in the air and so it may not be practical to do so. If most of the radon in the home is from the water, consider installing a water treatment system.

Private water treatment companies can provide quotes for treatment systems (see Hazard 4, Drinking Water: Private Wells). If you are concerned that radon may be entering a home through a public water supply, call the supplier. Contact the EPA or your state environmental or health agency for additional information or assistance (see Appendix 4). For further information, call the EPA's Safe Drinking Water Hotline (800/426-4791).

The Bottom Line

In most cases, radon entering a home through water poses lower health risks than radon entering through soil. However, if there is an indoor air radon problem and well water is used, have it tested for radon. If needed, radon treatment systems can successfully reduce high levels of radon in water (and hence the air). Even if there *isn't* a radon-in-air problem, high levels of radon in drinking water can pose increased health risks. The costs to address radon in water are high and the value of a property with a radon-in-water problem will be reduced.

20. SEPTIC SYSTEMS

Rural and semirural areas not served by public sewers
Risks: HEALTH ⊕   FINANCIAL $ $ $

Background

More than one-quarter of all homes in the United States (primarily rural ones) use on-site sewage disposal systems, the most common being septic systems. The phrase "out-of-sight, out-of-mind" describes most home owners' level of concern for their septic system—people never really pay attention to it until there is a foul odor in the backyard or they experience a sewage backup. That's the problem: when these symptoms are recognized, it's usually too late—the damage is already done, and the expense associated with the repairs can be tremendous. It is estimated that almost half of the septic systems in the United States are not working properly.

While most people generally know what a septic system is, few know how one works. Typical septic systems consist of two main components: a septic tank and a drainage system, known as the "leaching field." Many variations of the basic system we describe below are used, as are numerous other nonconventional systems. When properly designed, installed, and maintained, a septic system is a simple and (some might say) elegant way to dispose of wastes in an environmentally friendly manner.

The Septic Tank On average, we each produce about 50 gallons of wastewater per day. Wastewater flows, or is pumped from the home, into an underground tank, anywhere from 500 to 2,000 gallons in size and made of concrete, fiberglass, plastic, or steel (steel tanks are generally found in older—pre-1950—homes). Inside a properly operating tank, the solids settle out and are digested by bacteria and other naturally occurring microorganisms. Clear wastewater flows through the tank into the leaching field. Baffles and piping inside the tank help prevent solids and grease from escaping into and damaging the leaching field. Although many disease-causing organisms from the human digestive tract die within the tank, many get passed through to the leaching field.

The Leaching Field Clear water from the septic tank flows to the leaching field, where it is further treated before seeping into the surrounding soil and groundwater. Treatment within the leaching field consists of filtration of solid particles, final digestion of organic materials by bacteria living in the soil, and killing of disease-causing organisms that become trapped and die in the soil. The leaching field typically consists of a distribution box and perforated piping laid within stone-filled trenches, pits, dry wells, or beds of various sizes and configurations. Leaching fields can be very large—trenches can be one hundred feet long and four feet or more wide. It is critical that the design of the leaching field match soil conditions at the property. While requirements vary from state to state, the bottom of the leaching field usually must be at least eighteen inches above the groundwater level and a minimum of four feet above bedrock to allow for proper filtration of the effluent.

Key factors governing how well a septic system works are local soil conditions, proper maintenance, and "hydraulic loading," or the amount of water put through a septic system—one that works fine for an elderly couple may not work for a large family. A common septic system problem is overloading the septic tank. This can result in: clogging of the leaching field; backed-up plumbing; septic water pooling in the yard; and the pollution of local streams and lakes or groundwater supplies. Improperly sited or failing septic systems can impact nearby drinking water wells. In many states, faulty septic systems are the leading source of pollutants to inland and coastal bodies of water. For example, reports out of Arizona in 1995 indicate that leaks occurred in more than 80 percent of the septic tanks on properties tested along the Colorado River.

Cesspools are a simple type of on-site sewage disposal system that historically was used throughout the United States. Instead of a septic tank, a cesspool relies on a brick, stone, or concrete chamber, surrounded by a bed of gravel, which serves as a crude leaching field. Wastewater flows directly through a cesspool, which does not provide the level of treatment achieved by a septic system. Cesspools are no longer allowed in most areas.

Care and ongoing maintenance are required to keep septic systems working properly and to keep expenses and health problems to a minimum. If properly designed, installed, and maintained, septic systems can function problem-free for many years.

A major environmental impact from improperly operating septic systems that does not result in human health risks is the escape of high amounts of nitrogen and phosphates into streams, lakes, and other bodies of water. These compounds are nutrients that cause excessive growth of algae, which can impact aquatic life. Ponds and lakes with this problem can turn green and become oxygen-depleted, a process scientists call eutrophication.

Health Risks

Potential health problems from failing septic systems generally fall into the area of a public health nuisance, but in some cases are more serious. Failed systems can create ponds or seeps of sewage containing fecal material that usually stink and can contain harmful levels of disease-carrying bacteria and viruses. Improperly designed or failing systems can also pollute nearby drinking water wells with harmful bacteria, viruses, and nitrates (see Hazard 4, Drinking Water: Private Wells).

Financial Risks

Septic systems (particularly the leaching fields) will eventually need to be repaired or replaced; these costs should be considered when buying a home with a septic system. A properly designed, installed, and maintained septic system can last twenty-five years or longer, depending on soil conditions and how it is used. The costs to repair or replace a septic system vary greatly, depending on the problem and your location. Costs range from less than $100 to snake out a clogged line to $500 to replace broken pipes, to $1,000 to $2,000 to replace a faulty tank (steel tanks are more likely to need replacement than concrete), to $5,000 to $20,000 to design, obtain the permits for, and install a completely new septic system. These costs can be even higher if there are stringent local rules that mandate more complicated systems—communities relying extensively on groundwater for drinking, and those near bodies of water, typically have strict septic system rules.

Where sewer lines are close to a property with a faulty septic system, local municipalities may require you to connect to the sewer, often at a cost of $10,000 to $20,000 or more, instead of allowing you to fix the septic system. (These costs can usually be spread out over tén or more years.)

Routine maintenance of a system involves pumping the tank to remove accumulated solids and grease every two or three years (depending on use) at a cost of about $100 to $200. Some towns and counties require payment of annual fees to support a septic system inspection program by the local health agency. Professional inspections of a system can cost between $200 and $1,500, depending on how difficult the system is to locate and access.

In many cases, specific soil conditions, along with local health agency rules, will greatly impact a property's value by limiting the size of the leaching field and thereby how intensively the property may be developed. This affects landowners and developers, by setting the maximum number of homes allowed in a new development, as well as individual home owners, by setting the number of bedrooms allowed in a home (thereby limiting its number of occupants) and specifying where on a property a home may be built. If you're buying undeveloped land and there are no public sewers, make certain the lot can support a septic system or else you may not be able to build your home.

Buyers may be wary of properties with septic systems, particularly older systems. Where there is a known septic system problem, homes can be devalued and difficult to sell. Early in 1995, a home owner near Atlanta, Georgia, abandoned her home when she could not afford to fix a faulty septic system that had turned the yard into a sewage swamp and created a severe odor problem—the property was later foreclosed on and put on the market "as is." Banks and mortgage companies are likely to insist that problems with septic systems be resolved as a condition of the loan. Some buyers will walk away from a home with a faulty septic system, use it as a negotiating point, require the seller to fix it prior to closing, or ask for a credit at closing. For example, in Massachusetts, after strict new septic system rules went into effect in 1995, hundreds of deals soured and hundreds more were delayed after prospective buyers learned of septic system problems. After one buyer backed out when the septic system failed to meet state requirements, the seller had to spend more than $21,000 to replace the septic system, which included costs for the inspection, tests to determine the capability of the soil to support a septic system, engineering plans, and permit fees. Even if a problem is fixed a property may be devalued because of stigma.

In a real estate transaction, if a failing septic system is not disclosed, sellers and real estate agents may be liable, especially in a state that requires such disclosure (see Disclosure Obligations, pages 13–19). In Massachusetts, one buyer successfully sued an agent, seller, and builder over a faulty septic system under fraud and consumer protection laws, receiving $5,000 to repair the system as well as double damages as a punitive award for willful fraud by the seller and agent. And in a recent New York case, a buyer sued the bank that sold the home but did not tell him that the house had a septic system—the trial is pending.

Home owners with a faulty septic system or those who have been impacted by one at a nearby property may also incur costs for legal and expert fees, short- or long-term medical treatment and monitoring, temporary inconvenience and relocation, property damage, and to address contaminated well water.

Managing the Risks

Before you purchase a home, have the septic system inspected and evaluated by a professional. Buyers should put a clause in the contract requiring the seller to have the system pumped and inspected by the septic tank cleaning company before closing, or funds will be withheld at closing to cover such costs. Inlet and outlet baffles and piping and the distribution box, if accessible, should be inspected for damage after the pump-out. (Be aware that septic tank companies will not guarantee the condition or life expectancy of a system, even after pumping it out and finding nothing wrong.) Ask the seller to provide a copy of the septic pumping report and a signed and paid receipt from the company at closing. If the tank has not been pumped and inspected, ask your lawyer to withhold the money needed to cover the costs to have it done. In this way, you know you start off with a "clean" tank and can more accurately gauge when you'll need to have the tank pumped again.

Buyers of new homes and those who are building homes should require the builder to satisfy all septic system requirements exactly and to provide you with copies of the design plans, "as-built" drawings, and all required permits and approvals. Ensure that the local health or building inspector checks the installation thoroughly. Drawings are important because they allow you to locate the tank and leaching field. For buyers of undeveloped land, a professional engineer or soil scientist should be hired to verify that the property can support a septic system (if one is needed). Usually it is necessary to dig "test pits" and perform soil percolation (known as "perc") tests to determine the capability of the site to support a septic system.

A common problem with septic systems is that too much water passes through them. This causes two problems. First, bacteria in the tank don't have enough time to fully digest the wastes before they enter the leaching field. Second, excess water can stir up solids in the tank and cause them to pass into the leaching field. Either way, this can lead to a fouling and failure of the leaching field. With this in mind, when installing a new system or replacing a tank, purchase the biggest tank your budget allows—this will pay for itself by reducing the necessary frequency of pumping and could significantly prolong the useful life of the leaching field—the component of the system that is most costly to replace.

If a septic system is not well maintained, problems will arise, causing a failure. Typically, septic systems require little maintenance. Home owners can follow some basic precautionary measures and perform routine maintenance to ensure proper function and maximum life of their septic system.

- *Do* keep accurate records about the location of the septic system and dates of inspection and pump-outs, and pass them along to subsequent owners.
- *Do* clean out the septic tank every two to three years, or more frequently if you have a large family or there is lots of use.
- *Do* conserve water as much as possible (e.g., fix leaky faucets and use low-flow toilets and water fixtures).
- *Don't* put paper towels, sanitary napkins, disposable diapers, or other bulky items into the system.
- *Don't* put large amounts of grease and fats down the drain.
- *Don't* use a garbage disposal unless the septic system is designed to accept the grindings.
- *Don't* pour pesticides, disinfectants, paint thinners, or other toxic chemicals down the sink, toilet, or tub drains (these materials can significantly affect the needed bacterial action in the system or pollute the groundwater).
- *Don't* plant deep-rooted trees or bushes, or allow trucks or heavy equipment to drive, over the septic tank and leaching field.

Recognizing that many people are relatively ignorant of how their septic system works, hundreds of additives touted to improve or repair septic systems are on the market. Some companies actually have been investigated for fraud by consumer protection agencies. These products claim to clean out and unclog the system with chemicals like caustic, or "miracle" bacteria or fungi that supposedly enhance the action of the naturally occurring bacteria in the septic tank. Some of these products in fact may work, or, at a minimum, will do no harm to your system, but we are not aware of any independent studies or recommendations from government agencies that these additives really solve septic system problems. We suggest that buying such additives is like pouring money down the drain, so to speak—the natural biodegradation provided by the bacteria in the tank is more than sufficient to ensure proper digestion of wastes. Under no circumstances should strong solvents, acids, or caustics be poured into a septic system to unclog it, as these toxic compounds are a major problem once in the groundwater.

Some home owner's insurance policies may cover costs associated with faulty septic systems, but most do not—check your policy if there is a problem. You can sue neighbors if their faulty septic system contaminates your well or otherwise impacts your property (or vice versa), but lawsuits are costly and often take years to resolve. For example, several families in New York were embroiled for almost a decade in a lawsuit against a neighbor whose failing septic system contaminated their drinking water wells.

Regulatory Outlook

While many states set standards for septic system design, installation, and maintenance, the authority to ensure compliance and enforce these standards usually falls to the local level—to the town or county health department, the building or land use department, or the sanitarian. These agencies often have requirements for:

- septic system design and siting, usually by professional engineering firms
- construction and installation
- inspection and maintenance
- upgrades and expansions
- the reporting of, and repairs to, failing systems

Local requirements may also control use of a septic system by prohibiting discharges from water treatment systems or requiring that septic tanks be pumped out every few years. In fact, in many states, it is illegal to discharge backflow (such as salt brine) from a water treatment unit to a septic system because of potential impacts to groundwater. Home owners installing new systems or altering existing ones usually must obtain some type of permit beforehand and have the work inspected by local health officials, who then issue a certificate of compliance. In some towns, septic systems are managed on a community basis, where home owners are charged an annual user fee for the pumping. Other towns are served by public utilities or take responsibility themselves for managing and servicing all septic systems and replacing any that fail through a quarterly assessment of each home owner.

Local septic system requirements often place limitations on how a property gets developed and used. These requirements can, for example, prevent addition of a new bedroom, bathroom, or in-law apartment; or they can set rules limiting where and how land gets developed, or greatly increase the cost of building in an environmentally sensitive area. In some places, there are different requirements for large septic systems, such as those for multifamily properties.

Many state environmental and health agencies require licenses for septic system installers and pumpers, and prohibit the use of septic system additives that contain toxic chemicals (some develop and maintain a list of approved additives). Most state disclosure laws specifically require disclosure of septic system problems.

Rigid septic system laws aimed at protecting public and private drinking water supplies and inland and coastal bodies of water are being developed in many states. In Massachusetts, for example, a law went into effect in 1995 that imposes many stringent requirements on home owners with septic systems. This law impacts about half of the homes in that state and requires, among other things: (1) a septic system to be inspected prior to, or up to six months after, the sale of a property, or before there is an expansion or change in use of the property; (2) failed systems to be reported to the local board of health and upgraded or replaced within one year; (3) that septic systems be set back from water supplies, wetlands, and other bodies of water; and (4) state environmental agency approval of the soil evaluator for a septic system's design and siting.

In the near future, because of increased knowledge of the impacts of septic system failures on drinking water supplies and surface water, stringent septic system laws are likely to become more common throughout the country.

What to Look For

Sellers should know the precise location of their septic tank and leaching field. If you do not, a good starting point to find the location of the septic tank is the pipe carrying the sewage out of the house—go outside, and from that point look for bare spots or disturbed vegetation, flat rocks, or metal or concrete covers in the yard about fifteen to twenty-five feet away from the house. These may indicate the location of the clean-out port for the septic tank. Often the outline of the septic tank or leaching field may be discerned from shading, contours, or other features of the lawn, such as a dry, rectangular patch of grass or an area of thicker, greener grass.

Without actually uncovering the tank and distribution box, it is difficult to determine the general condition of the system. However, the following may indicate a septic system problem:

- slow-draining sinks, showers, or toilets, or even sewage backup
- persistent wet, overly green, or lush areas near the leaching field
- soggy areas on the ground, possibly with dark, ponded water
- "rotten egg" odors in the vicinity of the tank or leaching field

Where to Find Help and Further Information

The local health department or land use or building department will provide copies of regulations and available guidance material concerning septic system design and operation. Examine the builder's blueprints for the septic system that should be on file with the town's building inspector, health officer, or sanitarian. Civil or environmental engineering firms have experts in septic system design and inspection. Home inspectors may include a dye test as part of a home inspection to check for problems with a septic system; while a good starting point, this test, which entails putting food coloring down toilets and drains and inspecting around the septic tank and leaching field for evidence of dye "breakout," is not the same as a thorough inspection. Finally, local septic system contractors can provide services ranging from pumping and cleaning to inspections to design and installation of new systems—get several competitive bids.

If your state environmental or health agency requires septic system installers and pumpers to be licensed, verify that the one you choose is (see Appendix 4).

When you have your tank pumped, make note of the exact location of the tank. Ask the pumper about the size of the tank, whether it is concrete or steel, how full it was, and the condition of the baffles. Have the pumper check to ensure that water doesn't run back into the tank during pumping, which would indicate a clogging problem in your leach field. You can use this information to determine more accurately how frequently you need to pump it out—this may add up to significant savings over time.

The Bottom Line

A septic system, like a roof or heating system or any other major component of a house, should last twenty-five years or more if properly designed, installed, and maintained. Remember, no septic system will last forever—eventually they will cause you aggravation and require significant money to fix or replace. By following basic preventative measures, home owners should be able to maximize the useful life of their septic system—it is easier, and cheaper, to prevent a problem than to correct one. Homes with faulty septic systems will be devalued and difficult to sell and can present health hazards to you and your neighbors, especially if you rely on a well for your drinking water. Buyers should have septic systems checked as part of the inspection and include any repair or replacement costs in the valuation of a home.

21. TERMITES AND OTHER WOOD-DESTROYING PESTS

Throughout the United States
Risks: HEALTH   None (Direct) / ⊕ ⊕ (Indirectly, from pesticide use)
FINANCIAL $ $ $

Background

In almost every part of the country, termites and other wood-destroying pests cause millions of dollars of damage annually. While the termite problem is biggest in the warmer, southern parts of the country and in California, they (or other wood-destroying pests) can be found as far north as Alaska. These pests live in the ground or in wood structures. Although they typically cannot get into a house through a concrete foundation, pests can enter directly through wood surfaces in contact with the soil, such as fences or decks, or through wooden crawl spaces, or by building "shelter tubes"—thin mud tunnels running from the ground up along a foundation wall to wood structures.

There are more than sixty species of termites in the United States; subterranean termites account for more than 95 percent of all termite damage. Termites are almost half an inch long and resemble large ants. Up to five million can live in a single colony. Many, though not all, termites are of concern because they will damage almost any wooden structure in a home, including supporting walls, floors, and roofs. Termites eat wood and thereby weaken and destroy structures—they can cause damage that remains hidden for months or years without a home owner even being aware of them. Left untreated, major structural damage from termites or other pests can occur in a matter of a year, or even months. Termites will infest new as well as older homes.

Beside termites, other pests can cause major problems. For example, carpenter ants live in and destroy wood structures like rafters and walls not by eating the wood but by hollowing it out to build nests. Carpenter ants are common in the Pacific Northwest and throughout the northeastern quarter of the United States. "Pine borers" attack pine wood and are found in the middle Atlantic states. Certain beetles attack seasoned hardwoods like oak and maple. Carpenter bees and wasps usually attack softwoods and can burrow through cedar shingles on a house exterior wall where they build a nest. Almost every geographic area has some local species of wood-destroying pests.

Health Risks

The direct risks from termite and other pest infestation problems are to your bank account, not to your health. However, termites do carry a significant indirect health risk—contamination of a home, surrounding soil, or groundwater can result from improper use or disposal of *pesticides* used to treat a home for termite infestation (see Hazard 42, Pesticides, for a detailed discussion of the health and financial risks of pesticides).

There are a number of ways that pesticides can impact a property. If improperly used or overapplied, they can leave residues inside a home or in the surrounding soil that can enter the body through direct contact or by breathing airborne dusts. Pesticides can also contaminate well water if overapplied or improperly disposed of. The specific health risk depends on the pesticide used and the amount, duration, and pathway of exposure. Children, because of their size and active growth, are at greatest risk from accidental pesticide poisoning.

Nationwide there are many cases of pesticide contamination of homes caused both by home owners or commercial applicators who didn't know what they were doing. Some pesticides used to control termites, such as chlordane, have been banned because of their extremely toxic nature; others have their use restricted and may be applied only by licensed applicators. Chlordane belongs to a group of organic pesticides that includes heptachlor, aldrin, and dieldrin, which were banned by the EPA in 1983 because they were determined to be carcinogens. In several cases, drinking water supplies have become contaminated following spraying of pesticides in and around houses—in a Tennessee case, a family was awarded damages for mental anguish after they ingested pesticide-contaminated water for several months before learning of the problem. In August 1995, a family in Dayton, Ohio, filed a $5 million lawsuit against the prior owners and a pest-control company when they discovered chlordane contamination in their well water and inside their home.

Financial Risks

Homes with significant termite or other pest problems will be devalued due to costs to eliminate them. Buyers will be wary of homes with termite problems. Some buyers may make an offer far below the asking price, make a sale contingent on the seller addressing the termite problem, or walk away from a deal. Even if a termite problem is not significant or has been resolved, the mere fact that there is, or was, a termite problem can be a stigma issue for future buyers, and so the pool of potential buyers may be smaller.

Costs for a termite or other pest inspection generally range from $50 to $200, depending on the location and size of the home. Chemical treatment can prevent termite infestation or can be used if there is a termite problem. The costs for chemical treatments range from $200 to $1,500 or more depending on the location and size of house and kind and extent of pest problem at hand. Costs to repair termite and other pest damage can be even higher. Major structural damage may require a roof to be replaced or entire walls and floors to be rebuilt—repair costs can reach into the tens of thousands of dollars.

Many private banks and mortgage companies, and public lending institutions such as the Veterans Administration (VA) and the Federal Housing Administration (FHA), require a termite inspection and report prior to making a home loan (only licensed termite exterminators can inspect federally insured homes). Even when there is no requirement for a termite inspection from a lender, many buyers will require, via the contract or purchase offer, that an inspection be performed prior to closing and stipulate that the seller be responsible for any needed treatment or repairs. For this reason, a home seller may wish to address these issues before putting his or her home up for sale.

Financial risks can also arise in the context of disclosure obligations in the course of a transaction. Most state disclosure laws generally apply to pests, and some states specifically require disclosure of a pest problem. Failure to disclose a termite problem to a potential buyer may have serious legal ramifications for the seller and the real estate agent. There have been many disclosure lawsuits and court decisions related to termite problems—in many cases, the seller and agent have been found liable for significant damages. These cases almost always stem from subsequent discovery by a new home owner of termite infestation and damage, although the particulars of each case vary. Termite inspectors or exterminators may also face potential liability for property damage or injuries to buyers or tenants from faulty inspections or improper pesticide applications.

The cost to "fix" a home where unsafe levels of indoor pesticide residues are present may be nominal if only a minor cleanup is needed, or it may be thousands of dollars if major repairs, such as installing new carpets, cabinets, countertops, appliances, ventilation systems, or woodwork, are required. In a highly publicized case, since January 1995, the EPA has been involved in a $20 million cleanup of more than two hundred contaminated homes and apartments near Cleveland, Ohio, that were sprayed for years with methyl parathion, a highly toxic pesticide (see Hazard 42, Pesticides).

Managing the Risks

To help prevent termite and other pest problems, ensure that wood structures do not come into contact with the soil. Keep crawl spaces dry and well ventilated. Do not store firewood or other wood supplies against a building or inside your home or garage. Use of railroad ties for landscaping (even treated wood) can encourage pests to move into the house. And don't allow shrubs near a home to get overgrown, as they can provide a pathway by which insects get to wood walls.

Although in some cases it may be apparent even to an untrained eye that there is a pest problem, inspections are often the only way to determine if there is a problem and how bad it is. Remember that no inspection is foolproof—some areas in a home cannot be accessed easily and visually inspected for damage or infestation, such as the insides of walls. Sometimes inspectors use stethoscopes to locate insects inside walls.

Chemical treatment is an effective way to minimize the possibility of termite and other pest infestation. However, pesticides, if not properly applied, can impact well water or leave toxic residues in and around a home. Pesticide application is a very serious undertaking that should be done by experts—it is not a do-it-yourself project. State-approved pesticide application companies should always be used—they are trained and licensed to use stronger, more effective, and more toxic chemicals than are available to the home owner. Chemical treatment programs must often be repeated to be effective. Commercial applicators will often guarantee their work for a year or more, and some provide guarantees for the life of the house; in some cases, these guarantees may be transferred to subsequent owners. Remember that less toxic substitute products or pesticides may be available, and in some cases they are just as effective.

A variety of simple construction techniques are available to reduce the chance of insect damage. Avoiding soil-wood contact and the use of pressure-treated wood in new construction will reduce the possibility of future damage (but see Hazard 17, Pressure-Treated Wood). In termite-prone areas, alternatives to all-wood construction, such as brick, masonry, or aluminum or vinyl siding, can prevent pest problems. In addition, soil can be treated with pesticides before a house is built to prevent a termite problem later on.

Regulatory Outlook

Federal and state laws require commercial pest-control companies to be licensed or registered with a state environmental or agricultural agency. Usually, stringent training and experience are required to be licensed as an exterminator and to be authorized to apply certain pesticides (see Hazard 42, Pesticides, for more information about pesticides). Houses that are federally insured through HUD or the FHA require licensed termite exterminators to conduct the inspection. State disclosure laws generally or specifically apply to termites and other pest infestations.

What to Look For

Look at the inside and outside foundation walls for evidence of wood-destroying pests; inspect areas where wood is in direct contact with the ground as well as areas like crawl spaces and basements where soil and wood may touch; and look for fences, decks, and other wood structures that abut a house and may serve as a pathway by which insects can get into a home. Evidence of pest damage may include obvious structural weaknesses, like rotted or damaged wood. Use a screwdriver or ice pick to poke at exposed wood in a basement or crawl space—easily punctured wood will be evidence of termite infestation. Insect droppings, cast-off skins, and wood dust trails may indicate infestation, as may shelter tubes. Remember, termites and other pests can be overlooked if a home is inspected in the winter.

Evidence of a pest problem or improper pesticide use and disposal may include: many containers of pesticides under the sink or in a basement, garage, or outbuilding; chemical odors in the house or basement; stains along the foundation; and residues where walls meet floors and rafters.

If a well is in use, taste and smell the water; however, laboratory tests are usually needed to detect contamination (see Hazard 4, Drinking Water: Private Wells). If a water treatment system or bottled water is used, find out why.

Where to Find Help and Further Information

Buyers should ask the sellers and their agents if termites are, or have been, a problem. If they have been, the buyer should request additional information and copies of any pest inspection reports. If a home has been treated, ask to see the paperwork—guarantees can sometimes be transferred to subsequent owners. If you have or anticipate building or buying a wood home, a termite inspection is an inexpensive way to minimize financial risks. Sellers should remember that in all likelihood, a sale will hinge on whether a buyer's pest inspection is satisfactory, so you may as well find out beforehand and address any problems according to your own timetable.

Often pest-control companies will offer "free" inspections and consultations. When all you want is an inspection, we suggest that you pay for it and let the inspector know that someone else will do any follow-up extermination or repair work that is needed. Make sure you are dealing with a licensed, reputable firm, and get a second opinion. While the majority of pest-control firms are honest and qualified, the industry has had more than its share of consumer-related problems, such as exaggeration and lying about pest problems, the use of scare tactics to make a sale, and operation by unlicensed and inexperienced companies. Call your local Better Business Bureau or state consumer protection office to see if there have been any complaints about a company. Many reputable companies are members of the National Pest Control Association (703/573-8330). Your state environmental agency, agricultural office, or local college or university can also assist you in identifying pest inspectors and control companies. Look in the phone book under "pest control"—you'll have many companies to choose from. Be sure to check references or use a company recommended by someone you know. Pesticide registrations and licenses can be checked at your state environmental agency (see Appendix 4).

Tests can be conducted if you suspect pesticide contamination in a home. Indoor air can be sampled, "wipe samples" of residues can be obtained from floors and walls, and samples can be taken from soil outside a home or in an earthen basement, and tested for pesticides. Home owners and potential buyers of homes with wells should consider testing the water (see Hazard 4, Drinking Water: Private Wells). Coordinate tests with a qualified laboratory, consultant, or inspector. Contact the EPA or your state environmental or health agency for additional information or assistance (see Appendix 4).

The Bottom Line

In a short time, termites and other wood-destroying pests can cause major damage to a home that can cost thousands, or even tens of thousands, of dollars to repair. Home owners and buyers—be on the lookout! If you suspect a problem, contact a pest-control expert right away; delay will only increase your costs, because the size of the infestation will get bigger and the structural damage will get worse. In areas prone to pest problems, consider a proactive approach: preventative chemical treatment can pay for itself many times over when major damage and repair bills are avoided. Sellers should be prepared for the inevitable questions and inspection by the buyer. Don't fool yourself by thinking problems won't be discovered—even if they are not found in an inspection, you could find yourself liable under state disclosure laws. Because health risks from improper pesticide use and application can be severe, always use a reputable, licensed pest-control specialist.

22. WETLANDS

Throughout the United States
        Risks: HEALTH None   FINANCIAL $ $

Background

Wetlands, because of their ecological importance, are protected by a broad and diverse array of stringent federal, state, and local statutes and regulations that impose limitations on the use of private property. Thousands of home owners around the country have been made acutely aware of the reach of these wetlands laws and have been restricted in their ability to clear land, build or expand a home, build a deck or pier, install an in-ground pool, landscape a yard, subdivide a property, or make other physical changes, like filling a depression, draining a swamp, or building a pond. Because of the strict regulation of wetlands, placing a "wetlands" label on a property is a critical event that more often than not results in some controversy—a "swamp" that one person wants to fill and build on can be a "unique wetland habitat" that another person wants to preserve.

The term *wetland* encompasses many different types of ecological habitats, including inland marshes, creeks, mud flats, rivers, ponds, lakes, meadows, swamps, brooks, bogs, intermittent streams, and drainage ditches. These inland wetlands are broadly protected, as are coastal or tidal wetlands, which include estuaries, salt marshes, tidal flats, sand dunes, and barrier beaches. Wetlands are rigidly protected against certain types of development because they are important to a number of common public interests, such as: providing habitats and breeding areas for diverse plants, fish, and birds; acting as a sponge to absorb flood waters and a stabilizer against shoreline erosion; ensuring an adequate supply of groundwater and surface water; and protecting drinking water supplies from drought, overuse, pollution, misuse, and mismanagement.

There is much variation and debate in defining a wetland. In addition to its common usage, *wetland* is a regulatory term for land that is sometimes submerged by water. Regulatory definitions of wetlands encompass land that is wet enough, either due to flooding or soil saturation, to influence the types of plants that grow there. In addition, land that is flooded during periodic storms or serves to prevent flood damage may also be protected under wetlands regulations.

Wetlands are defined by federal, state, and local laws and regulations, but there is no unified approach to characterizing a wetland among the various levels of government. Some state and local agencies rely on a single parameter—for example, soil characteristics—to define a wetland. Other states, local agencies, and the federal government use a multiparameter approach including vegetation (the plants that live and grow in water or wet soil), soil (the amount of saturation in the soil throughout the year), and hydrology (how close the water table is to the surface at various times of the year), to determine whether an area is a wetland. These terms can be ambiguous, and their applications are often controversial and seem to defy common sense—the upland, wooded parcel of land you bought far from any waterway and that is dry most of the year can still meet some definition of a wetland. We can generally say that areas that are wet at times of the year may be considered wetlands. Wetlands subject to regulatory restrictions can be seasonal, isolated, and even artificially created.

Health Risks

Generally, wetlands pose no direct health risks, although some wetlands have serious insect problems that can be a nuisance. But wetlands regulations may cause heartburn and ulcers to landowners and developers!

Financial Risks

Although wetlands restrictions are significant to developers, individual property owners can also face restrictions that impact the ability to build a new home, plan improvements to an existing one which expand the footprint of the house, construct outbuildings (such as sheds or detached garages), or subdivide the property. By defining and limiting the types of activities allowed, wetlands directly impact property values and the ability to use, develop, expand, refinance, or sell a home. If land cannot be developed because of a wetland, the value of the property will be diminished, often by tens of thousands of dollars, or in rare instances, completely devalued. The restrictions will also reduce the pool of potential buyers, since a buyer will also be restricted in terms of what can and cannot be done on or to the property. However, sometimes a wetland may *increase* a property's value by limiting nearby development and increasing privacy and aesthetic value.

The costs to obtain the necessary approvals to develop a property with wetlands (including agency fees and consultant and legal costs), or to challenge a governmental or private wetland restriction, can run into tens of thousands of dollars. The permit process itself can be complicated and lengthy, and if you end up in a legal battle over a wetland issue, the process may be drawn out over many years, delaying your ability to develop the property and perhaps forcing you to make alternative housing arrangements until the matter is settled. In addition, if you conduct some activity in a wetlands area *without* obtaining the necessary permits, you may be directed, at your own expense, to restore the wetlands and/or seek a permit for the unauthorized work. (In rare cases, you may also be responsible for a prior owner's violations of wetlands laws.) Although a citation against a property owner for a violation may not necessarily result in legal action by a wetlands agency, a notice of violation could be attached to the property records and result in a "cloud" on the title, complicating future efforts to sell the property.

Land use restrictions due to the presence of wetlands may be subject to disclosure requirements for sellers and their agents. If a property has a wetland that cannot be developed, or if a permit application to expand a house was denied because of a wetland issue, sellers may be required to alert buyers—especially if a state's disclosure law requires it. For example, a Massachusetts couple who bought property to build a new home and a golf green were awarded triple damages because the seller deliberately failed to disclose significant wetlands restrictions that he knew about (from a letter he received from the town's wetlands agency before the sale).

Managing the Risks

Know and understand all of the wetlands issues and restrictions that apply to a property to determine if you will be able to develop it as you want. Know if your planned uses will require obtaining wetlands permits and what the chances of denial might be. Review the property's deed with a qualified land use attorney before signing a contract. Ask yourself if the wetlands restrictions will prevent you from doing what you want with your property or if you can live with them. If you need a variance from a wetlands restriction,* know up front what your chances are of getting one (in many areas, they are difficult to obtain), how long the process will take, and what it will cost.

The best scenario for a buyer is to require all wetlands permits and approvals to be in place before closing. Buyers should also factor the wetlands restrictions, as well as the associated time and costs for dealing with them, into a purchase offer. Sellers and their agents should ensure

---

* A variance is an exception granted by a land use agency because of special conditions, particularly where a literal interpretation or application of the law would result in exceptional difficulty or impose undue hardship.

that all aspects of the home and property use conform to applicable wetlands laws prior to putting the house on the market.

Developers should be certain that a site is buildable from the standpoint of wetlands regulations and understand all applicable requirements.

Regulatory Outlook

Wetlands are subject to an almost unbelievable number of regulatory controls—the permit process is very complex and at times falls under the simultaneous jurisdiction of federal, state, and local agencies. At the federal level, the U.S. Army Corps of Engineers (referred to here as the Corps) and the EPA have jurisdiction over land that meets the federal definition of a wetland. They can require a permit for almost any activity, including those by an individual home owner, impacting a wetland under the Clean Water Act Section 404 program and Section 10 of the Rivers and Harbors Act of 1899. These laws regulate excavation, dredging, and the placement of structures, fill, or dredged materials into wetlands, which are considered "waters of the United States."

To streamline the procedures for obtaining wetlands permits for the minor and low-impact activities that typically occur on many residential properties, the federal program provides for what are called "nationwide" permits. These permits are designed to apply to general categories of activities in wetlands that will have minimal environmental effect. In 1995, the Corps issued a new nationwide wetlands permit for single-family residential properties in an attempt to further streamline federal wetlands permitting and to provide relief from the perceived unfair burdens placed on residential property owners. Under this new permit, known as NWP 29, a residential property owner whose home building or restoration work, including garage and driveway construction, meets listed criteria will no longer have to submit detailed plans for review by multiple federal agencies that can require major design changes or even force a home owner to construct new, artificial wetlands.

Several conditions must be met for a project to qualify for NWP 29, including:

- the loss of wetlands will be less than half an acre
- the permit seeker is an individual owner or a couple, not a developer or a business
- the project is associated with a single-family home used for personal residential purposes
- all possible actions have been taken to minimize impacts

Be aware that NWP 29 applies only by default in those states that do *not* have a parallel, federally approved program.

Even if a proposed activity does not qualify for a nationwide permit, you can apply for an individual permit to conduct activities in a federal wetland. The Corps will review the application and determine the wetland's value and function in making its decision. The Corps cannot issue a permit for any wetlands activity unless the EPA or the state environmental agency with jurisdiction over water pollution certifies that the activity will not have an adverse effect on water quality. This water quality certification is a precondition to receiving federal wetlands approval to fill in a wetlands area, and can take a lot of time to obtain.

In addition to federal requirements, environmental agencies at the state level also regulate wetlands, as do towns and counties through zoning, wetlands, and conservation agencies. It is important to note that federal wetlands laws do *not* preempt state and local programs—just because your activity does not require a *federal* wetlands permit does not mean you're free and clear. (Recall that state and local agencies often define wetlands differently than the feds.) Thus, while you may not have a *federal* wetland, you may still have a wetland that needs a state and/or local permit. State and local wetlands agencies often specify the allowable uses in and around wetlands and usually administer their own permit programs. Of great significance to residential property owners, many local agencies have "setback" rules that specify a buffer zone (usually fifty or one hundred feet, or more, from a wetland) in which activities are limited. Be aware that costs to comply with wetlands rules can be high and penalties for violations can be severe—people have even gone to jail for flagrant violations.

Until recently, the trend in wetlands regulation was toward increasing restrictions and the diminution of private property rights. However, governmental regulation now appears to be heading in the other direction and toward greater protection of such rights. We've also seen an increase in court decisions favoring the protection of such rights. Many property owners denied permits to fill wetlands have successfully argued that the denials constitute "taking" of private property without just compensation, in violation of the U.S. Constitution. For example, in 1990, a property developer in New Jersey was awarded about $2.7 million having been denied a federal wetlands permit to fill 11.5 acres of wetlands in a 250-acre residential development.

New wetlands legislation at all governmental levels is making it easier for home owners to obtain permits. One of the most widely discussed environmental proposals before Congress in 1995 was a measure that would require the federal government to compensate private property owners if wetlands regulations prevented them from using more than a designated percentage of their land. Although the measure was not passed into law, similar provisions have been considered or approved in some states, and we may yet see it again in Congress. However, there is much variability at all levels of government, and the trends in your state or town may not be in harmony with national trends. And, as with everything political, in time, the winds will undoubtedly shift the other way.

What to Look For

Wetlands are typically low, wet places referred to as meadows, swamps, bogs, intermittent streams, or drainage ditches, and are often adjacent to a brook, river, pond, lake, ocean, or other body of water. However, seasonally dry areas and areas that do not look wet to the average person may be regulated wetlands. Therefore, only experts can truly identify and delineate a wetland through a field inspection; remember that the legal definition of a wetland is broad and complex. Soil characteristics, local plants, and hydrology—not common sense—determine whether an area is a wetland.

Home owners and buyers must also be aware of, and should identify, wetlands setbacks that carry over onto otherwise nonwet areas before buying or planning any construction activities.

Developers of large residential projects should be aware that wetlands are also wildlife habitats, and many species of plants and animals are protected by federal, state, and local laws governing endangered and threatened species. Because of such laws, the habitat value of wetlands can seriously affect the ability to develop the property.

Where to Find Help and Further Information

Do your homework—research the universe of federal, state, and local wetlands restrictions that may impact your ability to build on your land, to renovate or expand your home, or generally to use and enjoy your property as you desire. As a buyer, ask the owner to identify any wetlands (and associated setbacks) on the property. Find out if the property has ever been denied any type of wetlands permit approval, and if any activity has been undertaken that required a wetlands permit but was conducted without one.

Review all applicable agency regulations and the town's map of designated wetlands; be cautious, however, as these maps may not contain the locations of individual property lines and the scale of a map may not accurately portray wetlands boundaries—use the maps only as a guide. USGS maps and aerial photographs typically show features such as general locations of wetlands and waterways (see Appendix 3). The town's land use or building officials can also provide information about specific wetlands rules and whether or not a property has any known wetlands or is currently violating any wetlands regulations. Also, the federal government maintains a wetlands hotline (800/832-7828).

Experts in wetlands identification often work for environmental consulting or civil engineering firms and can identify, delineate, and map wetlands on your property. Hire only qualified wetlands soil scientists with a thorough working knowledge of the applicable federal, state, and local wetlands requirements. For a residential property, the cost for this type of survey should be between $200 and $500, although in many cases it can be more expensive.

The Bottom Line

Wetlands, while aesthetically and naturally pleasing to many people, can devalue a property by restricting its use and/or development. To some people, homes with or near wetlands are desirable because additional development in the future may be restricted—this means more privacy and space for existing homes. For most buyers of *existing* houses, wetlands will be a nonissue. However, buyers with plans to develop vacant land or further develop an existing home or property with wetlands need to understand all wetlands laws that could interfere with future plans. Buyers should account for any wetlands issues early in the property evaluation process to minimize delays and associated costs. Sellers should recognize that because of the restrictions they pose, some people will not want a property with wetlands. For all properties with wetlands, governmental restrictions can impact the value, your ability to refinance or sell it, and your overall ability to use and enjoy it in the manner you desire.

23. ZONING AND OTHER LAND USE RESTRICTIONS

All types of properties
         Risks: HEALTH   None   FINANCIAL $ $

Background

When you buy a home, you get the good with the bad; while home and land ownership entitle you to do many things on your property ("your home is your castle"), there are also limits on land use and development. These limits are of two types: governmental restrictions—land use controls imposed by state, county, or local governments; and private restrictions—typically recorded against a property in the deed (the legal document that is used to transfer title from seller to buyer) or in other legal documents.

Governmental Restrictions

Governmental regulations that affect your ability to use and/or develop your property can take many forms, including all of the following types of rules:

- planning
- zoning
- wetlands
- conservation
- forestry
- floodplain zoning
- historic district
- water pollution control
- airport zoning
- coastal zone and harbor management
- shoreline, watershed, and aquifer protection
- bird sanctuary and wildlife reserve
- public health
- underground storage tanks
- septic systems

Land use laws or ordinances are typically developed by local governments in accordance with state law. Although requirements vary considerably from town to town and from state to state, generally they all specify what, where, when, and how you can build on your property and what you can do there.

Depending on the situation and your political viewpoint, governmental land use restrictions can be burdensome and, in many instances, seem an intrusion into personal choice, but they are intended to enhance and protect the quality of life and property values for everyone in the community. Remember that while they may restrict you from doing certain things, they also protect you and your investment against things your neighbors might want to do. Land use agencies that apply and enforce these regulations have a difficult job: they must balance the competing interests of the public, the home owner, the developer, businesses, neighbors, and any opponents.

Private Restrictions

Private limitations on property use are essentially a form of regulation that can be imposed by contract, deed restrictions, community association bylaws, and other legal mechanisms. Just about every property has some type of private restriction. The deed may contain specific restrictions ("deed restrictions"), such as covenants and easements, which dictate how land is to be used or subdivided. These private restrictions generally must be followed. Sometimes private restrictions may reflect idiosyncratic wishes of prior owners. Utility easements are the most common type of private restriction—public utilities such as electric, gas, cable, telephone, and water or sewer companies often have continual access to your property through a strip of land set aside for their use. Community or cooperative associations for many condominiums, townhouses, and housing developments impose use and activity restrictions through their bylaws or other association documents.

Remember that land use regulation of *nearby* properties can also impact your health and finances (see Hazard 50, Zoning).

Health Risks

Land use restrictions do not cause health problems—except when your blood pressure rises when you find out about a restriction *after* you purchase a home and are prevented from doing something you had planned.

Financial Risks

By defining and often limiting the kinds of activities allowed, governmental and private land use restrictions directly impact property values and your ability to use, develop, expand, refinance, or sell a home. If, for example, land cannot be developed because of wetlands (see Hazard 22, Wetlands) or a home addition is not allowed because of setback or septic system requirements (see Hazard 20, Septic Systems), the value of the property will be diminished—often by thousands of dollars. These restrictions will reduce the pool of potential buyers for a property, since future buyers will also be restricted in what they can and cannot do on the property.

The costs to obtain the necessary permits and approvals to develop your property, including consultant and legal fees, or to challenge a governmental or private restriction, can run into thousands of dollars. In addition, if you end up in a legal battle over a land use issue, the process can be drawn out over many months or even years, delaying the ability to develop the property and perhaps forcing you to make alternative housing arrangements until the matter is settled.

Land use restrictions may be subject to disclosure requirements for sellers and their agents (see Disclosure Obligations, pages 13–19). For example, if a property has a conservation easement limiting development in a certain area of the property, or has been denied a permit to expand its septic system, the seller may be required to alert a buyer. To prevent problems at closing, sellers should inform buyers of governmental and private restrictions up front, rather than letting the buyer's lawyer find them out when doing a title search or reviewing community bylaws or other documents.

Managing the Risks

Be aware of and understand all of the land use restrictions that apply to a property to determine if you will be able to do with it what you want. Know if your planned uses will require a permit and what the chances of denial might be. Review the property's deed and other associated documents with a land use attorney before signing a contract. If there are restrictions, ask yourself which ones are really important and which are just bothersome. For example, if you want to work out of your home, find out if there are any restrictions on home businesses. If there are any restrictions, find out the likelihood of getting a variance,* how long the process will take, and what it will cost.

The best scenario for a buyer is to require that the seller have all

---

* A variance is an exception to a restriction granted by a land use agency because of special conditions, particularly where a literal interpretation or application of the law would result in exceptional difficulty or impose unusual hardship.

permits and approvals in place before closing. Because land use restrictions can significantly change, until you've received all necessary approvals, you cannot count on being able to use or develop your property in the future—even if what you've contemplated is permitted under the current regulations. Buyers should factor into a purchase offer the land use restrictions as well as the associated time and costs for dealing with them. Sellers and their agents should ensure that all aspects of the home and property use conform to applicable laws and codes. Otherwise there may be difficulty in selling the home or a disclosure lawsuit could arise later. Buyers should verify that the property and any structures comply with all local building codes and other land use laws.

Regulatory Outlook

The regulation of land use by state and local officials involves balancing traditional rights of property owners with the power of government to protect the health, safety, and welfare of the public. Since early in this century, courts have ruled that states may regulate land development in the public interest. In most states, land use decisions are often delegated to local officials in planning, zoning, wetlands, conservation, and other commissions, who presumably understand the issues associated with local private property. There are also special commissions and boards for historic districts, airport zoning, water pollution control, forestry, public health, coastal zones, and shorelines, and others who regulate specific aspects of land use. Recognize that the expertise of these officials varies tremendously; while some are experienced land use professionals, many commissions and boards are made up of elected or politically appointed volunteers with no special training.

Governmental restrictions cover a broad range of issues, including:

- the ability to subdivide land
- setbacks (the distance from the house to a property line, street, or body of water)
- the size of buildings and area of coverage
- building height
- fences
- pools
- types of animals allowed
- leases
- the number, and relationships, of occupants
- street parking
- parking boats, campers, or commercial vehicles in a driveway

- number of principal uses allowed (such as for home occupations or in-law apartments)
- historic issues, such as color, type of siding, shutters, or architectural design
- wetlands and watercourses
- coastal or lake areas
- dock or pier coverage
- aquifer protection
- endangered species
- conservation issues and easements (such as open space preservation, greenways, stream corridors, river encroachment, bird sanctuaries, and limits on fertilizer and pesticide use)
- public health, safety, and environmental issues (such as septic systems and underground storage tanks)

These are just some of the types of governmental restrictions; there are many more.

Private restrictions often cover many of the same issues as the governmental restrictions listed above and are acknowledged by buyers and attached to the property deed at closing. These restrictions are generally legally binding and typically withstand challenge in court, unless they are in any way discriminatory. Increasingly, newer residential communities utilize covenants and other restrictions to control a neighborhood's image and impose uniformity on a development. While the overall goals are to improve the quality of life and protect property values, these developments with their myriad restrictions have many critics. Enforcement of private restrictions, which can include warnings, fines, liens, and lawsuits, is generally in the hands of the community association.

Until recently, the trend in governmental land use regulation was toward increasing restrictions and the diminution of private property rights. Recently, there has been an increase in court decisions leaning toward the protection of private property rights, and new legislation at all levels is easing the burden on home owners in terms of private property use and restrictions. However, there is much variability at all levels of government, and the trends in your state or town may not be in harmony with national trends. Remember, too, that as with everything political, in time, the winds will undoubtedly shift the other way.

What to Look For

Make yourself aware of all governmental and private restrictions that may impact your ability to build on the land, lease or renovate a home, or generally to use and enjoy a property as you desire. First, check the state and local regulations for any restrictions. For example, if you want to further develop the land, add on to the house, have a home occupation, or lease out the home, check:

1. zoning issues such as setbacks, height limits, and use restrictions
2. public health requirements, such as your ability to expand the septic system to allow you to add on another bathroom
3. any wetlands or conservation requirements and
4. restrictions on the permissible number of occupants

Second, check the deed for any easements, covenants, or other restrictions. While deed restrictions should show up during your lawyer's title search—don't wait until the last minute to find out if there is a significant restriction. Remember that not all easements or restrictions are recorded, even if they should be; ask the current owner and neighbors if they are aware of any uses of the property that have been going on without formal approval (for example, public access across your property to a lake or stream). If you need to access *your* property by passing through another's property, make sure you have a recorded easement so that such access can continue. For example, if a driveway or drinking water well is shared, rights and responsibilities regarding use and maintenance costs should be defined in the deed. If there is a community association or housing authority of some type, review the bylaws and declarations for any restrictions, such as the ability to rent or sell the unit, the use of a basketball hoop, clotheslines, fences, above-ground pools or barbecue grills, the colors of drapes, blinds, or the exterior of houses, or whether children are allowed.

When buying undeveloped land, make sure you have direct access to utility hookups; you do not want to find out that you have to obtain an easement over a neighbor's property for access to utilities—you will have no leverage with the neighbor and it could end up costing you an arm and a leg. We have a friend who bought twelve acres on a northeastern resort island only to find out later that the property had no direct access to public utilities. This has delayed development of his property for years and could cost him thousands of dollars.

If you want to change the appearance or aesthetic features of your home, check zoning, historic requirements, and association bylaws that may restrict such things as the colors you may use for exterior paint, types of approved building materials, and the use or color of window treatments.

If you plan on remodeling, check state and local building codes for construction, plumbing, electrical, and other standards.

Where to Find Help and Further Information

A buyer should ask the owner to identify any governmental or private restrictions on the property or if he or she has ever been turned down for any type of land use permit or approval. The property survey may also identify recorded restrictions, such as easements—ask the owner for any site drawings or check with the local building department. Review local zoning and other applicable agency regulations, zoning maps, the town's plan of development, and flood insurance rate maps. Also, USGS and Sanborn Fire Insurance Maps may show the location of utility lines (see Appendix 3). Call the local utility to confirm utility easements and to find out whether there are any plans for additional work, such as moving utilities underground or the installation of cable hookups.

The Bottom Line

The impact of land use restrictions will vary with each situation, but for most home owners who do not anticipate changing the use of or structures on the property, the restrictions will have little bearing on you. However, you should always do your homework to identify all possible governmental and private restrictions and how you might be impacted—a good lawyer can help with this process. In the end, you need to ask yourself whether a particular restriction adds to the value of your property, has no effect on value, or makes the property unsuitable for your needs. In addition, it is critical that when buying a home you take into consideration how easy it will be to resell in the future. Governmental and private land use restrictions can impact the value of your home, your ability to refinance or sell it, and your overall ability to develop, use, and enjoy it in the manner you desire.

PART III

Off-Site Environmental Hazards

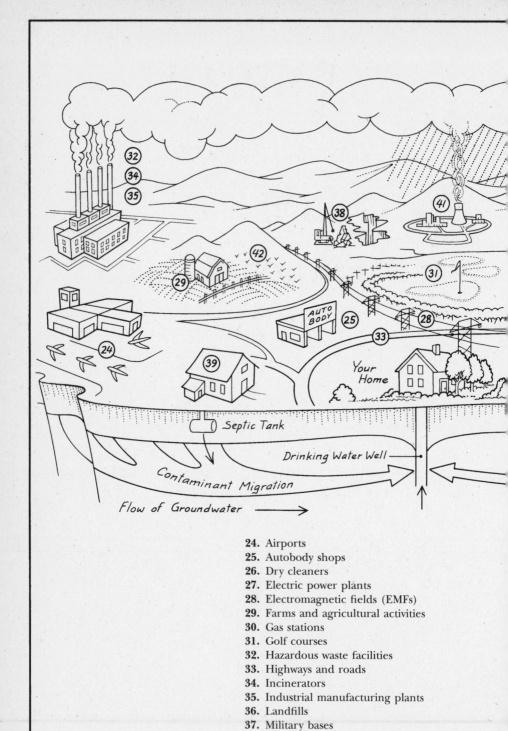

Septic Tank

Drinking Water Well

Contaminant Migration

Flow of Groundwater ⟶

Your Home

AUTO BODY

24. Airports
25. Autobody shops
26. Dry cleaners
27. Electric power plants
28. Electromagnetic fields (EMFs)
29. Farms and agricultural activities
30. Gas stations
31. Golf courses
32. Hazardous waste facilities
33. Highways and roads
34. Incinerators
35. Industrial manufacturing plants
36. Landfills
37. Military bases

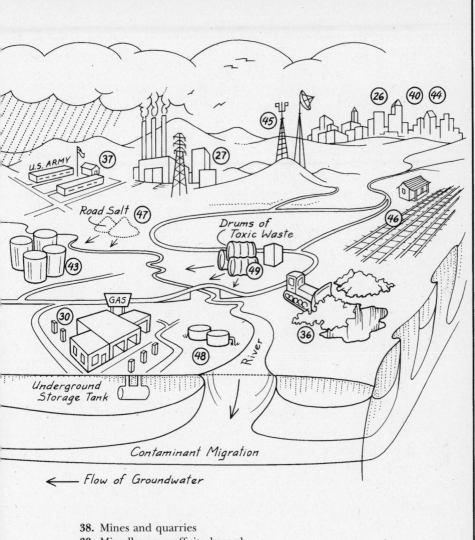

U.S. ARMY (37)

Road Salt (47)

(26) (40) (44)

(45)

(27)

(46)

Drums of
Toxic Waste

(43)

(49)

GAS

(30)

(48)

(36)

River

Underground
Storage Tank

Contaminant Migration

⟵ Flow of Groundwater

38. Mines and quarries
39. Miscellaneous off-site hazards
40. Municipal garages
41. Nuclear power plants
42. Pesticides
43. Petroleum storage terminals
44. Print shops
45. Radio and communication towers
46. Railroad yards and tracks
47. Salt storage areas
48. Sewage treatment plants
49. Superfund sites
50. Zoning issues (not shown)

24. AIRPORTS

Risks: HEALTH   FINANCIAL $ $

Background

Airports are located everywhere, from major cities to the least populated countryside. There are approximately thirteen thousand public and private airports in the United States (most are private). Due to increased population and the rising demand for air transportation—the number of passengers flying each year in the United States alone will almost double by the turn of the century—many new airports are being planned and existing ones are expanding. Environmental impacts and the financial and health risks to home owners who live near airports or are located in aircraft flight paths include noise pollution; soil, groundwater, and surface water contamination; traffic congestion; and, although extremely rare, aircraft accidents.

Noise, clearly the single most important issue associated with airports, will impact people living in homes close to many airports as a result of aircraft takeoffs and landings, and those in homes directly under the flight paths of aircraft. Since the 1940s, home owners have been embroiled in disputes with airport authorities over noise pollution and impacts to property and buildings. Today an estimated five million people in the United States are exposed to significant aircraft noise.

Airports often have soil and groundwater contamination problems from past use, disposal, or spills associated with underground or aboveground fuel storage tanks, PCB-containing transformers, maintenance facilities, deicing operations, on-site sewage treatment or septic systems, bulk storage and use of pesticides on rights-of-way and runways, and other sources. Contaminants from plane fueling and washing, aircraft ·and vehicle maintenance, and temporary waste storage often end up in wastewater or storm water drains. Airplanes use billions of gallons of fuel per year, and spills are common. Although many airports now use aboveground tanks, groundwater contamination from historic practices and the potential for new spills or leaks remain.

In addition to noise, aircraft also have an impact on the physical environment, including air emissions of particulates, nitrogen oxides, and carbon monoxide. These emissions are significant on both a local and global scale. Airports are a source of odors, fumes, lights, traffic, and other nuisances to nearby residential properties. A kerosene odor from jet fuel can often be smelled at nearby properties. Bright lights and traffic congestion around an airport can impact the daily life of nearby residents. Finally, crashes and other accidents, while infrequent, do happen, and they can force evacuations and harm people, property, and the environment. The lingering effects of these catastrophes can result in long-term surface and groundwater contamination problems.

Health Risks

Noise and vibrations can be significant for many homes situated near busy airports. At excessive levels, noise may lead to heart problems, exhaustion, mental illness, ulcers, indigestion, loss of equilibrium, nausea, high blood pressure, and loss of hearing, among many other problems. Some studies suggest a link between birth defects and low birth weight of babies and aircraft noise. However, not all airports have continuous air traffic—the amount of noise at any given airport will be related to the number, routes, and hours of flights, as well as the types of planes.

Pollution from a variety of airport activities can also impact human health through a number of exposure routes. Toxic chemicals, jet fuel, pesticides, cleaning solvents, runway and aircraft deicing chemicals (namely glycol, a hazardous waste in many states), and others can contaminate downgradient drinking water wells and cause health problems (see Hazard 4, Drinking Water: Private Wells). In addition, air inside homes located above groundwater containing high levels of certain organic compounds can become contaminated and pose a variety of health problems to occupants. Air pollution from "pesticide drift" from spraying of airport properties or vapors from jet fueling can also pose risks, especially to the young, the elderly, and people with respiratory ailments. Recently a woman in Virginia claimed she had developed chronic respiratory problems following a spill of more than thirty thousand gallons of jet fuel from a storage tank.

Other airport issues, such as odors, traffic delays, or interference with radio, TV, or telephone communications, can be a distraction, disturb your sleep, and disrupt the use and enjoyment of your home. In addition, obviously, the rare airplane crash can have catastrophic health impacts.

Financial Risks

Proximity to an airport or a heavily used flight path can devalue a home. Property (or rental) values may already reflect proximity to an airport and buyers (tenants) should be aware of noise issues before they make an offer or get to the deal stage. Properties close to airports may also be devalued because of stigma.

Residents who live near an airport may incur costs to soundproof a home; to repair property damage such as structural damage from vibrations or harm to livestock, crops, or landscaping; to provide lodging due to forced evacuation following an accident; and to pay legal and expert fees. For example, a home owner living near the end of a Pittsburgh airport runway sued (and won) for noise and vibration issues—the windows of his home rattled, plaster fell from the ceilings and walls, shelves and china cabinets toppled, and it was impossible to sleep in the house. Also, homes near airports may incur costs to address problems caused by storm water runoff containing oils, fuel, deicers, pesticides, and other pollutants that can cause erosion and harm a home's lawn and gardens, wetlands, ponds or lakes, and well water.

State or local governments, when developing or expanding an airport, often utilize their powers of eminent domain to buy out ("condemn" or "take") nearby property and relocate the residents, whether it be for a new or expanded terminal, a new runway, a new parking lot, a noise buffer zone, or radar or weather equipment. So after you've settled into your home, there is a chance that you could be uprooted. Home owners beware: the authority taking your property for airport use may first try to depress property values, through a technique known as "down-zoning," to reduce fair market value—several years ago the city of Los Angeles was unsuccessful in its attempt to do this.

There may also be zoning-type restrictions for property uses near airports. In addition to local zoning and building requirements, the Federal Aviation Administration (FAA) has rules that can control new construction near airports and will make a determination as to whether proposed construction will pose a "hazard to air navigation." For example, a California developer who owned 230 acres next to a runway was so restricted by a local zoning ordinance limiting the height of buildings (the highest he could build was twenty-four feet), he was awarded compensation for the value of his land. In similar instances, if the FAA prevents proposed construction because it would constitute a "hazard to air navigation," a home owner may have the basis for a compensable "takings" claim—of course, significant legal and expert costs would be incurred pursuing any claim.

Buyers may ask about noise, contamination, vibrations, odors, smoke, lights, and traffic. These and other issues can affect a buyer's decision and the negotiations, as can various aesthetic issues, such as an airport's visual impacts on a neighborhood. Airports around the country have paid hundreds of millions of dollars to compensate home owners for noise-related damages in addition to large sums expended for noise mitigation. However, court decisions vary—in some states, to be compensated you need to be directly under a flight path, while in others there is no such requirement.

Other financial risks:
- ► Liability for nondisclosure; see Disclosure Obligations, pages 13–19.
- ► Costs associated with contaminated drinking water; see Hazard 4, Drinking Water: Private Wells.
- ► Costs for short- or long-term medical treatment and monitoring; legal and expert fees; and inconvenience and relocation costs due to forced evacuation following an accident.

Managing the Risks

If you're looking at a home near an airport, expect traffic, noise, odors, lights, and vibrations. If you are concerned about these issues, make sure you're going to be far enough away and that there is substantial vegetation to act as a buffer to minimize them. When figuring out what "far enough away" means, consider that when an airport expands, it may need to "take" property, not just for a new runway or terminal, but for any of the other airport-related uses discussed above.

Contact the airport for financial and technical help in correcting any noise or contamination problem and in managing the associated risks. Remember, the noise caused by aircraft flying over a home is essentially an easement because public airports are government operations. Since the 1940s, numerous courts (including the U.S. Supreme Court) have determined that noise and lights from airports are a "taking" that diminishes property values and therefore requires airports to appropriately compensate home owners. In certain circumstances, and as governed by federal law, airports may pay for soundproofing of homes and compensate property owners for the loss of value due to noise. Construction of sound barriers around a residential development or soundproofing of individual homes may be an option (funds may be available from federal grants—check with the airport owner or operator); the use of well-placed shrubbery and trees can also muffle aircraft noise. Builders of residential developments should assess potential noise impacts and choose appropriate construction materials for the homes. For noise from private airports, home owners may choose to utilize private nuisance lawsuits to seek damages for impacts on property values. In general, those lawsuits based on nuisance or requesting "injunctive" relief (to shut down an operation) against *privately owned* airports have been more successful.

See Hazard 4, Drinking Water: Private Wells, for a discussion of how to manage risks if a drinking water well is contaminated.

Regulatory Outlook

Airports must comply with applicable federal laws and regulations and obtain necessary approvals. Where they are not preempted by the federal government, state and local agencies may also play roles in regulating airports. There are a number of agencies at all governmental levels that play some role in regulating airports and aircraft operations and their impacts to health, safety, and the environment.

Federal laws give jurisdiction to the FAA to regulate noise from aircraft and airports. Note that where not a restriction of interstate commerce, state and local governments often issue and enforce noise-abatement regulations, particularly when they own or operate an airport or where they apply to private airports. While the FAA long has had authority to approve aircraft and their engines, it was not until the late 1960s, when commercial jet engines came into use, that the FAA began to include noise issues in its evaluation process. Noise is the most heavily legislated issue for airports; federal laws include: the Federal Aviation Act of 1958 (and its amendments in 1968); the Noise Control Act of 1972 (which gave the EPA a role in regulating aircraft and airport noise, with the FAA retaining veto power); and the Aviation Safety and Noise Abatement Act of 1979. This last law includes provisions for reducing the impacts of aircraft noise by: developing a standardized system for measuring noise; determining appropriate land uses correlated with noise levels; requiring airport operators to develop noise exposure maps; and developing a noise compatibility program that incorporates use of preferential runways, restrictions on the use of some airports by certain types of aircraft, use of alternative flight procedures, construction of sound barriers, and acquisition of land.

Under federal law, airports can limit their potential liability to nearby property owners if they notified them of the potential for noise. Buyers of homes near an airport that has a noise exposure map generally cannot recover damages incurred due to aircraft noise if they knew about the airport or if the noise map was published in a local newspaper, as required by law. Home buyers can potentially recover damages if there has been a substantial change in the type or frequency of aircraft operations, a change in flight patterns, or an increase in night flights, among other factors that might result in damages to the home owner. (These laws do not apply to all airports—some municipally owned and operated airports, as well as private airports, are subject to different rules.)

In response to the growing problem of airport noise, Congress enacted the Airport Noise and Capacity Act of 1990. This law establishes a national aviation noise policy (preempting state and local authority by giving the FAA control of all noise restrictions on aircraft) and calls for a phasing in of more stringent noise standards by the year 2000, and a phasing out of aircraft that don't meet the new standards. To reduce impacts on residential areas, airports are using a number of measures, such as limiting hours of use (some impose strict night curfews), requiring aircraft to use noise-reducing equipment, using preferential runways, changing aircraft climbing gradients, and moving the takeoff points.

In the United States, the EPA and state environmental agencies, in conjunction with the FAA, regulate the use, storage, and disposal of jet fuel, pesticides, and other toxic materials; air emissions; the installation, monitoring, and removal of all fuel storage tanks; the generation, storage, and disposal of hazardous wastes; storm water, industrial, and sanitary wastewater discharges; emergency responses and reporting obligations (such as under community right-to-know programs); and the cleanup of contaminated soil and water supplies. Under the National Environmental Policy Act, some airports are required to prepare environmental impact reports, which are publicly available, before a new airport is planned or an existing airport undertakes certain activities, such as a major construction project or an expansion. These reports contain noise contour maps for surrounding areas that are affected.

Where not preempted by federal law, state, county, and local government agencies regulate land uses near some airports (such as municipal or city owned) and may set maximum noise level standards for interiors of buildings. These agencies also may "take" properties for developing and operating public airports. Airports are taking more steps to mitigate impacts on their neighbors; problems will further diminish as agency oversight and private lawsuits over noise, contamination, and other environmental, health, and safety issues increase. Nevertheless, lawsuits by residents near airports are common—home owners seek to recover damages for noise or halt the expansion of an existing one because of perceived effects on property values.

What to Look For

Airports are everywhere and most are highly visible as you drive around an area. In addition to commercial and private airports, many military bases have airports (see Hazard 37, Military Bases). If there is a nearby airport, inspect the home when it is busy and planes are taking off and landing. Returning at different times of the day and on different days should give you a good sense of what to expect in the way of noise, vibrations, odors, and traffic. Make sure you aren't inspecting the home on a particularly quiet day or when a nearby runway isn't in use. Even if a home is not close to an airport, find out about flight paths, as noise problems can extend for several miles. Remember that odors may also only be an intermittent problem, depending on flight patterns and the direction of the wind. Inside, look for cracks in plaster walls and ceilings, special soundproofing construction materials, and other signs of noise-related problems.

Environmental contamination will probably not be obvious. If a well is in use, taste and smell the water; however, laboratory tests are usually needed to detect contamination. If a water treatment system or bottled water is used, find out why (see Hazard 4, Drinking Water: Private Wells). If a home is very close to an airport, check for visible signs of contamination, such as stained soil, stressed vegetation, or an oil sheen on the surface of any body of water.

Where to Find Help and Further Information

Check with neighbors and town land use or building officials about the presence of a nearby airport, any problems associated with it, and any expansion plans. Historic aerial photographs, USGS maps (see Appendix 3), local zoning maps, and interviews with local officials can help confirm the past or current location of a nearby airport. However, little-used private airports may be difficult to spot in rural areas and may not be identified on maps. Some states require counties and towns to map airports, runways, and areas around them (often called "airport safety zones").

Find out who owns and operates the airport and ask them for information about flight paths, flight times, which runways are used and when, and any associated noise, odors, or vibration problems. Also ask if there is any history of spills from airport activities, such as from underground storage tanks, and known impacts to drinking water supplies. Owners and potential buyers of nearby homes with wells should test the water (see Hazard 4, Drinking Water: Private Wells). Coordinate tests with a qualified laboratory, consultant, or inspector. Contact the EPA or your state environmental or health agency for additional information or assistance (see Appendix 4).

The Bottom Line

Noise and other environmental issues from airports can be significant to nearby residents. Proximity to an airport can lower property values. The price of homes near airports usually reflects such concerns, and many buyers are willing to accept them. When you buy or build near an airport, know the risks. Noise, vibrations, odors, and traffic can disturb sleep, impair hearing, and cause other health effects, and affect the overall use and enjoyment of your home. Soil and groundwater contamination from past and present airport activities can pose significant health and financial risks to nearby home owners if drinking water wells are contaminated. Buyers of nearby homes with private wells should have the water tested to see if there is any reason for concern. The value of a property with a water problem will be significantly reduced. Finally, remember that *airports expand*—there is no guarantee that a property close to but not affected by an airport now will not be affected by changes in the future.

25. AUTOBODY SHOPS

Risks: HEALTH ⊕   FINANCIAL $

Background

Autobody shops, where vehicle repairs and painting are performed, may be located near residential properties. These shops often use paints and cleaners containing high levels of volatile organic compounds (VOCs). There are two possible environmental threats to nearby properties from VOC usage: (1) local air pollution and odors, and (2) groundwater contamination from spillage or improper storage and disposal of paint and other toxic chemicals.

When a car is painted, fumes containing VOCs are emitted from the paints as they dry. These fumes are exhausted out of the building using fans or blowers. If a home is nearby and the wind is blowing in the wrong direction, VOC fumes may be detected as an objectionable odor. Many autobody shops have been required to modify operations to reduce emissions; many have switched to less toxic paints, use special low-emitting spray guns, and have installed state-of-the-art pollution-control equipment to capture and filter emissions as they exit the building. However, some autobody shop operators may not be aware of (or are not covered by) newer environmental laws and regulations.

Autobody shops store paints, thinners, and cleaners on-site. In addition to VOCs, the paints often contain heavy metals. Strong acids and alkalies are used for removing rust from cars. Autobody shops must dispose of various hazardous wastes, such as contaminated blast abrasives (used in paint removal operations), dried paint filters, and spent rust removers, thinners, paints, and other coatings. Current or past spills or disposal of wastes in septic systems or dry wells, or the dumping of materials directly on the ground, can contaminate soil and groundwater.

Health Risks

There are a large number of VOCs used in paints and thinners. While many are relatively nontoxic, some are known to cause serious health problems. In most cases, VOC air emissions will be a nuisance but not a health problem, since, as with any chemical contaminant, health effects are based on the level and duration of exposure, which are usually extremely low and infrequent. Breathing low levels of organic solvents can cause headaches, loss of energy, or nausea.

Health risks from drinking VOC-contaminated water can be more serious, depending on the specific compound ingested, its level, and the amount of water consumed (see Hazard 4, Drinking Water: Private Wells). In addition, air inside homes located above groundwater containing high levels of VOCs can become contaminated and pose a variety of health problems to occupants. Laboratory studies, as well as the reports of people who have consumed VOC-contaminated water, have linked such exposure to birth defects, cancer, and many other health problems.

Financial Risks

Properties near an autobody shop, may be devalued due to concerns over potential health impacts and aesthetic issues resulting from air emissions. In addition, if an autobody shop, through improper use, storage, or disposal of hazardous materials, has contaminated the soil or groundwater, downgradient homes with private drinking water wells are at risk. Homes with contaminated wells will be devalued and difficult to sell. And even if a problem is addressed, a property may be devalued because of stigma. Buyers of properties near autobody shops may ask about odor problems or for information about possible contamination of drinking water supplies. This may be a point of contention in negotiations over price.

Other financial risks:

► Liability for nondisclosure; see Disclosure Obligations, pages 13–19.
► Costs associated with contaminated drinking water; see Hazard 4, Drinking Water: Private Wells.
► Costs for short- or long-term medical treatment and monitoring; and legal and expert fees.

Managing the Risks

See Hazard 4, Drinking Water: Private Wells, for a discussion of how to manage risks if a drinking water well is contaminated.

If there is an occasional odor problem, closing windows or modifying a home's ventilation system may reduce (but not eliminate) the amount of contaminants entering the home. State health and environmental agencies can force companies to eliminate air pollution and odor problems—autobody shops may need to change their activities or install an air treatment system.

Contact the autobody shop for financial or technical help to correct a problem and manage the associated risks.

Regulatory Outlook

Autobody shops must comply with applicable federal, state, and local environmental laws and regulations and obtain required permits. For example, under various environmental programs, the EPA and state agencies may regulate the storage and disposal of hazardous chemicals and wastes, air emissions, and the cleanup of contaminated soil and groundwater. State and local health and environmental agencies usually have rules about nuisance odors as well as emissions of hazardous air pollutants.

Larger autobody shops may face significant new requirements on air emissions as a result of the federal Clean Air Act Amendments of 1990. However, because most autobody shops are small operations, many have never been inspected by an environmental agency and are often exempt from certain regulations. In the past ten years, "environmentally friendly" paints (such as water-based paints or those formulated with fewer solvents and metals) and cleaners have become available and are being used as substitutes for products that typically contained high levels of toxic VOCs. Recycling is also becoming more common among autobody shops.

Also, all states have rules that require contaminated groundwater to be cleaned up. State and federal environmental agencies have authority to issue compliance orders to autobody shops that violate the law or that are contaminating soil or groundwater. Failure to comply with applicable requirements can subject an owner to both civil and criminal penalties.

What to Look For

A drive or walk around the area will allow you to locate any autobody shops. (Remember that many types of businesses that utilize, sell, or service vehicles, particularly fleets of vehicles, such as car dealerships, have an autobody repair shop as an ancillary operation at their facility.) If a well is in use, taste and smell the water; however, laboratory tests are usually needed to detect contamination. If a water treatment system or bottled water is used, find out why (see Hazard 4, Drinking Water: Private Wells).

Potential buyers should spend some time outside, on a day when the autobody shop is open, to see if they notice any unusual odors. Air pollution and odor problems are very localized—properties more than a few hundred feet away are not likely to experience problems. Remember that weather conditions, especially wind direction, influence whether or not an odor can be detected on a given day. If a home is close to an autobody shop, check for visible signs of contamination like stained soil, stressed vegetation, or an oil sheen on any surface body of water.

Where to Find Help and Further Information

Check with neighbors and the town land use or building officials to identify the location of existing or planned autobody shops. If there is an autobody shop nearby, find out about any odor problems or known impacts to drinking water wells at homes in the vicinity. Ask the state or local environmental agency if any air permits have been applied for by, or issued to, an autobody shop, and about known or suspected problems in an area.

If the home uses a well, a water analysis for VOCs can be performed for about $100 to $150 (see Hazard 4, Drinking Water: Private Wells). If needed, indoor air tests can also be performed for about $200 to $300 for a single test (see Hazard 12, Indoor Air Pollution Sources: Carpets and Building Materials). Coordinate tests with a qualified laboratory, consultant, or home inspector.

Contact the EPA or your state environmental or health agency for additional information or assistance (see Appendix 4).

The Bottom Line

Living close to an autobody shop can sometimes affect the use and enjoyment of your home. If odors are detected, they are likely to be more of a nuisance than a major health problem. However, odors can and do impact property values. Buyers of nearby homes that rely on private wells should have the water tested to see if there is any reason for concern. The costs to address contaminated water are high and the value of a property with a water problem will be significantly reduced.

26. DRY CLEANERS

Risks: HEALTH ⊕   FINANCIAL $ $

Background

Dry cleaners are often located near residential properties, whether in strip malls or shopping centers in the suburbs or in apartment and condominium complexes in cities. There are two general types of dry cleaners: laundry collection or drop centers (where no dry cleaning takes place on the premises), and those with dry-cleaning equipment on-site. While the laundry drop centers should pose no financial or health risks, facilities where dry cleaning takes place (or took place) pose a number of environmental concerns, such as air emissions; leaks of hazardous materials from equipment and solvent storage tanks; wastewater discharges and spills; and improper use, storage, or on-site disposal of dry-cleaning chemicals.

Dry-cleaning solvents, such as perchloroethylene ("perc" for short), are hazardous wastes under federal and state environmental laws. Of the roughly thirty-five thousand dry cleaners in the United States, about 85 percent use perc. Reports of perc or other solvents contaminating public and private drinking water supplies are common. Some dry cleaners use underground or aboveground tanks for bulk storage of cleaning solvents, and many older tanks have leaked. Contamination of groundwater has also occurred where dry-cleaning solvents have been dumped onto the ground or into septic systems, dry wells, or storm sewers. For example, the EPA recently spent more than $3 million to clean up contamination caused by a dry cleaner in New York after solvents, which had been dumped through a floor drain into a dry well for many years, polluted the city of Brewster's drinking water supply.

Under the federal Clean Air Act, perc is listed as a hazardous air pollutant. Annual perc emissions from U.S. dry cleaners are estimated at 100,000 tons. In homes near dry cleaners, and in apartment and condominium buildings that contain dry cleaners, continual exposure to low levels of perc in the indoor air is not uncommon.

Health Risks

Since the early 1980s, there has been growing concern about health problems resulting from exposure to perc, from drinking contaminated water or breathing contaminated air. Laboratory studies, as well as reports of people who have consumed perc-contaminated groundwater, link such exposures to birth defects, cancers, and a host of other health problems. Breathing air contaminated with low levels of perc emitted from a dry cleaner (or from volatilization of perc from contaminated groundwater) can cause headaches, dizziness, nausea, and fatigue. A study of New York City dry cleaners showed perc levels in nearby apartments that were 150 times higher than the city's guidelines of 0.4 parts per million (ppm). Perc has been found in certain fat-containing foods (such as butter, cheese, and cream) which can accumulate it in homes or stores located near dry cleaners. As with any chemical contaminant, the duration and level of exposure determine the possible health effects.

Financial Risks

A property near a dry cleaner and affected by air emissions can be devalued due to concerns about potential health impacts or for aesthetic reasons. In addition, if activities at a dry cleaner have contaminated soil or groundwater, then downgradient homes with private drinking water wells are at risk for perc contamination. Homes with contaminated wells will be devalued and difficult to sell. And even if a problem is addressed, a property may be devalued because of stigma. A buyer of a property near a dry cleaner may ask about odors, noise, and possible contamination of drinking water supplies. These factors may be a point of contention in the negotiations over price.

Other financial risks:

▶ Liability for nondisclosure; see Disclosure Obligations, pages 13–19.
▶ Costs associated with contaminated drinking water; see Hazard 4, Drinking Water: Private Wells.
▶ Costs for short- or long-term medical treatment and monitoring; and legal and expert fees.

Managing the Risks

See Hazard 4, Drinking Water: Private Wells, for a discussion of how to manage risks if a drinking water well is contaminated. Recently, perc contamination at levels two to ten times higher than allowed by law was discovered in five residential wells in one of our home towns, sparking an investigation of a nearby dry cleaner. Residents of impacted homes, some almost 1,000 feet away, have been put on bottled water pending the completion of the investigation by the state environmental agency and the local health department.

If there is an occasional odor problem, closing windows or modifying a home's ventilation or heating and cooling system may reduce (but not eliminate) the amount of contaminants entering the home. State health and environmental agencies can force a company to eliminate air pollution or odor problems by changing their activities or requiring the installation of air treatment systems.

Contact the dry cleaner for financial or technical help to correct a problem and manage the associated risks.

Regulatory Outlook

Dry cleaners must comply with applicable federal, state, and local environmental laws and regulations. For example, under various environmental programs, the EPA and state environmental agencies regulate the use, storage, and disposal of dry-cleaning solvents; air emissions; wastewater discharges; the installation, maintenance, and monitoring of storage tanks; and the cleanup of contaminated soil and drinking water supplies.

Spent dry-cleaning solvents are hazardous wastes under the Resource Conservation and Recovery Act; perc is specifically listed as a hazardous air pollutant under the Clean Air Act. New regulations will require reductions in perc emissions, which may force many dry cleaners to make operational changes and may put some smaller dry cleaners out of business. Many dry cleaners are passing on the ever-increasing costs to their customers through dry-cleaning surcharges to install state-of-the-art monitoring equipment and to meet and comply with environmental laws. In addition, some states have imposed taxes on dry-cleaning services to raise money for cleaning up sites contaminated by dry-cleaning activities.

State and federal environmental agencies have authority to issue compliance orders to dry cleaners that violate the law or that contaminate soil or groundwater. Failure to comply with applicable requirements can subject a dry cleaner to civil penalties, criminal fines, and even imprisonment for "knowing" violations, such as illegally discharging perc. Since 1984, the EPA has been looking at perc exposures and dry cleaners themselves have taken major steps to recycle cleaning solvents and reduce emissions. The dry-cleaning industry reports an approximately 10 percent reduction in perc usage over the past decade and is currently testing a nontoxic cleaning solvent that may be a viable alternative to perc.

What to Look For

A drive or walk around the neighborhood, or a walk through your apartment or condo building, will help to identify any nearby dry cleaners. Remember that many dry cleaners, particularly in some cities, are laundry collection centers only (they do not do dry cleaning on the premises). If a home is adjacent to a dry cleaner, inspect the property for stained soil, stressed vegetation, or an oil sheen on any surface body of water, which may indicate a history of dumping or discharge of dry-cleaning wastes.

Check for unusual odors if there is a nearby dry cleaner—perc has a distinctive, sweet smell. If a dry cleaner is located in your apartment building, find out how its ventilation system works. Perc emissions and odors are typically localized—properties more than a few hundred feet away should not experience any problems. Remember that weather conditions, especially wind direction, will influence whether or not an odor is detected on any given day.

If a well is in use, taste and smell the water; however, laboratory tests are usually needed to detect contamination. If a water treatment system or bottled water is used, find out why (see Hazard 4, Drinking Water: Private Wells).

Where to Find Help and Further Information

Check with neighbors and the town land use or building officials to identify existing or planned dry cleaners. If one is nearby, find out about any problems or complaints associated with it (such as odors and noise) or known impacts to drinking water supplies for homes in the vicinity. Ask the EPA or your state environmental or health agency about past complaints or known health or environmental problems from dry cleaners in the area (see Appendix 4).

If the house uses a well, a water analysis for perc should be considered; it will cost about $100 to $200 (see Hazard 4, Drinking Water: Private Wells). Indoor air tests can also be performed, for $200 to $300 for a single test (see Hazard 12, Indoor Air Pollution Sources: Carpets and Building Materials). Coordinate water and air tests with a qualified laboratory, consultant, or home inspector. Contact the EPA or your state environmental or health agency for additional information or assistance (see Appendix 4).

The Bottom Line

Odors from dry cleaners can affect the use and enjoyment of your home, and the improper disposal or spills of perc and other chemicals used in dry cleaning can contaminate private drinking water wells. Buyers of nearby homes that rely on private wells should have the water tested to see if there is any reason for concern. The costs to address contaminated water are high and the value of a property with a water problem will be significantly reduced. For apartments in a building with a dry cleaner, low levels of perc in the air may be a health concern. If odors from a nearby dry cleaner are detected, they are more likely to be a nuisance than a major health problem—but odors can, and do, impact property values.

27. ELECTRIC POWER PLANTS

Risks: HEALTH   ⊕ ⊕   FINANCIAL $ $

Background

Electric power plants that burn various fossil fuels—coal, oil, or natural gas—are located throughout the United States.* The major components of the exhaust gases from electric power plants, which are vented to the atmosphere via smokestacks, are carbon dioxide (the compound associated with the greenhouse effect) and water vapor (the white cloud that may be evident from a stack on a cold day). Pollutants emitted depend on the type of fuel used, but two that are always present in exhaust gases are carbon monoxide and nitrogen oxide.

Coal, by far the most polluting fossil fuel, is burned by over half of the electric-generating plants in the country—most are located in the Midwest. Emissions from coal-fired plants contain sulfur dioxide and hydrochloric acid (prime contributors to acid rain), particulates (fine solid particles), and trace levels of some heavy metals. In addition to air pollutants, environmental concerns at coal plants include the handling and storage of vast amounts of coal—dust control and contaminated soil, groundwater and storm water can be major problems. Air emissions from oil- and natural gas–fired electric plants are significantly lower than from coal plants (natural gas is cleaner burning than oil). At many oil-fired plants, large volumes of petroleum products are handled and stored, and fuel oil spills have polluted surface water and groundwater (see Hazard 43, Petroleum Storage Terminals).

All newer electric power plants use some type of pollution-control equipment, such as filters or wet scrubbers. However, some old plants were built before pollution controls were required and may not have installed them. Tall smokestacks are often used to get the exhaust gases high into the atmosphere, where they are dispersed and carried away from populated areas. All power plants have electrical substations and power lines that may be of concern because of PCBs and EMFs (see Hazard 16, PCBs, and Hazard 28, Electromagnetic Fields).

---

* Nuclear power plants are reviewed in Hazard 41, Nuclear Power Plants.

"Waste ash," the dustlike waste produced by most power plants, consists of particulates captured by air pollution collection equipment and those that drop to the bottom of the furnace. The ash contains small amounts of toxic heavy metals. Electric power plants almost always have elaborate systems to collect and store waste ash in ways that prevent it from escaping into the environment. However, some may blow off the site as a dust. Some power plants also have landfills located on their property where they dispose of waste ash (see Hazard 36, Landfills).

Power plants require huge volumes of water to make the steam necessary to generate electricity and for cooling. This water is often discharged into nearby bodies of water and its heat can create localized thermal impacts. Historically, many power plants used chromium, a toxic metal, to prevent buildup of bacteria in their water (chromium is rarely used today). Because of past disposal practices of chromium-contaminated water, soil, surface water, and groundwater supplies at some plants have been impacted.

Homes near electric power plants may be affected by storm water runoff containing oil or gasoline, solvents, heavy metals, and other pollutants. These pollutants can impact lawns and gardens, wetlands, ponds, and lakes. A power plant may also have many of the environmental problems common to all large industrial facilities, such as odors, noise from equipment, truck traffic, lighting, and possible soil and groundwater contamination from large chemical and fuel storage tanks or past on-site disposal practices.

Health Risks

Air pollution from fossil fuel–fired power plants is normally a *regional problem,* not a localized one that would target only nearby property owners and neighbors. However, under certain weather conditions, pollutants can be directed to and impact nearby areas; under these circumstances, respiratory problems may be experienced by children, the elderly, and those with existing health problems like asthma. A short summary of health risks associated with the major types of air pollutants follows.

Carbon Monoxide The most common air pollutant from any combustion process, carbon monoxide (CO) competes with oxygen to get into the blood, and at low levels will cause dizziness, weakness, and other problems (see Hazard 3, Combustion Sources and Carbon Monoxide). People with heart and cardiovascular diseases are particularly sensitive to CO.

Particulates Particulates from air emissions or from ash dust are readily inhaled and can irritate the lungs and respiratory tract. They are the compound associated with black lung disease, which plagues coal miners. They also act as carriers of heavy metals, allowing them to get deep into the lungs.

Nitrogen Oxides Nitrogen oxides (NOx) can irritate the lungs and increase the chances of respiratory infections. NOx is one of the major air pollutants that causes ozone problems. Breathing ozone is known to cause health problems such as asthma and is a particular concern for people who work or exercise outdoors as well as the elderly and children.

Sulfur Oxides At high levels, sulfur oxides (SOx) can cause or aggravate existing respiratory problems, like asthma. SOx are also the major culprits behind the acid rain problem.

If operations at a power plant impact groundwater and nearby drinking water wells are in use, there may be serious health risks to people drinking the water (see Hazard 4, Drinking Water: Private Wells). In addition, air inside homes located above groundwater containing high levels of certain organic compounds can become contaminated and pose a variety of health problems to occupants.

Financial Risks

Properties located close to a power plant may experience a decrease in value due to aesthetic concerns, the presence of power lines, traffic problems, or stigma. Properties near a power plant known to have air pollution, odor, or soil or groundwater contamination problems may be further devalued and difficult to sell. And even if a problem is addressed, a property may be devalued because of stigma.

A buyer of a property near a power plant may ask about air pollution and noise problems; these issues that may be points of contention in the negotiations over price.

Power plants (and other public utilities) have right-of-way authority. That means, if they want to expand, they can condemn some or all of your property. You'll get compensated for the value, but you may have to move.

Other financial risks:

▶ Liability for nondisclosure; see Disclosure Obligations, pages 13–19.

- ► Costs associated with contaminated drinking water; see Hazard 4, Drinking Water: Private Wells.
- ► Costs for short- or long-term medical treatment and monitoring; property damage (such as harm to livestock, crops, or landscaping); and legal and expert fees.

Managing the Risks

See Hazard 4, Drinking Water: Private Wells, for a discussion of how to manage risks if a drinking water well is contaminated.

If you are looking at a home near an electric power plant, expect some odors, noise, lights, and traffic. If you are concerned about these issues, make sure that the home is far enough away and that there are substantial vegetative buffers to minimize them. If there is an occasional odor problem, closing windows or modifying a home's ventilation system may reduce (but not eliminate) the amount of contaminants entering your home. State health and environmental agencies can require a power plant to reduce emissions and minimize odor, noise, and dust problems by requiring a change in its activities or the installation of air treatment systems.

Contact the power plant for financial or technical help to correct a problem and manage the associated risks.

Regulatory Outlook

Power plants are a highly regulated industry—day-to-day operations are controlled by federal, state, and local health and environmental agencies as well as by state public utility authorities. In addition to air pollution regulations, power plants are subject to rules governing how chemical wastes and waste ash are stored and handled; permits for wastewater discharges, noise levels, and underground storage tanks; and rules to protect groundwater from spills and to force cleanup of contaminated soil, groundwater, and surface water.

All power plants will have a permit from the EPA or a state or local environmental agency that defines acceptable levels of air pollutant emissions, sets certain operating conditions, requires pollution controls to be working, and may require regular sampling and testing of the smokestack's emissions. Most new power plants have "continuous emissions monitors" that sample and test certain stack emissions many times per hour. However, pollution problems can still result from improper operation or lax regulation.

The federal Clean Air Act, first passed in 1972, has encouraged great reductions in air pollution from power plants. Subsequent increased regulations and the use of control equipment and cleaner fuels have resulted in a net decrease in the emissions of all major pollutants from the power industry, even though the overall capacity has increased greatly. Changes in the law passed in 1990 set a layer of tough regulations requiring new and existing power plants to obtain and renew permits every five years and meet stricter limits on emissions for almost all pollutants. With the ever-tightening environmental regulations and changes in the financial structure of the industry, some plants will be shut down in the coming years.

State and federal environmental agencies have the authority to issue compliance orders to a facility that violates its permits or that contaminates soil or groundwater. Failure to comply with applicable requirements can subject the owner to both civil and criminal penalties.

What to Look For

Drive around the area—power plants are large industrial complexes that have power lines extending from them. There may be tall smokestacks, coal piles, large storage tanks, and other massive concrete structures.

If you've located a nearby power plant, spend some time in the neighborhood to see if there are any unusual odors, noises, or traffic problems. Remember that these problems may be intermittent and may vary with the time of day or local weather and wind conditions. If odors from a power plant are detected, it may be an indication that it is not operating properly and could be emitting high levels of toxic pollutants. Talk to the neighbors, but remember, people have varying tolerance levels for nuisance-type problems.

If a well is in use, taste and smell the water; however, laboratory tests are usually needed to detect contamination. If a water treatment system or bottled water is used, find out why (see Hazard 4, Drinking Water: Private Wells). If a home is close to an electric power plant, check for visible signs of contamination like stained soil, stressed vegetation, or an oil sheen on any surface body of water.

Where to Find Help and Further Information

Nearby power plants can be found by asking the local building department or by calling the utility directly. Often power plants are identified on USGS and Sanborn Fire Insurance maps and aerial photographs. (See Appendix 3.)

Check with the neighbors and the town land use or building officials to identify any existing or planned power plants, and ask if there are any anticipated expansion plans. Find out about any problems or complaints associated with them, or known impacts to drinking water wells for homes in the vicinity. A buyer should ask the owner if there have been any air pollution, odor, or other problems, such as heavy truck traffic, associated with a power plant.

Owners and potential buyers of nearby homes with wells should consider testing the water (see Hazard 4, Drinking Water: Private Wells). Coordinate tests with a qualified laboratory, consultant, or inspector. Contact the EPA or your state environmental or health agency for additional information or assistance (see Appendix 4).

These agencies will have specific departments responsible for air permits and can provide information about a particular facility's design and operation as well as known or suspected environmental problems.

The Bottom Line

Electric power plants that burn fossil fuels have the potential to create nuisances—odors, noise, and the like. Power plants have had more than their share of pollution problems, and they have impacted nearby homes through soil, groundwater, surface water, and air pollution. They can pose health and financial risks to nearby home owners if private drinking water wells are impacted—a buyer of such a home should have the water tested to determine if there is any need for concern. The costs to address contaminated water are high and the value of a property with a water problem will be significantly reduced. In this situation, or because of stigma, a property close to a power plant will be devalued.

28. ELECTROMAGNETIC FIELDS

Risks: HEALTH Uncertain   FINANCIAL $ $

Background

Electromagnetic fields (EMFs)* are forms of energy produced by electrical currents. EMF radiation is produced in various frequencies: high-frequency waves, such as X rays; middle-frequency waves, such as micro-

---

* EMFs can also be an on-site hazard, such as from household appliances or where electric transmission lines are located on, or pass over, the property.

waves; low-frequency waves, such as those from televisions; and extremely low frequency waves, such as those from utility power lines. EMFs are also produced by natural sources: the electromagnetic field from the earth's rotation, and even the minute electrical currents associated with cellular activity in our bodies. The biggest *nearby* source of EMFs for home owners is electric utility transmission (power) lines (also called high tension lines). There are over 600,000 miles of high-voltage transmission lines in the United States, and millions of people are exposed to EMF levels from them every day. In the home, all machines that use electricity, including TV sets, microwave ovens, electric blankets, clock radios, electric stoves, and hair dryers, emit EMFs, as does internal home wiring. While every electrical power line is an EMF source, large high-voltage transmission lines (as opposed to distribution lines located along most public streets) have received the most attention because they are a constant source of relatively high levels of EMF in their immediate vicinity.

EMF levels, which are measured in "milligauss," decrease rapidly as you move away from the source; levels from power lines usually drop to "natural" background levels at a distance of several hundred feet. Most EMFs inside a home are due to indoor wiring and appliances, not power lines that are several hundred or more feet away. For example, EMF levels twenty feet away from a typical high-voltage power line will be less than 100 milligauss; at three hundred feet, EMF levels will be under 2 milligauss. In contrast, the EMF field produced one inch from a hair dryer ranges from 60 to 2,000 milligauss; one foot from a microwave oven, EMF levels may be 40 to 80 milligauss.

A great deal of scientific research has been done on EMF exposure and potential health risks, yet today there is still no clear answer and controversy exists in the scientific community.* The primary research focus has been on transmission lines that operate at a specific frequency everywhere in the United States—namely 60 hertz (Hz). The scientific community has been looking at whether extended exposure to EMF fields in the 60 Hz frequency range increases the likelihood of getting cancer. While a few studies have implicated EMFs in general, and power lines in particular, with a small increased cancer risk, the majority of studies have found no increased health risks associated with EMFs. Regardless of the scientific uncertainty, or perhaps because of it, the potential for harm from power lines has, during the past few years, been the subject of widespread, adverse publicity, frequent lawsuits, and disputes concerning the siting of high-voltage lines.

---

* Except for high-frequency waves like X rays, none of the frequencies has been proven to cause cancer.

Health Risks

The current state of scientific knowledge does not allow a determination that exposure to EMFs presents an increased risk of cancer or other health effects. Although some studies claim that EMFs cause various forms of cancer, birth defects, and other health problems, many more suggest otherwise. Several epidemiological studies conducted since 1979 suggest that EMFs may result in a small increased risk of cancer and leukemia. In November of 1992, a Swedish study concluded that EMFs from high-power electric lines increased the risk of leukemia in children. The results of these studies were well publicized and are probably responsible for much of the current concern over EMFs. Publicity aside, the scientific community has generally not accepted these studies as conclusive. It is widely believed that the energy levels associated with EMFs from power lines are too low to cause genetic damage that triggers cancer.

Because of the controversy and public concern, there have been many official EMF studies commissioned by the EPA, OSHA, and various industry, academic, and environmental groups. One effort by the U.S. Department of Labor commissioned a panel of eleven experts on radiation to review more than one thousand EMF studies. The panel's final report, published in late 1993, concludes that "there is *no convincing evidence* in the published literature to support the contention *that exposures to EMFs* generated by such sources as household appliances, video display terminals, and local *power lines* are demonstrable health hazards" [emphasis added]. This conclusion was affirmed by a 1995 report of the American Physical Society. New state-of-the-science reports are due to be released by the EPA and other groups before the end of 1996.

Financial Risks

Homes near electric utility transmission lines may be devalued due to perceived health risks or for purely aesthetic reasons. Some buyers, particularly those with, or contemplating having, children, are wary of homes near utility power lines. Some buyers may make an offer below the asking price or walk away from a deal. Even if the power lines are not very close, their mere presence can be a stigma issue for future buyers and the pool of potential buyers may shrink. Whether founded or not, fears about possible health effects from EMFs can and do reduce property values. The uncertainty associated with EMF health risks also fuels future financial risk: in the event that scientific research brings us closer to concluding that EMFs *do* play a role in causing cancer, we expect to see even more significant decreases in the values of properties near power lines. If you buy a home near electric power lines, recognize that you may have to confront the EMF issue in the future.

Buyers may demand information about nearby power lines as part of the purchase and sale agreement; some will undoubtedly use the EMF issue as a bargaining chip during negotiations. Sellers and their agents may be required to disclose the presence of nearby power lines to potential buyers; disclosure may also be required if it is known that power lines are planned for a nearby right-of-way (see Disclosure Obligations, pages 13–19).

Several EMF court cases are now pending as neighbors sue utilities for alleged property devaluation and real or perceived impacts to their health. In a few property devaluation lawsuits, financial impacts from power lines to nearby property owners have been documented and upheld by the courts. In one case, an electric utility was required to compensate a landowner for reduced property values allegedly from public fears caused by a new power line easement. There even have been several so-called fear or cancerphobia lawsuits where utilities have been sued not for causing property devaluation or actual health impacts but merely for causing fear. To date, courts and juries have not awarded damages in fear lawsuits, but the suits continue. Depending on how the courts rule, these can greatly influence future financial risks. Home owners do, however, incur legal and expert fees to bring these lawsuits.

Managing the Risks

If you're considering a home near power lines and you don't like looking at them, or you have concerns about their possible health effects, all you can do is make sure it is far enough away to alleviate or minimize your concerns. The most conservative approach when choosing a home is to avoid being directly under or right next to these sources of EMFs— get five hundred or more feet away from transmission lines. This concept has been labeled in the EMF literature as "prudent avoidance." Once you're in a home, there is no way to reduce EMF levels caused by power lines. Utility companies can reduce the levels of EMFs emitted from existing power lines, but the cost to do so can be extremely high. Methods to minimize EMF levels from new power lines are also available—options include burying lines or changing the shape of transmission towers. Some utilities have adopted policies and practices to minimize EMF levels at the edge of their rights-of-way.

If power lines are being planned for your neighborhood, for your own comfort, and so you can respond to the questions and concerns of potential buyers, verify that they will be located an acceptable distance away and will be constructed, operated, and maintained correctly.

Contact the utility or the government agency with authority over the power lines for financial or technical help to correct a problem and manage the associated risks.

Regulatory Outlook

At present, there are no federal EMF exposure standards, although the issue has been raised before Congress in the past few years. The major federal role at present is to fund scientific research—the Department of Energy, the Food and Drug Administration, the National Cancer Institute, and the EPA, among others, are actively sponsoring research on EMF health impacts. Many EMF status reports are expected by the end of 1996 as regulators continue to grapple with the complexities of the EMF issue, including the lack of useful data for setting health-based exposure standards.

A number of states (including California, Colorado, Connecticut, Florida, Illinois, New Jersey, New York, Ohio, Rhode Island, Texas, and Wisconsin) have some kind of EMF standard, guideline, or policy. Many require utilities to avoid populated areas or places like schools or day-care centers when planning power lines. New York and Florida are the only states that have specific EMF standards for new and upgraded power lines—they set allowable EMF levels at the edge of the right-of-way. However, these are *not* health-based exposure standards but rather are based on averages for existing power lines.

The siting of power lines is a heavily regulated activity—state public utility agencies and local land use boards play a large role in the decision to locate or to expand existing rights-of-way. When siting and approving new rights-of-way, most state agencies follow a prudent avoidance strategy, requiring that power lines be sited at some minimum distance from homes as a precaution in light of the inconclusive nature of EMF research. Today, due in large part to the EMF controversy, siting of power lines is, to say the least, difficult.

What to Look For

Obviously you can't see EMFs, so you need to look for their source. It is hard to miss power lines close to a property—they are supported by tall steel or wood towers. Electrified rail tracks are also a potentially significant source of EMFs near residential properties. Keep in mind that

EMFs decrease quickly with distance—depending on the voltage and current, power lines located three hundred to one thousand feet away may not generate EMFs that are measurable on your property.

Where to Find Help and Further Information

Ask the neighbors and town land use or building officials about the presence of nearby power lines and check with the local zoning board or electric utility company to see if there are plans for future power line rights-of-way in the area. Historic aerial photographs, USGS and Sanborn Fire Insurance maps, and local land use maps can help confirm the presence of existing or proposed power lines (see Appendix 3). Although electric utilities are sensitive, for obvious reasons, about the EMF issue, they will provide additional information.

EMF levels can easily be measured using portable devices known as "gaussmeters." You can buy (for $100 to $200) or rent one (generally for under $75), or have an inspector take the measurement for you as part of the home inspection (for an additional cost, often up to $200). Once you have a measurement, what do you do with it? Remember, at present there is no way to interpret the results because there aren't any accepted and established safe standards in the United States to use as a benchmark. Recognize that inside a home, many electric appliances will give off higher readings than the power lines down the street. However, the readings *can* tell you how a home compares with the average home and might give you the comfort that a home's levels are no higher than the norm. The utility may perform these tests for home owners, sometimes at no cost; these tests may also be conducted by a qualified electrical engineering consultant.

Contact the EPA or your state environmental or health agency for additional information or assistance (see Appendix 4).

For more information, see National Institute of Environmental Health Sciences and U.S. Department of Energy, *Questions and Answers About Electric and Magnetic Fields Associated With the Use of Electric Power*, DOE/EE-0040, 1995; U.S. Environmental Protection Agency, *Questions and Answers About Electric and Magnetic Fields*, 402-R-92-009, 1992.

The Bottom Line

A clear bottom line is difficult to define for the complex and uncertain risks associated with EMFs. Proximity to utility power lines can devalue a home because of the fear of EMFs or because buyers may consider them an eyesore. However, the speculated health risks of EMFs may be exaggerated. Even if the experts finally agree that there isn't any health risk (remember, it is impossible to prove a negative), until the media and general public accept this, there will be some financial risk. Scientists are still studying the EMF issue, and they will be for a while. Since the scientific and regulatory community has not reached a definite conclusion about EMF safety, concerns remain, and in the absence of conclusive science, it is left to the courts to make decisions about health and financial impacts. To date, EMF personal injury lawsuits have not been successful due to the inability of claimants to demonstrate that their illness was caused by EMFs; however, many lawsuits are pending. If you already own property close to power lines, there isn't much you can do other than to get more information and be prepared to respond to the questions and concerns of potential buyers. Risk-adverse buyers should practice their own prudent avoidance to avoid unnecessary EMF exposures. Today's buyers should keep in mind that the EMF debate may still be unresolved when they want to sell in the future.

29. FARMS AND AGRICULTURAL PROPERTIES

Risks: HEALTH   ⊕ ⊕   FINANCIAL $ $

Background

Farms as covered here include all types of commercial and noncommercial crop and livestock farms, ranches, nurseries, vineyards, pastures, and any other agricultural venture—from a small Vermont dairy farm to a thousand-acre California citrus plantation. Farming, the bucolic, "natural" endeavor of the countryside, entails many operations and practices that can have serious environmental impacts on the farm and on neighboring properties.*

Recent studies identify agriculture as the greatest source of water pollution in the United States; it contributes more than half of the pollutants entering our rivers and lakes. Farm pollutants include fertiliz-

---

* Many existing and new residential developments are built on former farms or agricultural properties. We'd like a nickel for each time we've been told by friends and colleagues that the nice piece of property they just bought in the country has no environmental problems because there's no industry nearby—it's just old farmland. There are many issues to be aware of when considering "just" farmland. While this section deals with farms as an off-site hazard, if you're buying former agricultural property or a house on an old farm, the issues raised here should be reviewed in the context of on-site hazards, too.

ers, pesticides, and herbicides; animal wastes; petroleum products; and solvents. Storm water runoff can cause erosion or contain pollutants that impact nearby public drinking water supplies, private wells, and other bodies of water.

Groundwater pollution from farms is also a significant problem for rural areas without public water supplies; more than 95 percent of the rural U.S. population relies on groundwater for drinking water. Nitrates from fertilizers and manure, bacteria from livestock waste, and pesticides and herbicides can seep down through the soil and pollute groundwater. Actions such as soil tilling and irrigation can worsen the problem by increasing the leaching of contaminants.

The following are some of the major farm issues and activities that pose financial, health, and environmental problems for nearby property owners.

Chemicals Fertilizers and pesticides have long been, and continue to be, used extensively on farms. The mixing and application, and over-application, as well as the improper storage and disposal, of these chemicals have caused problems on many farms. Pesticides may also cause air pollution through what's called "pesticide drift" to nearby properties (see Hazard 42, Pesticides).

Noise and Odors Noise from animals and farm equipment and vehicles can disturb neighbors. Odors from animals and their wastes, manure piles, fertilizers, and pesticides applications are a part of life near most farms.

Fuel Storage Tanks Aboveground and underground fuel storage tanks for farm vehicles and machinery are common at farms. As elsewhere, many of these tanks leak and pollute the groundwater. In some cases, they are long forgotten and remain buried, slowly leaking their contents.

Outbuildings Storage sheds and other buildings where excess, expired, or banned farm chemicals and wastes are stored are also sources of groundwater pollution.

Vehicle and Equipment Maintenance Another common source of pollution at farms is vehicle and equipment maintenance. Petroleum-based wastes, such as fuels, oils, lubricants, and solvents, used for tractors and other farm machinery, were often dumped into septic systems, dry wells, and farm landfills, or straight onto the ground.

Landfills Farm landfills, where owners or others may have dumped toxic materials, are another source of concern. Before the 1970s and the birth of modern environmental law, which banned such dumps, many farms disposed of household garbage, building debris often contaminated with lead and asbestos, containers used to store farm chemicals, machinery parts, batteries, waste oils, hydraulic fluids, solvents, and other toxic chemicals on some remote portion of the farm. One family that spent $1.5 million to buy more than one hundred acres of "pristine" farmland in upstate New York later discovered buried batteries, underground fuel tanks, machinery, crankcases, garbage, and other junk all around the property.

Irrigation Farms often require a lot of water for irrigation, and it is often pumped from wells or nearby bodies of water. This water use can impact the availability (yield) of well water at nearby properties.

Health Risks

As discussed above, there are a number of ways that activities at farms can pollute groundwater, most commonly by use of fertilizers and pesticides. Nearby home owners using drinking water wells may face certain health risks if groundwater is contaminated (see Hazard 4, Drinking Water: Private Wells). For example, nitrates from fertilizers can cause serious problems. In 1986, a baby girl living near a farm in South Dakota died from a rare illness known as blue baby syndrome, caused by high nitrate levels in the blood; her home's drinking water had nitrate levels fifteen times higher than the EPA's drinking water standard. High levels of harmful bacteria from manure piles can contaminate drinking water supplies, as well as impact nearby streams, ponds, or lakes used for recreation.

Ingestion of or breathing pesticides can be hazardous to human health; problems range from skin irritation to chronic respiratory conditions to cancer and birth defects (see Hazard 42, Pesticides). "Pesticide drift" can especially affect the young, the elderly, and those with respiratory problems.

Finally, odors and noise from a farm can be objectionable and disrupt your use and enjoyment of your property. Often, impacts from farms may be of short duration or seasonal, depending on when activities, such as fertilizing and planting, occur.

Financial Risks

Proximity to a farm can devalue properties. For example, a home owner in Colorado was awarded $30,000 ($20,000 for property devaluation and the rest for "impairment to quality of life") for dust, odors, and other problems from a nearby hog farm. Homes with drinking water wells polluted by chemicals or storm water runoff from a farm will be devalued and difficult to sell. Even if a problem is addressed, a property may be devalued because of stigma.

Potential buyers may ask about soil or water problems from a nearby farm. Odors and noise from a farm can affect a buyer's decision and the negotiations.

Other financial risks:
- ▶ Liability for nondisclosure; see Disclosure Obligations, pages 13–19.
- ▶ Costs associated with contaminated drinking water; see Hazard 4, Drinking Water: Private Wells.
- ▶ Costs for short- or long-term medical treatment and monitoring; property damage (such as harm to livestock, crops, or landscaping); and legal and expert fees.

Managing the Risks

See Hazard 4, Drinking Water: Private Wells, for a discussion of how to manage risks if a drinking water well is contaminated.

If you're looking at a home near a farm, expect odors and noise. If you have concerns, make sure that you'll be far enough away and that there are substantial vegetative buffers to minimize them. If odors or pesticide drift are an occasional problem, closing windows or modifying a home's ventilation or heating and cooling system may reduce (but not eliminate) the amount of contaminants entering the home.

If there is a problem, contact the farm owner for financial or technical assistance to correct it and manage the associated risks.

Regulatory Outlook

Farms must comply with applicable federal, state, and local environmental laws and regulations. Although many historic problems linger, the EPA and other agencies at all levels regulate a farm's use, storage, and disposal of pesticides and fertilizers; installation, monitoring, and removal of fuel storage tanks; disposal of hazardous wastes; and cleanup of contaminated soil and water supplies. Note that wastewater and storm water discharges from farms are exempt from the permitting requirements under the federal Clean Water Act. Odor problems and complaints are typically handled by state and local environmental and health agencies.

In addition, federal agencies, including the EPA, the U.S. Department of Agriculture, the Department of the Interior, the Department of Commerce, and the U.S. Army Corps of Engineers, provide assistance to farmers to address existing problems, reduce their sources of pollution, and better manage their environmental impacts. Many farms now use various techniques to protect groundwater supplies, such as reducing water usage to limit leaching of farm chemicals, curtailing and even eliminating the use of certain fertilizers and pesticides, and using less harmful chemicals and natural methods to control weeds.

More and more farm owners are becoming sensitive to their environmental impacts on neighbors; problems will diminish as farmers improve their practices and regulatory agency oversight and private lawsuits over contamination and odors increase. However, we offer a word of caution: many lawsuits arise *after* people move near an existing farm. Recognize that many states have right-to-farm laws that prohibit "nuisance" lawsuits against farms that meet GAAP—generally accepted agricultural practices. (If you choose to move near a farm—"come to the nuisance"—make the move with your eyes open and your nose blocked.)

What to Look For

Farms are everywhere—they come in all sizes and types. Many home owners have small farms where they may keep horses, roosters, chickens, and other domestic animals that can have environmental impacts, though somewhat less than a large commercial farm. Some farms will be obvious, while others, especially former farms that have been developed for other uses, will be more difficult to spot. Remember that odors and noise may be only an intermittent problem, depending on the season, what operations are occurring at the farm, and which way the wind is blowing. Inspecting the home during planting and harvesting seasons may give you a good sense of the degree of odors and the level of noise that you can expect. If the home is very close to a farm, inspect the property for visible signs of contamination, such as stained soil, stressed vegetation, or an oil sheen on any body of water.

If a well is in use, taste and smell the water; however, laboratory tests are usually needed to detect contamination. If a water treatment system or bottled water is used, find out why (see Hazard 4, Drinking Water: Private Wells).

Where to Find Help and Further Information

Check with neighbors and town land use or building officials about any problems from a nearby farm. Ask about underground storage tanks and past spills, and known problems with drinking water supplies. Owners and potential buyers of homes with wells should test the water for chemicals such as pesticides, petroleum, metals, bacteria, nitrates, and other compounds. Tests for pesticides can be expensive. If you can find out about the history of the farm and what crops were grown, you may be able to limit your water tests to specific chemicals and pesticides as appropriate (for example, if apple trees were grown, you may need to look for lead, arsenic, and organic pesticides, among others). Coordinate water and soil tests with a qualified laboratory or consultant.

Historic aerial photographs and USGS and Sanborn Fire Insurance maps can help confirm the presence of a historic farm (see Appendix 3).

Contact the EPA or your state environmental or health agency for additional information or assistance (see Appendix 4).

The Bottom Line

Proximity to a farm or agricultural property can impact the value of a home. Farm chemicals and activities can contaminate private drinking water wells and pose significant health and financial risks. Buyers of homes with private wells that are near or on a farm or land that was a farm should have the water tested to see if there is any reason for concern. The costs to address contaminated water are high, and the value of a property with a water problem will be significantly reduced. Odors and noise can be overwhelming at times and affect the use and enjoyment of a home. If you move near a farm, accept the fact that you'll have to deal with these issues.

30. GAS STATIONS

Risks: HEALTH   ⊕ ⊕   FINANCIAL $ $

Background

Gas stations, whether new or old, can pose health and financial risks to nearby homes, especially those with private wells. Leaking underground storage tanks that may have contained gasoline, diesel fuel, kerosene, or waste oil; hazardous waste spills from vehicle maintenance activities; autobody repair (see Hazard 25, Autobody Shops); and air pollution from fuels and other chemicals used at gas stations are all potential problems.

The environmental concern over underground storage tanks is simple: they can leak. Historically, underground storage tanks at gas sta-tions were made from steel—with time, the tanks and their fittings rusted and leaked. Because of this, the EPA and state environmental agencies have set a fifteen-year life expectancy for underground storage tanks. It's safe to say that most gas stations have had a leaking tank or spill. When a tank leaks, the potential for contaminants to reach a nearby property's well depends on several factors: the amount of gas or waste oil released, when the leak occurred, soil conditions, the direction and distance from the gas station to the property, and the depth of the drinking water well. Leaking tanks from gas stations are known to have contaminated wells more than a mile away.

Over the past ten years or so, owners of gas stations everywhere have been forced to remove and replace their underground storage tanks, which had been "out-of-sight, out-of-mind" for so long. In most cases, soil or groundwater contamination has been found. Lucky gas station owners have been required to remove only small amounts of contami-nated soil; others have not been so fortunate—in situations where there is serious groundwater contamination, it requires years and hundreds of thousands of dollars to complete the cleanup. For example, the cleanup of soil and groundwater contamination from an old abandoned gas station in West Point, Indiana, that polluted wells at eleven nearby homes with gasoline is estimated to cost more than $2.5 million. The home owners are now seeking $12.4 million for property and personal injury damages from the oil companies that supplied gas to the now-deceased gas station owner. Leaking tanks at many other sites have yet to be discovered. In some cases, existing tanks have not reached their life expectancy or may not have been tested for leaks. In other instances, property owners may not even be aware that their property was formerly used as a gas station. For example, some corner lots in older cities and suburbs were gas stations at one time, and leaking tanks may still lurk beneath them.

Maintenance and repair activities at gas stations are also concerns. These activities require various chemicals and generate wastes like used motor oil, solvents (such as chlorinated cleaners and kerosene), lead acid batteries, freon, and antifreeze. Spills resulting from deliveries of fuels and other materials and improper storage and disposal of chemi-cals and wastes have polluted soil and groundwater at many sites. Past disposal of toxic wastes into floor drains or sinks connected to dry wells or septic systems is another common cause of groundwater pollution.

Air pollution, and associated odors from fuel storage and pumping, is sometimes a problem. Homes near gas stations may be affected by storm water runoff tainted with oil or gas, solvents, heavy metals, and other pollutants. These pollutants can impact lawns and gardens, wetlands, ponds, and lakes. Other issues, such as noise, traffic, and lights from a gas station, can also be a concern to nearby residents.

Health Risks

Spills and leaks of hazardous chemicals from a gas station can impact human health, particularly through contamination of drinking water sources. Gasoline, a mixture of many volatile petroleum products, is the major groundwater pollutant from gas stations. At relatively low levels, gasoline contamination can be smelled and tasted, thereby rendering water unpalatable. Health risks from drinking water with low levels of gasoline or associated contaminants range from headaches to cancer. The toxic components of gasoline include benzene, which is suspected of causing cancer and liver and kidney damage; toluene; and lead from gasoline that leaked before leaded fuels were banned. A relatively new gasoline additive known as methyl-tertiary-butyl-ether (MTBE) is being evaluated by the EPA as a possible cancer-causing chemical. The discovery of MTBE in a drinking water well is often the first clue of a nearby leaking gas tank. Other possible groundwater contaminants from gas stations that can pose health risks include diesel fuel, kerosene, waste oils, and solvents. In addition, air inside homes located above groundwater containing high levels of certain organic compounds can become contaminated and pose a variety of health problems to occupants.

Leaking tanks are also a potential health hazard if fumes migrate and build up in the basement of a nearby home. The fumes can be toxic when inhaled, and could be ignited by electrical sparks or the pilot light of a gas appliance. Finally, odors from fueling activities, noise, traffic, and lights, as well as a temporary road closing or evacuation after a spill incident, can cause minor health problems and disrupt the use and enjoyment of your property.

Financial Risks

Due to aesthetic concerns, stigma, or actual problems, proximity to a gas station can devalue properties and pose other financial risks. Nearby home owners using drinking water wells are at risk if the groundwater is contaminated. Stories of hapless home owners and their financial nightmares abound. For example, in 1988, gasoline from leaking tanks at a gas station on the Massachusetts Turnpike was discovered in a private drinking water well located more than half a mile away. The family incurred costs for well water testing, installation of a permanent water treatment system, and the use of bottled water. Additional costs included increased electricity bills and legal and consultant fees. The family was reimbursed for only some of these costs. In 1993, a family in Ottawa, Canada, was forced to abandon their home when more than one thousand gallons of gasoline leaked from a nearby gas station and contaminated the soil and groundwater beneath their house. The family never got to return home. Their financial losses (aside from physical and emotional problems) were estimated at more than $200,000, excluding legal fees. Their insurance company paid only a small fraction of their relocation and temporary housing expenses, which totaled more than $24,000. The family, who continued to pay the mortgage on their abandoned home until it was razed, ultimately sued for relocation costs and for devaluation of the home—their legal battle continues today. In another example, several families in Durham, North Carolina, whose wells were contaminated with fuel from a nearby gas station, had to use bottled water for bathing, cooking, and drinking for years before they were ultimately connected to a public water supply.

Homes with property or wells polluted by a gas station will be devalued and difficult to sell. Even if a problem is addressed and cleaned up, a property may be devalued because of stigma. Prospective buyers of a property that uses well water and is near a gasoline station may ask for information about possible contamination. Other issues, such as odors, lights, traffic, and noise, can also affect a buyer's decision and the negotiations.

Other financial risks:

- ▶ Liability for nondisclosure; see Disclosure Obligations, pages 13–19.
- ▶ Costs associated with contaminated drinking water; see Hazard 4, Drinking Water: Private Wells.
- ▶ Costs for short- or long-term medical treatment and monitoring; property damage (such as harm to livestock, crops, or landscaping); legal and expert fees; and inconvenience and relocation costs due to forced evacuation following an accident.

Managing the Risks

See Hazard 4, Drinking Water: Private Wells, for a discussion of how to manage risks if a drinking water well is contaminated.

In many states, publicly funded cleanup programs may provide financial assistance to home owners to respond to environmental problems from a gas station's leaking underground tanks; if a property qualifies, there may be money available for hooking up to a public water supply, for the installation of a water treatment system, or for the evaluation and cleanup of the contamination. If there is a problem, home owners should contact the gas station for financial or technical help to correct it and manage the associated risks. While the individual owners of many gas stations, both active and abandoned, may not be able to afford an expensive cleanup, the corporate parent or franchise may be able to do so.

If you're looking at a home near a gas station, expect some traffic, noise, odors, and lights. If you are concerned about these issues, make sure that you'll be far enough away and that there are substantial vegetative buffers to minimize them. If there is an occasional odor problem, closing windows or modifying a home's ventilation or heating and cooling system may reduce (but not eliminate) the amount of contaminants entering the home.

Regulatory Outlook

Gas stations must comply with federal, state, and local environmental laws and regulations that apply to underground and aboveground storage tanks, hazardous waste–generating activities, and air pollution sources. As with many federal environmental programs, the EPA often allows the states to run these programs so long as they are at least as stringent as the federal programs. The EPA and state environmental agencies regulate the storage and dispensing of flammable materials such as gasoline, and the storage and disposal of waste oils and hazardous wastes. Programs governing commercial underground gasoline and waste oil storage tanks cover notification, installation, spill prevention, corrosion protection, leak detection, recordkeeping, and cleanups. For example, existing tanks must be upgraded or replaced by 1998. New tanks must be designed and installed in ways that minimize the chance of leaks and tanks must now be monitored so that leaks are detected early. Tank owners must also post a bond, or use other financial mechanisms, so that money is available for any environmental problems that might arise.

Meeting requirements of the stringent new environmental laws is costly; many mom-and-pop gas stations have been forced to go out of business or sell to bigger oil companies. Because of the limited financial resources of many individual gas station owners, as well as the abundance of numerous abandoned old stations, "leaking underground storage tank cleanup programs" have been set up in many states as a way to fund investigations and cleanups.

Depending on the state, many of the hazardous vehicle fluids, such as waste oils and antifreeze, can be recycled for reuse, thereby minimizing disposal costs for gas station owners and eliminating some of the incentive to dispose of these materials illegally. Finally, recent changes to the Clean Air Act, such as requiring the use of vapor recovery systems—the equipment on gas pumps that captures gas vapors and minimizes their release into the air—will decrease air pollution from gas stations.

Federal and state environmental agencies can issue compliance or cleanup orders to owners of gas stations that violate laws or are contaminating soil or groundwater. Failure to comply can subject a gas station owner to both civil and criminal penalties.

What to Look For

Gas stations are everywhere—drive around the area to locate both active and closed ones. The sites of many former gas stations are now used for other businesses or are vacant—these sites may have leaking tanks that no one knows about. Look for other commercial businesses that may have gas tanks—auto dealerships, car rental companies, postal facilities, bus yards, airports, hospitals, police and fire stations, delivery companies, building contractors, laundries, or any company that uses a truck fleet. Residential properties may have underground gasoline tanks—some home owners installed such tanks for private use during the fuel crisis in the 1970s (see Hazard 9, Heating Oil Storage Tanks). Check the deed to ensure the property was not used as a gas station by a former owner.

If a well is in use, taste and smell the water; however, laboratory tests are usually needed to detect contamination. If a water treatment system or bottled water is used, find out why (see Hazard 4, Drinking Water: Private Wells). If a home is close to a gas station, check for petroleum and gasoline odors and visible signs of contamination like stained soils, stressed vegetation, or an oil sheen on any surface body of water.

Where to Find Help and Further Information

If you own or are thinking about buying a property with a drinking water well close to a gas station, talk to the station owner and ask how the underground tanks are installed and monitored. Ask, too, about waste handling and air pollution–control practices. Many station owners have spent thousands of dollars on such measures and may be willing to explain their operations and the relevant safety features.

Owners and potential buyers of nearby homes with wells should consider testing the water (see Hazard 4, Drinking Water: Private Wells). Coordinate tests with a qualified laboratory, consultant, or home inspector. A water analysis for oils and gasoline compounds will run about $100 to $200. Water should be tested for petroleum hydrocarbons, lead, and BTEX (toxic gasoline constituents—*b*enzene, *t*oluene, *e*thylbenzene, and *x*ylene).

State health and environmental agencies and the local fire marshal will have copies of reports filed by owners of underground tanks—these are public records available for review. Check the reports and ask the agencies about past complaints, spill reports, or known environmental problems at a specific gas station. See Appendix 3 for a discussion of relevant databases. While these reports are a good source of information, they are not infallible. Beware: reports are often not filed for historic or abandoned tanks. Historic aerial photographs and Sanborn Fire Insurance maps may depict the presence of above- or underground tanks (see Appendix 3). Contact the EPA or your state environmental or health agency for assistance or additional information (such as available state cleanup funds) (see Appendix 4).

The Bottom Line

Proximity to a gas station can impact the value of a home due to aesthetic or stigma issues. Traffic, noise, odors, and lights can affect the use and enjoyment of a home. While catastrophic accidents such as explosions are rare, leaking tanks or spills are common and can pose significant health and financial risks if drinking water wells are contaminated. Buyers of nearby homes with wells should have the water tested to see if there is any reason for concern. The costs to address contaminated water are high and the value of a property with a drinking water problem will be significantly reduced. Buyers of all homes should check to ensure that the property was not previously used as a gas station.

31. GOLF COURSES

Risks: HEALTH ⊕   FINANCIAL $

Background

There are about fifteen thousand public and private golf courses in the United States and more than three hundred new courses are built each year. Because of the boom in the game's popularity, residential developments are springing up around and even on golf courses. Golf courses can be desirable neighbors; they generally provide aesthetically pleasing, open, quiet recreational spaces. A vision of golf courses as pristine green landscapes is deceiving, however; to achieve that look means years of excessive use of fertilizers, pesticides, herbicides, and other chemicals. A study of golf courses on Long Island, New York, found that more than fifty thousand pounds of pesticides (about eighteen pounds per acre) are used per year—more than seven times the amount that local farmers use for the same acreage!

Environmental hazards posed by golf courses arise from the improper use, storage, and disposal of pesticides and fertilizers, which can contaminate public drinking water sources or private wells at nearby homes. Golf courses are often built near bodies of water, and storm water runoff carrying pollutants can impact groundwater and surface water as well as natural resources, like plants and wildlife. For example, migratory birds often land on golf courses, and pesticides have been linked to many bird deaths.

Other issues, such as the improper use, storage, and disposal of chemicals and oil at vehicle and equipment maintenance garages, leaking underground fuel storage tanks, and large septic systems, can pose threats to groundwater and nearby homes. Golf courses require a lot of water for irrigation; it is often pumped from wells or a nearby body of water. These water uses can impact the availability (yield) of well water at nearby properties. Odors from pesticides and fertilizers, decomposing landscaping wastes, and manure may be a concern at some golf courses. Other aesthetic issues include noise and traffic.

Health Risks

Pesticides and fertilizers used at golf courses, as well as pollution from vehicle maintenance and fuel storage activities, can impact human health, particularly through contamination of drinking water sources (see Hazard 4, Drinking Water: Private Wells, and Hazard 42, Pesticides). Also, on certain days (especially holidays, weekends, and when the course holds a special event), the noise and traffic associated with a golf course may be bothersome and disrupt the use and enjoyment of a property.

Financial Risks

While proximity to a golf course can actually enhance residential property values, golf courses with environmental problems will probably devalue nearby properties. Residents of nearby homes with private wells on or near a golf course are at risk if groundwater is contaminated. Water usage at a golf course can affect the availability and quality of water for nearby homes. Homes with contaminated wells will be devalued and difficult to sell. And even if the problem is addressed, the property may be devalued because of stigma.

Buyers of properties near golf courses may ask about odors, traffic, noise, and water usage. These aesthetic issues can also impact property values.

Other financial risks:

▶ Liability for nondisclosure; see Disclosure Obligations, pages 13–19.
▶ Costs associated with contaminated drinking water; see Hazard 4, Drinking Water: Private Wells.
▶ Costs for short- or long-term medical treatment and monitoring; property damage (such as harm to livestock, crops, or landscaping); and legal and expert fees.

Managing the Risks

See Hazard 4, Drinking Water: Private Wells, for a discussion of how to manage risks if a drinking water well is contaminated.

Buyers who are looking at a property near a golf course and are concerned about potential impacts should make sure that the home is far enough away from the golf course and that there is sufficient vegetative buffers to minimize noise, sight, and pollutant runoff problems. Buyers should also consider future expansion plans by the golf course.

If there is a problem, contact the golf course for financial or technical assistance to correct it and manage the associated risks.

Regulatory Outlook

All golf courses must comply with applicable federal, state, and local environmental laws and regulations. For example, under various environmental programs, the EPA and state agencies regulate: the types of pesticides that may be used (although actual use goes relatively unchecked) and how they are stored and disposed of; the installation, maintenance, and monitoring of underground fuel storage tanks; and the cleanup of contaminated soil, surface water, and drinking water supplies. Golf course owners are becoming more sensitive to their environmental impacts on neighboring land, including private homes; in time, others will, too, as regulatory agency oversight and private lawsuits increase.

Not all golf courses have environmental problems. In fact, many are not just looking green, they're actually being "green." The Audubon Cooperative Sanctuary Program for Golf Courses, created by the Audubon Society of New York and funded by the United States Golf Association, is working with more than eleven hundred public and private U.S. and Canadian golf courses to improve their environmental practices. These golf courses are being managed to promote and protect the environment by minimizing or eliminating pesticides, properly selecting and applying fertilizers, reducing water usage, and creating habitats for birds and other wildlife.

What to Look For

Drive around the neighborhood and beyond to locate any golf courses. If a well is in use, taste and smell the water; however, laboratory tests are usually needed to detect contamination. If a water treatment system or bottled water is used, find out why (see Hazard 4, Drinking Water: Private Wells). If the home is adjacent to a golf course, inspect the property for stressed or burned-out vegetation, which may indicate pesticide or fertilizer contamination.

Where to Find Help and Further Information

Check with the neighbors and the town land use or building officials to identify existing or planned golf courses (also ask if there are any anticipated expansion plans). Find out about any problems associated with the golf course or known impacts to drinking water wells for homes in the vicinity. If wells are in use, find out if there are any problems with the water supply, especially during the summer months.

Owners and potential buyers of nearby homes with wells should consider testing the water (see Hazard 4, Drinking Water: Private Wells).
Coordinate tests with a qualified laboratory, consultant, or home inspector. Contact the EPA or your state environmental or health agency for
additional information or assistance (see Appendix 4).

The Bottom Line

A golf course will generally make a good neighbor—and may even increase property values. However, existing and planned golf courses can
impact the use and enjoyment of your home, and pesticides, fertilizers,
and underground fuel tanks used at golf courses can contaminate
nearby drinking water wells. Buyers of nearby homes that rely on private
wells should have the water tested to see if there is any reason for concern. The costs to address contaminated water are high and the value of
a property with a drinking water problem will be significantly reduced.

32. HAZARDOUS WASTE FACILITIES

Risks: HEALTH ⊕ ⊕   FINANCIAL $ $

Background

Triggered largely by the public outcry over the toxic waste dumping at
Love Canal in upstate New York, Congress passed the Resource Conservation and Recovery Act (RCRA) in 1976. RCRA places stringent controls on the treatment, storage, and disposal of hazardous chemical
wastes produced by industry as well as the wastes generated at
Superfund sites (see Hazard 49, Superfund Sites) undergoing cleanup.
RCRA is a complicated and lengthy law with complex definitions of
"hazardous waste" and a program that specifies "cradle-to-grave" requirements for how hazardous waste is tracked and handled from generation to disposal. Under the law, companies that generate hazardous
waste must either be permitted to treat or dispose of the waste themselves or send it to licensed treatment, storage, or disposal facilities
(TSDFs). Once delivered to a TSDF, wastes may be temporarily held in
drums or large holding tanks, treated by physical or chemical means,
burned in special hazardous waste incinerators, or buried in approved
landfills. Many TSDFs recycle valuable resources from wastes, allowing
them to be reused instead of disposed of. TSDFs with operations that

may impact groundwater (such as landfills or treatment lagoons) often install test wells to monitor groundwater quality.

There are numerous commercial TSDFs located all over the country, and many more businesses that manage their own hazardous wastes on-site. In order to get a permit, all TSDFs must go through a complex and lengthy permitting procedure that includes public hearings, and must meet strict operating procedure guidelines. TSDF operations vary widely—where one operation may present a myriad of risks, another may have none. The possible environmental concerns that neighbors may have with TSDFs include soil and groundwater contamination, which may occur as a result of past practices, accidental spills, or poor design and operating practices; air pollution and odors from storage and treatment processes or as a result of waste incineration (see Hazard 34, Incinerators); and trucks bringing hazardous waste into the facility, and the associated noise and risk of accidents and spills.

Health Risks

There are numerous possible soil, groundwater, and air contaminants that could be associated with a TSDF, depending on exactly what has been and is done at the site—some of the more common hazardous compounds include metals, waste acids, cyanide, and organic compounds. If past or present operations at a TSDF have impacted groundwater, there may be serious health risks to the people relying on private drinking water wells. In addition, air inside homes located above groundwater containing high levels of certain organic compounds can become contaminated and pose a variety of health problems to occupants. As with groundwater, toxic air pollutants from TSDF operations have the potential to be released to nearby properties, depending on the specific operation. Health risks to neighbors could also result if a spill occurred when loading or storing wastes at a TSDF or in the event of a major truck accident or spill (see Hazard 4, Drinking Water: Private Wells, for a discussion of health risks associated with contaminated well water; Hazard 34, Incinerators; Hazard 43, Petroleum Storage Terminals; and Hazard 49, Superfund Sites).

Financial Risks

Properties near a TSDF known to have air pollution, odor, noise, or soil or groundwater contamination problems may be devalued and difficult to sell. Due to stigma, some buyers will be wary of any property close to a TSDF, even if there are no actual environmental problems.

Potential buyers may ask a home owner about any environmental problems at a nearby TSDF (such as spills, polluted well water, odors, air pollution, heavy truck traffic, or noise); these may be a point of contention in negotiations over price.

Other financial risks:
- ▶ Liability for nondisclosure; see Disclosure Obligations, pages 13–19.
- ▶ Costs associated with contaminated drinking water; see Hazard 4, Drinking Water: Private Wells.
- ▶ Costs for short- or long-term medical treatment and monitoring; property damage (such as harm to livestock, crops, or landscaping); legal and expert fees; and inconvenience and relocation costs due to forced evacuation following an accident.

Managing the Risks

See Hazard 4, Drinking Water: Private Wells, for a discussion of how to manage risks if a drinking water well is contaminated.

If you're looking at a home near a TSDF, expect some odors, noise, lights, and traffic. If you are concerned about these issues, make sure the home is far enough away and that there are substantial vegetative buffers to minimize them. If there is an occasional odor problem, closing windows or modifying a home's ventilation system may reduce (but not eliminate) the amount of polluted air entering the home. State health and environmental agencies can force a TSDF to minimize odor, noise, or other problems by changing its activities or requiring the facility to install control systems.

If there is a problem, contact the TSDF for financial or technical help to correct it and manage the associated risks.

Regulatory Outlook

TSDFs are heavily regulated: day-to-day operations are governed by RCRA permits issued by the state environmental agency or by the regional EPA office. In addition, specific state rules to protect groundwater from spills and to force cleanup of groundwater, if necessary, will apply to TSDFs. Hazardous waste incinerators and some other TSDFs will have an air permit that defines acceptable levels of air pollutant emissions, sets operating conditions, and may require pollution controls and testing of the stack emissions. Most new incinerators will have "continuous emissions monitors" that sample and test air emissions many times.per hour. Changes to the federal Clean Air Act in 1990 specifically targeted TSDFs as an industry category requiring air pollution controls and, in some cases, permits.

State and federal environmental agencies have authority to issue compliance orders to a facility that violates its permits or that contaminates soil or groundwater. Failure to comply with applicable requirements can subject the TSDF owner to both civil and criminal penalties.

What to Look For

The location of a permitted TSDF may or may not be apparent. Commercial TSDFs that specialize in managing hazardous waste should be easiest to identify; however, keep in mind that many industrial plants are also TSDFs because they manage their wastes on-site. Spend some time in the neighborhood to see if there are unusual odor, noise, or traffic problems. Remember that these problems may be intermittent and vary with the time of day or local weather and wind conditions. Talk to the neighbors, but remember that people have varying tolerance levels for nuisance problems.

If a well is in use, taste and smell the water; however, laboratory tests are usually needed to detect contamination. If a water treatment system or bottled water is used, find out why (see Hazard 4, Drinking Water: Private Wells). If a home is close to a TSDF, check for visible signs of contamination like stained soil, stressed vegetation, or an oil sheen on any surface body of water.

Where to Find Help and Further Information

The EPA and state environmental agencies maintain records of all permitted and proposed TSDFs in a given area and should be able to tell you about a particular facility and any known or suspected environmental problems (see Appendix 4). The EPA maintains a computerized database of TSDFs known as RCRIS, which can be used to identify companies that produce, treat, or dispose of hazardous waste in your area (see Appendix 3). Another tool for finding out what wastes are treated are the annual reports that must be filed by TSDFs with the EPA or state environmental agencies. The local health department may also be able to provide information about complaints or problems associated with a nearby TSDF.

Owners and potential buyers of nearby homes with wells should consider testing the water (see Hazard 4, Drinking Water: Private Wells). Coordinate tests with a qualified laboratory, consultant, or home inspector. Costs will vary from $50 to $200, depending on the number of constituents tested.

The Bottom Line

Proximity to a TSDF can lower property values. While homes near some TSDFs are not at any significant health risk, many TSDFs managed wastes for years prior to passage of the strict regulations under RCRA, so significant soil and groundwater contamination from past practices may exist. Financial and health risks for neighboring properties will depend on the specific situation. If you rely on a private well for drinking water and there is a TSDF nearby, have the water tested. Homes with contaminated wells or soil problems from a TSDF can be devalued and costs to clean up the problems will be significant. Noise, odors, and traffic from TSDF operations can affect the use and enjoyment of your home.

33. HIGHWAYS AND ROADS

Risks: HEALTH ⊕ FINANCIAL $

Background

It may be obvious that highways and roads can be a source of nuisances, like noise, light, vibrations, and odors, to nearby residential properties. However, not so well known is the fact that transportation routes can be plagued with soil and groundwater contamination from maintenance activities, past accidents, and spills.

Road-related spills of gasoline, toxic chemicals, or hazardous waste occur frequently. While most spills are quickly cleaned up and short-term impacts localized, distant drinking water supplies are sometimes affected. Even a gasoline spill from a car accident can contaminate groundwater. Disastrous spills and explosions from tanker trucks carrying large quantities of toxic chemicals or waste have forced the closing of roads and the evacuation of nearby homes, polluted streams and lakes, and contaminated groundwater reserves.

Homes located near a highway can have other environmental problems. Localized air pollution from vehicle emissions can affect indoor air quality in nearby homes. Storm water runoff can cause erosion, and often carries pollutants such as asphalt by-products, oils, gasoline, and salts, which can harm vegetation and pollute wells. In some areas, herbicides are heavily used on roadsides to keep vegetation from encroaching, and can contaminate private drinking water wells (see Hazard 42, Pesticides). Soil along major roads may also contain lead from past vehicle emissions (when lead was used as an additive in gasoline) or as a result of lead-based paint contamination from bridge renovation and de-leading activities (see Hazard 13, Lead-Based Paint).

Some properties situated along rural routes may have contaminated soils and groundwater from historic spraying of oil (sometimes contaminated with toxics such as PCBs or solvents) on dirt roads as a dust suppressant. For example, from 1964 to 1978, more than forty-one thousand gallons of waste oil containing PCBs were applied to local roads in a one-hundred home residential development in Brant, a town in upstate New York—the area became a Superfund site in 1985 (see Hazard 49, Superfund Sites).

Health Risks

Spills of hazardous chemicals or waste on a highway are inevitable and can affect human health, particularly through contamination of drinking water sources (see Hazard 4, Drinking Water: Private Wells). In addition, air inside homes located above groundwater containing high levels of certain organic compounds can become contaminated and pose a variety of health problems to occupants. The most common contaminants from traffic-related accidents are gasoline and other petroleum compounds. For example, in 1992, a tanker truck overturned and released more than ten thousand gallons of gasoline, which spread into a nearby wetlands area and contaminated a significant aquifer that provided drinking water to the town of Reading, Massachusetts. It's still being cleaned up.

Those most at risk from air pollution from highways include the young, the elderly, and those with respiratory problems. The risks are greatest along the most congested roads and vary with geographical area and weather conditions.

With the introduction of unleaded gasoline in the 1970s, lead in soil has decreased and is generally not a significant problem along new roads or in new housing developments. However, lead in soil near some highways may pose a health threat. Although leaded gasoline was banned from use in post-1975 vehicles, soil lead levels still remain high from the decades of emissions from cars using leaded gasoline. One study of homes near heavily traveled roads in Baltimore found soil lead levels as high as 10,900 ppm (more than twenty times the EPA's widely accepted maximum level of 500 ppm). Children living and playing near major roads may be at risk from lead poisoning (see Hazard 13, Lead-Based Paint).

Finally, noise, traffic, odors, vibrations, and sight impacts from a highway, as well as the temporary road closing and evacuation after an accident or spill, can disrupt the use and enjoyment of a property.

Financial Risks

Proximity to a major road or highway can devalue a property regardless of environmental concerns. A home with property or a well polluted by chemicals or storm water runoff from a highway will be further devalued and difficult to sell. And even if a problem is addressed, a property may be devalued because of stigma.

Home buyers may ask about soil or water problems. Other issues, such as odors, lights, traffic, vibrations, and noise from a highway, can also affect a buyer's decision and negotiations over price. The widening or relocation of roads can also impact your ability to use your property and present financial issues.

Other financial risks:
- ▶ Liability for nondisclosure; see Disclosure Obligations, pages 13–19.
- ▶ Costs associated with contaminated drinking water; see Hazard 4, Drinking Water: Private Wells.
- ▶ Costs for short- or long-term medical treatment and monitoring; property damage (such as harm to livestock, crops, or landscaping); legal and expert fees; and inconvenience and relocation costs due to forced evacuation following an accident.

Managing the Risks

See Hazard 4, Drinking Water: Private Wells, for a discussion of how to manage risks if a drinking water well is contaminated.

If the soil around your home or near the road has been contaminated with lead, keep the yard well vegetated and monitor the activities of children in those areas closely. If the soil lead levels are high, consider removing or replacing the topsoil.

Buyers looking at a property near a highway who are concerned about noise, odors, vibrations, or traffic should make sure that the home is far enough away from the highway (factor in any planned expansion) and that there is enough vegetation to act as a buffer and minimize any impacts.

Chemical spills from traffic accidents are rare and impossible to predict. Unless a particular road has a history of such problems, there is only a small risk of a chemical spill at a given location. However, areas where there have been accidents or spills in the past may still have lingering soil or groundwater contamination problems.

If there is a problem with soil or water, contact the appropriate department of transportation (DOT) for financial or technical assistance to correct a problem and manage the associated risks.

Regulatory Outlook

Trucks and other vehicles carrying petroleum products and hazardous chemicals are subject to strict transportation and environmental laws and regulations. The EPA and federal and state DOTs regulate highway safety and the transport of hazardous materials and waste. Transporters of hazardous chemicals must comply with rules concerning training, labeling, handling, packaging, and transportation; they must report and be qualified and prepared to respond to an accident, including demonstrating financial ability to fund a cleanup. Watersheds and other environmentally sensitive areas are sometimes designated as off-limits for transportation of toxic materials. The EPA and state or local environmental agencies respond to spills and provide for emergency cleanups. Most towns also have plans for responding to hazardous spills and for containment along roads.

What to Look For

Drive around the neighborhood and beyond to get a feel for a highway's impact. Inspect a home during rush hour to get a sense of the level of traffic and associated noise and vibrations. If a well is in use, taste and smell the water; however, laboratory tests are usually needed to detect contamination. If a water treatment system or bottled water is used, find out why (see Hazard 4, Drinking Water: Private Wells).

If the home is very close to a highway, inspect the property for stressed or burned-out vegetation, which may be an indication of contamination from past spills, deicing salts, pesticides, or lead in the soil.

Where to Find Help and Further Information

Check with neighbors and town land use or building officials about the impacts of a nearby highway and find out if it is a hazardous waste transportation route. Ask if there are plans for new roads, road widenings, or highway expansions. Inquire about past spills and, if a well is used, their impact on drinking water supplies.

Owners and potential buyers of homes with wells located near a highway should consider testing the water (see Hazard 4, Drinking Water: Private Wells). In addition, if a home is adjacent to a major road or steel bridge, you should consider testing the soil for lead, especially if you have, or are contemplating having, children. Coordinate tests with a qualified laboratory, consultant, or inspector. Contact the EPA or your state environmental or health agency for additional information or assistance (see Appendix 4).

The Bottom Line

Proximity to a highway or busy road can impact property values, as traffic, noise, odors, lights, and vibrations will likely affect the use and enjoyment of a home. Spills of toxic chemicals and hazardous waste— although rare—can pose significant health and financial risks, including the contamination of private drinking water wells. For homes with private wells, water should be tested to see if there is any reason for concern. The costs to address contaminated water are high and the value of a property with a water problem will be significantly reduced. Buyers of all homes should check to ensure that a new highway (or a highway relocation) is not planned for the neighborhood.

34. INCINERATORS

Risks: HEALTH   ⊕ ⊕   FINANCIAL $ $

Background

Incinerators come in all types and sizes and are used to burn a variety of wastes. In addition to incinerators that burn solid waste (trash), there are numerous other special-purpose municipal, commercial,* and industrial incinerators that burn hazardous chemicals, waste oils, sewage sludge, wood waste, old tires, or medical or biological waste. Historically, solid waste incinerators were used by many cities for trash disposal; because of air pollution problems and the availability of relatively low cost landfills, their use decreased drastically through the 1960s. However, since the late 1970s, as existing landfills began to reach capacity and the

---

* Hazardous waste incinerators are also covered in Hazard 32, Hazardous Waste Facilities.

siting of new landfills became more difficult, "resource recovery facilities" ("trash-to-energy" incinerators that produce steam and/or electricity) have been built and continue to be considered as a waste disposal option by communities throughout the country. According to an EPA study, there are more than two hundred municipal waste incinerators in the United States, and about two-thirds of these are resource recovery facilities.

Incinerators produce waste gases that are vented to the atmosphere using tall chimneys or "stacks." The major components in the exhaust gas from an incinerator (or any combustion source, for that matter) are carbon dioxide and water vapor. Nitrogen oxide, one of the pollutants that contributes to ozone and smog problems, is an unavoidable by-product of the combustion process, as are sulfur dioxide and acid vapors, pollutants associated with acid rain. Depending on what is incinerated, exhaust gases may also contain a large variety of other toxic compounds. Toxic components in waste gases from solid-waste incinerators include trace heavy metals (like lead and mercury, from batteries and electrical devices) and organic compounds (dioxin can be produced when plastics are burned; other organic compounds may be components of materials in the garbage, like inks, paints, or household cleaners). The exhaust gases from incinerators will also contain small solid particles, called particulates, some of which will pass through pollution-control equipment. Particulates are composed mostly of inert inorganic materials but may also contain trace levels of toxic metals like cadmium and lead.

Almost all newer incinerators are equipped with air pollution–control equipment, such as filters to remove particles or wet scrubbers to remove other chemical constituents. Older incinerators often had pollution-control devices added on to meet changing laws. Many incinerators operate at very high temperatures, which helps to destroy the toxic organic compounds. Proper operating practices, such as monitoring the materials burned and maintaining a high internal temperature, are important if an incinerator is to operate without pollution problems. Tall stacks are often used at incinerators to get the waste gases high into the atmosphere, where they are diluted and carried away from nearby population centers. However, depending on distance, direction of prevailing winds, and weather conditions, air pollution from incinerators can impact nearby residential areas and nuisance odors can be a problem if an incinerator is improperly designed or operated.

Other possible environmental problems may exist at incinerators. "Waste ash," the dustlike waste produced by all incinerators, contains some toxic heavy metals and may be classified as hazardous waste. Incinerators almost always have elaborate scrubber or filter systems to collect and store waste ash to prevent it from escaping into the environment. However, some ash may blow off the site as a dust; at some incinerator plants, ash may be disposed of on-site.

Solid-waste incinerators, which can take in hundreds of tons of trash daily, often have many of the same problems common to landfills, such as noise, odors, and truck traffic (see Hazard 36, Landfills). Many incinerators also have aboveground or underground tanks to store fuel or chemicals used for pollution control, and these can leak and endanger groundwater supplies. A home near an incinerator may be affected by storm water runoff containing various pollutants that can cause erosion and harm a home's lawn, gardens, wetlands, ponds, lakes, and well water.

Health Risks

Pollution from an incinerator can affect human health through a number of exposure routes. The toxic compounds found in air emissions will depend on what is being burned. Hazard 27, Electric Power Plants, summarizes the health risks from common pollutants associated with almost any combustion process. Air pollution is particularly problematic for the young, the elderly, and those with respiratory ailments.

The most significant toxic compounds from incinerators burning trash can be dioxins (specifically chlorinated dioxins) and trace metals like cadmium, chromium, and arsenic. Scientific debate over the health risks associated with these incinerators is very controversial. Millions of dollars have been spent studying the dioxin issue and there is still no agreement—the EPA's final risk assessment of dioxin is long awaited. Most scientists would agree that the risk from dioxin is probably more significant than the risks posed by other contaminants in an incinerator's exhaust. Although a small increase in cancer risk has been suggested by studies of chemical workers exposed to very high levels of dioxin for extended periods of time, there have been no conclusive studies on the health risks posed to the general population by exposure to very low levels of dioxin released into the air by an incinerator. Until more studies are completed, dioxin is considered a probable human carcinogen. Note that dioxin emissions from older incinerators (those over twenty or so years old) are significantly higher than from new facilities.

If toxic chemicals from various operations at an incinerator pollute groundwater and drinking water wells are in use, there may be serious health risks to people drinking the water (see Hazard 4, Drinking Water:

Private Wells). In addition, air inside homes located above groundwater containing high levels of certain organic compounds can become contaminated and pose a variety of health problems to occupants. Other incinerator issues, such as noise, odors, and traffic, can disrupt the use and enjoyment of a home.

Financial Risks

Properties near an incinerator and affected by its air emissions can be devalued due to concerns about health impacts and aesthetic issues, such as odors. In addition, if an incinerator, through improper storage or disposal of hazardous materials, has contaminated soil or groundwater, downgradient homes with private drinking water wells are at risk. Homes with contaminated wells will be devalued and difficult to sell. And even if a problem is addressed, a property may still be devalued because of stigma. Even if there is no problem, properties may be devalued because of buyers' fears of incinerators and their combustion byproducts, especially dioxin.

A buyer of a property near an incinerator may ask about odors, noise, traffic, or any known contamination of drinking water supplies. Any of these issues may be a point of contention in the negotiations over price.

Other financial risks:
- Liability for nondisclosure; see Disclosure Obligations, pages 13–19.
- Costs associated with contaminated drinking water; see Hazard 4, Drinking Water: Private Wells.
- Costs for short- or long-term medical treatment and monitoring; property damage (such as harm to livestock, crops, or landscaping); legal and expert fees; and inconvenience and relocation costs due to forced evacuation following an accident.

Managing the Risks

See Hazard 4, Drinking Water: Private Wells, for a discussion of how to manage risks if a drinking water well is contaminated.

If you're looking at a home near an incinerator, expect some odors, noise, lights, and traffic. If you are concerned about these issues, make sure the home is far enough away and that there are substantial vegetative buffers to minimize them. If there is an occasional odor problem, closing windows or modifying a home's ventilation system may reduce (but not eliminate) the amount of contaminants entering the home.

State health and environmental agencies may be able to force an incinerator owner or operator to minimize odor, noise, dust, or other problems by changing its activities or requiring the installation of air treatment systems. Unfortunately, an easy, affordable, and quick solution to odors may not be available.

Contact the incinerator for financial or technical help to correct a problem and manage the associated risks.

Regulatory Outlook

Day-to-day operations at incinerators are heavily regulated by the EPA and state or local health and environmental agencies. In addition to requirements for air pollution controls, there are rules for how wastes are received and handled, wastewater discharges, noise levels, storage and management of waste ash and other wastes shipped off-site, and underground storage tanks, as well as rules to protect groundwater from spills and to force the cleanup of soil and groundwater if necessary.

Incinerators are required to have a permit from the EPA or a state or local environmental agency that defines acceptable levels of air pollutant emissions, sets certain operating conditions, and may require pollution controls and regular testing of the stack emissions. Most new incinerators have "continuous emissions monitors" that sample and test certain stack emissions many times per hour. However, pollution problems can result from improper operation or lax regulation. The Clean Air Act Amendments of 1990 set a whole new layer of requirements that will impact new and existing large incinerators. The EPA recently issued regulations that require incinerators to obtain and renew permits every five years and meet stricter limits on emissions for dioxin, particulates, and other pollutants.

State and federal environmental agencies can issue compliance orders to a facility that violates its permits or that contaminates soil or groundwater. Failure to comply with applicable requirements can subject the owner of an incinerator to both civil and criminal penalties.

What to Look For

It should be easy to spot a nearby incinerator—just look for a tall smokestack (usually two hundred feet or more high) next to large industrial-type buildings. However, smaller commercial and industrial incinerators may not be evident at all from the outside. Problems like odors, noise, or traffic may be intermittent and vary with the time of day and local weather and wind conditions. It may be necessary to visit the home you're considering several times to determine if any of these issues are a concern. Talk to the neighbors, but remember that people have varying tolerance levels for nuisance-type problems.

If a well is in use, taste and smell the water; however, laboratory tests are usually needed to detect contamination. If a water treatment system or bottled water is used, find out why (see Hazard 4, Drinking Water: Private Wells). If a home is close to an incinerator, check for visible signs of contamination like stained soil, stressed vegetation, or an oil sheen on any surface body of water.

Where to Find Help and Further Information

Check with neighbors and the town land use or building officials to identify existing or planned incinerators. Often incinerators are depicted on USGS and Sanborn Fire Insurance maps and aerial photographs (see Appendix 3). If there is one nearby, find out about any air pollution or odor problems or any known effects on drinking water supplies for homes in the vicinity. State or local health or environmental agencies may also have information about the location of nearby incinerators and if there are any known or suspected problems in an area; EPA and state environmental databases may also contain useful information (see Appendix 3). If your property is near a sewage treatment plant, find out if it burns sludge (see Hazard 48, Sewage Treatment Plants). Contact the EPA or your state environmental agency for additional information (such as a nearby incinerator's design and operations) or assistance (see Appendix 4).

Contact the owner or regulatory agency to find out what is being done if there are noise, odor, traffic, or other problems. Owners and potential buyers of nearby homes with wells should consider testing the water (see Hazard 4, Drinking Water: Private Wells). Coordinate tests with a qualified laboratory, consultant, or home inspector. Costs will vary from $50 to $200, depending on the number of constituents tested.

The Bottom Line

A home near an incinerator may be devalued due to air pollution, odors, groundwater contamination, or mere stigma. Potential impacts from incinerators will vary depending on what they burn, where they are located, and how they are operated. Odors from incinerators can be a nuisance that will affect the use and enjoyment of a home. In some cases, air pollutants from an incinerator, such as dioxins and heavy metals, may pose serious health risks. Buyers of nearby homes with private wells should have the water tested to see if there is any reason for concern. The costs to address contaminated water are high and the value of a property with a water problem will be significantly reduced.

35. INDUSTRIAL MANUFACTURING PLANTS

Risks: HEALTH   ⊕ ⊕   FINANCIAL $ $

Background

In response to environmental regulations, public concern, and the overall environmental awareness that has developed over the past twenty years, many industries have adopted management practices to minimize pollution and associated risks to human health and the environment. Nationally, companies now spend billions of dollars on pollution prevention, treatment of air and water discharges, and proper management of their waste streams. Nonetheless, nearby residential properties can be impacted by historic activities as well as by ongoing practices at many active industrial facilities.

There is a wide variety of types of manufacturing operations. While the majority of manufacturing plants employ fewer than one hundred people at small facilities, there are thousands of large industrial complexes as well. Operations like automobile manufacturers, steel and paper mills, petroleum refineries, and chemical, electronics, and aircraft manufacturers employ thousands of people and are located on hundreds of acres or more. A facility's age, its history, the types of chemicals used, and the operations and controls at a site will determine possible environmental risks—where one facility may present a myriad of risks, another may have virtually none. Acknowledging that it is impossible to talk about risks from a specific operation, we make a few general observations about health and financial risks associated with manufacturing operations.

- *Soil and groundwater contamination* at industrial sites is, unfortunately, not uncommon. Uncontrolled waste disposal, chemical spills, and underground tanks can contaminate soil and groundwater with metals, solvents, oils, and other toxic pollutants. Since groundwater moves, drinking water wells at properties located hundreds or even thousands of feet away from a pollution source can be impacted.

- *Air pollution* from industrial operations may occur when compounds are emitted without proper controls. Some industrial plants may store and use hazardous chemicals that could be released in the event of a catastrophic accident or spill.
- *Surface water pollution* from wastewater discharges or storm water runoff from manufacturing operations can impact downstream properties.
- *Aesthetic issues* that can impact nearby neighbors include traffic, odors, lighting, visual impacts, and noise.

Local land use laws attempt to segregate residential areas from industrial zones. However, in many parts of the country, homes literally surround industrial plants—they were built because people wanted to live close to where they worked. In other areas, there may be almost no buffer distance at all as residences were developed close to historic industrial land. Industries are critically important to the economic well-being of communities—a challenge for the community and corporate executives has been to keep industries (often the older facilities) located near residences viable without unduly impacting their neighbors.

Almost all of the off-site activities discussed in this section of the book could apply to a particular industrial facility that is near your home or one you are interested in. We refer you to these hazards for more details on concerns like:

- Landfills and Superfund Sites (Hazards 36 and 49)—many companies have active or closed landfills where hazardous wastes have been disposed;
- Hazardous Waste Facilities (Hazard 32)—some companies manage their hazardous waste on-site;
- Incinerators (Hazard 34)—companies may burn wastes on-site;
- Electric Power Plants (Hazard 27)—many manufacturers usually have large boilers to make steam;
- Gas Stations (Hazard 30)—underground fuel storage tanks for fueling fleet vehicles or for on-site use are common at manufacturing plants;
- Municipal Garages (Hazard 40)—many companies usually have large maintenance shops on-site;
- Print Shops (Hazard 44)—companies often have in-house printing (or painting) operations; and
- Petroleum Storage Terminals (Hazard 43)—many companies have large aboveground fuel or chemical storage tanks.

Health Risks

The compounds found in air emissions from an industrial facility depend on the site-specific activity. Air pollutants can present localized health concerns which vary with the weather or plant operating conditions. Odors associated with industrial plants can be a nuisance or an indication of an air pollution problem that may present real health risks. Major health problems can result in the rare event of a catastrophic industrial accident, such as toxic fumes being emitted after a chemical spill.

If past or present operations at an industry pollute groundwater and a nearby downgradient home relies on a private well for its drinking water, there may be serious health risks to people drinking the water (see Hazard 4, Drinking Water: Private Wells). Possible toxic groundwater pollutants include the universe of industrial chemicals and wastes; they include fuels from leaking tanks, chlorinated solvents, heavy metals, cyanide, and PCBs, among others. In addition, air inside homes located above groundwater containing high levels of certain organic compounds can become contaminated and pose a variety of health risks to occupants.

Financial Risks

In any real estate market, property values of homes near industrial sites will be reduced relative to similar homes not so situated. Due to environmental issues, proximity to an industrial facility can further devalue a property and pose other financial risks. If operations at a plant have contaminated groundwater, nearby private wells may be at risk. For example, drinking water wells in a Texas residential development were severely contaminated with hydrogen sulfide gas coming from a nearby natural gas company. The contamination forced home owners to use bottled water for several years, corroded appliances, and created overwhelming odor problems. A jury recently awarded the home owners more than $200 million for property damage, inconvenience costs, and other damages.

Homes with property or wells polluted by an industrial facility will be devalued and difficult to sell. Even if a problem is addressed and cleaned up, a property may be devalued because of stigma. Due to stigma, many people are wary of any property very close to any industrial plant, even if there are no actual environmental problems. Properties near an industrial facility known to have odor, noise, or traffic problems may also be devalued and difficult to sell.

Buyers of properties that use well water may ask for information about possible contamination from nearby industrial plants. Other issues, such as odors, lights, traffic, visual impacts, and noise, can also affect a buyer's decision and the negotiations.

Other financial risks:
- ▶ Liability for nondisclosure; see Disclosure Obligations, pages 13–19.
- ▶ Costs associated with contaminated drinking water; see Hazard 4, Drinking Water: Private Wells.
- ▶ Costs for short- or long-term medical treatment and monitoring; property damage (such as harm to livestock, crops, or landscaping); legal and expert fees; and inconvenience and relocation costs due to forced evacuation following an accident.

Managing the Risks

See Hazard 4, Drinking Water: Private Wells, for a discussion of how to manage risks if a drinking water well is contaminated.

If you're looking at a home near an industrial facility, expect some odors, noise, lights, and traffic. If you are concerned about these issues, make sure the home is far enough away and that there are substantial vegetative buffers to minimize them. If there is an occasional odor problem, closing windows or modifying a home's ventilation system may reduce (but not eliminate) the amount of contaminants entering the home. State health and environmental agencies may require a company to minimize odor, noise, dust, or other problems by changing its activities or requiring the installation of air treatment systems.

Contact the industrial facility for financial or technical help to correct a problem and manage the associated risks.

Regulatory Outlook

Day-to-day operations at industrial manufacturing sites are heavily regulated by federal, state, and local health and environmental agencies. There are rules and permits governing air and wastewater emissions; how chemicals and wastes are received, stored, and handled; noise levels; storage and management of hazardous and other wastes; and underground storage tanks, as well as rules to protect groundwater from spills and to require the cleanup of soil and groundwater if necessary.

Most industrial plants with air or water emissions have permits from the EPA or state or local environmental agencies that define acceptable levels of pollutant emissions, set certain operating conditions, require pollution controls to be working, and require regular sampling and testing. Many manufacturers generate hazardous waste and are subject to specific rules about how these wastes are stored, handled, and disposed of. However, pollution problems can result from improper operation or lax enforcement.

State and federal environmental agencies can issue compliance orders to a facility that violates its permits or that contaminates soil or groundwater. Failure to comply with applicable requirements can subject plant owners to stiff penalties, including criminal sanctions in some instances.

What to Look For

Drive around the area to locate nearby industrial parks and plants. Spend some time in the neighborhood to see if there are any unusual odor, noise, or traffic problems. Remember that these problems may be intermittent, varying with the time of day or local weather and wind conditions—you may need to visit the property more than once. Talk to the neighbors, but remember that people have varying tolerance levels for nuisance-type problems.

If a well is in use, taste and smell the water; however, laboratory tests are usually needed to detect contamination. If a water treatment system or bottled water is used, find out why (see Hazard 4, Drinking Water: Private Wells). If a home is close to an industry, check for visible signs of contamination like stained soil, stressed vegetation, or an oil sheen on any surface body of water.

Where to Find Help and Further Information

Large industrial plants are often shown on USGS and Sanborn Fire Insurance maps and aerial photographs (see Appendix 3). The EPA or your state environmental agency should be able to tell you about known problems in your area and provide information about a specific company, as well as copies of its records, permits, or reports (see Appendix 4). You will normally have to contact many departments within an agency to get the complete picture—the air department will be able to tell you only about air issues, the water bureau about wastewater permits, and so on.

There are many useful databases and files at the EPA and state environmental agencies that can help you find out what chemicals are used and emitted by local industries (see Appendixes 3 and 4). These include: RCRIS, a database of facilities that generate, treat, store, or dispose of hazardous waste; spill reports and underground tank notifications; and annual reports on toxic chemicals used and emitted by manufacturers, known as EPCRA Form R and Tier II reports.

Owners and potential buyers of nearby homes with wells should test the water (see Hazard 4, Drinking Water: Private Wells). Coordinate tests with a qualified laboratory, consultant, or home inspector. Costs will vary from $50 to $200 or more, depending on the number of constituents tested.

The Bottom Line

A central theme of this book—that buyers must keep their eyes open and be fully aware of a home's surroundings—is critical for homes located close to industry. Homes near some industrial plants may be devalued due to air, soil, or water pollution problems and their associated health and financial risks; other facilities may not pose any real health risks, but due to aesthetic issues or stigma, the homes may be devalued nonetheless. In some instances, the list price of such homes reflects these concerns. A buyer of a nearby home relying on a private well should test the water to see if there is any reason for concern. The cost to treat contaminated water or replace a well can be great, and the resale value of a property with a groundwater problem will be significantly reduced.

36. LANDFILLS

Risks: HEALTH   ⊕ ⊕ ⊕   FINANCIAL $ $ $

Background

Over the years, thousands of landfills have been used by every town, city, and county for the disposal of solid waste (garbage), including household trash, yard waste, bulky wastes (such as appliances or construction debris), and sewage sludge. Landfills may be owned by local governments, private companies, or individuals. With tightening governmental regulations, many have been forced to close—the number of active landfills is dwindling. Many of the almost twenty thousand active landfills operating in the late 1970s have closed, reached capacity, or are planning to close. Still, as of 1993, more than two-thirds of the solid waste generated in the United States is sent to landfills (most of the rest goes to incinerators).

Landfill is a nice word for *dump*. Technically speaking, a landfill is designed and operated to minimize environmental impacts, while a dump is not. Regardless of what we call them, landfills, whether active or closed, present a number of issues, ranging from odors to contaminated groundwater to methane gas seeps, that can impact nearby properties.

Of particular concern are the older landfills (most are now closed) that operated before the advent of environmental awareness and strict regulatory controls. Toxic groundwater contaminants from landfills may include natural by-products of solid waste like nitrate or ammonia, or compounds like solvents, PCBs, or heavy metals that were often disposed of, along with the trash, by local businesses, industry, or residents. Groundwater pollution from landfills can present significant health risks if nearby drinking water wells are contaminated. Stories abound about the problems home owners have faced from landfills seriously impacting nearby drinking water wells. Over the years, many landfills accepted—often unknowingly—toxic wastes; many have become Superfund sites (see Hazard 49, Superfund Sites).

Depending on distance, direction of prevailing winds, and weather conditions, odors can be a major problem for residences near (and even those at some distance from) landfills, particularly active ones. Given what landfills are used for, odors cannot be completely eliminated. However, when properly designed and operated, odors should be minimal. Other problems at active landfills that can impact nearby neighbors include truck traffic, noise, and dust generated by landfill equipment, blowing debris, and pests like mosquitoes, flies, and rats. For example, home owners in an Atlanta suburb near a landfill were awarded thousands of dollars due to nuisance odors, pests, and wild animals, which were attracted to the landfill, loss of fair rental value, and actual damages (including legal fees). A home near a landfill may also be affected by storm water runoff containing sediments, pesticides, oil, and other pollutants that can cause erosion and harm a home's lawn and gardens, wetlands, ponds, lakes, and well water.

Health Risks

It is a safe bet to assume that the groundwater underneath all but the newest of landfills is contaminated. Drinking water wells on downgradient properties may be at risk, depending on local water table conditions. Since a variety of materials are put into landfills, there are many possible contaminants, including bacteria, nitrates, dissolved salts, heavy metals, petroleum hydrocarbons, volatile organic compounds (VOCs), and pesticides. If a drinking water well is contaminated, a wide range of health risks may be encountered, depending on the pollutants, their concentration in the water, and the amount consumed (see Hazard 4, Drinking Water: Private Wells). For example, pollution from the Lipari Landfill in New Jersey was linked to increased levels of leukemia and low birth weight in babies in nearby homes. Local residents also suffered various respiratory problems and nausea, among other health problems. This landfill, which was shut down in 1971, was later ranked as the nation's worst Superfund site (see Hazard 49, Superfund Sites). In addition, air inside homes located above groundwater containing high levels of VOCs can become contaminated and pose a variety of health risks to occupants.

Contaminated groundwater is not the only possible pathway for human exposure to toxic pollutants from a landfill. Uncontrolled surface water runoff (such as rainwater or "leachate"—polluted water that seeps out of the sides and bottom of a landfill) can be highly contaminated. This runoff can pond up, seep into the ground, or get into nearby streams or other bodies of water. Direct contact with contaminated soil or uncovered waste materials (like sewage sludge that was used to cover garbage) is also possible at active and closed sites if the owner doesn't take measures to prevent unauthorized access and properly cap the landfill. In these cases, children could be exposed to toxic chemicals if they get onto the site (say, to ride dirt bikes).

Methane is an odorless gas that is produced at landfills as wastes decompose. Under certain conditions, methane gas can migrate from a landfill into the basements of nearby homes, causing a risk of explosion. For example, Seattle was recently forced to close its landfill and relocate and buy out many home owners because of methane gas migration problems. Odors generated by landfills may be objectionable and can cause such health problems as eye irritation or respiratory ailments. (Usually it is the sulfur compounds present in landfill gas that cause the distinctive odor, not methane.)

Finally, noise and traffic impacts from a dump can be objectionable and disrupt the use and enjoyment of your property.

Financial Risks

Due to the nature of real estate supply and demand, any property located close to a landfill will be devalued to some degree. Properties near a landfill with odor, groundwater, or other problems may be devalued even more, and can be difficult to sell. In a recent case in Ohio, a landfill owner agreed to a $5-million settlement with thirty-five hundred nearby home owners (up to $4,500 per home) to resolve claims for diminished property values because of known toxic dumping at the landfill. Because of stigma, buyers may be wary of any property close to a landfill, particularly if the homes rely on private drinking water wells, even if there are no actual environmental problems.

If a landfill pollutes drinking water wells, property owners will experience a significant loss in value. For example, in a 1990 case, two families in Madison, Wisconsin, won a lawsuit against owners of a landfill that had contaminated their wells with solvents and were awarded $1.6 million for damages, including medical expenses, cancerphobia, relocation costs, and loss of property values.

Buyers of properties near landfills may ask about odors, noise, and possible contamination of drinking water supplies—all possible points of contention in negotiations over price. If a known problem is not disclosed, sellers and real estate agents may be liable, especially where a state requires such disclosure (see Disclosure Obligations, pages 13–19). Whether a nearby landfill is active or closed, its presence alone may be information that a seller must disclose to a buyer. In New Jersey, for example, a court recently ruled that builders and real estate developers had a duty to tell potential buyers that their homes were built near a closed landfill (see pages 16–17).

By their very nature, landfills expand with time. Because of their age, growth, and changes in nearby property uses (especially the expansion of residential areas), homes and even schools and playgrounds will often abut, and sometimes even sit on, former landfills. Due to cleanup costs or stigma alone, the value of any property located *directly on* a former landfill will be severely reduced.

Other financial risks:
- Costs associated with contaminated drinking water; see Hazard 4, Drinking Water: Private Wells.
- Costs for short- or long-term medical treatment and monitoring; property damage (such as harm to livestock, crops, or landscaping); and legal and expert fees.

Managing the Risks

See Hazard 4, Drinking Water: Private Wells, for a discussion of how to manage risks if a drinking water well is contaminated.

If you're looking at a home near a landfill, expect some odors, traffic, and noise. If you are concerned about these issues, make sure the home is far enough away and that there are substantial vegetative buffers to minimize them. If there is an occasional odor problem, closing windows or modifying a home's ventilation system may temporarily reduce (but not eliminate) contaminated air entering the home. State health and environmental agencies may require a landfill owner to minimize odor problems by changing the facility's operations or requiring the installation of air treatment systems.

Contact the landfill owner or operator for financial or technical help to correct a problem and manage the associated risks. For example, the landfill owner may be responsible for providing a safe water supply or bottled water, or for paying the cost of individual water treatment systems. Fixing methane seepage problems costs thousands of dollars and is the responsibility of the landfill owner. For example, a Georgia home owner was recently awarded almost $200,000 by a court for complete loss of property value, emotional distress, and legal fees, after methane gas from a nearby closed landfill seeped into his home.

Finally, if you live near a closed landfill or an old dump, unless it has been properly closed and access is allowed by local health or environmental authorities, *never* use it as a recreational area and *do not allow your kids to play there.*

Regulatory Outlook

Day-to-day operations at active landfills are heavily regulated by the EPA, and state and local health or environmental agencies. Active landfills are required, under Subtitle D of the federal Resource Conservation and Recovery Act of 1976 (RCRA), to have permits and meet strict operational controls that include plans to monitor and protect groundwater and to properly close when out of space. Remember that past controls were much less strict than they are now; consequently, even a landfill now using the best available controls may have problems from past practices. Landfill owners are spending hundreds of thousands of dollars to comply with this law; however, because costs to comply are so high, many have closed. Most states require closed landfills to undertake environmental studies to determine if past operations caused problems. However, many inactive landfills have not been thoroughly looked at, either because they closed before strict requirements were in place or because they aren't thought to be causing any problems.

State and federal environmental agencies can issue compliance orders to landfills that violate their permits or that contaminate soil or groundwater. Failure to comply with applicable requirements can subject a landfill to both civil and criminal penalties. Some states require property deeds to indicate if a property has been used as a landfill.

What to Look For

It should be easy to find the local landfill if it's still open—just ask a neighbor where it is or call the local sanitation department. Drive around the area—landfills are usually large (several acres or more), but their appearances vary considerably. While many appear as large man-made hills, others may be old quarries. Former dumps may be more difficult to locate—again, check with local officials.

Problems like odors, noise, and traffic will be intermittent and will vary with the time of day or local weather and wind conditions. It may be necessary to visit the location more than once. Talk to the neighbors, but remember that people have varying tolerance levels for this type of problem.

If a well is in use, taste and smell the water; however, laboratory tests are usually needed to detect contamination. If a water treatment system or bottled water is used, find out why (see Hazard 4, Drinking Water: Private Wells). If a home is close to a landfill, check for visible signs of contamination like stained soil, stressed vegetation, or an oil sheen on any surface body of water.

Where to Find Help and Further Information

The location of active and some older, closed landfills can often be found by looking at aerial photographs or USGS, Sanborn Fire Insurance, or local maps (see Appendix 3) or by calling or visiting the local public works department, or the EPA or your state environmental agency (see Appendix 4). Many agencies have a specific department responsible for solid waste disposal issues, and that department may publish a map or listing of landfill locations as well as a list of sites with contamination problems. Check the EPA's NPL and CERCLIS lists to see if a landfill is a Superfund site or a candidate to be one (see Appendix 3 and Hazard 49, Superfund Sites). These agencies can also provide information about a particular landfill's design and operation as well as known or suspected environmental problems. Contact the landfill owner or operator or the EPA or your state environmental or health agency to find out additional information and if there are pollution, noise, odor, traffic, or methane problems (see Appendix 4).

Owners and potential buyers of nearby homes with wells should test the water (see Hazard 4, Drinking Water: Private Wells). Coordinate tests with a qualified laboratory, consultant, or inspector. Costs to test water are $50 to $200 or more, depending on the number of constituents tested. Tests for soil contaminants or methane gas can also be performed if you suspect a problem.

The Bottom Line

Proximity to an operating or closed landfill can lower property values because of actual contamination, odors, noise or traffic problems, or stigma. For active sites, odors, noise, and traffic can be overwhelming at times, affecting the use and enjoyment of a home. Groundwater contamination from landfills can pose significant health and financial risks if private drinking water wells are contaminated. Methane gas seepage from a landfill can also pose significant problems for nearby homes. Buyers of homes with private wells that are near (or on) a landfill should have the water tested to see if there is any reason for concern. The costs to address contaminated water are high and the value of a property with a water problem will be significantly reduced.

37. MILITARY BASES

Risks: HEALTH   FINANCIAL $ $ $

Background

Military bases, with their firing ranges and missile test areas, arsenals, laboratories and research centers, and stockpiles of munitions and chemicals, are plagued with environmental problems that can pose health and financial risks to nearby home owners. Many are undergoing, or are targeted for, cleanup, estimated to cost more than $50 billion. There are more than ten thousand contaminated military sites nationwide (with many in Alaska, California, Pennsylvania, Texas, and Virginia), often located in areas where groundwater is the source of drinking water.

Environmental problems at military bases are similar to those at large industrial sites; many military bases have been likened to small cities, as they have their own landfills, incinerators, gas stations, maintenance and plating shops, dry cleaners, and airports. The major concern is groundwater pollution from:

- the improper use, storage, and disposal of toxic chemicals
- contamination from activities conducted at research labs
- underground storage tanks
- stockpiled munitions
- electroplating operations

There are also more than two million acres of military firing range lands in the United States. Spent munitions left out on the firing ranges leach toxics (such as lead) into the soil and groundwater. There are periodic explosions from buried, unexploded ordnance.

Department of Energy (DOE) military sites pose even larger problems—many are sites where nuclear weapons were developed. From the 1940s, when the United States began to develop nuclear weapons, through the late 1980s, little attention was paid to their environmental consequences. Nuclear waste was stored in buildings, tank farms, ponds, and burial pits across the country (especially in California, Colorado, Florida, Idaho, Missouri, Nevada, New Mexico, Ohio, South Carolina, Tennessee, Texas, and Washington). As a result, DOE sites are now contaminated with radioactive and hazardous wastes, and the DOE faces an astounding cleanup effort—estimated to cost up to $1 trillion. The DOE already has spent more than $23 billion, although not one nuclear weapons facility has been fully cleaned up.

With the increase in base closings, more environmental problems will be discovered during the shutdown process. These base closings will have their own environmental issues, such as on-site incineration or hazardous waste transportation problems. The Department of Defense (DOD) is engaged in the cleanup of over seventeen hundred bases targeted for closure, of which ninety-two are listed as Superfund sites by the EPA (see Hazard 49, Superfund Sites). The DOD has estimated costs of over $5 billion just to clean up eighty-four of the ninety-two sites. In a study of seventy-nine army, air force, and navy bases targeted for closure, twenty-one were federal Superfund sites (that's more than one in four!), fifty-one had groundwater contamination problems, sixty-seven had on-site landfills, and twenty-five contained unexploded ordnance. And that's just *some* of the bases being closed, never mind the others that will follow or the facilities that will remain active.

Health Risks

Toxic chemicals (such as petroleum products, PCBs, cyanides, mercury, pesticides, metals, and solvents), radioactive and hazardous waste, chemical and biological weapons, and various activities at a military base can impact human health, particularly through contamination of drinking water sources (see Hazard 4, Drinking Water: Private Wells). For example, in Florida, chemicals from the Cecil Field Naval Base landfill were linked to numerous health problems (including cancers and deaths) of nearby residents who drank polluted water. A court awarded more than $7 million in damages to seventy-four residents. And in Massachusetts, groundwater pollution from decades of toxic chemical disposal and leaking underground tanks at the twenty-one-thousand-acre Otis/Camp Edwards National Guard base on Cape Cod contaminated private wells in several nearby towns and is believed to be the cause of numerous serious health problems. Air inside homes located above groundwater containing high levels of certain organic compounds can become contaminated and pose a variety of health problems to occupants.

Some homes and recreational fields have been built near, and even on, former military bases. In southern California, two children were killed in the early 1980s when a buried artillery shell exploded in the backyard of a home built on what had once been a military base. In many states, commercial developments and office parks have been built on former government arsenals where unexploded ordnance and other chemicals remain buried beneath the site. And a current case making its way through the courts in Pennsylvania alleges serious personal injuries, including leukemia, by more than one hundred people who worked on, played soccer at, or lived near a field the army previously used as a toxic waste dump.

Finally, the noise, odors, vibrations, and traffic from routine operations at a military base can be bothersome and disruptive to the use and enjoyment of a property.

Financial Risks

Proximity to a military base can devalue a property. Private wells for homes near military bases with groundwater problems are at risk from chemical contamination. For example, home owners near the Rocky Mountain Arsenal, an army chemical and munitions facility outside of Denver that is contaminated with pesticides, chemical weapons, metals, and incendiaries, have had to deal with contaminated drinking water, destruction of crops, and cattle deaths. And a family in Nebraska has been battling the government for years over contamination of their home's drinking water and crops from toxic chemicals coming from a nearby air force missile facility.

Homes with wells contaminated by military bases will be devalued and difficult to sell. Even if a problem is addressed, a property may be devalued because of stigma. Buyers of homes near military bases may ask about water issues. Aesthetic issues, such as odors, noise, vibrations, and traffic, can also impact property values.

Other financial risks:

- ► Liability for nondisclosure; see Disclosure Obligations, pages 13– 19.
- ► Costs associated with contaminated drinking water; see Hazard 4, Drinking Water: Private Wells.
- ► Costs for short- or long-term medical treatment and monitoring; property damage (to buildings, livestock, crops, or landscaping); legal and expert fees; and inconvenience and relocation costs due to forced evacuation following an accident.

Managing the Risks

See Hazard 4, Drinking Water: Private Wells, for a discussion of how to manage risks if a drinking water well is contaminated.

If you're looking at a home near a military base and don't want to deal with noise, odors, or traffic, make sure that the home is far enough from the base and any expansion area and that there are substantial vegetative buffers to minimize any impacts.

Contact the military base for financial or technical help to correct a problem and manage the associated risks.

Regulatory Outlook

Except where specifically exempted and subject to other rules (there is a lot of debate and disagreement in this area), military bases must comply with the federal environmental laws and regulations that apply to their activities. Under various environmental programs, the EPA rules that may apply to military bases include those that govern the use, storage, and disposal of various chemicals and wastes; the installation, maintenance, and monitoring of underground fuel storage tanks; and the cleanup of contaminated soil, groundwater, and surface water and drinking water supplies.

As military bases close, many are or will be sold to towns or the private sector for new uses. The federal agencies closing the bases and selling the properties must meet applicable environmental standards. Special advisory groups, which include citizen representatives, are being formed by the government to monitor the base closure and restoration process, resolve the cleanup and liability issues, and see if these sites can be safely reused.

What to Look For

Military bases are located all over the country; drive around the neighborhood to locate any nearby (they are usually fenced in and well marked). Check for noise, traffic, odors, and vibrations. If a home is close to a military base, look for visible signs of contamination like stained soils, stressed vegetation, or an oil sheen on any surface body of water. If a well is in use, taste and smell the water; however, laboratory tests are usually needed to detect contamination. If a water treatment system or bottled water is used, find out why (see Hazard 4, Drinking Water: Private Wells).

Where to Find Help and Further Information

Check with neighbors and the town land use or building officials to identify nearby active or closed military bases. USGS maps and aerial photographs should identify their location (see Appendix 3). Ask if there are plans for expansion, and about any known problems from the base, especially impacts to drinking water supplies. Owners and potential buyers of nearby homes with wells should consider testing the water (see Hazard 4, Drinking Water: Private Wells). Coordinate tests with a qualified laboratory, consultant, or inspector. Contact the EPA or your state environmental or health agency for additional information or assistance (see Appendix 4).

The Bottom Line

Proximity to a military base can impact the value and use and enjoyment of a home. Toxic chemicals, munitions, and various activities at these facilities can pose significant health and financial risks if they contaminate private drinking water wells. A buyer of a nearby home that relies on private well water should have the water tested to see if there is any reason for concern. The costs to address contaminated water are high and the value of a property with a water problem will be significantly reduced.

38. MINES AND QUARRIES

Risks: HEALTH   ⊕⊕   FINANCIAL $ $

Background

Mines and quarries located throughout the United States range from large open coal mines covering thousands of acres to small "sand and gravel" quarries. Mining operations involve the removal and then extraction of the desired material (such as coal and metal ores) from the surface or belowground while quarries are open operations that remove bulk materials (usually sand or rock) from the earth without extraction. Operations at mines and quarries and related activities can impact neighboring properties in many ways—and, contrary to what many people think, they aren't always in remote or rural areas. The potential for problems is very site specific and depends on the type of operations and local geology.

Soil, surface, and groundwater contamination resulting from a variety of activities at mines and quarries can pose significant health and financial risks for nearby home owners. Blasting can affect local bedrock and disrupt the volume or quality of water in nearby wells. In 1994, a Pennsylvania coal mine was ordered to undertake groundwater monitoring because of possible impacts to a well and spring on a residential property located hundreds of feet away. Mine "tailings"—the leftover rock and debris—are often deposited on the site. Drainage of acidic water is a by-product of many mining operations, such as coal mining, and is a major source of pollution in certain areas of the country. Also, contaminants like hydrogen sulfide, copper, nickel, zinc, arsenic, and lead can pollute groundwater as they leach from the mines themselves, the mine spoil piles, or ore-processing activities. Since many old mine sites are "reclaimed," they may be developed for other uses—including residential. For example, a California subdivision that was built directly on top of a former gold mine waste pile has arsenic-contaminated soil.

In the West, old uranium mines have serious problems with radioactive soil and groundwater pollution. Over one thousand former uranium mines are located on Navajo Indian lands in the Southwest, many of which are seriously contaminated with radioactive waste. Many former mines and sand and gravel pits are now Superfund sites (see Hazard 49, Superfund Sites). For example, in southeastern Kansas, large areas of former mines are now Superfund sites with contaminated soil, mine drainage, and impacted groundwater supplies, and a Colorado town named Leadville has more than sixteen square miles of hazardous mine-tailing piles.

Some mines use large ponds to process water to extract ores—contaminated water from these ponds can migrate into the groundwater. Groundwater can also become contaminated from ancillary operations at a mine, such as improper waste disposal practices, leaking underground fuel storage tanks, chemical or oil leaks from equipment, and spills. Also, because old mines and quarries were historically used as dumps, many are severely contaminated.

Other common types of problems associated with mines and quarries include:

- *Noise* and *vibrations* from drilling, blasting, and material handling, crushing and sorting operations, and trucks and other heavy equipment;
- *Dust* from truck traffic, waste disposal piles, blasting, and other extraction operations, or from rock or ore crushing and processing operations.
- *Subsidence* and *landslides* which can damage walls, foundations, and other structures at nearby homes;
- *Aesthetics*—mines and quarries, especially open-pit operations, can be rather ugly to look at or live near; and
- *Storm water runoff,* which may contain metals, sediments, cyanide, oil, and other pollutants, can contaminate downstream properties, cause erosion problems, and harm a home's lawn and gardens, wetlands, ponds, lakes, and well water.

Mines and quarries expand with time. What was once a distant mine may expand to a point where it can affect a home. However, in these times of suburban growth, the more likely scenario is new residential development coming to an area where an old mine or quarry is located.

There are tens of thousands of inactive or abandoned mines and quarries that can pose risks just as significant as those at active facilities. Over time, many of these facilities have become informal dump sites with serious environmental contamination problems but for which no responsible owner may readily be identified.

Health Risks

Pollution from a mine or quarry can impact human health through contamination of drinking water sources, skin contact, or inhalation of contaminants. Potential pollutants from mines and quarries include cyanide, hydrogen sulfide, radioactive materials, heavy metals, waste oil, solvents, and gasoline. Potential health problems vary with the type of contaminant, and range from skin irritation to chronic respiratory problems to cancer and birth defects. See Hazard 4, Drinking Water: Private Wells, for a general discussion of health concerns associated with contaminated well water. In addition, air inside homes located above groundwater containing high levels of certain organic compounds can become contaminated and pose a variety of health problems to occupants. For example, home owners near an open-pit coal mine in Wyoming complained of medical problems and illnesses from methane and hydrogen sulfide gases; homes were evacuated and the residential development was declared a disaster area.

Noise and vibration can be irritating and can affect the use and enjoyment of a home in some circumstances; in others they can create significant disruptions of daily activities and affect the structural integrity of a home. Noise and vibration can disrupt sleep or damage structures to the point where they could cause personal injury. Subsidence of land near underground mines can also damage structures and present health risks. For example, old mine shafts in one Pennsylvania mountain town are being filled in with a concrete mixture at a cost in excess of $20 million because virtually the whole town was in danger of collapse.

Dusts from active mining operations can contain trace levels of heavy metals that if breathed or otherwise ingested can pose serious health risks. Also, waste piles of soil at former mine dumps may contain unsafe levels of certain compounds (like arsenic or radioactive metals); these hazards are a special concern for children who may play in these areas.

If access to a mine or quarry is not restricted (and, sometimes, even if it is), there may be dangers to those who venture onto the property— abandoned quarries are notorious for (often fatal) accidents, especially involving children using them for recreation.

Financial Risks

Proximity to a mine or quarry can devalue a property. Private wells for nearby homes are at risk if groundwater is contaminated. Homes built directly on mine sites with contaminated soil or drinking water wells may require cleanup and will be significantly devalued and difficult to sell. For example, cleanup costs for seventy-five homes located on a former gold mine in Sacramento, California, are estimated to be as much as $25,000 per site. And even if a problem is addressed, a property may be devalued because of stigma.

Blasting operations are a prime source of vibrations that can damage personal property like dishes and pictures and can weaken foundations and crack walls in nearby homes. For example, blasting activities at an underground limestone mine located near an Indianapolis suburb is claimed to be damaging nearby homes and causing serious local dust problems. Throughout the country, courts have awarded "nuisance" damages to neighbors who have documented that problems from mines and quarries have reduced property values or impacted their ability to use and enjoy their property.

Subsidence can cause sinkholes; in 1994, an underground salt mine near Rochester, New York, collapsed and caused sinkholes throughout thousands of acres of residential property. In 1988, federal officials ordered a West Virginia mine operator to cease operations after several homes began to sink (the mine owned "subsurface rights" while the home owners owned "surface rights").

Potential buyers may ask about soil or water problems from a nearby mine. Noise, vibrations, dust, traffic, and odors can also affect a buyer's decision and the negotiations over price.

Other financial risks:
- ▶ Liability for nondisclosure; see Disclosure Obligations, pages 13–19.
- ▶ Costs associated with contaminated drinking water; see Hazard 4, Drinking Water: Private Wells.
- ▶ Costs for short- or long-term medical treatment and monitoring; property damage (such as harm to livestock, crops, or landscaping); legal and expert fees; and inconvenience and relocation costs due to forced evacuation following an accident.

Managing the Risks

See Hazard 4, Drinking Water: Private Wells, for a discussion of how to manage risks if a drinking water well is contaminated.

If you're looking at a home near an active mine or quarry, expect noise, traffic, dust, and vibrations. If you don't want to deal with them, make sure that the house is far enough away and that there is substantial vegetation to act as a buffer to minimize impacts.

Contact the owner or operator of the mine for financial or technical help to correct a problem and manage the associated risks.

Regulatory Outlook

Mines and quarries must comply with applicable federal, state, and local environmental laws and regulations. Under a variety of programs, most states and the Bureau of Land Management, the Bureau of Mines, the Office of Surface Mining (under the Department of Interior), the U.S. Mine Safety and Health Administration (under the Department of Labor), and the EPA regulate mining activities including dust and erosion control, land reclamation, use of explosives, and air and water pollution. Most states have mining acts that set limits on mining activities and restrict mines from impeding nearby land uses. These rules may require a facility owner to obtain permits and regulate operations including rock crushers and sorters, boilers, and trucking operations. Operators are often required to develop and follow an "operations plan," which, among other things, defines how close they can come to populated areas and how impacts to neighboring properties will be reduced.

State and federal environmental agencies can issue compliance orders to a mine or quarry that violates its permits or contaminates soil or groundwater. Failure to comply with applicable requirements can subject the owner or operator of a mine or quarry to both civil and criminal penalties.

At the local level, zoning, wetlands, and noise ordinances often control, to some extent, operations at local mines or quarries, such as when blasting and other noisy operations may take place. Zoning can be a major factor in setting buffers and controlling future expansions of mines and quarries.

Nuisance lawsuits have often been used by neighbors to control activities at a mine or quarry; courts have issued injunctions—enforceable limits on activities—and awarded damages to home owners. Where mining or quarrying activities change the stability of land that affects nearby homes, property owners may be able to sue for damages; however, courts around the country differ on questions of competing rights and land uses. The Office of Surface Mining has proposed a program to buy out owners of homes damaged by abandoned mines.

What to Look For

Mines and quarries are found throughout the United States. Quarrying and open-mining operations typically take place in nonurban areas, although they can also be located near suburbs and are sometimes even within city limits.

Take a drive around the area and look for large open pits, piles of rock and debris, or road signs that suggest some type of mine or quarry operation. In areas historically used for mines and quarries, verify, if possible, whether or not there are any abandoned sites on or near your property.

Noise, vibration, odors, and dust problems from a nearby mine or quarry may be evident after spending time in the area. Remember that blasting—the worst actor in terms of noise and vibration—may occur on a regular schedule; however, it may also be sporadic and even frequent visits to inspect a property may not coincide with blasting operations. Also, weather conditions will influence how strongly noise is heard and vibrations are felt. If you are looking at a home close to a facility where blasting takes place, make sure your home inspector looks carefully for structural damage.

If a home is close to a mine or quarry, check for visible signs of contamination like stained soil, stressed vegetation, or an oil sheen on any surface body of water.

If a well is in use, taste and smell the water; however, laboratory tests are usually needed to detect contamination. If a water treatment system or bottled water is used, find out why (see Hazard 4, Drinking Water: Private Wells).

Where to Find Help and Further Information

Talk with neighbors and town land use or building officials to find out about any historic contamination or known impacts to drinking water supplies, expansion plans, as well as noise, vibration, and traffic problems from a mine or quarry. Often, companies will provide their blasting schedule to local officials—check with your town hall or call the company directly. If the home is close to a mine, review the deed and land records carefully to ensure that no one has previously sold the subsurface rights to the property.

The locations of mines and quarries are often shown on aerial photographs and USGS or local maps (see Appendix 3).

All states with significant mining operations have a state agency or agencies responsible for controlling environmental, health, and safety aspects of mine operations. In addition, the federal Office of Surface Mining, 1951 Constitution Avenue, N.W., Washington, D.C. 20240 (202/208-4006), and the Mine Safety and Health Administration, 4015 Wilson Boulevard, Arlington, VA 22203 (703/235-1385), may be able to provide you with general information or with details on a specific mining site. Owners and potential buyers of nearby homes with wells should test the water (see Hazard 4, Drinking Water: Private Wells). Coordinate tests with a qualified laboratory, consultant, or home inspector.

Contact the EPA or your state environmental or health agency for additional information or assistance (see Appendix 4).

The Bottom Line

Proximity to a mine or quarry can significantly impact the value of a home. Remember, mines and quarries may expand over time. Noise, vibrations, traffic, and odors can affect the use and enjoyment of a home; sometimes the level of nuisance may go beyond aggravation and present real health and financial risks. Stigma from merely being near a mine or on a former mine can also impact property values. Activities associated with mines and quarries can pose significant health and financial risks if they contaminate groundwater. Buyers of homes on or near former mine sites should be particularly aware of the potential for soil and groundwater contamination. Property owners relying on well water located near mines or quarries should have their water tested. The resale value of any property with a soil or groundwater problem will be significantly reduced.

39. MISCELLANEOUS OFF-SITE HAZARDS

Risks: HEALTH ⊕   FINANCIAL $

Background

All of the hazards in Part III of this book cover the common off-site activities that can impact nearby homes and pose health and financial risks. The main concern is possible groundwater contamination of drinking water wells, but these activities can also contaminate soil from chemical storage or disposal or can be a source of objectionable noise, odors, vibrations, lights, visual impacts, or traffic. Our discussion of miscellaneous off-site hazards that may pose similar risks follows; there may be others, depending on a property's location.

The House Next Door

Nearby homes and associated activities can pose health and financial risks. Leaking underground heating oil storage tanks and failing septic systems are two common problems whose impacts do not honor property lines. Others include: storm water runoff eroding soil, blasting and other site work decreasing the yield of a well, improper removal of exterior lead-based paint contaminating soil and indoor air, and disposal of waste oil or household chemicals polluting soil and groundwater. Finally, businesses and hobbies conducted at nearby homes sometimes involve the use of hazardous chemicals that can contaminate groundwater and may result in noise and odors.

Other Nearby Activities

Various commercial, light manufacturing, and other nonresidential activities can impact groundwater via discharge of various wastes to septic systems or dry wells or from past or current waste disposal practices. They may also impact neighboring properties in other ways, such as from noise, odors, lights, vibrations, and traffic. Examples of nearby activities and associated specific hazards include:

- barbershops and beauty salons—water usage, detergents
- bridges—lead-based paint, vibrations, noise
- butcher shops—brine, detergents, odors
- car washes—oils, nitrates, salts
- fire stations—water usage, petroleum fuels and lubricants, solvents
- funeral homes and cemeteries—formaldehyde, metals, incinerators
- furniture repair shops—solvents
- gun clubs and shooting ranges—lead contamination, noise
- hospitals and clinics—laboratory and medical waste, incinerators, underground storage tanks
- junkyards—solvents, PCBs, gasoline and oil spills, miscellaneous dumping
- marinas and shipyards—underground storage tanks, fungicides, paints, solvents, wood preservatives
- medical and dental offices—formaldehyde, medical waste, metals
- mobile homes and trailer parks—underground storage tanks, sewage, drinking water problems, noise
- photoprocessing—chemical solutions, silver
- pipelines—oil spills, gas leaks, explosions, PCBs, land use restrictions
- plating or printed circuit board shops—chemical wastes, metals
- prisons—underground tanks, dry cleaners, maintenance shops
- restaurants—oils, cleaners, septic systems
- shopping malls—traffic, noise, underground storage tanks

- sports complexes and ski resorts—traffic, noise, underground storage tanks, septic systems, groundwater depletion, herbicides
- universities—underground storage tanks, labs, maintenance shops, swimming pool chemicals, PCBs, incinerators
- veterinary offices—medical wastes, pesticides
- water towers—lead-based paint
- welding and machine shops—metals, solvents

Health Risks

Spills of toxic chemicals or waste at an off-site location can impact human health, particularly by contaminating drinking water wells (see Hazard 4, Drinking Water: Private Wells). In addition, air inside homes located above groundwater containing high levels of certain organic compounds can become contaminated and pose a variety of health problems to occupants. Air pollution from any of these activities can be significant, and can especially affect the young, the elderly, and those with respiratory problems. Noise, traffic, lights, odors, vibrations, and visual impacts from some activities can disrupt the use and enjoyment of a property.

Financial Risks

Nearby homes with private wells are at risk if groundwater is contaminated. Homes with contaminated wells will be devalued and difficult to sell. Proximity to an activity can devalue a home by the mere threat of a problem. And even if a problem is addressed, a property may be devalued because of stigma.

Buyers of homes near any of these activities may ask about possible drinking water contamination. Noise, vibrations, dust, traffic, odors, and other impacts can also affect a buyer's decision and the negotiations over price.

Other financial risks:
- Liability for nondisclosure; see Disclosure Obligations, pages 13–19.
- Costs associated with contaminated drinking water; see Hazard 4, Drinking Water: Private Wells.
- Costs for short- or long-term medical treatment and monitoring; property damage (such as harm to buildings, livestock, crops, or landscaping); and legal and expert fees.

Managing the Risks

See Hazard 4, Drinking Water: Private Wells, for a discussion of how to manage risks if a drinking water well is contaminated.

If you're looking at a home close to any of the commercial activities listed above and you are concerned about noise, lights, odors, or traffic, make sure that the home is far enough away and that there are substantial vegetative buffers. Keep in mind that commercial sites may expand. If there is a problem, contact the facility owner or operator for financial or technical help to correct it and manage the associated risks.

Regulatory Outlook

Commercial and industrial activities must comply with applicable federal, state, and local environmental laws and regulations. Under various environmental programs, the EPA and some state and local agencies regulate the use, storage, and disposal of various hazardous materials; the installation, maintenance, and monitoring of underground fuel storage tanks; and the cleanup of contaminated soil, surface water, and drinking water supplies. Business owners are becoming sensitive to their environmental impacts on neighbors; as regulatory agency oversight and private lawsuits increase, others will too.

What to Look For

Drive around the neighborhood to locate nearby commercial activities. If a home is adjacent to a commercial activity, check for odors and noise, and inspect the property for visible signs of contamination like stained soil, stressed vegetation, or a sheen on any surface body of water.

If a well is in use, taste and smell the water; however, laboratory tests are usually needed to detect contamination. If a water treatment system or bottled water is used, find out why (see Hazard 4, Drinking Water: Private Wells).

Where to Find Help and Further Information

Check with neighbors and the town land use or building officials to identify any historic, existing, or planned commercial activities and whether there are any plans for expansion. Find out how the area is zoned and what the local zoning laws are that will determine if and how an activity can expand. If necessary, contact a qualified land use attorney. Find out about any problems associated with a nearby activity, including any known impacts to drinking water supplies for homes in the vicinity. Check relevant environmental databases, USGS and Sanborn Fire Insurance maps, and aerial photographs for the area (see Appendix 3).

Owners and potential buyers of nearby homes with wells should consider testing the water (see Hazard 4, Drinking Water: Private Wells). Coordinate tests with a qualified laboratory, consultant, or home inspector. Contact the EPA or your state environmental or health agency for additional information or assistance (see Appendix 4).

The Bottom Line

Most of these off-site activities should make good neighbors. However, some can impact the use and enjoyment of a home, or worse, contaminate its drinking water well. Buyers of homes that rely on private well water should have the water tested to determine if there is any need for concern about health issues. The costs to address contaminated water are high and the value of a property with a water problem will be significantly reduced.

40. MUNICIPAL GARAGES

Risks: HEALTH   ⊕   FINANCIAL $

Background

Most counties, towns, and cities operate centralized garage and service centers to repair and maintain vehicles and equipment used by various governmental departments such as public works, schools, parks and recreation, police, and fire. Issues of potential concern at municipal garages include:

- leaking aboveground and underground fuel storage tanks (see Hazard 30, Gas Stations);
- pesticides (see Hazard 42, Pesticides);
- storage of road salt (see Hazard 47, Salt Storage Areas);
- storage and (sometimes) disposal of paints, degreasers, solvents, cleaners, PCBs, used oil, batteries, waste freon, and antifreeze; and

- dumping of waste oils, tires, paints, asbestos, solvents, and other toxic chemicals in a remote area of the property or in on-site septic systems or dry wells.

The major environmental concern for properties close to a municipal garage is groundwater contamination from leaks, spills, and improper waste disposal. A drinking well at a residential property close to a municipal garage can be impacted, as can public drinking water supply wells, which are often located near the town garage. Homes near a municipal garage may also be affected by noise, lights, odors, and traffic, as well as by contaminated storm water runoff, which can impact lawns and gardens, wetlands, ponds, and lakes.

Health Risks

Spills or leaks of hazardous chemicals from a municipal garage can impact human health, particularly through contamination of drinking water sources (see Hazard 4, Drinking Water: Private Wells). Gasoline, the major groundwater pollutant from leaking fuel tanks at municipal garages, can present a variety of health risks, including cancer, and render water unusable (see Hazard 30, Gas Stations). Other possible groundwater contaminants from municipal garages include diesel fuel or kerosene, waste oils, pesticides, and solvents. In addition, air inside homes located above groundwater containing high levels of certain organic compounds can become contaminated and pose a variety of health problems to occupants.

Finally, odors from fueling activities and noise, traffic, and lights can cause minor health problems or disrupt the use and enjoyment of a property.

Financial Risks

Proximity to a municipal garage can devalue a property and pose other financial risks. Nearby homes with drinking water wells are at risk if groundwater is contaminated. Homes with soil or wells polluted by a spill or leak from a municipal garage will be difficult to sell. Even if a problem is addressed, a property may be devalued because of stigma.

A buyer of a property that uses well water near a municipal garage may ask for information about possible contamination. Other issues, such as odors, lights, traffic, and noise, can also affect a buyer's decision and negotiations over price.

Other financial risks:

- ► Liability for nondisclosure; see Disclosure Obligations, pages 13–19.
- ► Costs associated with contaminated drinking water; see Hazard 4, Drinking Water: Private Wells.
- ► Costs for short- or long-term medical treatment and monitoring; property damage (such as harm to livestock, crops, or landscaping); legal and expert fees; and inconvenience and relocation costs due to forced evacuation following an accident.

Managing the Risks

See Hazard 4, Drinking Water: Private Wells, for a discussion of how to manage risks if a drinking water well is contaminated.

If you're looking at a home close to a municipal garage, make sure that it is far enough away and that there are substantial vegetative buffers if you are concerned about noise, lights, odors, or traffic. Contact the municipality for financial or technical help to correct a problem and manage the associated risks.

Regulatory Outlook

Municipal garages must comply with applicable federal, state, and local environmental laws and regulations, including obtaining required permits. Under various environmental programs, the EPA and state and local agencies regulate:

- • the installation, maintenance, and monitoring of underground fuel storage tanks;
- • the use, storage, and disposal of hazardous waste generated from vehicles and machinery;
- • the use, storage, and disposal of pesticides;
- • storm water runoff; and
- • the cleanup of contaminated soil, groundwater, and surface water.

Municipalities are becoming sensitive to the environmental impacts of their activities on neighbors; in time, others will too, as regulatory agency oversight and private lawsuits increase.

What to Look For

Drive around the neighborhood to locate a nearby municipal garage, look for locations where municipally owned vehicles—buses, snowplows, street sweepers—are parked. If a home is adjacent to a municipal garage, inspect the property for visible signs of contamination like stained soil, stressed vegetation, or a sheen on any surface body of water.

If a well is in use, taste and smell the water; however, laboratory tests are usually needed to detect contamination. If a water treatment system or bottled water is used, find out why (see Hazard 4, Drinking Water: Private Wells).

Where to Find Help and Further Information

Check with neighbors and the town land use or building officials to identify an existing or planned municipal garage; also ask if there are any anticipated expansion plans. Municipal garages may also be identified on USGS, county, town, and city maps (see Appendix 3). Find out how the area is zoned and review the local zoning laws to determine if and how the municipal garage can expand. If necessary, contact a qualified land use attorney. If a municipal garage is nearby, find out about any problems associated with it, including known impacts to drinking water supplies for homes in the vicinity.

Owners and potential buyers of nearby homes with wells should test the water (see Hazard 4, Drinking Water: Private Wells). Coordinate tests with a qualified laboratory, consultant, or inspector. Contact the EPA or your state environmental or health agency for additional information or assistance (see Appendix 4).

The Bottom Line

Proximity to a municipal garage can impact the value of a home. Traffic, noise, odors, and lights can affect the use and enjoyment of your home. Leaking tanks or spills of chemicals or wastes are common and can pose health and associated financial risks if drinking water wells become contaminated. Buyers of nearby homes with wells should have the water tested to see if there is any reason for concern. The costs to address contaminated water are high and the value of a property with a water problem will be significantly reduced.

41. NUCLEAR POWER PLANTS

Risks: HEALTH   ⊕ ⊕ ⊕   FINANCIAL $ $ $

Background

There are about three hundred nuclear power plants producing electricity in thirty-four states. The environmental risks associated with nuclear power plants have been well publicized since the accidents at Three Mile Island (Pennsylvania) in 1979 and Chernobyl (Ukraine) in 1988. Environmental risks from nuclear power plants stem from the transportation and storage of radioactive materials and wastes, soil and groundwater contamination from a plant's operations, and the potential for catastrophic accidents, which can release radioactive gases into the atmosphere. Due to the high cost to build these plants, difficulties in siting and permitting them, as well as a general oversupply of electrical generating plants, no new nuclear plant has been built for more than a decade.

The potential for catastrophic accidents that release large quantities of radiation is probably the biggest issue for neighbors of nuclear power plants. There are many possible ways that radiation could be released in the event of a serious accident—a worst case scenario is a core meltdown followed by an explosion, sending huge quantities of radiation into the air. This is partially what happened at Chernobyl. Significant amounts of radiation could also be released during less catastrophic accidents. Except for Three Mile Island, no major accidents have occurred in the United States. All nuclear power plants are required to have elaborate control and backup systems designed to minimize and contain radioactive releases.

The storage and transportation of spent nuclear fuel is a major issue for nuclear power plants. In the 1960s and 1970s, when most nuclear plants were built, it was assumed that a final resting place for the large quantities of high- and low-level radioactive waste produced would be found by the federal government. This hasn't happened. Because siting of radioactive waste facilities has been bogged down for years, many nuclear power plants have had to store such wastes on-site using temporary methods. Although these on-site storage activities are regulated, the potential for accidents or groundwater contamination from such practices exists. The closing of old nuclear power plants is likewise a concern. Many are reaching the end of their expected lives, and proper closure of these facilities will undoubtedly uncover significant soil and groundwater contamination problems.

Nuclear power plants use huge volumes of water to cool their reactors. This water is often discharged to nearby bodies of water, sometimes creating localized thermal impacts. Historically, some plants used chromium, a toxic metal, to prevent buildup of bacteria in their cooling water (chromium is rarely, if ever, used today). Because of past disposal practices, some plants have contaminated nearby surface water and groundwater supplies with chromium. As with any power plant, large electrical substations and power lines can present PCB and EMF issues (see Hazard 16, PCBs, and Hazard 28, Electromagnetic Fields).

Nuclear power plants have many of the environmental problems common to all large industrial facilities, such as noise from equipment, truck traffic, lighting, and possible soil and groundwater contamination from underground fuel storage tanks or waste disposal practices.

Health Risks

The central issues with respect to nuclear safety are the risk of a catastrophic accident that could release dangerous levels of radiation into the air and the long-term impacts on the environment after a plant closes. The long-term storage of high-level radioactive wastes and the transportation of radioactive material to and from a plant also pose potential health risks. Exposure to high amounts of radiation can cause immediate health problems (vomiting, skin disease), and cancers, genetic defects, and deaths.

Radiation released by normal operation of a nuclear power plant is negligible compared to the routine exposure to radiation we all get from natural background sources (cosmic radiation or radon, for example) or from activities like air travel, smoking, and X rays. A typical radiation exposure cited by the nuclear industry to a person who lived at the property line of a nuclear power plant for a year is about 1 millirem; the average X ray gives a dose of about 6 millirem, and exposures from breathing background radon levels in a home are about 100 millirem.

If day-to-day operations at a nuclear power plant pollute groundwater, and drinking water wells are in use, there may be serious health risks to people drinking the water (see Hazard 4, Drinking Water: Private Wells). In addition, air inside homes located above groundwater containing high levels of certain organic compounds can become contaminated and pose a variety of health problems to occupants.

Financial Risks

Properties located close to a nuclear power plant are likely to experience a decrease in value due to aesthetic concerns, presence of high power lines, traffic problems, and especially stigma. Reductions in local property taxes for home owners may offset devaluation somewhat. And, if another serious accident were to occur at any nuclear facility, we would expect difficulties in selling any property near any nuclear power plant. However, the overall financial risks associated with a catastrophic nuclear accident cannot truly be evaluated in the context of an individual residential real estate transaction—one accident could wipe out individual property values for miles and severely impact human health.

Buyers of properties near a nuclear power plant may ask about the safety record of the plant or about traffic and noise problems. This may be a point of contention in negotiations over price. If past or current problems have polluted drinking water wells, a home will be significantly devalued.

Home owners who have been impacted by a nuclear power plant may also incur other costs for short- or long-term medical treatment and monitoring; damage to livestock, crops, or landscaping; legal and expert fees; and inconvenience and relocation costs due to forced evacuation following an accident. In 1995, more than sixteen years after the Three Mile Island nuclear accident, over twenty-one hundred residents finally began their personal injury and punitive damages class-action lawsuit.

Other financial risks:
- ▶ Liability for nondisclosure; see Disclosure Obligations, pages 13–19. The mere presence of a nearby nuclear power plant may be information that must be disclosed to buyers.
- ▶ Costs associated with contaminated drinking water; see Hazard 4, Drinking Water: Private Wells.

Managing the Risks

If you live, or choose to live, near a nuclear power plant, we suggest contacting the plant to discuss your concerns. Owners of plants will be able to provide information (propaganda, some might say) about the plant's operation and safety record. This will include information about how the plant will communicate with the public if there is an accident, actions to take at home, and where to go if a problem requires evacuation.

See Hazard 4, Drinking Water: Private Wells, for a discussion of how to manage risks if a drinking water well is contaminated.

If there is a soil, groundwater, or air pollution problem, contact the nuclear power plant for financial or technical help to correct the problem and manage the associated risks.

Regulatory Outlook

Nuclear power plants are perhaps the most heavily regulated industrial activity around. The federal Nuclear Regulatory Commission (NRC) has primary jurisdiction over their operation and issues operating as well as closure permits. In addition, state environmental agencies, state utility boards, and the Federal Emergency Management Agency (FEMA) are responsible for ensuring that their operations do not present undue risks. NRC regulations govern the safe operation of these plants and the storage and handling of radioactive materials. The EPA and state and local environmental agencies govern noise levels, wastewater discharges, underground storage tanks, and the protection and cleanup of groundwater. The NRC and environmental agencies have authority to issue compliance orders to any facility that violates its permits or contaminates soil or groundwater.

What to Look For

Nuclear power plants are large facilities that have high-voltage power lines extending from them. There may be large storage tanks or concrete structures (cooling towers, reactor domes, and so forth). Nuclear plants are often located near a large body of water.

Spend some time in the neighborhood to see if there are any unusual noise or traffic problems. Remember that these problems may be intermittent and may vary with the time of day or local weather and wind conditions. Talk to the neighbors about these concerns.

If a home is near a nuclear power plant, inspect the property for visible signs of contamination like stained soil, stressed vegetation, or a sheen on any surface body of water. If a well is in use, taste and smell the water; however, laboratory tests are usually needed to detect contamination. If a water treatment system or bottled water is used, find out why (see Hazard 4, Drinking Water: Private Wells).

Where to Find Help and Further Information

Aerial photographs and USGS, Sanborn Fire Insurance, and local maps should show the location of a nearby nuclear power plant (see Appendix 3). Or ask the local building department or utility directly. Contact the NRC or state environmental agencies for information about a particular facility's design and operation, when it is due to go "off-line," and any known or suspected environmental problems. A buyer should ask the seller if there have been any problems, such as truck traffic, associated with a plant, as well as call the local health department to find out if there have been complaints or if they know of problems. If a private well is used, contact state or local health agencies to find out about groundwater problems in the area.

Owners and potential buyers of nearby homes with wells should consider testing the water (see Hazard 4, Drinking Water: Private Wells). Coordinate tests with a qualified laboratory, consultant, or inspector. Costs will be from $50 to $200, depending on the number of constituents tested. Contact the EPA or your state environmental or health agency for additional information or assistance (see Appendix 4).

The Bottom Line

Regardless of your feelings about nuclear power, the presence of a nearby nuclear power plant will impact property values. Even if there is no actual problem, stigma is a major issue for homes near a nuclear power plant; because of fears of a catastrophic accident, however unlikely, homes close to nuclear plants may be devalued and difficult to sell. Potential buyers of homes close to nuclear power plants are making a personal statement about their acceptance of certain risks. While daily operations at nuclear power plants generally do *not* present radiation hazards to nearby homes, they can pose health and financial risks like those of a major industrial complex, such as groundwater contamination from leaky underground storage tanks or improper disposal practices. Buyers of homes with private wells that are near a nuclear plant should have the water tested to determine if there is any need for concern about health issues. The costs to address contaminated water are high and the value of a property with a water problem will be significantly reduced.

42. PESTICIDES

Risks: HEALTH   FINANCIAL $ $

Background

By the term *pesticides* we mean all the "-cides" (which is Latin for "to kill")—insecticides, herbicides, fungicides, rodenticides, mildewcides, algicides, nematocides, and many others. Farmers, lawn- and tree-care companies, utilities, government agencies, commercial property owners, among others, extensively use pesticides to control or kill weeds, insects, and other pests on residential lawns and gardens; farms, orchards, and nurseries; utility and railroad corridors and rights-of-way; highways and roads; and golf courses, athletic fields, and other recreational areas.*

Although some pesticides, such as arsenic, have been used for centuries, most of the more than sixty thousand chemicals that are used to control pests in the United States today were not developed until after World War II. The EPA estimates that more than two billion pounds of pesticides are used in the United States each year—this is almost ten pounds per person. Because of health and environmental concerns, chemical companies have developed new pesticides that are less toxic and persistent than those used extensively in the past.

Some home owners, in their quest to eliminate weeds and insects and have the "perfect" lawn (or simply because it's faster and easier), apply excessive amounts of synthetic chemicals on their lawns (or use private companies to do so). Various pesticides are also used as disinfectants and for insect control indoors in homes, clinics and hospitals, beauty salons and barbershops, kennels and animal hospitals, and other places.

Many pesticides are notorious, such as the soil fumigant ethylene dibromide (EDB), used in tobacco fields; malathion, which is routinely used for insect control; the herbicide atrazine, used on cornfields; and the herbicide dimethyl tetrachloroterephthalate (DCPA), used on residential lawns and golf courses to control crabgrass. Yet there are thousands of others that are not so common. Over the years, many pesticides have been banned by the EPA and state environmental agencies due to health concerns. For example, DDT, which was widely used for mosquito control throughout the country (and is a much-written-about pesticide—see Rachel Carson's classic 1962 book *The Silent Spring*), was

---

* Although this chapter is placed in the off-site category, on-site uses of pesticides, indoors and out, present similar issues of concern.

banned in 1972. Similarly, in the mid-1970s, chlordane use was limited to termite control; in 1988, it was banned. However, many banned pesticides continue to show up on fruits and vegetables—in 1995, there were findings across New England of blueberries that were sprayed with methiocarb, a pesticide and bird repellent that was banned from use on all foods in 1988.

Pesticides can contaminate indoor air, public drinking water supplies, and private wells. They end up in drinking water supplies as a result of wind drift, storm water runoff, leaching from soil, and their improper use and disposal. Studies of pesticides in groundwater have been conducted all around the United States, and the results are disconcerting: high levels of pesticides have been discovered in public water supplies and private drinking water wells near all types of land use. The EPA estimates that more than 10 percent of all community water system wells and about 5 percent of the more than 10.5 million private wells in the United States have some level of pesticide contamination.

Health Risks

Pesticides are, by definition, toxic—they are purposely designed and used to kill something. When applied and used properly, pesticides generally should not pose a threat to human health. However, pesticides are not very discriminatory and can have unintended health consequences to humans and pets, especially where they have been overused or misused. Almost all pesticides will cause health problems at some level of exposure. And residues from previously applied pesticides can persist in soil and groundwater for years, and can pose a variety of health risks. Routes of pesticide exposure include drinking tainted water, eating contaminated food, direct skin contact (from lawns, soils, carpets, or woodwork), and inhaling fumes or dusts during application (outside and indoors).

Possible health problems range from skin irritation to chronic respiratory problems, cancer, and birth defects. There is mounting evidence that many pesticides can disrupt reproduction and cause cancer in laboratory animals and humans. For example, chlordane causes cancer in laboratory animals and adversely affects the central nervous system. Exposure to high levels of DDT, even for short periods, is known to cause tremors, rashes, and irritation of the nose, throat, and eyes; it is also known to cause cancer in lab animals. It is impossible to generalize about the health risks of pesticides as a group. Information about the particular chemical used in a specific situation must be considered to predict potential short-term (acute) or long-term (chronic) health effects.

The levels at which some pesticides cause health problems are very low. As with any toxicant, the degree of risk depends on the exposure level and the route of exposure. Children playing in areas where pesticides have recently been applied or overused may be at particular risk. Some recent studies have shown a link between home pesticide use (where pest strips, pesticide bombs, and flea collars were used) and childhood brain and soft-tissue cancers. In an extreme example, a Los Angeles teenager developed severe, permanent eye injuries from excessive exposure to malathion during aerial sprayings in 1990 for a Mediterranean fruit fly infestation (a helicopter unloaded such significant amounts of the pesticide that the boy was drenched in his yard). In 1984, two children died and five others became ill when methyl parathion was sprayed in their Mississippi homes to kill spiders.

There is no way to predict if groundwater in areas where pesticides are used is impacted without detailed information about the specific types of pesticides used and unless local soil and groundwater data are known. Some pesticides degrade rapidly while others do not; some are absorbed into the soil and are immobilized, others may dissolve rapidly and enter the groundwater.

Even today, many of the banned pesticides persist and still cause health problems. For example, soil samples recently taken from twelve homes near Los Angeles contained high levels of DDT. The source of the DDT is unknown; the EPA is investigating several potential sources, including a nearby Superfund site and a nearby former pesticide-manufacturing site. Or the DDT may have been sprayed directly on the properties, which were farms before being developed for residential use.

Financial Risks

Proximity to a property that uses pesticides extensively can affect the value of your home. A home with a contaminated well or indoor air problem will be devalued and difficult to sell. Pesticide-contaminated soil will be expensive to clean up (into the thousands of dollars) to prevent groundwater contamination or direct human exposure. And even if a problem is addressed, a property may be devalued because of stigma.

Buyers of homes near sites that use pesticides may ask about odors, pesticide drift, and possible contamination of drinking water. A home owner may also face increased landscaping costs; storm water runoff containing pesticides can damage lawns, gardens, ponds, and lakes.

The cost to "fix" a home where indoor pesticide residues are present may be nominal if only a minor cleanup is needed, or thousands of dollars if major repairs are required, such as installing new carpets, cabinets, countertops, appliances, ventilation systems, or woodwork. For example, in 1994, an Ohio family suffered health problems and was forced to evacuate its home less than a year after they bought it because of pervasive exposure to chlordane. The home's well water was heavily contaminated, and samples taken from the air, carpets, and other areas around the house reportedly exhibited excessive levels of chlordane. The family recently filed a $5 million lawsuit against the former owners for failing to disclose the termite problem and the large amounts of pesticides used, and against the termite company, who they claim illegally used chlordane, which had been banned for all uses in 1988. And in an almost unbelievable situation, since January 1995, the EPA has been involved in a $20 million cleanup of more than two hundred contaminated homes and apartments near Cleveland that were sprayed for years with methyl parathion, a highly toxic pesticide also banned from indoor use. The unlicensed exterminator faces criminal charges for his actions. Decontamination and restoration costs are more than $70,000 per home, and families were relocated at the government's expense to nearby hotels for almost two months. Costs for disruption of daily life and activities are immeasurable. While the reported health effects to date have been minimal (nausea, headaches, and diarrhea), the potential long-term health effects and their associated costs are unknown.

Other financial risks:
- Liability for nondisclosure; see Disclosure Obligations, pages 13–19.
- Costs associated with contaminated drinking water; see Hazard 4, Drinking Water: Private Wells.
- Costs for short- or long-term medical treatment and monitoring; property damage (such as harm to livestock, crops, or landscaping); legal and expert fees; and inconvenience and relocation costs due to forced evacuation following a problem pesticide application.

Managing the Risks

If soil or groundwater is known to be contaminated by pesticides, some short-term precautions are in order. Do not grow vegetables in soil with high pesticide levels. If groundwater is contaminated by pesticides, treatment of the drinking water from your well may be possible (see Hazard

4, Drinking Water: Private Wells). Recently several residential properties in northern Connecticut were determined to have high levels of the pesticide EDB, which was commonly used as a soil fumigant by tobacco farmers from the 1950s through the 1980s. The families in these homes had to use bottled water for several years while studies were being conducted. Subsequently, at a cost of tens of thousands of dollars, the town installed a water treatment system for each home and is maintaining the systems and monitoring the pesticide levels in the water at no cost to the home owners.

If there is an occasional odor problem, closing windows or modifying the home's ventilation system may temporarily reduce (but not eliminate) the amount of contaminated air entering the home.

A buyer should require the seller to dispose of any unneeded pesticides and their containers before closing the deal.

If pesticides are a problem, contact the responsible party for financial or technical help to correct it and manage the associated risks.

Regulatory Outlook

Commercial and agricultural properties that use pesticides must comply with applicable federal, state, and local environmental laws and regulations. Under various environmental programs (including our favorite-named statute, the Federal Insecticide, Fungicide, and Rodenticide Act [FIFRA], which governs the registration, labeling, and other aspects of pesticides), the EPA and state agencies regulate which pesticides may be used (although actual use goes relatively unchecked) and how they are stored, handled, and disposed of. State agencies can require soil or groundwater contaminated with pesticides to be cleaned up. The EPA, the Food and Drug Administration, and the Department of Agriculture share responsibility for controlling pesticide residues in food. However, even government experts who monitor the use (and misuse) of pesticides state that there is no reliable way to know the amount of illegal pesticides still used on farms and other sites today. And the EPA has no guidelines to assess the health effects of human exposure to pesticides after they are applied outdoors or indoors. In fact, many pesticides that have been banned continue to be used by applicators who either do not know that they are illegal or choose to use them despite the ban.

Many states and municipalities have their own pesticide laws and regulations (which must be at least as strict as the federal government's)— these vary widely from location to location. The EPA and state environmental agencies typically regulate which pesticides can be sold to the public and which are available for use only by certified and licensed applicators and have lists of prohibited pesticides as well as restricted-use pesticides—those that can be purchased and used only by certified applicators. The state agency with jurisdiction over pesticides may also require the licensing and certification of those applicators who can apply special pesticides. Although many states do not require a permit for the purchase and use of most pesticides, some state, local, and county agencies do. Farmers and commercial applicators must report the usage of certain chemicals.

More than half of the states (and many local governments) have notification programs. Some of these programs require pesticide applicators to notify only customers, while others require notification of neighboring property owners or tenants of the time and date of application. Some states require advance notification of pesticide application, while others require notification at the time of application.* Some state programs also require commercial applicators to post signs at entry points and along property frontages warning the public of the pesticide use (although there may be certain exemptions from the notification requirements for utilities, railroads, or municipalities when applying pesticides to rights-of-way or roadsides). Pesticide application may be limited or banned outright in certain environmentally sensitive areas, such as in public water supply watersheds or near recreational lakes, rivers, and streams.

Under the Safe Drinking Water Act, public drinking water supplies are routinely monitored for some pesticides. However, tests are not required for many common pesticides. Many states and the EPA have adopted standards (or "action levels") for acceptable amounts of certain pesticides in drinking water (see Appendix 2).

Many pesticide users are becoming more aware of their environmental impacts on neighboring properties, including private homes; in time, as regulatory agency oversight and private lawsuits increase, others will too. Also, the EPA appears to be reconsidering its long-held view that pesticides pose little risk to home owners and their families. In a recent study, the EPA indicated that it is particularly concerned about the effects of pesticides on children, who may play on or around treated lawns or indoor areas. In its study, the EPA found thirteen lawn-care pesticides in groundwater and identified four potential carcinogens among the eighteen major lawn-care pesticides. We expect the EPA to become more active in the arena of public education, especially concerning ways to reduce pesticide use, increasing the use of best management prac-

---

* In some places, the burden is on the neighbor to request notification.

tices for pesticide applications, and assisting home owners with the testing and monitoring of drinking water supplies.

What to Look For

Drive around the neighborhood to locate places where pesticides may have been used in significant amounts—look for nearby active or historic farms, commercial lawns, utility or railroad rights-of-way, golf courses, parks, and other areas where pesticides are used intensively. Some commercial activities are required to post signs indicating pesticide use; however, signs may not be required by utilities or departments of transportation spraying public rights-of-way.

Spend some time in the neighborhood to see if there are any unusual odors. Remember that odors may be a problem only on days when pesticides are used, and will vary with the time of year and local weather and wind conditions. Talk to neighbors about any concerns. If possible (and it may not be), find out if and when pesticides are routinely applied on a nearby property and try to visit the property then.

If a home is close to a property that uses pesticides heavily, inspect the property for visible signs of contamination like stained soil or stressed or burned-out vegetation, which may indicate pesticide overuse. If a well is in use, taste and smell the water; however, laboratory tests are usually needed to detect contamination. If a water treatment system or bottled water is used, find out why (see Hazard 4, Drinking Water: Private Wells).

For on-site pesticide issues, check the basement, garage, barns, and other outbuildings for evidence of improper use or storage of pesticides. Large quantities of pesticide containers or pesticidelike odors inside a house may be a telltale sign of improper or excessive pesticide use on the property.

Where to Find Help and Further Information

Owners and potential buyers of homes with wells near agricultural properties or other areas of heavy pesticide use should test the water (see Hazard 4, Drinking Water: Private Wells). Recognize that it is *very* expensive to do a comprehensive test of groundwater or soil for pesticides; costs can range from a few hundred dollars to over one thousand dollars per test. However, costs can be greatly minimized if you can find out which pesticides were previously applied (this may be difficult to do).* Coordinate tests with a qualified laboratory, consultant, or inspector. Testing of groundwater for agricultural pesticides should also be considered before residential development on or near a site of historic pesticide use.

If a home has had an interior pest problem, you might consider testing indoor air levels for pesticides. A consultant can test for indoor pesticide residues by doing a simple wipe test. Contact the EPA or your state environmental or health agency for additional information or assistance (see Appendix 4).

Aerial photographs and USGS and Sanborn Fire Insurance maps may show historic farmland, rights-of-way, or other areas of pesticide use (see Appendix 3).

Agricultural agencies are a great source of information about specific types of pesticides used in an area or on a particular farm—if you can find out what crops were grown, you might be able to identify specific pesticides to test for. State and local health and environmental agencies usually have general information about pesticides and may be able to tell you about any known problems in your area. These agencies can also answer your questions about the use of specific pesticides and about rules applying to commercial application of pesticides. A local pesticide applicator may be willing to provide information about the specific chemicals used nearby. The EPA's National Pesticide Telecommunications Network Hotline (800/858-PEST) can also be of assistance.

The Bottom Line

Misuse or overuse of pesticides, whether at nearby properties or on your property, can contaminate drinking water wells and indoor air. In these situations, health and financial risks can be significant. Home owners and buyers of properties that have private wells should find out about nearby (or on-site) pesticide use and possible problems, and should consider testing the water and indoor air to determine if there is any need for concern about health issues. The costs to address contaminated soil and groundwater are high and the value of a property with a water problem will be significantly reduced.

---

* Conducting a general pesticide scan may not be sufficient because only a few of thousands of possible pesticides are identified.

43. PETROLEUM STORAGE TERMINALS

Risks: HEALTH   ⊕⊕   FINANCIAL $ $

Background

Petroleum storage terminals are common around the country. They provide a central distribution point where large volumes of petroleum products (like crude oil, gasoline, kerosene, and diesel fuel), natural gas, and propane are delivered by ship, pipeline, rail, or truck and stored in large aboveground tanks (groups of tanks are often referred to as "tank farms") prior to distribution to delivery companies or consumers for home or business use.* Terminals range from huge complexes owned by the major oil companies to small tank yards owned by local fuel suppliers.

Many petroleum terminals utilize practices and state-of-the-art technology to minimize pollution threats. However, nearby residential properties can be impacted by past spills, leaking tanks, or by poor ongoing environmental practices that lead to large oil spills and to soil, groundwater, and surface water contamination. Oil spills may harm surrounding wildlife and plant habitats, contaminate groundwater supplies, and cause air pollution. Unfortunately, groundwater contamination from petroleum storage terminals is not uncommon and even drinking water wells at residential properties located thousands of feet away can be impacted. For example, in Virginia, petroleum products from a tank farm leached into the groundwater and formed an underground pollution plume beneath a nearby residential development of almost three hundred families. And in North Carolina, thousands of residents have sued several oil companies that use a huge tank farm (containing more than one hundred tanks that store more than 125 million gallons of oil), claiming that it contaminated a residential neighborhood, devalued properties, and poses health risks. The suit claims that numerous spills, totaling about 1.5 million gallons, have contaminated groundwater in the area and caused significant air pollution.

Homes near a petroleum storage facility may be affected by storm water runoff containing petroleum products that can cause erosion and harm a home's lawn, gardens, wetlands, ponds, lakes, and well water.

Aesthetic concerns from petroleum storage facilities include odors

---

* In addition to petroleum products, numerous other chemicals are often stored in bulk at aboveground tank farms.

produced when loading or unloading materials, visual impacts from large storage tanks, lighting, traffic, and noise.

Health Risks

Pollution from petroleum storage facilities can impact human health through a number of exposure routes. Petroleum compounds can contaminate drinking water sources or emit toxic fumes (volatile organic compounds, or VOCs) that cause health problems ranging from headaches and nausea to respiratory problems and various cancers (see Hazard 4, Drinking Water: Private Wells). In addition, air inside homes located above groundwater containing high levels of VOCs can become contaminated and pose a variety of health problems to occupants. Air pollution from VOC vapors can especially pose risks to the young, the elderly, and those with respiratory ailments. Recently a woman in Virginia claimed she developed chronic respiratory problems following a spill of more than thirty thousand gallons of jet fuel from a petroleum tank farm. Odors from petroleum storage terminals are not normally associated with health problems, but under certain conditions, such as in the event of a large spill where toxic fumes are emitted, there could be problems. Even minor odors can disrupt the use and enjoyment of a home. Residents may find their lives disrupted from forced evacuations due to a spill, fire, or explosion at a nearby petroleum storage facility.

Financial Risks

Proximity to a petroleum storage facility can affect property values. Private wells at homes near a petroleum storage facility are at risk if groundwater is contaminated. A home with a well polluted by oil will be devalued and difficult to sell. And even if a problem is addressed, a property may still be devalued because of stigma.

Buyers may ask about contamination issues from a nearby petroleum storage facility. Aesthetic concerns such as noise, odors, or traffic problems can also affect a buyer's decision and the negotiations over price.

Other financial risks:

► Liability for nondisclosure; see Disclosure Obligations, pages 13–19.
► Costs associated with contaminated drinking water; see Hazard 4, Drinking Water: Private Wells.
► Costs for short- or long-term medical treatment and monitoring; property damage (such as harm to livestock, crops, or landscap-

ing); legal and expert fees; and inconvenience and relocation costs due to forced evacuation following an accident.

Managing the Risks

See Hazard 4, Drinking Water: Private Wells, for a discussion of how to manage risks if a drinking water well is contaminated.

If you're looking at a home near a petroleum storage facility, expect traffic, noise, odors, and lights. If you are concerned about these issues, make sure that the home is far enough away and that there are substantial vegetative buffers. If there is an occasional odor problem, closing windows or modifying a home's ventilation system may reduce (but not eliminate) the amount of contaminants entering the home. State health and environmental agencies may require the owner of a petroleum storage terminal to minimize odors and noise by changing its activities or requiring the installation of a treatment system.

Contact the petroleum storage facility for financial or technical help to correct a problem and manage the associated risks.

Regulatory Outlook

Petroleum storage facilities must comply with applicable federal and state environmental, health, and safety laws and obtain any necessary permits. Most important, the EPA and most state environmental agencies require all owners of bulk petroleum storage tanks to develop and maintain special spill prevention and control plans to minimize the possibility of polluting groundwater or surface waters. These plans identify possible sources of spills, outline control strategies to reduce the potential for accidental spills to get into the environment, and spell out emergency procedures to follow in the event of a spill or other accident. The EPA and most states also have strict spill reporting laws that require owners to immediately notify agencies in the event of spills. Under the federal Community Right-to-Know law (EPCRA), owners of large tanks are required to submit annual reports (Tier II forms) to local emergency planning authorities (usually the local fire marshal) and to the state environmental agency. These forms, which are available to the public, list the types and amounts of petroleum products stored.

Federal and state environmental agencies can issue orders to a facility that violates its permits or contaminates soil or groundwater. Failure to comply with rules or an order can subject the owner and operator of a petroleum storage facility to both civil and criminal penalties.

What to Look For

A drive around the area should allow you to locate the large tanks that indicate a petroleum storage terminal. Often these terminals are supplied via barges and thus are located on rivers or other large waterways. Spend some time outside to see if there are any odors or problem noises associated with a facility. Remember that noise and odor problems are dependent on weather and wind—what may be an offensive problem one day may not be evident the next.

If a home is close to a petroleum storage terminal, check for visible signs of contamination, like stained soil, stressed vegetation, or an oil sheen on any surface body of water.

If a well is in use, taste and smell the water; however, laboratory tests are usually needed to detect contamination. If a water treatment system or bottled water is used, find out why (see Hazard 4, Drinking Water: Private Wells).

Where to Find Help and Further Information

The location of a nearby petroleum storage terminal can be found by asking the fire marshal or building department or looking at aerial photographs or USGS or Sanborn Fire Insurance maps (see Appendix 3). Ask neighbors and the town land use or building officials about odors, noise, lights, and traffic. Find out if there are any planned petroleum storage terminals, and if there are anticipated expansion plans. Check how the area is zoned and review the local zoning laws that will determine if and how the facility can expand. If necessary, contact a qualified land use attorney. If a petroleum storage terminal is nearby, find out about any problems associated with it or known impacts to drinking water supplies for homes in the vicinity.

The local emergency personnel or the fire marshal should be able to provide detailed information about the facility's operations and the nature of the petroleum (or other chemicals) stored there. State environmental agencies have an emergency or spill response department that maintains files on reported spills and cleanup actions (see Appendix 3). These agencies can also provide copies of any permits, information about a particular facility's design and operation, and details of any known or suspected environmental problems.

If a well is used, contact a state or local environmental or health agency to inquire about known groundwater problems in an area. Owners and potential buyers of nearby homes with wells should test the water (see Hazard 4, Drinking Water: Private Wells). Coordinate tests with a qualified laboratory, consultant, or inspector. Costs range from $50 to $200, depending on the number of constituents tested. Contact the EPA or your state environmental or health agency for additional information or assistance (see Appendix 4).

The Bottom Line

Proximity to a petroleum storage terminal can impact the value of a home due to air or groundwater pollution or by mere stigma. Leaking tanks that contaminate groundwater are common and can pose significant health and financial risks if nearby drinking water wells are impacted. Buyers of nearby homes with wells should have the water tested to see if there is any reason for concern. The costs to address contaminated water are high and the value of a property with a water problem will be significantly reduced. Traffic, noise, odors, and lights from a nearby petroleum storage terminal can affect the use and enjoyment of a home.

44. PRINT SHOPS

Risks: HEALTH ⊕   FINANCIAL $

Background

Print shops are often located near residential neighborhoods, whether in strip malls or shopping centers in the suburbs, or in apartment or condominium complexes, as they are in many cities. There are also a wide variety of facilities with print shops—large commercial "job" shops that print anything from wedding invitations to weekly national magazines; large newspaper or book printers; companies that produce consumer goods; and some manufacturing plants maintain small internal printing or graphic arts facilities. Print shops use and store petroleumbased inks, thinners, and cleaners. There are two possible environmental concerns from chemicals used at print shops: air pollution and associated odors, and groundwater contamination.

Print shops vent fumes from their operations out of the buildings using fans or blowers. Many printers have been required to modify their operations, switch to water-based inks to minimize emissions, or install pollution-control equipment (such as carbon filters) to capture fumes as they exit the building. Volatile organic compounds (VOCs) in the exhaust are usually diluted by the outside air to safe levels and so do not present a health problem. However, fumes may be detected as an objectionable odor.

Current or past spills, improper disposal of wastes into septic systems or dry wells, or on-site waste disposal at print shops may contaminate soil and groundwater. Nearby homes that use well water may be at risk if there is groundwater contamination.

Health Risks

There are a large number of VOCs in the inks, thinners, and cleaners used in print shops. While some are relatively nontoxic, others are known to cause serious health problems. In cases where an odor can be detected, air emissions of VOCs will be a nuisance but are usually not a health problem, since the level and duration of exposure are typically low and infrequent. Breathing low levels of organic solvents can cause short-term health effects such as headaches, loss of energy, and nausea. Health risks from drinking VOC-contaminated water can be more serious, depending on the specific compound ingested, its level, and the amount of water consumed. Laboratory studies, as well as reports of people who have consumed VOC-contaminated groundwater, have linked such exposures to birth defects, cancer, and a host of other health problems (see Hazard 4, Drinking Water: Private Wells). In addition, air inside homes located above groundwater containing high levels of VOCs can become contaminated and pose a variety of health problems to occupants.

In response to environmental concerns, many print shops have converted to water- or soybean oil–based inks, which have significantly less odor and are less toxic than compounds historically used in inks and cleaners.

Financial Risks

Properties near a print shop and impacted by air emissions can be substantially devalued due to concerns over health impacts or aesthetic issues. In addition, if activities at a print shop have contaminated soil or groundwater, nearby private drinking water wells may be at risk. Homes with contaminated wells will be devalued and difficult to sell. And even if a problem is addressed, a property may be devalued because of stigma.

Buyers of properties near print shops may ask about odor problems or for information about possible contamination of drinking water supplies. This may be a point of contention in negotiations over price.

Other financial risks:

▶ Liability for nondisclosure; see Disclosure Obligations, pages 13–19.

▶ Costs associated with contaminated drinking water; see Hazard 4, Drinking Water: Private Wells.

▶ Costs for short- or long-term medical treatment and monitoring; and legal and expert fees.

Managing the Risks

See Hazard 4, Drinking Water: Private Wells, for a discussion of how to manage risks if a drinking water well is contaminated.

When there is an occasional odor problem, closing windows or modifying a home's ventilation system may reduce (but not eliminate) the amount of polluted air entering the home. State health and environmental agencies can force companies to minimize air pollution or odor problems—a print shop may need to change its activities or install an air treatment system.

Contact the print shop for financial or technical help to correct a problem and manage the associated risks.

Regulatory Outlook

Print shops must comply with applicable federal, state, and local environmental laws and regulations. For example, under various environmental programs, the EPA and state environmental agencies regulate the use, storage, and disposal of hazardous chemicals and wastes; air emissions; and the cleanup of contaminated soil and groundwater.

Large print shops using inks and cleaners with VOCs are likely to be required to have air permits issued by the EPA or a state or local agency. These operations may face significant new requirements as a result of the federal Clean Air Act Amendments of 1990. State and local health and environmental agencies usually have rules about "nuisance" odors as well as emissions of hazardous air pollutants. However, many smaller printing operations may be exempt from certain rules.

Federal and state environmental agencies have authority to issue compliance orders to any company that violates the law or contaminates soil or groundwater. Failure to comply with applicable requirements can subject an owner to both civil and criminal penalties.

What to Look For

A drive or walk around the area will allow you to locate commercial print shops. Remember that many types of manufacturers may have a print shop at their plant.

If a well is in use, taste and smell the water; however, laboratory tests are usually needed to detect contamination. If a water treatment system or bottled water is used, find out why (see Hazard 4, Drinking Water: Private Wells).

A potential buyer should spend some time outside (when the print shop is operating) to detect any unusual odors. Air pollution and odor problems are localized—properties more than a few hundred feet away should not experience problems unless there is a large commercial printing facility in the area. Remember that weather conditions, especially wind direction, influence whether or not an odor is detected on a given day. If a home is close to a print shop, check for visible signs of contamination like stained soil, stressed vegetation, or a sheen on any surface body of water.

Where to Find Help and Further Information

Check with the neighbors and the town land use or building officials to identify any existing or planned print shops, and ask if there are any anticipated expansion plans. Find out how the area is zoned and about the local zoning laws that will determine if and how the print shop can expand. If necessary, contact a qualified land use attorney. If a print shop is nearby, find out about any odor problems or known impacts to drinking water supplies for homes in the vicinity. State or local health or environmental agencies may have information about known or suspected problems in an area, as well as whether any permits have been applied for by, or issued to, a printing operation.

Owners and potential buyers of nearby homes with wells should consider testing the water (see Hazard 4, Drinking Water: Private Wells). For $100 to $200, water can be tested for VOCs. Coordinate tests with a qualified laboratory, consultant, or inspector. Indoor air testing for VOCs can also be performed—costs for this type of testing can be high ($300 or more). Contact the EPA or your state environmental or health agency for additional information or assistance (see Appendix 4).

The Bottom Line

Living close to a print shop can affect the use and enjoyment of a home. If odors from a print shop are detected, they'll likely be a nuisance rather than a major health problem. But frequent odor problems can impact property values. Buyers of nearby homes that rely on private wells should have the water tested to see if there is any reason for concern. The costs to address contaminated water are high and the value of a property with a water problem will be significantly reduced.

45. RADIO AND COMMUNICATION TOWERS

Risks: HEALTH   Uncertain   FINANCIAL $

Background

Radio and communication towers—we call them R/C towers—are used for a variety of purposes and are sprouting up everywhere today across the United States. Traditionally they have been used to broadcast public safety (police, fire, and other emergency public service departments), radio, and television signals using various types of transmitting antennas. More recently, R/C towers have been built to support various types of technologies, such as cable, cellular telephone, paging, two-way radio, and newly licensed personal communication systems. Since the mid-1980s, telecommunications towers are being sited everywhere following the explosion in the demand for cellular telephones; it is reported that more than twenty-five thousand new cell phone customers sign up every day. The number of cell phones used nationwide has gone from 300,000 in 1985 to over thirty million today—paralleling the number of users has been a growth in companies providing these services and the number of cellular phone towers needed to provide coverage. It is estimated that there are about 20,000 cellular phone sites today (many are stand-alone towers—antennas are also placed on structures like water towers and tall buildings) and that more than 100,000 additional cell sites and 15,000 more towers will be needed over the next ten years.

A common local conflict pits companies wishing to site R/C towers against local residents not wanting them in their backyards or neighborhoods. Residents everywhere are fighting the siting of towers because of concerns about visual impacts, electromagnetic fields (EMFs), tower collapses, and impacts to property values. In addition, the companies erecting R/C towers cannot *take* property because they are not the government; rather they must negotiate a lease or purchase the property to site a tower. Because of this, property owners who enter into leases or sales with these companies are ending up in battles (legal and personal) with neighbors.

R/C towers range in height from short (fifty feet) to midsize (two hundred to five hundred feet) to huge (one thousand feet or more). Towers may be simple poles (called monopoles), lattice towers, or guyed towers (supported by wires). The most common R/C towers are cellular telecommunications towers that can hold anywhere from one to dozens of transmitting and receiving antennas, are one hundred to two hundred feet tall, and are located near major roads and highways. The height of a tower is determined by many factors, such as the type of communication devices it supports, the distance to the nearest tower, and the local terrain.

Not all R/C towers are the same. Radio and television towers have powerful transmission devices (tens of thousands of watts of power) and a single tower will provide service to a huge geographical area. Cellular telecommunications towers, on the other hand, are significantly less powerful (tens or hundreds of watts), and depending on local terrain and other factors, the towers may need to be as close as one-quarter mile or as far as fifty miles apart.

R/C towers and their associated communications equipment emit a type of EMF known as radio frequency (RF) radiation. RF radiation is nonionizing, which, unlike ionizing radiation associated with X rays or nuclear power, has not been shown to create health problems except when large exposures occur in occupational settings, such as to electrical workers. RF radiation is normally not a health risk to home owners living near an R/C tower because RF radiation levels decrease quickly with distance from the source. Since cellular antennas require very little power (around 100 watts), RF radiation levels from cellular towers are relatively insignificant even at the base of a tower, and are negligible at property boundaries.

The major impact to residential real estate from R/C towers is aesthetics—many people consider these towers "visual pollution." Visual impacts from a specific tower vary with a home's location and other factors, such as the height of trees, topography, the distance to nearby properties, and the location of buildings, roadways, and other properties in the sight line of the tower. For the most part, R/C towers are tall steel structures that may be lit at night. Since they are often located on ridgelines (to increase their effective height), they can be especially visible. In response to complaints about eyesores, some companies have tried to soften the visual impact by hiding the towers in barns, silos, or other structures, or camouflaging them to look like flagpoles, bell towers, clock towers, or trees. Other concerns include interference from tower transmission to radios, TVs, electric garage-door openers, baby monitors, and cordless phones, and noise from associated electrical equipment (such as heating, air-conditioning, and ventilation systems or generators housed in nearby equipment buildings) or periodic vehicle access to the site.

Because R/C towers are typically sited on high elevations, the construction of the access road and site itself can increase storm water runoff. Thus, homes near or below towers that are being developed may be affected by storm water runoff containing sediments from the construction site itself or from the access road, which can cause erosion and harm a home's lawn and gardens, wetlands, ponds, lakes, and well water.

Health Risks

Whether justified or not, the main health issue concerning the general public about R/C towers is EMFs. The EMF issue and potential related health risks are discussed in greater detail in Hazard 28, Electromagnetic Fields. The American National Standards Institute (ANSI), 655 15th Street, N.W., Suite 300, Washington, D.C. 20005 (202/639-4090) and the Institute of Electrical and Electronics Engineers (IEEE), 1828 L Street, N.W., Suite 1200, Washington, D.C. 20036 (202/785-2180) have published standards for safe levels of exposure to RF radiation. For the siting and operation of towers containing high-powered transmitters, for example, the Federal Communications Commission (FCC) (202/418-0200) utilizes the ANSI standards to set maximum allowable exposure (power density) at the base of a tower by requiring a worst-case approximation of RF levels that assumes all antennas are transmitting simultaneously on all channels at full power. Note that the RF radiation levels at the base of a *cellular* tower are less than 5 to 10 percent of the allowable standard; this level drops off rapidly with distance and is usually negligible at the property boundary. Therefore, the FCC specifically excludes cellular towers from the requirement to perform RF power density calculations because of their relatively low power (although state or local agencies may require such a demonstration).

RF radiation from towers generally should pose no hazards to human health or risk to the public because nearby homes and residents are not exposed to excessive levels. The same applies to towers having microwave communication antennas (point-to-point forms of communication used in lieu of transmitting communications through landlines). These antennas are typically located high up on the tower and angled in such a way that they "see" (point at) a receiver on a distant tower and emit a very narrow microwave beam that transmits the signal—this beam does *not* come in contact with people (. . . unless you're parachuting through the beam). While some uncertainty surrounds the scientific evidence about the health effects of EMFs, the RF radiation levels associated with R/C towers are so low as to present minimal, if any, risks.

Home owners have also raised concerns about falling R/C towers. However, reported instances of tower collapses are rare—most state and local agencies require that they be built to withstand certain inclement weather conditions, including hurricane-force winds, ice buildup, and so forth. We are aware of no instances of personal injuries from a falling R/C tower.

Noise associated with the construction or operation of an R/C tower (many claim these towers "hum") and related equipment can be a distraction, disturb your sleep, and disrupt the use and enjoyment of your home.

Financial Risks

Proximity to an R/C tower can devalue a residential property. Due to concern over visual impacts, the pool of potential buyers for properties visually impacted by R/C towers may be reduced. Studies by real estate appraisers and other experts have shown property devaluations from proximity to R/C towers (the amount of devaluation is difficult to predict—one study showed properties declined in value by 3 to 12 percent); industry experts maintain that the studies are flawed and that there is no measurable effect on property values. Properties may be devalued because of stigma—mere uncertainty or lack of complete knowledge about the EMF health issue can affect real estate values (see Hazard 28, Electromagnetic Fields).

Potential buyers may ask about problems such as EMF health issues, noise, and lights from a nearby R/C tower—these can all affect a buyer's decision and the negotiations over price. If a nearby tower's fall zone— that is, the largest circle that can be drawn around a tower *assuming* it could break off at its base and fall over in any direction—would be on a portion of the property, this may be another concern for potential buyers. In a real estate transaction, if there is a known issue that could affect property values, such as the planned siting of a tower in the neighborhood, and it is not disclosed, the seller and the agent may be liable for failure to disclose the problem, especially where a state requires such disclosure (see Disclosure Obligations, pages 13–19).

Other financial risks:
  ▶ Damage to property or landscaping; and legal and expert fees to challenge a tower siting or bring a property damage or personal injury claim.

Managing the Risks

If an R/C tower is being sited, find out if the company has considered sharing space on nearby towers to eliminate the need for a new one (some state or local siting laws may require companies to do this). If a tower will be built, talk to the owner to verify that it will be constructed, operated, and maintained correctly (for your own concern or so you can respond to the questions and concerns of potential buyers).

Get involved with the siting process—whether at the state or local level—to ensure that your concerns are addressed. The two most common issues concerning the siting of R/C towers are health and safety, and visual impacts. To minimize visual impacts, ensure that the tower is:

- built only as high as absolutely necessary;
- a monopole rather than a lattice tower or guyed tower;
- when possible, painted a blue-gray to blend in with the sky; and
- landscaped with vegetation and an inoffensive fence that hides the tower and associated equipment buildings.

Also make sure that the tower's fall zone does not extend onto your property.

If the tower is already built, contact the tower owner or the appropriate state or local authority and request proof that RF radiation on your property does not exceed applicable safety standards and that all other requirements are met. While there is nothing that a home owner can do to reduce RF levels, there are many ways that the tower owner or operator can lower RF radiation levels.

If you're considering a home near an R/C tower and have concerns about visual impacts, make sure that the house is far enough away and that there are substantial vegetative buffers to minimize sight and noise impacts.

Contact the tower owner and the government agency with authority over the tower for financial or technical help to correct a problem and manage the associated risks.

Regulatory Outlook

R/C towers must comply with applicable federal, state, and local communications, environmental, and land use laws and regulations. Presently, R/C towers are regulated at the federal level by the FCC and at the state level often by public utilities commissions and by county and local zoning agencies.

In regard to health and safety issues—namely, concerns over EMFs—FCC-regulated towers must meet the ANSI standards for RF radiation (discussed above—see pages 298–299) at the property line. Many state and local agencies responsible for siting these towers have adopted these standards.

The Federal Aviation Administration (FAA) also has jurisdiction over R/C towers and reviews proposed tower construction plans to ensure that they will not be a hazard to air navigation. In certain cases (based on proposed tower height or proximity to an airport) the FAA may require a tower to be marked (painted with stripes) and/or lighted (with beacons or strobe lights), which can create additional visual impacts for nearby residents.

Some states, counties, and towns have stringent laws and regulations; others have none. At either the state or local level, some form of agency permit or approval, such as a certificate of environmental compatibility and public need, may be required for the construction, maintenance, and operation of an R/C tower. These approvals typically require notification of nearby property owners and the submittal of an application or an environmental impact assessment that evaluates the effects of the tower on issues such as the environment; public health and safety; scenic, historic, and recreational values and activities; forests and parks; air and water (including wetlands); and fish and wildlife. Public hearings may be required. Many other aspects of R/C towers may also be regulated, such as type of tower, height, fall zone location, ability to withstand certain weather conditions, and so forth.

In some states, the siting process is controlled by the county or the town or city; in other states, a state-level agency (a "super"–zoning board or siting commission) may have superseding jurisdiction over local authority. Because of the variability and uncertainty in the siting process, the telecommunications industry recently attempted to have federal law preempt state and local authority governing the siting of

R/C towers. The industry lost, and for now the siting of towers remains controlled by state laws and local land use requirements.

Many owners of R/C towers are becoming sensitive to their environmental, financial, and health impacts on neighboring land uses, including private homes; in time, as regulatory agency oversight and private lawsuits increase, others will too. However, until satellite technology for mass communication becomes a reality, more towers will need to be sited in the future.

What to Look For

Today R/C towers are just about everywhere; most will be obvious as you drive around the neighborhood. However, in rural areas that are heavily wooded, the towers may be difficult to spot and may not be identified on local maps. It is usually hard to miss R/C towers close to a property, as they are fifty- to one-thousand-foot structures; however, some companies have begun to camouflage them as barns, silos, or other structures. Often towers are situated on hilltops and placed in groupings (sometimes referred to as "tower farms"). If there is a tower nearby, remember, it may be much more visible in the winter than it is in the summer.

Where to Find Help and Further Information

Check with the neighbors and the town land use or building officials to identify any existing or planned R/C towers. Find out how the area is zoned and about the state and local zoning laws that will determine if a tower can be sited. If necessary, contact a qualified land use attorney. If an R/C tower is nearby, find out about any problems associated with it or any known impacts to homes in the vicinity. Historic aerial photographs and USGS and local zoning maps may show the location of a nearby tower (see Appendix 3).

If there is a tower, find out who owns and operates it and call with your questions. State or local public utility, environmental, or land use agencies can assist you in identifying problems and possible solutions (see Appendix 4).

The R/C tower owner may be willing to take RF radiation measurements for you on your property. These tests may also be conducted by a qualified electrical engineering consultant.

The Bottom Line

Proximity to an R/C tower can impact the value of a home, as most people consider them eyesores. Visual impacts, noise, and lights from these towers can affect the use and enjoyment of a home. Radiation from R/C towers is negligible and is generally not considered to pose a health risk to nearby residents. However, health risks from EMFs are still being debated. Keep in mind that the number of towers will increase as the demand for cellular phones and other communications technologies increases. In addition, local zoning may play no role in the siting of these towers, as state agencies may dictate where they go—check thoroughly for any towers planned in your neighborhood.

46. RAILROAD YARDS AND TRACKS

Risks: HEALTH   ✚✚   FINANCIAL $ $

Background

Railroads have been around a long time and are found everywhere, from downtown areas of cities to the least populated countryside. Although railroad corridors pass through some of the most pristine and scenic areas of the United States, environmental problems abound, often tracing back to when the yards and tracks were first built. Environmental impacts and the financial and health risks from railroads arise from railroad yards, tracks, and trains.

At railroad yards, contaminants from locomotive fueling and washing, maintenance, and temporary waste storage often end up in wastewater discharges. Railroads use more than three billion gallons of diesel fuel per year—spills from fueling and leaks from underground storage tanks are common. Although many railroads now use aboveground tanks, past contamination exists, and the potential for spills or leaks remains. One railroad recently had to pay $2.5 million in criminal environmental fines for a significant spill of oil and grease that polluted a river near Boston.

Often, chemicals used in railroad yards, such as waste oils, solvents, and diesel fuel, have migrated to nearby properties through soil and groundwater contamination as well as from storm water runoff, which can cause erosion and harm a home's lawn, gardens, wetlands, ponds, lakes, and well water. In the past, most railroads operated their own tie-treating plants (some still do). Toxic wood preservatives like creosote have contaminated soil and groundwater at many railroad yards and along many tracks. In addition, contamination from PCBs (see Hazard 16, PCBs), in the fire-resistant dielectric fluid used in the electrical transformers under some older railroad cars (as well as in transformers at rail yards and along tracks), is common. The severity of environmental problems at railroad yards is underscored by the report that one railroad company recently had to pay more than $7 million in fines and costs to assess contamination at railroad yards in Alabama, Florida, Georgia, Kentucky, South Carolina, and Tennessee. In addition, many railroad yards have become federal or state Superfund sites (see Hazard 49, Superfund Sites).

Railroad tracks and rights-of-way have environmental problems that pose threats to drinking water wells from contaminated fill materials used to support tracks, railroad ties preserved with toxic chemicals, and rights-of-way sprayed with pesticides and other defoliants. Also, EMFs *may* pose health risks to residents who live along electrified rails (see Hazard 28, Electromagnetic Fields).

Trains have environmental impacts: emissions include diesel particulates, hydrocarbons, nitrogen oxides, and carbon monoxide. Trains transport large quantities of solid and hazardous waste and toxic chemicals; and derailments, spills, explosions, and other accidents, while rare, do happen, often resulting in evacuations and harm to people, property, and the environment. The Federal Railroad Administration reported about 2,000 accidents involving trains carrying hazardous materials from 1985 to 1989, of which about 250 resulted in a spill. In some places, the lingering effects of these accidents result in long-term soil, surface water, and groundwater contamination problems.

Finally, railroads are also a source of noise, vibrations, odors, smoke, and lights for nearby residential properties.

Health Risks

Pollution from railroad yards or tracks can impact human health through a number of exposure routes. Toxic chemicals, including petroleum compounds, pesticides, solvents, and others, can contaminate drinking water wells and cause health problems (see Hazard 4, Drinking Water: Private Wells). In addition, air inside homes located above groundwater containing high levels of certain organic compounds (VOCs) can become contaminated and pose a variety of health problems to occupants. Health problems can also arise from the historic discharge of sanitary wastes from trains; high levels of nitrogen and bacteria can contaminate water to levels above drinking water standards, rendering it unsafe.

Air pollution from railroad yards, "pesticide drift" from spraying railroad rights-of-way, and train emissions can pose risks, especially to the young, the elderly, and those with respiratory ailments. For example, a Tennessee woman was repeatedly hospitalized for severe reactions to what were claimed were creosote fumes from an adjacent railroad yard that treated and stored wooden railroad ties with preservatives.

In addition, historic and recent chemical spills from train derailments can have catastrophic health impacts. Some examples:

- in 1995, a train carrying toxic and potentially flammable and explosive chemicals derailed near Miami, Oklahoma, and forced the evacuation of more than five hundred people from their homes;
- in 1993, a spill created a sulfuric acid cloud more than six miles long that drifted over a residential development in Richmond, California (the home owners and others settled for $180 million to cover personal injury and property-related claims);
- in 1993, after more than sixty thousand people in Minnesota and Wisconsin were evacuated following a spill of benzene and other chemicals from a derailed train, the railroad company agreed to settle a lawsuit for more than $2 million for personal injuries, property damages, inconvenience for evacuation, and other issues; and
- in 1986, a train derailed in Ohio, released toxic phosphorus gas, and forced the evacuation of thousands of homes—a class action for personal injury claims is pending.

Other railroad issues, such as odors and delays at train crossings, can disrupt the use and enjoyment of a home. Noise and vibrations can also be significant; many homes are situated near railroad tracks where trains pass as frequently as every thirty minutes or less. Trains produce low-level but continuous vibrations and noise, and their whistles in the middle of the night are a shock to anyone who's not used to them.

If access to an active railroad track is not restricted (and, sometimes, even if it is), there may be dangers to those who venture near them (especially young children).

Financial Risks

Proximity to a railroad yard or tracks can devalue properties. Nearby homes with private wells are at risk if groundwater is contaminated. For example, nine families in Paoli, Pennsylvania, are trying to recover damages for soil and groundwater contamination and property devaluation (including stigma damages) caused by PCB contamination from a nearby railroad yard (the estimated cost to clean up the yard and their property is more than $25 million). Homes with wells polluted by chemicals from a railroad yard, tracks, or a spill will be devalued and difficult to sell. And even if a problem is addressed, a property may be devalued because of stigma. Recently, many home owners have raised claims of property devaluation due to concerns about potential EMF health hazards from nearby electrified rails.

A buyer may ask about soil or water contamination issues from a nearby railroad yard or tracks. Odors, noise, smoke, lights, or traffic can affect a buyer's decision and the negotiations over price.

Other financial risks:

- ▶ Liability for nondisclosure; see Disclosure Obligations, pages 13–19.
- ▶ Costs associated with contaminated drinking water; see Hazard 4, Drinking Water: Private Wells.
- ▶ Costs for short- or long-term medical treatment and monitoring; property damage (such as structural damage to a home from vibrations, or harm to livestock, crops, or landscaping); legal and expert fees; and inconvenience and relocation costs due to forced evacuation following an accident.

Managing the Risks

See Hazard 4, Drinking Water: Private Wells, for a discussion of how to manage risks if a drinking water well is contaminated.

If you're looking at a home near a railroad yard or track, expect noise, odors, and vibrations. Soundproofing may be an option (and there may be funds available—check with the railroad company). If you're considering a home near a railroad yard or track and have concerns about visual and noise impacts, make sure that the house is going to be far enough away and that there are substantial vegetative buffers to minimize them.

Contact the railroad for financial or technical help to correct a problem and manage the associated risks.

Regulatory Outlook

Railroads must comply with applicable federal environmental, health, and safety laws, and obtain the necessary permits. The U.S. Department of Transportation (which includes the Federal Railroad Administration and the National Transportation Safety Board), the Interstate Commerce Commission, the EPA, and OSHA all play some role in regulating the environmental, health, and safety aspects of a railroad, such as:

- the use, storage, and disposal of diesel fuel, pesticides, and other materials;
- air emissions;
- the installation, monitoring, and removal of all fuel storage tanks;
- the disposal of hazardous wastes;
- emergency responses; and
- the cleanup of contaminated soil, surface water, and groundwater.

Environmental impact reports, which are available to the public, must be prepared before a railroad undertakes a significant activity (such as track abandonment, expansion, or renovation). Where not preempted by federal law, state and local agencies and private entities also play roles in regulating railroads.

Although railroads have reduced their locomotive emissions by more than 25 percent over the last several years, the EPA is looking for greater reductions (as high as 65 percent) by the turn of the century. Railroads are also addressing noise and other environmental impacts, including:

- cleaning up historic spills and reducing operating pollution;
- using state-of-the-art fueling stations, oil-water separators, and fuel storage tanks; and
- responding more efficiently to spills and emergencies, and disseminating information to property owners following a spill.

Today, railroads employ environmental management personnel to assist with these efforts and budget tens of millions of dollars a year for environmental programs. In some areas, partnerships between railroads, agencies, and chemical manufacturers speed up responses to hazardous materials spills.

The railroad industry is becoming more sensitive to its impacts on neighbors; problems will diminish as agency oversight and private lawsuits over contamination and other environmental, health, and safety issues increase.

What to Look For

Railroads are everywhere; trains and railroad yards will be obvious as you drive around an area. However, little-used or abandoned railroad tracks become overgrown with brush and are difficult to spot; just because you can't see them does not mean that there is no reason for concern about contamination from past activities. Inspect a home when the railroad is busy or a train is going by; it should give you a good sense of what to expect in the way of odors, noise, traffic, and vibrations. Remember that odors and noise may be only an intermittent problem, depending on what operations are occurring at the railroad yard and which way the wind is blowing.

Environmental contamination will not be obvious. If a well is in use, taste and smell the water; however, laboratory tests are usually needed to detect contamination. If a water treatment system or bottled water is used, find out why (see Hazard 4, Drinking Water: Private Wells). If a home is close to a railroad yard or tracks, check for visible signs of contamination, such as stained soil, stressed vegetation, or an oil sheen on any surface body of water.

Where to Find Help and Further Information

Aerial photographs and USGS and Sanborn Fire Insurance maps should show the location of railroad yards and tracks (see Appendix 3). Check with neighbors and town land use or building officials about any problems from a nearby railroad yard or tracks and about any expansion plans. Find out when the trains run. Ask about associated noise, odors, vibration problems, underground storage tanks, and historic spills (and known impacts to drinking water wells). Owners and potential buyers of nearby homes with wells should consider testing the water (see Hazard 4, Drinking Water: Private Wells). Test the water (and soil, if necessary) for chemicals such as petroleum, pesticides, PCBs, or other compounds. Coordinate tests with a qualified laboratory, consultant, or home inspector. Contact the EPA or your state environmental or health agency for additional information or assistance (see Appendix 4).

The Bottom Line

The railroad industry is not environmentally benign. Proximity to a railroad yard or tracks can impact the value of a home. Soil and groundwater contamination from past or present railroad activities can pose health and financial risks if nearby drinking water wells are impacted.

Buyers of homes with private wells near a railroad yard or that have tracks on or near the property should have the water tested to see if there is any reason for concern. The costs to address contaminated water are high and the value of a property with a water problem will be significantly reduced. Noise, odors, vibrations, and traffic can all affect the use and enjoyment of a home.

47. SALT STORAGE AREAS

Risks: HEALTH   ⊕   FINANCIAL $

Background

Salt is routinely applied to road surfaces in various areas of the United States to melt ice and snow to ensure safe winter travel. While beneficial, road deicing salt can cause significant environmental damage to forests and to aquatic life in lakes and streams, contaminate groundwater, and corrode pipes and appliances in a home. Road salt can get into drinking water supplies from runoff at salt storage sites (or from heavily salted roads) by seeping through soil into underground drinking water sources. Historically, state and local departments of transportation (DOTs) stored road salt on the bare ground and without the use of any type of cover. Because of this, uncovered salt washed into the ground, and many public and private drinking water supplies became contaminated.

Health Risks

Drinking water with high sodium levels can increase the risk of, or exacerbate, hypertension (high blood pressure) or heart disease.

The EPA and state environmental or health agencies set standards for acceptable levels of salt in drinking water. The EPA recommends, as a National Secondary Drinking Water Standard (which are unenforceable guidelines), that chloride levels not exceed 250 mg/L (=ppm) (see Appendix 2). However, federal law does not require either the states or public water systems to comply with secondary drinking water standards. In addition, some states have set sodium standards for drinking water (often 20 mg/L; standards vary from state to state—check your state's drinking water rules).

Financial Risks

Nearby homes with drinking water wells are at risk if groundwater is contaminated. Homes with contaminated wells will be devalued and difficult to sell. Proximity to a salt storage area can devalue a home by the mere threat of a problem. And even if a problem is addressed, a property may be devalued because of stigma. Salt that gets into a private well can severely corrode a home's pipes and appliances (such as dishwashers and washing machines), requiring them to be replaced.

A recent Michigan case shows how significantly a home can be devalued when a well is contaminated with salt, sometimes beyond the value of the property. In this case, twelve home owners who had been living on bottled water for more than ten years were awarded about $120,000 each—more than the fair market value of their homes—for damages resulting from the town's improper storage of road salt, which contaminated their drinking water wells.

Buyers of homes near salt storage areas may ask about possible drinking water contamination. A home owner may also face increased landscaping costs if lawns, gardens, and trees are damaged from heavy applications of salt or substantial runoff from a storage area. In addition, any wetlands or body of water on or adjacent to a property (and associated wildlife) may be threatened.

Other financial risks:
- ▸ Liability for nondisclosure; see Disclosure Obligations, pages 13–19.
- ▸ Costs associated with contaminated drinking water; see Hazard 4, Drinking Water: Private Wells.
- ▸ Costs for short- or long-term medical treatment and monitoring; and legal and expert fees.

Managing the Risks

If salt has contaminated a public water supply, the supplier should address the problem. See Hazard 4, Drinking Water: Private Wells, for a discussion of how to manage risks if a *private* drinking water well is contaminated.

Contact the salt storage facility for financial or technical help to correct a problem and manage the associated risks.

Regulatory Outlook

Today, most state and local DOTs are required to use enclosed, covered sheds with impermeable floors to store their salt supplies. The siting of new salt storage facilities and the use of salt is also banned in many environmentally sensitive areas, such as water-supply watersheds or near wetlands and lakes. Overall, problems should decrease as more and more DOTs and state environmental agencies develop rules to control the storage and application of road salt to minimize damage to water supplies and the environment, and as salt substitutes and other application methods (such as varied sand-salt ratios) are used. But remember that past practices of salt storage can still cause problems today.

What to Look For

Drive around the neighborhood to locate any nearby salt storage areas. If a well is in use, taste the water—if it's salty, investigate. If a water treatment system or bottled water is used, find out why. However, laboratory tests will usually be needed to determine salt levels (see Hazard 4, Drinking Water: Private Wells). If a home is near a salt storage area, inspect the property for stressed or burned-out vegetation, which may indicate salt contamination.

Where to Find Help and Further Information

Since there is usually only one salt storage area in a town, or at most a few, a call to the town hall (land use or building department) should quickly get you the locations. Aerial photographs and USGS and Sanborn Fire Insurance maps may show the location of salt storage areas (see Appendix 3). Ask neighbors if they know of any nearby salt storage areas. Remember to ask not just about current storage areas, but where salt was stored in the past. If a salt storage area is or was nearby, find out about any problems associated with it or if there are reports of impacts to drinking water wells for homes in the vicinity. If a home relies on a private well and there is or was a nearby salt storage area, have the water tested for salinity and inspect the appliances for evidence of corrosion. Contact the EPA or your state environmental or health agency, or DOT, for additional information or assistance (see Appendix 4).

The Bottom Line

Problems concerning road salt arise from its storage and use near homes with private drinking water wells. Although road salt contamination of private wells is not common, there are many reported incidents of salt storage facilities causing groundwater contamination. To minimize financial risks and eliminate health concerns, buyers of homes with drinking water wells should test the water. Contaminated water is expensive to deal with and any property with a well contaminated by salt will be devalued.

48. SEWAGE TREATMENT PLANTS

Risks: HEALTH ⊕ ⊕   FINANCIAL $ $

Background

Billions of gallons of domestic wastewater produced every day in communities throughout the country are collected in sewers and routed to publicly owned sewage treatment plants (which we call STPs but are also known as POTWs, publicly owned treatment works), where it is purified so that it can be safely released to the environment. There are thousands of public STPs in the country that have been built with the help of over $10 billion in federal assistance since the late 1960s. Privately owned STPs are also common, especially at mobile home parks, condominium developments, university campuses, and malls where there are no available public sewers. STPs provide a valuable service—they treat the wastewater we produce so the water can be discharged without harming human health or the environment. Sewage-pumping stations may be located in residential areas (and often far from the STP itself); they house the pumps needed to transfer the sewage across hilly terrain.

Odors are the major environmental problem from STP operations that can impact neighboring homes. Odors may occur within sewers, at sewage-pumping stations, or at the STP itself, where air mixed with wastewater or sludge is eventually released into the atmosphere. Also, STPs sometimes handle their waste sludge on-site in ways that can generate odors—they may burn it in incinerators, compost it, or maintain on-site lagoons or landfills. Given what they do, STPs cannot completely eliminate odors. However, many plants now include expensive systems to capture and treat offensive odors. STPs are usually located far from residential developments, but not always. Depending on distance, direction of prevailing winds, and weather conditions, odors from an STP can sometimes be detected at some distance.

STP discharges, if not treated properly, will pollute waterways, rendering them unsafe for drinking, fishing, shellfishing, or recreation. Downstream waterfront property owners can be significantly impacted in these situations. In some cases, instead of flowing to waterways, STP wastewater is discharged into the ground using leaching fields or other structures, or reused for irrigation. In these situations, groundwater supplies can become contaminated. Groundwater contamination at STPs can also result from on-site disposal of sludge as well as leaks from the underground fuel or chemical tanks that are typically located at these facilities.

STPs often use large quantities of chemicals during the water treatment process—some of these chemicals, like chlorine or chlorine dioxide gas, present environmental risks if not handled and stored properly. Additional environmental concerns at STPs include noise (usually large blowers must run continuously to provide the air needed to run the plant), lighting, and truck or rail traffic associated with chemical deliveries.

Homes near STPs may be affected by storm water runoff contaminated with wastes or other pollutants, which can impact lawns, gardens, wetlands, ponds, and lakes.

Health Risks

The odors associated with STPs and pumping stations, while offensive to some, are usually not linked to health problems. Some odors may be due to a compound called hydrogen sulfide which produces a rotten egg–like smell. At low levels hydrogen sulfide can cause symptoms like eye irritation and nausea; at extremely high levels it can be toxic and even explosive. Due to dilution in the air before it reaches neighboring properties, hydrogen sulfide often falls in the category of a nuisance that, while certainly significant and offensive, is not known to cause serious health problems. In an extreme example, odors from a Tennessee STP and its sewage lagoon were so strong that habitation of the nearby homes was almost impossible—the odor was found to be a nuisance, and the city was forced to correct the problem and pay damages to the home owners.

Potential water contaminants from an STP discharge include bacteria, nitrates, oxygen-depleting organics, and metals. Exposure via drinking polluted water, skin contact, or eating tainted fish or shellfish can cause a variety of health problems from rashes to diarrhea to hepatitis. For water discharges, the common route of exposure would be from swimming in inadequately treated wastewater before it is diluted in the waterway. In the case of on-site disposal systems, such as when treated sewage effluent is used for irrigation, there is a chance of direct exposure if access to the area is not properly restricted.

Bacteria and nitrates can get into groundwater and impact nearby drinking water wells if the STP uses a poorly designed or failing on-site leaching field or other disposal system. See Hazard 4, Drinking Water: Private Wells, for a discussion of health risks associated with contaminated groundwater. In addition, beach closings as a result of STP discharges happen every summer throughout the United States.

Financial Risks

Due to the nature of real estate supply and demand, any property located close to an STP will be devalued to some degree. Properties known to be impacted by major odors from an STP (or a sewer line or pumping station) may be devalued more and may be difficult to sell. Because of stigma, buyers may be wary of any property very close to an STP, even if there are no actual environmental problems. Waterfront property values can be impacted if recreational or other uses are limited due to pollution caused by an upstream STP.

Potential buyers of a property near an STP may ask about odors, noise, and possible contamination of drinking water supplies—all possible points of contention in negotiations over price.

Other financial risks:
▶ Liability for nondisclosure; see Disclosure Obligations, pages 13–19.
▶ Costs associated with contaminated drinking water; see Hazard 4, Drinking Water: Private Wells.
▶ Costs for short- or long-term medical treatment and monitoring; property damage (to buildings, livestock, crops, or landscaping); legal and expert fees; and inconvenience and relocation costs due to forced evacuation following an accident.

Managing the Risks

See Hazard 4, Drinking Water: Private Wells, for a discussion of how to manage risks if a well is contaminated.

If you're looking at a home near an STP, expect some odors, noise, and traffic. If you are concerned about these issues, make sure that the home is far enough away and that there are substantial vegetative buffers to minimize them. If there is an occasional odor problem, closing windows or modifying a home's ventilation system may temporarily reduce (but not eliminate) the amount of contaminated air entering the home. State health and environmental agencies can require an STP to eliminate air pollution or odor problems by changing its activities or installing an air treatment system. Unfortunately, easy, affordable, and quick solutions to odors may not be available, as significant problems are often caused by the design of already installed sewers and treatment plants.

Contact the STP for financial or technical help to correct a problem and manage the associated risks.

Regulatory Outlook

Day-to-day operations at STPs are heavily regulated by federal, state and local environmental agencies, and STP owners are legally responsible for the proper design and operation of their plants. Under the Clean Water Act, all STPs must have permits for wastewater discharges to waterways and must file reports regularly about plant operations and the quality of their discharges. Wastewater discharges to the ground are subject to state and local permit requirements that usually require monitoring wells to ensure there are no impacts to groundwater. EPA and state environmental agencies have authority to issue compliance orders to STPs that contaminate soil or groundwater from wastewater disposal or other activities (like leaking underground tanks). Failure to comply with applicable requirements of permits or orders can subject an STP owner to both civil and criminal penalties.

Air emissions from STPs are regulated in many ways. First, there are usually general state laws or rules prohibiting anyone from causing "nuisance odors." Second, there may be specific requirements on air emissions of possible toxic compounds (such as hydrogen sulfide). Finally, if the STP has an incinerator, composting facility, or any air pollution–control device, the STP will be required to operate it according to the permit issued by the state or local agency. At the federal level, air emissions from STPs, which have historically not been regulated, are a target of the Clean Air Act Amendments of 1990—under this law, the EPA is expected to require many STPs to obtain air permits and take steps to reduce and control air emissions.

What to Look For

STPs are often located near large bodies of water. They are normally fenced complexes ranging in size from one acre to hundreds of acres.

Pumping stations may be below-grade vaults or small, nondescript buildings; they have vents which exhaust the noxious gases produced within sewers. Private STPs (at, for example, nearby malls or condominium complexes) may be more difficult to locate, but the local health department or state environmental agency should be able to help.

If a home is adjacent to an STP, inspect the property for visible signs of contamination like stained soils, stressed vegetation, or a sheen on any surface body of water.

If a well is in use, taste and smell the water—however, laboratory tests are usually needed to detect contamination. If a water treatment system or bottled water is used, find out why (see Hazard 4, Drinking Water: Private Wells).

Odor problems at a plant may be intermittent, and whether they are detected at a particular location on a given day is dependent on weather and wind. What may be an offensive problem one day may not be evident the next.

Where to Find Help and Further Information

Call the sewer department and ask where the STP is located or look on a USGS map for an area labeled "sewage disposal" (see Appendix 3). Also find out if there are any sewage-pumping stations close to your property. Ask the town land use or building officials if there are any anticipated expansion plans; find out how the area is zoned and check the local zoning laws that will determine if and how an STP can expand. If necessary, contact a qualified land use attorney.

If there is an STP or pumping station nearby, potential buyers should find out about known problems, including any known impacts to drinking water wells for homes in the vicinity. Ask the owner if there are or have been odors or other problems—better yet, ask the neighbors. Hydrogen sulfide levels can be measured using handheld gas meters—if your local STP has a hydrogen sulfide problem, the operator probably has a meter; otherwise contact a local lab or consulting firm.

Buyers of waterfront properties should find out if upstream STPs have caused problems that could limit their use and enjoyment of the water. State or local environmental agencies should be able to provide information on a particular STP's design and operation, data on the quality of its effluent, and any known problems associated with the STP.

Owners and potential buyers of nearby homes with wells should consider testing the water (see Hazard 4, Drinking Water: Private Wells).
Well water can be tested for a variety of compounds indicative of pollution from an STP. Bacteria and nitrates are two common indicator parameters of pollution from wastewater. Coordinate tests with a qualified
laboratory, consultant, or inspector. Contact the EPA or your state environmental or health agency for additional information or assistance
(see Appendix 4).

The Bottom Line

Proximity to a sewage treatment plant can impact the value of a home.
Odors, which can be a problem for homes near an STP or pumping
station, can be overwhelming at times and can affect the use and enjoyment of a home. Some STPs will have major odor problems, while others will not. Improper wastewater discharges or chemicals used at STPs
can pose significant health and financial risks to nearby home owners
whose drinking water wells are impacted. Buyers of homes with private
wells that are near an STP should have the water tested. The costs to
address contaminated water are high and the value of a property with a
water problem will be significantly reduced.

49. SUPERFUND SITES

Risks: HEALTH   ✚ ✚ ✚   FINANCIAL $ $ $

Background

"Superfund" refers to the federal law passed in 1980 (and revised in
1986), known as the Comprehensive Environmental Response, Compensation and Liability Act (CERCLA), that created a national program
for cleaning up the most serious hazardous waste disposal sites in the
United States. As of the middle of 1995, the EPA reported almost sixteen thousand sites in its inventory, of which about fourteen hundred
are considered the most hazardous. Superfund sites are locations that
the EPA or a state agency has targeted for cleanup due to a real or
potential threat to the environment or human health. At all of these
sites, there is an elevated health risk as a result of the presence of toxic
wastes. The EPA estimates that more than two million people live within
one mile of a Superfund site and one in five live within four miles of a

site. Some experts estimate that more than 400,000 other sites pose threats to human health and the environment, and these may ultimately become Superfund sites.

Many Superfund sites present significant risks to the environment and to neighboring properties and those who reside there. Ground-water contamination poses the greatest real health threat, although air pollution and contact with contaminated soils are also significant concerns. Homes near a Superfund site may also be affected by storm water runoff that can cause erosion and also may contain toxic chemicals that can harm a home's lawn, gardens, wetlands, ponds, lakes, and well water. A Superfund cleanup can take decades to complete, during which time construction activities can impact local neighborhoods with air pollution, noise, dust, odors, and truck traffic.

The impacts to home owners from Superfund sites are well known and well publicized; a few examples follow.

- At the infamous Love Canal Superfund site in upstate New York, which was contaminated from 1942 to 1953 with twenty-two thousand tons of buried toxic waste from various industries and the war effort, hundreds of residents were evacuated and relocated, and their homes destroyed, after toxic chemicals contaminated the yards and basements. Although much of the contamination has been cleaned up, potential buyers are leery of repopulating the area, and banks are reluctant to lend money to potential buyers because of past contamination and stigma.
- More than ninety neighbors of a 190-acre industrial park Superfund site in Monterey Park, California, contaminated with toxic wastes filed suit in 1994 against the responsible parties for various health damages (respiratory disorders, nausea, and other health effects), property damage, and devaluation of their homes.
- At the Brio Superfund site near Houston, toxic chemicals such as chloroform, xylene, and various solvents have been responsible for numerous serious health problems, including a cluster of birth defects (in one four-month stretch, eleven deformed children were born and many others suffered serious heart and reproductive problems), and forced more than seventeen hundred residents from their homes.
- Between 1964 and 1978, about forty-one thousand gallons of waste oil contaminated with PCBs were applied to local roadways for dust control in a residential community of about one hundred homes in upstate New York. In 1980, the installation of

sanitary sewer lines in the neighborhood required the excavation of highly contaminated soil, much of which was then reused as fill on the properties. The area was placed on the Superfund National Priorities List (NPL) in 1983 because of potential for human PCB exposure from dust, surface water, and groundwater. The EPA performed an emergency removal, which included paving the roads and driveways, decontamination of homes, and installation of water treatment systems on private wells.

• An eighty-home residential development known as Carver Terrace, in Texarkana—an old railroad town on the Texas-Arkansas border—was built right on top of a former wood treatment plant that had contaminated the ground and water with creosote, a toxic chemical. After moving into the homes built during the late 1960s, residents observed a number of strange things: grass and gardens wouldn't grow, pipes corroded, there were constant odors, black gunk appeared from faucets, and chemicals bubbled up from the ground after rainstorms. People began to get sick—headaches; respiratory problems; liver, heart, kidney, and thyroid problems; cancer clusters; and more. Many even died, as did numerous cats and dogs. After an investigation, the EPA placed the site on the Superfund list, then proceeded to study it for eight years. It took several more years before the government finally agreed to close off the development, buy out the home owners, and relocate them. In the meantime, more had died or were suffering serious health problems, not to mention all of the financial losses the residents suffered.

We could go on and on, with stories from every part of the United States. Suffice it to say that residential real estate and Superfund sites are *not* compatible.

Health Risks

Pollution from a Superfund site can impact human health through a number of exposure routes: ingestion, inhalation, and skin contact. Many Superfund sites pose health risks serious enough to warrant cleanup. The EPA considers the risk serious enough to warrant cleanup if it finds that (1) there is more than a one in ten thousand chance for exposed persons to develop cancer from the site's contaminants or (2) if exposures to the site's contaminants might exceed the level humans can tolerate without developing other ill-health effects, such as birth defects or nerve or liver damage.

Contaminants at Superfund sites include the whole universe of toxic chemicals and wastes, such as petroleum compounds, PCBs, asbestos, pesticides, solvents, heavy metals, and cyanide, that can contaminate soil, groundwater, surface water, and the air—and, most critically, lead to impairment of drinking water sources (see Hazard 4, Drinking Water: Private Wells). Known health risks include various types of cancers, birth defects, nerve or liver damage, and others. In addition, air inside homes located above groundwater containing high levels of volatile organic compounds (VOCs) can become contaminated and pose a variety of health problems to occupants.

Air pollution and odors can also pose risks, especially to the young, the elderly, and those with respiratory ailments. Also, elevated methane and VOC levels from toxic waste dumps are potential fire and explosion hazards; the gas can build up in basements of nearby homes and create these risks. And although Superfund sites are typically fenced in to restrict access, people, especially children, may still be at risk from direct contact with contaminated soil or water from the site. Many people living near Superfund sites have also suffered psychological impacts from the effects of stress, fear, and anxiety.

Other issues at Superfund sites, such as odors, forced relocation, and noise from traffic, construction, and cleanup activities, can disrupt the use and enjoyment of a home.

Financial Risks

Properties near a Superfund site—even those several miles away in some instances—can be substantially devalued due to concerns about potential health impacts and associated financial costs. Downgradient homes with private drinking water wells may be at serious risk from contamination. Homes with contaminated wells will be devalued and difficult to sell. And even if there is no problem on a property, a home may still be devalued because of stigma (homes near some Superfund sites have been completely devalued). For example, in 1994 an Ohio jury awarded 1,713 home owners whose properties were *not* contaminated almost $7 million in stigma damages based solely on property devaluation from mere proximity to a toxic waste site. Even *after* cleanup of a Superfund site, stigma may depress real estate values in the area for a long time.

This is especially critical because if you end up buying a home that is near a property that is severely contaminated, your property could become part of the Superfund site. Under the Superfund law, the EPA can require owners of residential property to clean up their properties if they are contaminated, whether or not they caused the contamination. An EPA 1991 policy document, "Homeowners Exempted From Superfund Cleanup Costs: Policy Towards Owners of Residential Property at Superfund Sites" [Publication 9230.0-23FS], spells out the EPA's guidance to home owners for residential property located on a Superfund (NPL) site.* The bottom line of this policy statement is that the EPA will not require home owners to clean up their contaminated properties unless the home owner caused the contamination or fails to cooperate with the EPA.

Potential buyers of a property near a Superfund site may ask about odors, noise, and possible contamination of drinking water supplies—all possible points of contention in negotiations over price.

Other financial risks:

- ► Liability for nondisclosure; see Disclosure Obligations, pages 13–19. Depending on your state, the presence of a *nearby* Superfund site may need to be disclosed in a transaction.
- ► Costs associated with contaminated drinking water; see Hazard 4, Drinking Water: Private Wells.
- ► Costs for short- or long-term medical treatment and monitoring; property damage (to buildings, livestock, crops, or landscaping); legal and expert fees; and inconvenience and relocation costs.

Managing the Risks

See Hazard 4, Drinking Water: Private Wells, for a discussion of how to manage risks if a drinking water well is contaminated.

Contact the owner or operator of the Superfund site for financial or technical help in correcting any problem and in managing the associated risks. The EPA, the state environmental agency, or the responsible parties conducting the cleanup may provide a safe water supply or bottled water, or pay for the cost of individual water treatment systems. In addition, where necessary, the EPA or the responsible parties may provide funds for medical monitoring and treatment, compensate home owners for financial impacts and property devaluation, or buy out home owners for fair market value and relocate them. If you own a home near a Superfund site, check your home's tax assessment, as it probably does not factor in the proximity to the toxic dump, so you may be successful

---

* Note that the policy document defines residential property as single-family residences of one to four dwelling units; thus, multifamily properties *would not* be covered by this policy.

in getting the assessment lowered—a small financial savings, but a savings nonetheless (see Environmental Hazards and Taxes, pages 28–30).

If you live near a Superfund site, never use it as a recreational area and do not allow your children to play there.

Regulatory Outlook

Under Superfund, the EPA is authorized to force "responsible parties" (those who own or operate a site or who generated or transported wastes to a site for disposal) to clean up a site. When these parties can't be found, won't agree to do the cleanup, or do not have the finances, the EPA conducts the cleanup using money from a trust fund (hence the name "Superfund") to finance the cleanup and then seeks to recover these costs from the responsible parties through court actions. This trust fund, currently at more than $15 billion, is financed by a tax on crude oil and chemicals. Through 1994, the EPA has spent more than $10 billion for cleaning up Superfund sites and estimates spending another $40 billion or so before the year 2019.

For a property to be considered as a possible Superfund site, the EPA considers the *potential* for health and environmental risks. Based on some previous report or information that there may be an environmental problem, the EPA will place a site on a potential problem list called the CERCLIS list (this computerized database is used by the EPA to evaluate sites; sites that appear on the list do not necessarily pose health or safety risks to the public). There are over thirty-five thousand listed CERCLIS sites—most town dumps are on the list; *any* "bad" information (whether verified or not) about a site, such as a chemical spill or a leaking underground storage tank, can qualify a site to be placed on the CERCLIS list. The EPA then goes through a rigorous and costly screening procedure to identify the worst sites. The EPA studies the specific risks at CERCLIS locations and scores the dangers—if a site has minimal risks, it will score low; if it scores high, the EPA can propose it to be an NPL site for priority cleanup. After a formal procedure, where the site owner and the public are offered the opportunity to comment on the EPA's evaluation, the site can be legally placed on the NPL. The process of identifying responsible parties and conducting environmental studies to determine the nature and scope of the contamination and the best way to clean up the site then begins. Only afterwards does the EPA actually start cleaning up a site.

Our description of the Superfund process is general, and many states have adopted their own version of Superfund to tackle sites which the EPA does not prioritize or take the lead in cleaning up. Nevertheless, state-listed Superfund sites may present the same concerns as those on the EPA's lists. Recognize that state-listed sites may be called something different than Superfund sites in your state.

For various reasons, the Superfund program has been severely criticized for being slow and inefficient. Many of the criticisms are justified. For example, as of 1994, fewer than sixty of the most serious sites have been fully cleaned up, and a huge amount of money is spent for EPA oversight and on legal and consulting fees—funds that could be better spent on cleaning up the environment. However, the reasons behind the delays in cleanups are complex and in many cases result from problems with the law itself. Congress extended the Superfund program in 1990 and is now considering substantial changes, which may eliminate some of the past problems and help expedite site cleanups.

What to Look For

Superfund sites are everywhere, but most will not be readily obvious to the untrained eye as you drive around the area. Many are closed landfills or are located in industrial areas. Active Superfund sites undergoing evaluation and cleanup are usually fenced in and have signs posted. Ongoing cleanup activities resemble construction work with heavy equipment and truck traffic. Check for odors, noise, and traffic. Remember that odors and noise may be only an intermittent problem, depending on which way the wind is blowing.

Environmental contamination will not be obvious. If a well is in use, taste and smell the water; however, laboratory tests are usually needed to detect contamination. If a water treatment system or bottled water is used, find out why (see Hazard 4, Drinking Water: Private Wells). If a home is close to a Superfund site, look for visible signs of contamination, such as stained soil, stressed vegetation, or an oil sheen on any surface body of water.

Where to Find Help and Further Information

Ask neighbors and town land use or building officials about Superfund sites in the area and any known contamination, noise, odors, and traffic problems associated with them. As the location of a Superfund site may not be obvious, it may be useful to conduct some library research and look through back issues of local newspapers for any stories relating to a nearby Superfund site. In addition, you can easily find out if a nearby property is a Superfund site by calling the EPA or your state environmental agency. Ask whether it is a CERCLIS site that is being investigated for *possible* placement on the NPL, an NPL site already targeted for cleanup, or is on your state Superfund list (see Appendix 3). States will usually rank their sites by severity of contamination. If a site is on the CERCLIS list or NPL (or an equivalent state list), contact the EPA, the state environmental agency, or the specific site cleanup contractor to find out the status of the site and any cleanup plans. Remember, although sites on the CERCLIS list may be significantly contaminated, many are not. Less than 10 percent of CERCLIS sites pose environmental threats significant enough to warrant cleanup as an NPL site. However, for any site on the CERCLIS list or a state list, you really have no way of knowing what the problems are and what the eventual outcome of the site investigation and cleanup will be. The EPA maintains a Superfund Hotline (800/424-9346), which can provide information about the Superfund program generally or particular sites.

Owners and potential buyers of homes with wells near a Superfund site should test the water (see Hazard 4, Drinking Water: Private Wells). Costs will range from $50 to $200 or more, depending on the number of constituents tested—the EPA, state environmental agencies, or the cleanup contractor may be willing to perform and pay for these tests for you. Coordinate tests with a qualified laboratory, consultant, or inspector. Contact the EPA or your state environmental or health agency for additional information or assistance (see Appendix 4).

The Bottom Line

Proximity to a Superfund site can seriously impact the value of a home—in many cases homes have been completely devalued. Soil and groundwater contamination from a Superfund site can pose significant health and financial risks if private drinking water wells are impacted. Noise, odors, and traffic associated with a Superfund site cleanup can affect the use and enjoyment of a home. Home owners with private wells near a Superfund site should have the water tested. The costs to address contaminated water are high and the value of a property with a water problem will be significantly reduced. No matter what the price is, you do not want to buy a property on or next to a Superfund site—whether or not there is contamination on the property or a threat of contamination, any home close to a Superfund site is not a wise investment. This is one instance where the financial risks are high and the health risks may be severe.

50. ZONING

Risks: HEALTH None   FINANCIAL $ $

Background

Zoning is a local governmental technique typically authorized by the state and used to control land use in the interest of the public. Specifically, zoning is a means by which a town or community is divided into districts—zones—and regulations are developed that govern the activities and types of uses and buildings that can take place or be constructed within each district. Most towns and counties have some or all of the following basic types of zones: residential, multifamily residential, commercial, industrial, and recreational. However, there are a variety of zoning classifications used throughout the United States. Some areas have "mixed" zones, permitting more than one type of land use, and in other areas there is no zoning at all.

How a neighborhood and its surroundings are zoned can affect residential property values and the quality of life in the area. Financial and aesthetic impacts to a home owner vary with the types of permitted land uses on nearby properties. Stories abound about home owners who have been living peacefully in their homes for many years, only to suddenly find out that a retail plaza, office building, or manufacturing plant is being sited across the street. And it's not just commercial or industrial activities that can cause a stir—residential zones where farming activities (including keeping of cows, pigs, horses, roosters, and other sorts of domestic animals, and the storage of fertilizer and manure), multifamily uses, and home-based businesses (such as pet kennels, day-care centers, beauty salons, and professional offices) are allowed can increase traffic and noise and negatively affect property values.

Zoning laws are governmental restrictions on private property. Depending on the situation and your personal stake in a matter, they can be viewed as good or bad. As discussed in Hazard 23, Zoning and Other Land Use Restrictions, while a home owner typically does not welcome any restrictions on what can be done on his or her property, at the same time, the home owner does not want any activity to be undertaken on a nearby property that can impact the value or use and enjoyment of his or her property. Although zoning laws can be burdensome or an intrusion into personal choice when applied to your property, they are intended to enhance the community and protect property values. Remember that while they may restrict you from doing certain things on your property, they also protect you and your property's value against things your neighbors—whether other home owners or commercial or industrial operations—might do. On the other hand, remember that what some may view as undesirable neighbors, like manufacturing, landfills, and subsidized housing, are specifically allowed by the same zoning laws in certain areas.

Health Risks

Aesthetic issues, such as noise, odors, and traffic, associated with certain nearby land uses allowed by zoning rules can disrupt the use and enjoyment of a property. Otherwise there are no direct health risks associated with off-site zoning itself. However, if a facility that poses potential environmental hazards is located nearby, then the health risks associated with the particular facility should be reviewed (see Hazards 24–49 as appropriate).

Financial Risks

The biggest financial risk from off-site zoning is its effect on property values. If you purchase a home in or adjacent to an industrial or commercial zone, in a mixed-use zone, or even in a residential zone where a nearby land use is disruptive, the property may be devalued. A colleague purchased a home in a rural town only to find out later that an asphalt manufacturing plant was being sited nearby. This same unfortunate individual has neighbors who raise farm animals—including roosters— that disturb him every morning . . . and when the wind blows in the "wrong" direction. Resale value is critical to all home owners, particularly for young home owners who have incurred substantial debt to purchase a home in today's down economy. Therefore, the zoning classification of nearby property can directly impact your property's value and your ability to use, refinance, or sell your home. Nearby zoning classifications and allowed land uses can also reduce the pool of potential buyers for a property.

Home owners and buyers should be aware that demographic shifts and changing regional economics can lead to wholesale zone changes that can radically affect property values and living standards. For instance, many neighborhoods that were once zoned exclusively for single-family residences have been transformed into mixed-use and multi-family areas. The result is often increased taxes and lower property values—as well as a loss of those intangible factors that make living in a quiet residential community so attractive to many home owners.

While it is difficult to predict how the zoning regulations in a particular area may change over time, potential buyers should be aware of recent zoning changes that may not yet have impacted the neighborhood.

The costs to challenge a facility siting, zoning classification change, or variance can run into thousands of dollars in legal and expert fees. If you end up in a legal battle over a nearby land use, the process can be drawn out for many years and force you to expend significant money to attempt to preserve your property's value.

Potential buyers of properties may ask about odors, traffic, noise, lights, view obstructions, and other aesthetic issues that can impact property values. Significant off-site zoning issues or controversies may be subject to disclosure requirements for sellers and their agents. For example, if there is a gas station or telecommunications tower being sited nearby, that can affect the property's value, and sellers and agents may be required to alert potential buyers. To prevent problems at closing, sellers and their agents should inform buyers of significant nearby land use or zoning issues up front, rather than letting buyers find out when the deal is done—or a messy and expensive lawsuit could follow (see Disclosure Obligations, pages 13–19).

Managing the Risks

Know and understand all of the zoning classifications for properties that abut your land, are in your neighborhood, or are even beyond (remember, it is not uncommon for commercial and industrial entities to buy up surrounding land and expand operations). Don't assume that the vacant land next door or down the road is reserved for residential use only.

If you're looking at a home and the zoning classification for nearby properties allows other, potentially disruptive, land uses, recognize that these uses are likely to occur. If you are concerned, make sure the home is far enough away from any potential activity that can impact the value of your home and your ability to use and enjoy it and that there are substantial vegetative buffers to minimize problems.

Regulatory Outlook

The regulation of land use by state and local officials involves balancing the traditional rights of property owners with the power of government to protect the health, safety, and welfare of the public. Since early in this century, courts have ruled that states may regulate land development in the public interest. In most states, the land use decisions are often delegated to local officials, such as zoning commissions, who (presumably) understand the issues associated with the use of private property. Zoning requirements are often set at the local (town or county) level, although many state agencies can make decisions that override local zoning commissions. Governmental land use regulations cover a broad range of topics—of importance here are the zoning laws and regulations that characterize land uses and specify the types of activities that may be conducted in different areas. Knowledge of an area's zoning classification scheme and its underlying regulations is critical in the home-buying process.

What to Look For

Drive around the neighborhood and beyond to try and spot nonresidential land uses (if possible, try to come back at different times of day—many activities take place only at night, or certain animals make noise only early in the morning). We're not just talking about industrial or commercial uses; many rural areas allow horses and other farm animals on certain-size lots. Some people don't mind animal smells and sounds; many do. Ask the current owner and neighbors if they are aware of any nonresidential (or nontraditional) uses of nearby properties. However, the only way to determine whether a manufacturing plant could be sited next door is to review the zoning classifications of nearby properties and identify what activities are and are not permitted.

Where to Find Help and Further Information

Ask the seller and agent to identify any nearby properties that are zoned for anything other than residential use (be careful—some properties may be zoned residential but current commercial or industrial activities may be allowed as grandfathered, nonconforming uses that preexisted the zoning scheme). Visit the land use or building department and review site-specific tax maps, zoning and other applicable agency regulations, zoning maps, the town's comprehensive plan or plan of development, and the plan for economic development. Ask if there is any rezoning going on in the area, whether any nearby properties have submitted building applications, and if any zoning amendments, applications for variances, or appeals have been filed for nearby properties. Review back issues of the local newspaper to get a feel for any zoning issues that may be of concern. If the property you are considering is near a town line, find out what's going on in the nearby town and how the nearby properties in that town are zoned. If your property is part of a subdivision, look at the documents related to the creation of the subdivision and find out what restrictions exist and what may be built next in the subdivision.

Also ask the local land use or building department whether any new or expanding commercial or industrial activities are anticipated, or if any highways or roads will be constructed or expanded nearby. Also, find out what other property uses are allowed in a residential zone—you may be shocked at what you learn.

Finally, *don't just check local zoning laws and records*—many state agencies have taken siting of certain facilities, such as cellular towers and hazardous waste operations, out of the hands of local agencies. Thus, you or your attorney may want to review the zoning regulations of your town, county, state, and any other pertinent political subdivision as they may affect you.

The Bottom Line

The bottom line for the off-site environmental hazards discussed in this book is simple: before you buy a home, take a look at what's next door. Here, we add a corollary to the bottom line: before you buy a home, find out what *can be* next door. Impacts to property values from off-site land uses—especially commercial or industrial—can be significant and will vary with the situation. Although home owners generally will be safe in a residential zone, thereby limiting the possibility of impacts from unexpected nearby commercial or industrial development, homes located on the fringe of a residential zone (where it abuts a zone that allows other uses) may not be so protected. Also, residential zoning in some areas allows more than meets the eye, and this can also affect property values. Always identify nearby zoning for surrounding properties and how you might be impacted—off-site zoning can affect the value of your home, your ability to refinance or sell it, and your overall ability to use and enjoy it as you desire.

PART IV

Appendixes

APPENDIX 1

Acronyms and Abbreviations

ACM	asbestos-containing material
ANSI	American National Standards Institute
ASHI	American Society of Home Inspectors
ASHRAE	American Society of Heating, Refrigerating and Air-Conditioning Engineers
BANANA	build absolutely nothing anywhere near anything
BTEX	benzene, toluene, ethylbenzene, and xylene
CCA	chromated copper arsenate
CDC	Centers for Disease Control
CERCLA	Comprehensive Environmental Response, Compensation and Liability Act
CERCLIS	Comprehensive Environmental Response, Compensation and Liability Information System
CO	carbon monoxide
CPSC	Consumer Product Safety Commission
DCPA	dimethyl tetrachloroterephthalate
DOD	Department of Defense
DOE	Department of Energy
DOT	Department of Transportation
EDB	ethylene dibromide
EMF	electromagnetic field
EPA	Environmental Protection Agency
EPCRA	Emergency Planning and Community Right-to-Know Act
ERNS	Emergency Response Notification System
FAA	Federal Aviation Administration
Fannie Mae	Federal National Mortgage Association
FCC	Federal Communications Commission
FDA	Food and Drug Administration
FEMA	Federal Emergency Management Agency
FHA	Federal Housing Administration
FIFRA	Federal Insecticide, Fungicide, and Rodenticide Act
FIRM	Flood Insurance Rate Map
FMV	fair market value
FOIA	Freedom of Information Act
Freddie Mac	Federal Home Loan Mortgage Corporation
GAAP	generally acceptable agricultural practices

GAC	granular activated carbon
HEPA	high-efficiency particulate air filter
HUD	Department of Housing and Urban Development
HVAC	heating, ventilation, and air-conditioning system
IEEE	Institute of Electrical and Electronics Engineers
IRS	Internal Revenue Service
LBP	lead-based paint
MCL	maximum contaminant level
MTBE	methyl-tertiary-butyl-ether
NAR	National Association of Realtors®
NFIP	National Flood Insurance Program
NIMBY	not in my backyard
NOPE	not on planet Earth
NO_2	nitrogen dioxide
NOx	nitrogen oxides
NPL	National Priorities List
NRC	Nuclear Regulatory Commission
NWP	nationwide permit [wetlands]
OSHA	Occupational Safety and Health Administration
PCBs	polychlorinated biphenyls
pCi/L	picocuries per liter
POTW	publicly owned treatment work
ppb	parts per billion
ppm	parts per million
PTW	pressure-treated wood
R/C	radio and communication tower
RCP	Radon Contractor Proficiency program
RCRA	Resource Conservation and Recovery Act
RCRIS	Resource Conservation and Recovery Information System
RF	radio frequency
RMP	Radon Measurement Proficiency program
RO	reverse osmosis
SDWA	Safe Drinking Water Act
SOx	sulfur oxides
STP	sewage treatment plant
TSCA	Toxic Substances Control Act
TSDF	treatment, storage, or disposal facility
TSP	trisodium phosphate
UFFI	urea formaldehyde foam insulation
UL	Underwriters Laboratory Inc.
USDA	United States Department of Agriculture
USGS	United States Geological Survey
UST	underground storage tank
UV	ultraviolet light
VA	Veterans Administration
VOC	volatile organic compound
XRF	X-ray fluorescence

EPA Primary and Secondary Drinking Water Standards

NATIONAL PRIMARY DRINKING WATER STANDARDS

(From EPA, 810-F-94-001A, February 1994)

Contaminants	MCLG (mg/L)	MCL (mg/L)	Potential Health Effects from Ingestion of Water	Sources of Contaminant in Drinking Water
Fluoride	4.0	4.0	Skeletal and dental fluorosis	Natural deposits; fertilizer, aluminum industries; water additive
Volatile Organics				
Benzene	zero	0.005	Cancer	Some foods; gas, drugs, pesticide, paint, plastic industries
Carbon Tetrachloride	zero	0.005	Cancer	Solvents and their degradation products
p-Dichlorobenzene	0.075	0.075	Cancer	Room and water deodorants, and "mothballs"
1,2-Dichloroethane	zero	0.005	Cancer	Leaded gas, fumigants, paints
1,1-Dichloroethylene	0.007	0.007	Cancer, liver and kidney effects	Plastics, dyes, perfumes, paints
Trichloroethylene	zero	0.005	Cancer	Textiles, adhesives and metal degreasers
1,1,1-Trichloroethane	0.2	0.2	Liver, nervous system effects	Adhesives, aerosols, textiles, paints, inks, metal degreasers
Vinyl Chloride	zero	0.002	Cancer	May leach from PVC pipe; formed by solvent breakdown
Coliform and Surface Water Treatment				
Giardia lambia	zero	TT	Gastroenteric disease	Human and animal fecal waste
Legionella	zero	TT	Legionnaire's disease	Indigenous to natural waters; can grow in water heating systems
Standard Plate Count	N/A	TT	Indicates water quality, effectiveness of treatment	
Total Coliform*	zero	<5%+	Indicates gastroenteric pathogens	Human and animal fecal waste
Turbidity*	N/A	TT	Interferes with disinfection, filtration	Soil runoff
Viruses	zero	TT	Gastroenteric disease	Human and animal fecal waste
Phase II—Inorganics				
Asbestos (>10um)	7MFL	7MFL	Cancer	Natural deposits; asbestos cement in water systems
Barium*	2	2	Circulatory system effects	Natural deposits; pigments; epoxy sealants, spent coal
Cadmium*	0.005	0.005	Kidney effects	Galvanized pipe corrosion; natural deposits; batteries, paints
Chromium* (total)	0.1	0.1	Liver, kidney, circulatory disorders	Natural deposits; mining, electroplating, pigments

NOTES: * Indicates original contaminants with interim standards which have been revised.
TT = Treatment Technique requirement   MFL = Million Fibers per Liter
MCL = maximum contaminant level   MCLG = maximum contaminant level goal

Phase II—Organics (continued)

Contaminant			Health effects	Sources
Lindane	0.0002	0.0002	Liver, kidney, nerve, immune, circulatory	Insecticide on cattle, lumber, gardens; restricted 1983
Methoxychlor	0.04	0.04	Growth, liver, kidney, nerve effects	Insecticide for fruits, vegetables, alfalfa, livestock, pets
Pentachlorophenol	zero	0.001	Cancer; liver and kidney effects	Wood preservatives, herbicide, cooling tower wastes
PCBs	zero	0.0005	Cancer	Coolant oils from electrical transformers; plasticizers
Styrene	0.1	0.1	Liver, nervous system damage	Plastics, rubber, resin, drug industries; leachate from city landfills
Tetrachloroethylene	zero	0.005	Cancer	Improper disposal of dry cleaning and other solvents
Toluene	1	1	Liver, kidney, nervous, circulatory	Gasoline additive; manufacturing and solvent operations
Toxaphene	zero	0.003	Cancer	Insecticide on cattle, cotton, soybeans; cancelled 1982
2,4,5-TP	0.05	0.05	Liver and kidney damage	Herbicide on crops, right-of-way, golf courses; cancelled 1983
Xylenes (total)	10	10	Liver, kidney; nervous system	By-product of gasoline refining; paints, inks, detergents

Lead and Copper

Contaminant			Health effects	Sources
Lead*	zero	TT†	Kidney, nervous system damage	Natural/industrial deposits; plumbing, solder, brass alloy faucets
Copper	1.3	TT‡	Gastrointestinal irritation	Natural/industrial deposits; wood preservatives, plumbing

Phase V—Inorganics

Contaminant			Health effects	Sources
Antimony	0.006	0.006	Cancer	Fire retardants, ceramics, electronics, fireworks, solder
Beryllium	0.004	0.004	Bone, lung damage	Electrical, aerospace, defense industries
Cyanide	0.2	0.2	Thyroid, nervous system damage	Electroplating, steel, plastics, mining, fertilizer
Nickel	0.1	0.1	Heart, liver damage	Metal alloys, electroplating, batteries, chemical production
Thallium	0.0005	0.0002	Kidney, liver, brain, intestinal	Electronics, drugs, alloys, glass

Organics

Contaminant			Health effects	Sources
Adipate, (di(2-ethylhexyl))	0.4	0.4	Decreased body weight; liver and testes damage	Synthetic rubber, food packaging, cosmetics
Dalapon	0.2	0.2	Liver, kidney	Herbicide on orchards, beans, coffee, lawns, road/railways
Dichloromethane	zero	0.005	Cancer	Paint stripper, metal degreaser, propellant, extraction
Dinoseb	0.007	0.007	Thyroid, reproductive organ damage	Runoff of herbicide from crop and non-crop applications
Diquat	0.02	0.02	Liver, kidney, eye effects	Runoff of herbicide on land & aquatic weeds

Notes: † Action Level = 0.015 mg/L   ‡ Action Level = 1.3 mg/L   TT = Treatment Technique
* Indicates original contaminants with interim standards which have been revised.

Contaminants	MCLG (mg/L)	MCL (mg/L)	Potential Health Effects from Ingestion of Water	Sources of Contaminant in Drinking Water
Phase II—Inorganics (continued)				
Mercury* (inorganic)	0.002	0.002	Kidney, nervous system disorders	Crop runoff; natural deposits; batteries, electrical switches
Nitrate*	10	10	Methemoglobulinemia	Animal waste, fertilizer, natural deposits, septic tanks, sewage
Nitrite	1	1	Methemoglobulinemia	Same as nitrate; rapidly converted to nitrate
Selenium*	0.05	0.05	Liver damage	Natural deposits; mining, smelting, coal/oil combustion
Phase II—Organics				
Acrylamide	zero	TT	Cancer, nervous system effects	Polymers used in sewage/wastewater treatment
Alachlor	zero	0.002	Cancer	Runoff from herbicide on corn, soybeans, other crops
Aldicarb*	0.001	0.003	Nervous system effects	Insecticide on cotton, potatoes, others; widely restricted
Aldicarb sulfone*	0.001	0.002	Nervous system effects	Biodegradation of aldicarb
Aldicarb sulfoxide*	0.001	0.004	Nervous system effects	Biodegradation of aldicarb
Atrazine	0.003	0.003	Mammary gland tumors	Runoff from use as herbicide on corn and non-cropland
Carbofuran	0.04	0.04	Nervous, reproductive system effects	Soil fumigant on corn and cotton; restricted in some areas
Chlordane*	zero	0.002	Cancer	Leaching from soil treatment for termites
Chlorobenzene	0.1	0.1	Nervous system and liver effects	Waste solvent from metal degreasing processes
2,4-D*	0.07	0.07	Liver and kidney damage	Runoff from herbicide on wheat, corn, rangelands, lawns
o-Dichlorobenzene	0.6	0.6	Liver, kidney, blood cell damage	Paints, engine cleaning compounds, dyes, chemical wastes
cis-1,2-Dichloroethylene	0.07	0.07	Liver, kidney, nervous, circulatory	Waste industrial extraction solvents
trans-1,2-Dichloroethylene	0.1	0.1	Liver, kidney, nervous, circulatory	Waste industrial extraction solvents
Dibromochloropropane	zero	0.0002	Cancer	Soil fumigant on soybeans, cotton, pineapple, orchards
1,2-Dichloropropane	zero	0.005	Liver, kidney effects; cancer	Soil fumigant; waste industrial solvents
Epichlorohydrin	zero	TT	Cancer	Water treatment chemicals; waste epoxy resins, coatings
Ethylbenzene	0.7	0.7	Liver, kidney, nervous system	Gasoline; insecticides; chemical manufacturing wastes
Ethylene dibromide	zero	0.00005	Cancer	Leaded gas additives; leaching of soil fumigant
Heptachlor	zero	0.0004	Cancer	Leaching of insecticide for termites, very few crops
Heptachlor epoxide	zero	0.0002	Cancer	Biodegradation of heptachlor

NOTES: * Indicates original contaminants with interim standards which have been revised.
TT = Treatment Technique requirement   MFL = Million Fibers per Liter

Phase V—Organics (continued)

Contaminant	MCLG	MCL	Health effects	Sources
Dioxin	zero	0.00000003	Cancer	Chemical production by-product; impurity in herbicides
Endothall	0.1	0.1	Liver, kidney, gastrointestinal	Herbicide on crops, land/aquatic weeds; rapidly degraded
Endrin	0.002	0.002	Liver, kidney, heart damage	Pesticide on insects, rodents, birds; restricted since 1980
Glyphosate	0.7	0.7	Liver, kidney damage	Herbicide on grasses, weeds, brush
Hexachlorobenzene	zero	0.001	Cancer	Pesticide production waste by-product
Hexachlorocyclopentadiene	0.05	0.05	Kidney, stomach damage	Pesticide production intermediate
Oxamyl (Vydate)	0.2	0.2	Kidney damage	Insecticide on apples, potatoes, tomatoes
PAHs (benzo(a)pyrene)	zero	0.0002	Cancer	Coal tar coatings; burning organic matter; volcanoes, fossil fuels
Phthalate, (di(2-ethylhexyl))	zero	0.006	Cancer	PVC and other plastics
Picloram	0.5	0.5	Kidney, liver damage	Herbicide on broadleaf and woody plants
Simazine	0.004	0.004	Cancer	Herbicide on grass sod, some crops, aquatic algae
1,2,4-Trichlorobenzene	0.07	0.07	Liver, kidney damage	Herbicide production; dye carrier
1,1,2-Trichloroethane	0.003	0.005	Kidney, liver, nervous system	Solvent in rubber, other organic products; chemical production wastes

Other Proposed (P) and Interim (I) Standards

Contaminant	MCLG	MCL	Health effects	Sources
Beta/photon emitters (I) and (P)	zero	4 mrem/yr	Cancer	Decay of radionuclides in natural and man-made deposits
Alpha emitters (I) and (P)	zero	15 pCi/L	Cancer	Decay of radionuclides in natural deposits
Combined Radium 226/228 (I)	zero	5pCi/L	Bone cancer	Natural deposits
Radium 226* (P)	zero	20 pCi/L	Bone cancer	Natural deposits
Radium 228* (P)	zero	20 pCi/L	Bone cancer	Natural deposits
Radon (P)	zero	300 pCi/L	Cancer	Decay of radionuclides in natural deposits
Uranium (P)	zero	0.02	Cancer	Natural deposits
Sulfate (P)	400/500	400/500	Diarrhea	Natural deposits
Arsenic* (I)	0.05	0.05	Skin, nervous system toxicity	Natural deposits; smelters, glass, electronics wastes; orchards
Total Trihalomethanes (I)	zero	0.10	Cancer	Drinking water chlorination by-products

NOTES: * Indicates original contaminants with interim standards which have been revised.

pCi = picocurie—a measure of radioactivity   mrem = millirems—a measure of radiation absorbed by the body

NATIONAL SECONDARY DRINKING WATER STANDARDS
(From EPA, 810-F-94-001A, February 1994)

Contaminants	Suggested Levels	Contaminant Effects
Aluminum	0.05–0.2 mg/L	Discoloration of water
Chloride	250 mg/L	Salty taste; corrosion of pipes
Color	15 color units	Visible tint
Copper	1.0 mg/L	Metallic taste; blue-green staining of porcelain
Corrosivity	noncorrosive	Metallic taste; fixture staining; corrosion of pipes (corrosive water can leach pipe materials, such as lead, into drinking water)
Fluoride	2.0 mg/L	Dental fluorosis (a brownish discoloration of the teeth)
Foaming agents	0.5 mg/L	Aesthetic—frothy; cloudy; bitter taste; odor
Iron	0.3 mg/L	Bitter metallic taste; staining of laundry, rusty color; sediment
Manganese	0.05 mg/L	Taste; staining of laundry, black to brown color; black staining
Odor	3 threshold odor	"Rotten egg," musty, or chemical smell
pH	6.5–8.5	Low pH: bitter metallic taste; corrosion High pH: slippery feel; soda taste; deposits
Silver	0.1 mg/L	Argyria (discoloration of skin); graying of eyes
Sulfate	250 mg/L	Salty taste; laxative effect
Total dissolved solids (TDS)	500 mg/L	Taste and possible relation between low hardness and cardiovascular disease; also an indicator of corrosivity (related to lead levels in water); can damage plumbing and limit effectiveness of soaps and detergents
Zinc	5 mg/L	Metallic taste

NOTE: Secondary Drinking Water Standards are unenforceable federal guidelines regarding the taste, odor, color, and certain other, nonaesthetic, effects of drinking water. EPA recommends them to the states as reasonable goals, but federal law does not require water systems to comply with them. States may, however, adopt their own enforceable regulations governing these concerns. To be safe, check your state's drinking water rules.

APPENDIX 3

Environmental
Databases, Maps, and Photos

Environmental Databases

Some examples of the most useful publicly available environmental databases are summarized below.

NPL and CERCLIS Sites

The National Priorities List (NPL) is the EPA's list of the more than thirteen hundred most toxic Superfund (or CERCLA) sites that are targeted for cleanup (703/603-8852). The Comprehensive Environmental Response, Compensation and Liability Information System (CERCLIS) is an EPA database that identifies more than thirty-five thousand potentially hazardous facilities and properties (800/424-9346—follow menu prompts; in D.C. area, call 703/421-9810). Both lists are sorted by town and site name—look for sites in your town to see if a property you are considering is near a listed site (see Hazard 49, Superfund Sites). There are also state hazardous waste site lists that should be reviewed. Each state lists sites differently, so you will need to check with your state environmental agency, local library, or nearest EPA office.

RCRIS

The EPA maintains a database, called the Resource Conservation and Recovery Information System (RCRIS), of all companies that generate, treat, store, and dispose of hazardous waste (800/535-0202). Use this list to identify companies that are involved with hazardous waste in your area. Possible issues and associated risks will vary depending on the type of facility and history of operations (see Hazard 32, Hazardous Waste Facilities; Hazard 34, Incinerators; and Hazard 35, Industrial Manufacturing Plants).

Spill Reports

The EPA and state environmental agencies keep records of reported spills and emergency responses listed by town, location (street address), and company name. One national database, the Emergency Response Notification System (ERNS), is a collection of oil and hazardous waste spills reported to several federal agencies. The information about a spill may be filed by address or by the name of the company.

EPCRA

EPCRA, short for the Emergency Planning and Community Right-to-Know Act, is a federal law that requires industries to report on toxic chemicals used or made at the site and how much is released into the environment. This information is available to interested citizens. If you are looking at a property near an industrial area, these reports (called Form R and Tier II reports) can provide you with some information about the chemicals used and emitted into the environment (800/535-0202; in D.C. area call 703/412-9877).

Landfills and Solid Waste Sites

State and local environmental agencies maintain records of landfills, transfer stations, recycling centers, and other solid waste sites (see Hazard 36, Landfills). You will want to know where the town dump is (or was) located—many accepted commercial and industrial waste in addition to household trash. Check if there were any "informal" dumps nearby; many sites, particularly undeveloped properties, became dump sites over time without any formal designation.

UST Programs

State environmental agencies have files or databases of underground storage tanks (USTs), including leaking USTs. Check these to find out if your property or any nearby property is on the list.

Maps and Photos

There are a number of publicly available maps and photos that can be used to find out about historic uses of a property or about a nearby industry.

USGS Maps

The United States Geological Survey (USGS) prints and updates detailed topographic maps for the entire country that typically cover an area about five miles by ten miles. These maps give elevations in feet (or meters), and show features such as general locations of wetlands and waterways, buildings, mines, quarries, landfills, airports, military bases, railroads, and power line and utility rights-of-way. USGS maps can be found at and/or purchased from the USGS—call its customer service office in Denver (800/435-7627) for a free index and catalogue of available USGS maps for your state—federal and state environmental agencies, libraries, universities, and outdoor sporting goods stores. Make sure the map you review is up-to-date; some USGS maps have not been changed for twenty years or more.

Sanborn Fire Insurance Maps

Sanborn maps are historic insurance maps, dating as far back as 1867, that are available for most cities and developed suburbs in the United States. The maps show a lot of useful information about individual properties, including locations of sewer lines and other utilities, building foundations, railroad lines, and underground storage tanks. Sanborn maps are generally available at state and university libraries. For additional information contact: Sanborn Mapping and Geographic Information Service, 629 Fifth Avenue, Pelham, NY 10803 (914/738-1649).

Flood Zone Maps

Maps printed by the National Flood Insurance Program (800/638-6620) identify various flood zones and document this information in Flood Insurance Rate Maps (FIRMs) and/or flood zone studies. You can check these maps and the local floodplain study at your town hall (check with the town's building or wetlands department, the conservation commission, or the state wetlands agency). These maps rank properties based on expectations of flooding during certain-size storms, which are categorized by the expected frequency of occurrence. For example, is the property within an area expected to be flooded by storms that, on average, occur every twenty or one hundred years?

Aerial Photographs

Many state environmental or natural resource agencies undertake statewide aerial surveys once every five or ten years. These photographs are often available dating as far back as the 1940s and are a useful supplement to USGS maps. The photographs are often keyed to a state map and can be used to develop a site history about a property over time—they often show the location of old buildings, agricultural activities, aboveground storage tanks, wetlands, and other features of a property or its use. Aerial photographs can be reviewed at university libraries and at state or local environmental agencies.

APPENDIX 4

Federal and State Environmental and Health Agency Hotlines and Phone Numbers

Note: The telephone numbers listed below are subject to change.

U.S. Environmental Protection Agency (EPA) Offices

EPA Regional Offices

Region 1
Connecticut, Maine, Massachusetts,
   New Hampshire, Rhode Island, and
   Vermont:
John F. Kennedy Federal Building
One Congress Street
Boston, MA 02203
(617) 565-3420

Region 2
New Jersey, New York, Puerto Rico,
   and the Virgin Islands:
Jacob K. Javits Federal Building
26 Federal Plaza
New York, NY 10278
(212) 637-3000

Region 3
Delaware, Washington, D.C.,
   Maryland, Pennsylvania, Virginia,
   and West Virginia:
841 Chestnut Building
Philadelphia, PA 19107
(215) 597-9800

Region 4
Alabama, Florida, Georgia, Kentucky,
   Mississippi, North Carolina, South
   Carolina, and Tennessee:
345 Courtland Street NE
Atlanta, GA 30365
(404) 347-4727

Region 5
Illinois, Indiana, Michigan, Minnesota,
   Ohio, and Wisconsin:
77 West Jackson Boulevard
Chicago, IL 60604-3590
(312) 353-2000

Region 6
Arkansas, Louisiana, New Mexico,
   Oklahoma, and Texas:
First Interstate Bank Tower
1445 Ross Avenue, 12th Floor, Suite
   1200
Dallas, TX 75202-2733
(214) 665-6444

Region 7
Iowa, Kansas, Missouri, and Nebraska:
726 Minnesota Avenue
Kansas City, KS 66101
(913) 551-7000

Region 8
Colorado, Montana, North Dakota,
    South Dakota, Utah, and Wyoming:
999 18th Street, Suite 500
Denver, CO 80202-2405
(303) 312-6312

Region 9
Arizona, California, Hawaii, and
    Nevada:
75 Hawthorne Street
San Francisco, CA 94105
(415) 744-1305

Region 10
Alaska, Idaho, Oregon, and
    Washington:
1200 Sixth Avenue
Seattle, WA 98101
(206) 553-1200

U.S. Consumer Product Safety Commission (CPSC) Offices

CPSC Headquarters
4330 East West Highway, Room 519
Bethesda, MD 20814
(301) 504-0580

Eastern Regional Center
6 World Trade Center
Vesey Street, Room 350
New York, NY 10048
(212) 466-1612

Central Regional Center
230 South Dearborn Street, Room
    2944
Chicago, IL 60604-1601
(312) 353-8260

Western Regional Center
600 Harrison Street, Room 245
San Francisco, CA 94107
(415) 744-2966

Environmental and Health Information Hotlines

- Asbestos Ombudsman Clearinghouse, (800) 368-5888
- Bureau of Explosives Hotline, (202) 639-2222
- Center for Hazardous Materials, (412) 826-5320
- CERCLIS (Comprehensive Environmental Response, Compensation and Liability Information System) Helpline, (800) 424-9436 (follow menu prompts); (703) 421-9810 (Washington, D.C., area only)
- Chemical Emergency Preparedness Program, (800) 535-0202; (703) 412-9877 (Washington, D.C., area only)
- Consumer Product Safety Commission Hotline, (800) 638-2772
- DOT Hotline, (202) 366-4488
- Emergency Planning and Community Right-to-Know, (800) 535-0202; (800) 424-9346; (703) 412-9877 (Washington, D.C., area only)
- Energy Efficiency and Renewable Energy Clearinghouse, (800) 428-2525; (800) 428-1718 (Montana only)
- EPA Public Information Center, (202) 260-2080
- EPA Safe Drinking Water Hotline, (800) 426-4791
- Hazardous Waste Ombudsman, (800) 262-7937; (202) 260-9361 (Washington, D.C., area only)
- Indoor Air Quality Information Clearinghouse, (800) 438-4318
- Information Exchange HAZMAT, (800) 752-6367; (800) 367-9592 (Illinois only)

- National Capital Poison Control Center, (202) 625-3333 (collect calls accepted)
- National Lead Information Center, (800) 532-3394 (general information); (800) 424-5323 (technical assistance)
- National Lead Information Clearinghouse, (800) 424-LEAD
- National Pesticide Telecommunications Network, (800) 858-7378 (PEST); (806) 743-3091
- National Priorities List (NPL) Helpline, (703) 603-8852
- National Response Center/U.S. Coast Guard Hotline, (800) 424-8802; (202) 267-2675
- Occupational Safety and Health Administration (OSHA), (800) 321-6742 or (202) 219-8148
- Office of Pesticide Program, Registration Division (Ombudsman), (703) 305-5446
- Radon Hotline, (800) 767-7236
- RCRA/Information Hotline, (415) 744-2074
- RCRA/Superfund Hotline, (800) 424-9346; (800) 535-0202
- RCRIS Hotline, (800) 535-0202
- Solid Waste Information Clearinghouse Hotline, (800) 677-9424
- TSCA Asbestos Hotline, (800) 835-6700; (202) 554-1404
- Wetlands Hotline, (800) 832-7828

State Environmental and Health Agencies

Note: The following are useful numbers for state-specific questions that you may have about any of the environmental hazards discussed in this book. For each state, we have provided general numbers for the state environmental agency and the health agency as well as specific numbers where available for state-level asbestos, lead, radon, and drinking water contacts. Recognize that numbers and addresses change; if so, you can always use your local telephone directory or call information.

Alabama
Environmental Management Department, (334) 271-7706
Public Health Department, (334) 316-5200
Asbestos, (334) 271-7861
Lead, (334) 271-7706
Radon, (334) 613-5391
Drinking water, (334) 271-7773

Alaska
Environmental Conservation Department, (907) 465-5050
Environmental Health Division, (907) 465-5280
Asbestos, (907) 465-5100
Lead, (907) 465-5280
Radon, (907) 465-3019 or (800) 478-8324
Drinking water, (907) 465-5300

Arizona
Environmental Quality Department, (602) 207-2300
Health Services Department, (602) 542-1025
Asbestos, (602) 207-2301
Lead, (602) 207-4153
Radon, (602) 255-4845
Drinking water, (depends on the county)

Arkansas
Pollution Control and Ecology Department, (501) 682-0744
Health Department, (501) 661-2111
Asbestos, (501) 682-0744
Lead, (501) 661-2000
Radon, (501) 661-2301
Drinking water, (501) 661-2000

California
Environmental Protection Agency, (916) 445-3846
Health and Welfare Agency, (916) 654-3345
Asbestos, (916) 445-3846
Lead, (916) 445-3846
Radon, (916) 445-3846 or (800) 745-7236
Drinking water, (916) 445-3846

Colorado
Environment and Public Health Department, (303) 692-2100
Health Office, (303) 692-2700
Asbestos, (303) 692-3150
Lead, (303) 692-3150
Radon, (303) 692-3150 or (800) 846-3966
Drinking water, (303) 692-3500

Connecticut
Department of Environmental Protection, (860) 424-3001
Department of Health, (860) 509-8000
Asbestos, (860) 509-7367
Lead, (860) 509-7745
Radon, (860) 509-7367
Drinking water, (860) 509-7333

Delaware
Natural Resources and Environmental Control Department, (302) 739-4403
Health and Social Services Department, (302) 577-4502
Asbestos, (302) 739-4791
Lead, (302) 739-4735
Radon, (302) 739-3028
Drinking water, (302) 739-5410

District of Columbia
Environmental Regulation Administration, (202) 645-6617
Public Health Commission, (202) 673-7700
Asbestos, (202) 645-6093
Lead, (202) 727-9850
Radon, (202) 727-7791
Drinking water, (202) 645-6601

Florida
Environmental Protection Department, (904) 488-4805
Health and Rehabilitative Services Department, (904) 448-0004
Asbestos, (800) 227-9908
Lead, (904) 488-0114
Radon, (904) 488-1525 or (800) 543-8279
Drinking water, (904) 487-1762

Georgia
Natural Resources Department, (404) 656-3500
Human Resources Department, (404) 657-2700
Asbestos, (404) 363-7026
Lead, (404) 362-2713 (lead paint); (404) 656-2750 (lead in water)
Radon, (404) 657-6534 or (800) 745-0037
Drinking water, (404) 656-5660

Hawaii
Land and Natural Resources Department, (808) 548-6550
Health Department, (808) 580-4400
Asbestos, (808) 586-4576
Lead, (808) 586-4576
Radon, (808) 586-4700
Drinking water, (808) 586-4258

Idaho
Environmental Quality Division, (208) 334-1450
Health and Welfare Department, (208) 334-5500
Asbestos, (208) 334-1626
Lead, (208) 334-1626
Radon, (208) 334-5927 or (800) 445-8647
Drinking water, (208) 334-9509

Illinois
Environmental Protection Agency,
(217) 782-3397
Public Health Department, (217) 782-
4977
Asbestos, (217) 782-7326
Lead, (217) 782-7326 (lead paint);
(217) 782-9470 (lead in water)
Radon, (217) 785-9900 or (800) 325-
1245
Drinking water, (217) 782-5830

Indiana
Environmental Management
Department, (317) 232-8162
Health Department, (317) 383-6400
Asbestos, (317) 232-8232
Lead, (317) 232-8232 (lead paint);
(317) 233-4263 (lead in water)
Radon, (317) 383-6510 or (800) 272-
9723 (in-state)
Drinking water, (317) 233-4222

Iowa
Department of Natural Resources,
(515) 281-5385
Public Health Department, (515) 281-
5605
Asbestos, (515) 281-5145 (recorded
menu)
Lead, (515) 281-5145 (recorded
menu)
Radon, (515) 281-5145 (recorded
menu) or (800) 383-5992
Drinking water, (515) 281-5145
(recorded menu)

Kansas
Health and Environment Department,
(913) 296-1535
Environmental Health Services, (913)
296-5599
Asbestos, (913) 296-1550
Lead, (913) 296-1550
Radon, (913) 296-1567
Drinking water, (913) 296-5514
(public water); (913) 296-5599
(private wells)

Kentucky
Environmental Protection
Department, (502) 564-2150
Health Services Department, (502)
564-3970
Asbestos, (502) 573-3382
Lead, (502) 573-3382 (lead paint);
(502) 573-2150 (lead in water)
Radon, (502) 564-3970
Drinking water, (502) 564-2150

Louisiana
Environmental Quality Department,
(504) 765-0741
Health and Hospital Department,
(504) 568-5054
Asbestos, (504) 765-0899
Lead, (504) 765-0151
Radon, (504) 765-0160
Drinking water, (504) 342-9500

Maine
Environmental Protection
Department, (207) 287-2812
Human Services Department, (207)
287-2736
Asbestos, (207) 287-7688
Lead, (207) 287-7688
Radon, (800) 287-5676
Drinking water, (207) 287-2070

Maryland
Environment Department, (410) 631-
3000
Environmental Health Coordinator,
(410) 631-3851
Asbestos, (410) 631-3200
Lead, (410) 631-3825
Radon, (410) 631-3302
Drinking water, (410) 631-3702

Massachusetts
Environmental Protection
Department, (617) 292-5500
Public Health Department, (617) 727-
0201
Asbestos, (617) 292-5631
Lead, (617) 522-3700

Radon, (617) 727-6214
Drinking water, (617) 292-5770

Michigan
Department of Environmental Quality,
(517) 373-9400
Department of Public Health, (517)
335-8024
Asbestos, (517) 335-8246
Lead, (517) 373-9215
Radon, (517) 335-8914 or (800) 723-6642
Drinking water, (517) 335-9216

Minnesota
Pollution Control Agency, (612) 296-7301; (612) 296-6196
Department of Health, (612) 623-5460
Asbestos, (612) 296-7331
Lead, (612) 296-7333 (lead paint);
(612) 627-5017 (lead in water)
Radon, (612) 627-5012 or (800) 796-9050
Drinking water, (612) 623-5000

Mississippi
Environmental Quality Department,
(601) 961-5000
Environmental Health Bureau, (601)
960-7518
Asbestos, (601) 961-5171
Lead, (601) 961-5517
Radon, (601) 961-5171
Drinking water, (601) 960-7518

Missouri
Department of Natural Resources,
Technical Assistance Number, (800)
361-4827
Health Department, (314) 751-6001
Asbestos, (800) 361-4827
Lead, (800) 361-4827
Radon, (800) 361-4827 or (800) 669-7236
Drinking water, (800) 361-4827

Montana
Department of Environmental Quality,
(406) 444-2544
Health and Environmental Services,
(406) 444-2544
Asbestos, (406) 444-3454
Lead, (406) 444-2544
Radon, (406) 444-2406 or (800) 546-0483
Drinking water, (406) 444-2544

Nebraska
Environmental Quality Department,
(402) 471-2186
Health Department, (402) 471-2133
Asbestos, (402) 471-2186
Lead, (402) 471-2186
Radon, (402) 471-2186 or (800) 334-9491
Drinking water, (402) 471-2541

Nevada
Division of Environmental Protection,
(702) 687-4360
Health Division, (702) 687-4740
Asbestos, (702) 687-5872 (recorded
menu)
Lead, (702) 687-5872 (recorded
menu)
Radon, (702) 687-5872 (recorded
menu)
Drinking water, (702) 687-5872
(recorded menu)

New Hampshire
Environmental Services Department,
(603) 271-3505
Public Health Services Division, (603)
271-4664
Asbestos, (603) 271-3505
Lead, (603) 271-3505
Radon, (603) 271-3505 or (800) 852-3345
Drinking water, (603) 271-3505

New Jersey
Environmental Protection
  Department, (609) 292-2885
Health Department, (609) 292-7837
Asbestos, (609) 292-2885
Lead, (609) 292-2885
Radon, (609) 292-2885 or (800) 648-
  0394
Drinking water, (609) 292-2885

New Mexico
Environment Department, (505) 827-
  2771
Health Department, (505) 827-2613
Asbestos, (505) 827-0197
Lead, (505) 827-2900 (lead paint);
  (505) 827-7536 (lead in water)
Radon, (505) 827-1564
Drinking water, (505) 872-7536

New York
Environmental Conservation
  Department, (518) 457-3446
Health Department, (518) 474-2011
Asbestos, (518) 457-2051
Lead, (518) 457-5768
Radon, (518) 458-1158
Drinking water, (518) 457-5768
  (recorded menu)

North Carolina
Environmental, Health, and Natural
  Resources Department, (919) 733-
  4984
Environmental Health Division, (919)
  715-4125
Asbestos, (919) 733-4125
Lead, (919) 733-4125
Radon, (919) 571-4141
Drinking water, (call your county
  health department)

North Dakota
Health and Consolidated Laboratories
  Department, (701) 328-2372
Department of Health, (701) 328-5188
Asbestos, (701) 328-5188
Lead, (701) 328-5188
Radon, (701) 328-5188
Drinking water, (701) 328-5210

Ohio
Environmental Protection Agency,
  (614) 644-2782*
Health Department, (614) 466-2253

Oklahoma
Environmental Quality Department,
  (405) 271-8056 or (800) 869-1400
Department of Health, (405) 271-4200
Asbestos, (405) 271-1500
Lead, (405) 271-5205
Radon, (405) 271-4200
Drinking water, (405) 271-5205

Oregon
Environmental Quality Department,
  (503) 229-5300† or (503) 229-5395
Health Division, (503) 731-4000

Pennsylvania
Environmental Resources Department,
  (717) 787-2814‡
Health Department, (717) 787-6436

Rhode Island
Environmental Management
  Department, (401) 277-2771
Health Department, (401) 277-2231
Asbestos, (401) 277-2438
Lead, (401) 277-2313
Radon, (401) 277-2438
Drinking water, (401) 277-6867

---

* Ohio splits the state up into districts; for asbestos, lead, or drinking water, call (614) 644-2782
for the correct number for your district. For radon, call (800) 523-4439.
† Oregon splits the state into three districts; call (503) 229-5300 for the number for a specific
district.
‡ Pennsylvania splits the state up by regions based in part on counties; call (717) 783-2300 for
the specific number for your region. For radon, call (800) 237-2366.

South Carolina
Environmental Quality Control
    Division, (803) 734-5360
Health Regulation Division, (803) 737-
    7200
Asbestos, (803) 734-4730
Lead, (803) 734-7200
Radon, (803) 734-7401 or (800) 768-
    0362
Drinking water, (803) 734-5377

South Dakota
Water and Natural Resources
    Department, (605) 773-3151
Health Department, (605) 773-3361
Asbestos, (605) 773-3151
Lead, (605) 773-3151
Radon, (605) 773-3151 or (800) 438-
    3367
Drinking water, (605) 773-3754

Tennessee
Environmental and Conservation
    Department, (615) 741-0109
Department of Health, (615) 741-3111
Asbestos, (615) 532-0554
Lead, (615) 532-8011
Radon, (615) 532-0733 or (800) 232-
    1139
Drinking water, (615) 532-0191

Texas
Natural Resource Conservation
    Commission, (512) 239-1000
Health Department, (512) 458-7111
Asbestos, (512) 239-1457
Lead, (512) 458-7111
Radon, (512) 834-6688
Drinking water, (512) 239-6020

Utah
Environmental Quality Department,
    (801) 536-4402
Health Department, (801) 538-6111
Asbestos, (801) 536-4000
Lead, (801) 536-4000
Radon, (801) 536-4250 or (800) 458-
    0145
Drinking water, (801) 536-4200

Vermont
Environmental Conservation
    Department, (802) 241-3600
Health Department, (802) 863-7220
Asbestos, (802) 241-3888
Lead, (802) 241-3888
Radon, (802) 241-7730 or (800) 640-
    0601
Drinking water, (802) 241-3770

Virginia
Environmental Quality Department,
    (804) 762-4198
Health Department, (804) 786-3559
Asbestos, (804) 376-8595
Lead, (804) 376-8595
Radon, (800) 468-0138; (804) 318-
    5932 (greater Richmond area)
Drinking water, (call your local health
    department)

Washington
Ecology Department, (206) 407-7000
Health Department, (206) 586-5212
Asbestos, (206) 649-7107
Lead, (360) 407-6755
Radon, (360) 586-5846
Drinking water, (360) 753-3466

West Virginia
Environmental Protection Bureau,
    (304) 759-0515
Department of Environmental Health,
    (304) 558-2981
Asbestos, (304) 558-2981
Lead, (304) 558-2981
Radon, (304) 558-2981 or (800) 922-
    1255
Drinking water, (304) 558-2981

Wisconsin
Natural Resources Department, (608)
    266-2121
Bureau of Public Health, (608) 266-
    3681
Asbestos, (608) 266-2621
Lead, (608) 266-2621
Radon, (608) 266-2621
Drinking water, (608) 266-2621

Wyoming

Environmental Quality Department,
  (307) 777-7938

Department of Health, (307) 777-7656

Asbestos, (307) 777-7391

Lead, (307) 777-7391

Radon, (307) 777-6015 or (800) 458-
  5847

Drinking water, (307) 777-7781

APPENDIX 5

Self-Help Checklist

This checklist is a guide only in that it is intended to assist you with spotting possible environmental hazards. Photocopy and use it as you walk around your home or one you're considering buying. Check off those hazards that warrant further consideration, and then read the referenced section.

In many cases, testing will be needed to identify suspect materials or contaminants. Always seek the help of a qualified consultant or home inspector when evaluating these or other environmental hazards at a home.

Indoors—General

————— 1. *Asbestos* [Hazard 1]
   • In homes built before around 1980, are there walls with blown-in insulation, vinyl floors, acoustical ceiling tiles, decorative coatings sprayed or troweled on walls or ceilings, or vinyl wall paper? These materials may contain asbestos.

————— 2. *Combustion Sources and Carbon Monoxide* [Hazard 3]
   • Are there any gas or wood-burning fireplaces, space heaters, gas clothes dryers or refrigerators, fuel-burning ranges, water heaters, or woodstoves? These are potential sources of carbon monoxide.
   • Are all fuel-burning appliances properly exhausted?
   • Do you detect any odors in rooms where they are located?
   • Are there black stains above fireplaces and space heaters, or at vent pipes and flues, or where they connect to the chimney?
   • Are exhaust pipes securely attached to each other and the flue?
   • Is the chimney or exhaust blocked?
   • Are there smoke and carbon monoxide detectors in the home?
   • Have the chimneys and stove pipes been inspected and cleaned recently?

————— 3. *Formaldehyde Insulation* [Hazard 8]
   • In homes built or renovated during the 1970s, is there any hardened foam insulation in the walls? Check behind electrical outlet covers and light switch plates. It may be UFFI. Also look for uniformly separated, sealed holes on the outside of the house.

_____ 4. *Indoor Air Pollution Sources: Carpets and Building Materials* [Hazard 12]
  • Are subfloors and walls constructed of particleboard or plywood?
  • Are there new cabinets, carpets, or paneling? If the house is new construction, or has recently been renovated, these may be potential sources of indoor air pollutants.

_____ 5. *Lead-Based Paint* [Hazard 13]
  • In homes built before 1978, are any painted surfaces, such as window and door sills, chipped, flaking, or peeling? Unless renovated, homes built before 1960 will almost always have some lead-based paint.

Indoors—Kitchen and Bath

_____ 6. *Asbestos* [Hazard 1]
  • For pre-1980 homes, are there any stoves or ovens? Gaskets inside these appliances may have asbestos.
  • Is there any vinyl flooring (tiles or linoleum)?

_____ 7. *Biological Contaminants* [Hazard 2]
  • Do kitchen and bath exhausts vent outside? Is there any sign of mold?

_____ 8. *Drinking Water—General* [Hazards 4, 5, 14, 19]
  • Does the water have an unusual color, odor, or taste?
  • Are there stains (blue-green, black, or rust colored) in sinks, baths, toilet tanks, clothes washer, or dishwasher?
  • Is bottled water used? Is there a water treatment system under the sink or installed at a faucet? Find out why. Get copies of instructions and warranties.
  • How is the water pressure and flow in the house? Check during and after running water for several uses at the same time.
  • Are there any brass fixtures? These may contain lead.

_____ 9. *Household Chemicals/Pesticides* [Hazards 11, 42]
  • Are there large amounts of cleaners or pesticides under the sinks?

_____ 10. *Septic Systems* [Hazard 20]
  • Are sinks and toilets slow in draining? These are signs of a possible septic system problem.

_____ 11. *Termites and Other Wood-Destroying Pests* [Hazard 21]
  • Are there any household pets? Are there any ants or other insects in the kitchen? Are there any ant traps or unusual quantities of insecticides in the room or under the sink?

Indoors—Basement/Crawl Space

_____ 12. *Asbestos* [Hazard 1]
  • For pre-1980 houses, is there insulation around the furnace, wood-stove, or other heaters, steam and hot water pipes, and air ducts? It

may contain asbestos. Look for coatings that are sprayed or troweled on, or paper-type insulation with many air pockets.
* Are there gaskets on a wood or coal stove or a furnace? These may contain asbestos.

_____ 13. *Biological Contaminants* [Hazard 2]
* Is the basement damp and musty? Look for white powder ("efflorescence") on the foundation walls—this is a sign of a moisture problem.
* Is a humidifier or dehumidifier in use?
* Is the clothes dryer exhausted outside?
* Is mold or mildew growing on walls or floor joists? Are there stains on wood, concrete, or wall surfaces?
* Any mold or mildew or accumulated dust in the air system or ductwork?

_____ 14. *Combustion Sources* [Hazard 3]
* Are there any gas, coal-burning, wood-burning, or fuel oil–burning appliances (furnace, space heaters, clothes dryer, or water heater) in the basement? These are potential sources of carbon monoxide.
* Are all fuel-burning appliances properly exhausted?
* Do you detect any fuel-like odors in the basement?
* Are there any black soot or smoke stains around vent pipes, flues, or where they connect to the chimney?
* Is the chimney or exhaust blocked?
* Are all exhaust pipes and flues attached to each other and the flue?
* Is there any corroded piping, loose-fitting equipment, or cracks in the flue or chimney?
* Is there a smoke or carbon monoxide detector in the basement?
* Are there any bedrooms on the lowest level of the home?
* Have the chimneys and stove pipes been inspected and cleaned recently?

_____ 15. *Drinking Water—General* [Hazards 4, 5, 14, 19]
* Is the water supplied by a private well?
* If a well is used, locate the pressure tank. The water pump, if not at the bottom of the well, may be next to this tank. Are there any leaks or signs of rust?
* Is there a whole-house water treatment system? What is it used for? These systems may have various size and shape tanks or cartridges next to the water pressurization tank or connected to the public water supply pipe as it enters the basement. Get copies of instructions and warranties. What kind of chemicals and maintenance does it require?
* Is any water piping corroded, patched, or recently replaced? These could indicate corrosive water.

_____ 16. *Flooding* [Hazard 7]
* Is the basement wet or are there signs of water staining?
* Is there a drain or sump pump in the basement?

- Are there any cracks or gaps in the foundation or floor?
- Are stored objects raised off the floor?

_____ 17. *Heating Oil Storage Tanks* [Hazard 9]
- If there is an oil-burning furnace, is there a fuel oil tank in the basement?
- Are there any oil stains on the floor near the tank?
- Are there any strong petroleum odors?
- Is the tank leaking or badly rusted?
- Is the tank well supported and in good condition?
- Is the fuel line between the tank and furnace underground?
- Does the fuel line run through a wall to the outside or is there an abandoned pipe or patch marks on the foundation? These may be signs that there is or was an underground storage tank.

_____ 18. *Household Chemicals/Historic Disposal/Miscellaneous* [Hazards 10, 11, 15]
- Are there any utility sinks, floor drains, toilets, or sumps in the basement connected to a septic system or dry well?
- Is there a home hobby shop or darkroom?
- Are there any stockpiles of paints, cleaners, pesticides, or other chemicals?

_____ 19. *Lead in Water* [Hazard 14]
- For homes built before 1950, are water pipes made of lead? Lead pipes are soft metal pipes with a dull gray color that may scratch easily with a key.
- Is solder used to join copper or steel water pipes in pre-1988 homes? It likely will contain lead.

_____ 20. *PCBs* [Hazard 16]
- Are there any fluorescent light ballasts manufactured before 1979? They may contain PCBs.

_____ 21. *Radon in Air* [Hazard 18]
- Is there an earthen basement floor or crawl space?
- Are there any cracks or gaps in the basement floor?
- Is there a floor sump or drains with soil beneath?
- Are there any bedrock outcrops directly into the basement?
- Are there any bedrooms on the lowest level of the home?

_____ 22. *Septic Systems* [Hazard 20]
- Where does the waste plumbing leave the house? Any evidence of leakage into the basement at this point?

_____ 23. *Termites and Other Wood-Destroying Pests* [Hazard 21]
- Are there any holes in wood or sawdust piles next to woodwork?
- Is there any rotted or damaged wood?
- Are there any insect droppings or cast skins?

Indoors—Attic

_____ 24. *Asbestos/Formaldehyde Insulation* [Hazards 1, 8]
 • Any suspect insulation materials in the attic?

_____ 25. *Biological Contaminants* [Hazard 2]
 • Is the attic damp or musty?
 • Are bathroom exhaust fans or clothes dryers exhausted to the attic?
 • Are walls or rafters coated with mold or mildew?
 • Does the attic appear to be well vented?

_____ 26. *Termites and Other Pests (see Number 23.)* [Hazard 21]
 • Any indication of insect problems?

Garage and Outbuildings

_____ 27. *Historic Disposal/Household Chemicals/Miscellaneous* [Hazards 10, 11, 15]
 • Are there any utility sinks, floor drains, toilets, or sumps connected to a septic system or dry well?
 • Is there an auto repair or home hobby shop?
 • Are there any stockpiles of waste oil, paints, cleaners, or pesticides?

Outside the Home

_____ 28. *Asbestos* [Hazard 1]
 • In homes built before around 1980, are there any old roofing, shingles, or clapboard siding? These materials may contain asbestos.

_____ 29. *Drinking Water: Private Wells/Lead in Water* [Hazards 4 and 14]
 • Where is the well located? The top of a well may be a vertical stand-pipe, four or six inches in diameter, or it may be located in an out-building, or, if a "dug well," the top of the hole may be covered by a steel or concrete plate.
 • Is the well properly sealed to protect it from surface contamination?
 • For a dug well, is the well casing above grade and is the surrounding area landscaped and sloped to prevent surface water from entering the well?
 • Is there a well pump with brass parts? They can leach lead.
 • Is there a pre-1979 well pump? It may contain PCBs.

_____ 30. *Erosion and Flooding* [Hazards 6, 7]
 • Is the house in a low-lying area or near any body of water?
 • Are there any washed-out gullies, exposed rock, or sand with little vegetation?
 • Do areas around foundations and walls and other structures show signs of erosion damage? Look at natural drainage patterns and signs of soil disturbance.
 • Does the property appear to drain onto the neighbor's property (or vice versa)?

- For waterfront properties, are there any signs of shore erosion (damage caused by waves, storm water runoff, steep slopes, large storms, human and vehicle traffic, ice, or tidal fluctuations)?
- Are there any sinkholes or large depressions on the property?

_____ 31. *Heating Oil Storage Tanks* [Hazard 9]
- Are there any outdoor aboveground tanks or outside fuel-filling or vent pipes?
- Where is the tank located? Where are the fill and vent pipes?
- What is in the tank (fuel oil, kerosene, gasoline, propane, etc.)?
- Are there any fuel stains on the ground near the tank or near a fill or vent pipe?
- Are aboveground tanks leaking, badly rusted, not well supported, or in poor condition?
- Does the fuel line to the furnace run underground?
- Do fill pipes, concrete pads, or patches in the yard or outside paved area suggest that there is an old underground tank?
- Is the vent line clogged or restricted?

_____ 32. *Historic Disposal/Household Chemicals* [Hazards 9, 10]
- On larger tracts of land, are there any discarded drums, mounds of rubble or debris, or other areas where waste disposal may have taken place?
- Are there any piles of debris, old paint cans, or drums or stockpiles of paints, cleaners, or pesticides?
- Is there any soil staining or suspiciously dead or stressed vegetation?

_____ 33. *PCBs* [Hazard 16]
- Are there utility poles with transformers on them? PCB-containing transformers usually have square yellow labels with black lettering. If the transformer is not labeled or you are uncertain, write down the number on the pole so you can call the utility to ask.
- Is there any oil-stained soil or pavement beneath or adjacent to a transformer?

_____ 34. *Pressure-Treated Wood (PTW)* [Hazard 17]
- Is there any PTW debris lying around that might be eaten by children or pets?
- Is PTW used for children's play areas, near any drinking water supplies, or close to vegetable gardens?
- If there is PTW, is it newly manufactured and intended for home use or is it derived from old telephone poles or railroad ties?

_____ 35. *Septic Systems* [Hazard 20]
- Where are the septic tank and leaching field located? The outline of the septic tank or leaching field may be discernable from shading, contours, or other discrepancies in the lawn.

- Are there damp, especially green, or lush or soggy areas on the ground near the leaching field?
- Are there any septic odors in the area of the tank or leaching field?

_____ 36. *Termites and Other Wood-Destroying Pests* [Hazard 21]
- Are there any woodpiles adjacent to the house?
- Are there any holes in wood or sawdust piles next to wood siding?
- Is there any rotted or damaged wood?
- Are there any piles of insect droppings or cast skins?
- Are there any "shelter tubes"—thin termite tunnels running from the ground up along a foundation wall to wood structures?
- Are there places where the ground directly contacts wood parts of the house? Look at crawl spaces, fences, and decks.

_____ 37. *Wetlands* [Hazard 22]
- Are there any low, wet areas with matted, dark-stained leaves or areas adjacent to bodies of water, swamps, bogs, or intermittent streams or drainage ditches that may be classified as wetlands?

_____ 38. *Zoning and Other Land Use Restrictions* [Hazard 23]
- Are there any sewers, manholes, drainage ponds, utilities, or other public or private rights-of-way on the property?

Neighborhood/Nearby

_____ 39. *Off-Site Hazards* [Hazards 24–50]
- From the property, can you see any of the off-site activities listed in Hazards 24–50?
- Can you hear any unusual noises or smell any odors? If possible, come back to the property on different days and at different times of the day.
- What is the local traffic situation? Are there any major roads or frequent truck activity? Remember to inspect the property more than once.
- Walk and drive around the area. Are there any nearby off-site activities of possible concern?
- For properties using well water, are there any off-site activities that represent possible soil or groundwater pollution threats that occur upgradient (in an uphill location from your property)?

APPENDIX 6

Title X Lead
Warning Statements

Under Title X, the Residential Lead-Based Paint Reduction Act of 1992, the following lead warning statement must be included as part of the *sales* contract. The required text for a *sale* is:

> Every purchaser of any interest in residential real property on which a residential dwelling was built prior to 1978 is notified that such property may present exposure to lead from lead-based paint that may place young children at risk of developing lead poisoning. Lead poisoning in young children may produce permanent neurological damage, including learning disabilities, reduced intelligence quotient, behavioral problems, and impaired memory. Lead poisoning also poses a particular risk to pregnant women. The seller of any interest in residential real property is required to provide the buyer with any information on lead-based paint hazards from risk assessments or inspections in the seller's possession and notify the buyer of any known lead-based paint hazards. A risk assessment or inspection for possible lead-based paint hazards is recommended prior to purchase.

The required text of the lead warning statement for *leases* is somewhat different:

> Housing built before 1978 may contain lead-based paint. Lead from paint, paint chips, and dust can pose health hazards if not managed properly. Lead exposure is especially harmful to young children and pregnant women. Before renting pre-1978 housing, lessors must disclose the presence of lead-based paint and/or lead-based paint hazards in the dwelling. Lessees must also receive a federally approved pamphlet on lead poisoning prevention.

INDEX